Strategies for S█

About the author

James Mitchell is director of a Politics Research Centre at Strathclyde University. He is the author of *Conservatives and the Union* (published by EUP).

Strategies for Self-Government

The Campaigns for a Scottish Parliament

James Mitchell

Polygon
EDINBURGH

©James Mitchell 1996

Published by
Polygon
22 George Square
Edinburgh

Set in Monotype Garamond by Bibliocraft, Dundee
Printed and bound in Great Britain by Short Run Press Ltd, Exeter

A CIP record for this title is available

ISBN 0 7486 6113 1

Contents

Preface

This book originated in a conversation with Martin Spencer, Secretary to Edinburgh University Press, in 1989. Our conversation took place only months after Jim Sillars had won the Govan by-election and just as the Constitutional Convention was about to meet. His interest in these events was considerable, as was his keenness to contribute as a publisher to our understanding of contemporary Scotland and the debate on its future. During the conversation I expressed my doubts in fairly negative terms as to the likelihood of either the SNP or the Constitutional Convention living up to the expectations that many people then had of them. Only a publisher of Martin's quality could have seen a publishing opportunity in what I had to say. He convinced me to write a short, provocative piece raising questions about the prospects for Scottish self-government. The conversation with Martin Spencer which set this book in motion was over six years ago. Martin died not long afterwards and I am only one of many authors who still acknowledge the debt owed.

The work that I have written is not as originally intended. It is longer. It is less polemical and more thoughtful. It involved far more primary research, many more hours in libraries, attending more meetings and interviewing more people than I had initially thought. But I hope it is better for that. When I started to work on the book I became aware of a number of failings in earlier works on the national movement. There had been a tendency to follow certain works uncritically and accept accounts of events unquestioningly. John

MacCormick's *Flag in the Wind*, published in 1955, is a fascinating statement by a central figure but the fact that he gave only his personal account of what happened seems to have been overlooked all too often. I also found that there were even more instances than I had expected of strategies and tactics being repeated. It therefore became necessary to write a quite different book. This is much more a research-driven book than the personal account of events I had envisaged.

The work is based on reading over many years and speaking, sometimes in formal interviews but more often informally, to people involved in debates on Scotland's constitutional future throughout that time. I used the *Glasgow Herald* index as a major source and trawled through issues of the paper covering the best part of a century. I also used other newspapers as sources, particularly the *Scotsman* which I used fairly systematically to cover the last twenty years. In addition, I had access to papers held in the National Library of Scotland, especially the Scots Secretariat's massive collection of files, as well as those held in the Public and Scottish Records Offices. It is little appreciated how much work goes into documenting and organising an archive. Anyone who has written a work such as this soon becomes very well aware of the immense debt owed to librarians and archivists.

Numerous people helped in different ways in the preparation of the book. Marion Sinclair, Editorial director at Polygon, was typically politely firm and her comments on my style, or lack of it, were appreciated. The copy editor did an excellent and meticulous job. Ruth Drost's comments on an earlier draft were extremely helpful especially the period before the first world war. Richard Finlay provided comments and pointed me in the direction of very useful additional information. Richard's book *Independent and Free* is the most reliable work on the national movement in the inter-war period. Eilidh Whiteford read one of the chapters and offered valuable advice and suggestions for improvements. Diarmid O'Hara's journalistic experience proved invaluable for the most recent period. Academics often look down on journalists while relying heavily on them for source material. My association with many journalists has been fruitful and often entertaining. I am happy to acknowledge their assistance. The Royal Society of Edinburgh must be thanked for funding a research fellowship during which I was able to do the research on which this book is based.

Many people involved with the national movement over many years were very helpful. It would be impossible to list them all but a few deserve to be mentioned. I interviewed Dr Robert McIntyre and my respect for him grew the more I studied this subject. James Halliday is one of the most charming men to have led a political party and also one of the most helpful in answering queries. I have had privileged access to senior members of the SNP and others in the national movement despite my occasional public criticisms of the party and sections of the movement. I am grateful to Laura Cram who helped me in the final stages. Others I should mention include Robert Hall from Milnathort, David and Mark Allan from Balmullo and Billy Hislop from Wishaw.

I have never hidden my support for Scottish self-government but I hope that I have never been an uncritical supporter. This book does not explain how self-government will be attained, at least not directly, but raises questions about each of the strategies. My conclusion is pluralistic, in keeping with my understanding of what self-government means.

My Dad played a part in the origins of this book. He was a supporter of the Labour Party for most of his life who latterly turned towards the SNP, if somewhat warily. I regret that he died before I finished the book but I regret more that he never saw the Scottish Parliament he hoped would create the radically different Scotland he believed in. This book is dedicated to him.

James Mitchell
August 1995

Introduction

Debate on Scotland's constitutional status has been a feature of Scottish politics for most of this century. Various attempts to articulate the demand for some legislative body to allow the Scots to govern themselves have been made. The national movement is the catch-all term which will be used here to describe those who have campaigned in whatever way for some degree of autonomy, the minimum criterion being the establishment of a directly elected legislative forum. This definition obviously includes the Scottish National Party (SNP), the main organisation within the movement today, but also embraces a range of other bodies. I have made no attempt to list all the organisations which have sprung up over the years. It is, however, worth noting the variety and number of such bodies, as this in itself testifies to the difficulties and frustrations of the movement.

This study of the national movement focuses on the strategies and tactics used in its attempts to achieve its goals. Reviewing these attempts can be confusing. Different organisations at different times have shared the same name and similar organisations at different times have had different names. Whatever they have called themselves, certain key themes and practices are evident. This differs from previous studies which have either provided a broad narrative recounting the development of the movement or attempted to explain the reasons for its origins and growth, with particular reference to the SNP. It is not, therefore, intended as a comprehensive account of the national movement.

A deceptively simple question lies at the heart of this book: how does a movement with the potential or actual support of majority opinion translate this into an effective political force? In particular, the book is concerned with attempts over the course of a century to translate the potential or actual support for Scottish self-government into a force for political change. The question is deceptively simple in a number of respects. It might be contended that in any democracy the support of a majority would automatically translate itself into effect through institutions such as political parties, elections and pressure groups. It would be tempting to state that the translation of public support into political action defines a political system as more or less democratic. However, that would involve a crude, institutional definition of democracy.

It is deceptively simple in another respect. Potential or actual majority support for a cause may exist, but to understand its potential or actual force it is necessary to take account of its context. There are few occasions when one issue alone dominated the political scene. Issues are as much in competition with one another as are rival political parties. Majority support may prove less important than the salience of an issue, and it is crucially important to appreciate the nature of the case for the *status quo* as well as the case for change. The strength of British nationalism and unionism in Scotland is often understated. The case for the union in its present form, as much as the case against it, has changed and this must be understood to make sense of the case for reform.

This question kept recurring in the letters, papers and speeches of people who devoted much of their lives to the movement. In 1952, a private memorandum for members of the national committee of the Scottish Covenant Association, a home rule pressure group, articulated the issue:

> The problem with which the Association is clearly confronted is how to translate the general public sympathy for a measure of self-government into an active force capable of bringing effective influence to bear on the major political parties. In other words, unless the political parties can be compelled to take action it does not matter how many people in Scotland may urgently desire self-government.[1]

The body of academic literature which this book draws upon is

wide-ranging. Various studies of Scottish and British politics, nationalism and nationalist movements, democratic theory and practice,
political parties and pressure groups have been important sources.
In addition, the branch of political sociology concerned with social
movements has influenced this work. Heberle's classic definition
of a social movement is useful. He wrote that the term connotes
'a commotion, a stirring among the people, an unrest, a collective
attempt to reach a visualized goal, especially a change in certain
social institutions' and that it differs from a political party or pressure
group because although it contains 'certain groups that are formally
organized, the movements *as such* are not organized groups'.[2] Tilly
argued that:

> (a) Social movement is neither a party nor a union but a political
> campaign. What we call a social movement actually consists in a series
> of demands or challenges to power-holders in the name of a social
> category that lacks an established political position.[3]

A social movement is essentially a catch-all term. Social movement
organisations will exist within the broad movement including parties
and pressure groups. The study of social movements has been vast as
has the range of questions addressed. Much of the social movement
research will act as an unseen guide throughout this book.[4]

The Scottish self-government movement is a fascinating test case
to explore the extent to which political activity makes a difference
for a number of reasons. First, this is a movement which has existed
throughout most of this century with fluctuating levels of support.
This temporal dimension allows us to see the extent to which changing circumstances require changing strategies and the ways in which
a movement's 'collective memory' of past campaigns conditions its
contemporary approach. Second, the movement is concerned with
establishing a Parliament in Scotland. In this respect, it aims to
extend democracy and so a theoretical concern, regarding the nature
and meaning of democracy itself, is closely related to its practical
concerns. Third, the evidence that exists overwhelmingly suggests
that this is a movement which has had widespread support over the
course of the century. Every legitimate poll taken on the subject
has shown majority support for some measure of self-government.
Finally, the nature of the movement gives rise to important issues.

Self-government is a contestable concept and is not one which can easily be defined institutionally, though without some institutional definition it becomes meaningless. This gives rise to difficulties for a movement which is necessarily diffuse and disparate. Battles over the definition of the ideal become important.

This work begins with a discussion of what is meant by Scottish self-government. The nebulous nature of nationalism and its relationship to self-government are considered. This is followed by a chapter on Scotland's existing constitutional status and the changing contexts which have influenced debates on future strategies. This includes some consideration of the nature of contemporary Britain. Studies of Scottish nationalism have generally ignored that most pervasive alternative to it: British nationalism. It is a major contention of this work that no appreciation of the Scottish national movement and its methods can ignore the strengths and weaknesses of British nationalism. The different movement organisations and strategies are then discussed in turn: pressure groups, constitutional conventions, referendums and plebiscites, an independent national party, and direct action and Parliamentary disruption. The final chapter discusses the strategies since 1992 and draws some general conclusions. Inevitably there is some degree of overlap but as far as was possible the book follows a thematic rather than a strictly chronological path.

It might have been possible to organise the study differently. A chapter on working through the existing parties might have been included but instead this approach is touched on in other chapters. The reason for this is not to diminish the importance of other parties in Scottish politics but to focus on the movement itself. Some of the most dedicated campaigners for self-government have, of course, been members of British parties. However, the other parties – Conservative, Labour, and Liberal Democrat – contain people who believe in self-government although the party does not prioritise it. In addition, as the above quotation demonstrates, the British parties are the focus of the movement's activities rather than part of the movement. Separate studies already exist looking at Labour and Conservative parties' attitudes towards Scotland, and it is my intention to turn my attention to the Labour party at a later date.[5]

1. NLS, Acc. 7505, No. 20, Memorandum for Members of the National Committee of the Scottish Covenant Association.
2. Rudolf Heberle, *Social Movements*, New York, Appleton-Century-Croft, 1951.
3. Charles Tilly, 'Models and realities of popular collective action', *Social Research*, vol. 52, 1985, pp. 735–6.
4. Given the potential readership of the book, it was decided to omit a large section discussing social movement theory, especially as it would have to come in the introduction. The following works are a selection of some of the most useful, in particular those which discuss resource mobilisation theory: Peter Eisinger, 'The Conditions of Protest Behavior in American Cities' *American Political Science Review*, vol. 67; William Gamson, *The Strategy of Social Protest*, Homewood, IL, Dorsey; J. Craig Jenkins, 'Resource Mobilization Theory and the Study of Social Movements', *Annual Revue of Sociology*, Vol. 9, 1983; Alberto Melucci, 'The Symbolic Challenge of Contemporary Movements', *Social Research*, Vol. 52, 1985; Bert Klandermans, 'New Social Movements and Resource Mobilization: The European and the American Approach', *International Journal of Mass Emergencies and Disasters*, vol. 4, 1986; Bert Klandermans and Sidney Tarrow, 'Mobilization into Social Movements: synthesizing European and American Approaches', *International Social Movement Research*, vol. 1, 1988; Doug McAdam, John D. McCarthy and Mayer N. Zald, 'Social Movements' in Neil Smelser (ed.), *Handbook of Sociology*, London, Sage, 1988; Russell J. Dalton and Manfred Kuechler (eds.), *Challenging the Political Order*, Cambridge, Polity Press, 1990; Aldon D. Morris and Carol McClurg Mueller (eds.), *Frontiers in Social Movement Theory*, London, Yale University Press, 1992.
5. Michael Keating and David Bleiman, *Labour and Scottish Nationalism*, London, Macmillan, 1979; James Mitchell, *Conservatives and the Union*, Edinburgh, Edinburgh University Press, 1990.

The Meaning of Self-Government

Introduction: Outlining Some Problems

This chapter considers the changing meaning of self-government, with reference to the origins and development of the ideas of self-government and democracy and to the nature of Scottish identity. Democracy is not simply about institutions and the right to vote but has a more sociological meaning. It is concerned with the distribution of power. Democratic politics is concerned with the manner in which issues arrive or fail to arrive on the political agenda, the extent to which an identity may or may not have a political meaning, and the degree to which people are made to feel self-confident.

Popular sovereignty may not be the term used in everyday political discourse but it is the central idea of the self-government movement. Its roots lie in the French Revolution. Since then, popular sovereignty has developed along two ideological paths, towards nationalism and democracy. Nationalism and democracy are terms which have been used in debates on Scotland's constitutional status over the course of the century but the meaning of each has been disputed and has undergone change. Each is important as part of the wider context in which the movement has operated but also because these terms define the movement's objectives. They come together in the Scottish demand for self-government: the idea that Scotland is politically distinct and that this must be acknowledged in democratic institutions.

Any claim for self-government raises two conceptual questions: one concerns the identity of the 'self', and the other the type of rule which should exist. Following from these, three problems with the concept of national self-determination have been identified:

(a) The extent of the principle of national self-determination is ambiguous, (b) there is no justification for restricting the principle of self-determination to nations only, and (c) there is no justification for giving the principle of national self-determination unqualified support.[1]

It has also been suggested that the credibility of any claim to self-government is an empirical question.[2] The principles involved are relatively straightforward but, as Birch points out, it is their practical application that is controversial.

The Evolution of the Idea of Democracy

The doctrine of self-government is founded in the democratic ideal. The core meaning of democracy may be vague but at its root 'lies the idea of popular power, of a situation in which power, and perhaps authority too, rests with people'.[3] Beyond this basic definition, the term has many different meanings and its accepted use has changed over time. For most of history, democracy was seen as a dangerous, revolutionary notion – giving power to the uneducated mob. As late as the 1880s, advocates of franchise extension were careful in how they articulated their case. Gladstone was offended to be described as a 'democrat' when his government introduced measures to extend the franchise in 1884. Yet, within a century, democracy had become a label which regimes of all kinds attached to themselves in an attempt to gain legitimacy. During the twentieth century it became almost universally synonymous with the best form of government, but there has been less agreement on its meaning.[4] In addition, although the twentieth century has seen great advances towards the democratic ideal, the weaknesses of that ideal have simultaneously become increasingly evident. Many critics of self-government make exactly the same criticisms as earlier critics made of democracy. Indeed, it has often been the case that critics of self-government hide behind rhetoric attacking nationalism. It is important, therefore, to understand the motives of those opposed to self-government.

Potentially unpalatable consequences of democracy were well known in earlier centuries, and the ancient contempt for the *demos* – the people – and criticisms of democratic rule found in Plato's *Republic* are not far from the surface today. As Arblaster has reminded us, opposition to democracy is 'not as moribund as public rhetoric might lead us to suppose'.[5] The rhetoric, more than anything else, has changed. A survey after the second world war found that there were 'no adverse replies to democracy'.[6] The likelihood is that a similar survey conducted today would give an equally unequivocal vote in favour of self-government. As with democracy, with which it is inextricably linked, the case for self-government is more often asserted than put into effect while behind the facade of unity there exist differences of opinion and, again as with democracy, the idea of self-government raises as many questions as it provides answers.

For the early Fabians in Britain democracy was a 'faith, not a subject of argument'.[7] What was not always clear was the precise purpose of extending the franchise. Was the franchise an instrument for empowering greater numbers of people to improve their physical well-being? Or would extending the franchise transform politics in a more fundamental manner? Was it the political system or the people who would be changed? This tension between the instrumental and developmental purposes of democracy has been a persistent theme in debates. The work of the father and son James and John Stuart Mill in the nineteenth century brings this out.[8] James Mill's philosophic radicalism envisaged an extended franchise as a means of preventing the aristocracy from governing in their own interests against those of the greater number. But this, he felt, did not necessitate universal suffrage: exclusion of all women, men under forty, and the working class was justified on the grounds that the interests of these groups would be looked after by the enfranchised male middle classes. Mill could thus, in Macauley's words, 'dogmatise away the interests of half the human race'. The interests of the unenfranchised would be represented by those with the vote. This theory of democracy retains its appeal amongst a sizeable proportion of thinkers today though they accept a much extended franchise. The idea that the interests of a group can best be looked after by another group has been the most persistent corruption of the democratic ideal in the twentieth century and is evident amongst opponents of self-government.

Empiricists, Economists and Elitists

In this century, critics of democratic politics have had to be more subtle than those of previous times. Attacks on democracy have had to take place within the rhetoric of democracy. As a result the term has been revised to give it an elitist slant. Such elitist versions of democracy stemmed from what were perceived as the failings and dangerous consequences of popular rule, the results of empirical analysis combined with conservative attitudes and the fear of change. Some thinkers simply saw democracy as inefficient. Empiricists, economists and elitists undermined and revised the meaning of democracy to remove its essence, popular control. This is not to dismiss some genuine concerns about the weaknesses of democracy. Five basic problems have been identified which have plagued the modern public and given rise to doubts about democracy: 'two relate to its potential superficiality – lack of competence and lack of resources – and three concern its potential susceptibility – to the tyranny of the majority, to propaganda or mass persuasion, and to subtle domination by elite minorities.'[9]

The 'lack of competence' argument focuses on the public's perceived lack of active involvement in and inattention to public affairs. Lippmann commented that the private citizen has 'come to feel rather like a deaf spectator in the back row, who ought to keep his mind on the mystery off there, but cannot quite manage to keep awake.'[10] The 'lack of resources' argument is similar. The problem is seen as the lack of means to convey the appropriate information to the public which would make them fit to govern themselves. The public's potential for genuine self-government was accepted, but the nature of mass democracy made it unlikely.

The 'tyranny of the majority' problem has long been acknowledged and the emergence of mass democracy did not abate such fears. Rather it exacerbated the concern that politicians were 'likely to occupy themselves, not in forming opinion, but in discovering and hastening to obey it', as Bryce suggested.[11] The 'susceptibility to persuasion' of the masses has also been identified as a problem. Emotional appeals and the manipulation of mass communications were evident in inter-war Europe. The 'domination by elites' is another, quite different concern: this argues that mass passivity will allow government and society to be dominated by elites. But questions of competence and knowledge, of tyranny and susceptibility to persuasion may be features of elite politics as much as of mass politics. Nonetheless, evidence at different times in different places suggests that each of these concerns has validity, and advocates of self-government need to be as conscious of the weaknesses of their ideal as their critics are of their unspoken alternatives.

Schumpeter's *Capitalism, Socialism and Democracy* was first published in 1942, just after Hitler's rise to power through representative democratic institutions and the use of plebiscites. Against this background, Schumpeter argued that stability should replace the popular will as the main aim of the democratic process. His chief problem was that he could not accept that 'the people' could hold a definite and rational opinion about every individual question. His solution was to allow the people to choose 'representatives' who would express authoritative opinions.[12] A revisionist version of democracy was thus developed which involved competing elites instead of direct government by the people:

> The democratic method is that institutional arrangement for arriving at political decisions in which individuals acquire the power to decide by means of a competitive struggle for the people's vote.[13]

American students of politics, armed with the findings of public opinion surveys, argued that the 'masses' harboured illiberal attitudes. Kornhauser's study of 'mass society' reached the conclusion that mass politics in democratic society must be undemocratic.[14] Other influential works concluded that low levels of public participation in politics signalled satisfaction, made government possible, or did not matter so long as a plurality of interest groups operated in a competitive environment.[15] According to this view, the role of the people should be limited. The students faced a dilemma:

> Either they had to admit that most Americans failed to live up to the

high standards of democratic citizenship, a shortcoming that John Stuart Mill warned would lead to the loss of liberty; or else they had to declare that, notwithstanding claims to the contrary, the United States simply was not a true democracy. Needless to say, most found neither of these alternatives palatable.[16]

Schumpeter's revisionist view of democracy attempted to straddle the divide. Variants on this theme emerged and each contained an elitist element in their understanding and prescription of what democracy was.[17] These ideas took root without difficulty throughout Western liberal democracies.

Critiques of 'Democratic' Elitism

The reaction to revisionist theories of democracy came from a number of sources. Some have written about retrieving democracy, or superseding liberal democracy, creating 'strong democracy', and discovering new forms of democracy.[18] There have been several attempts to create opportunities for greater participation in the political process and to widen the scope of politics. Self-government in its widest sense has been the root of these radical democratic aims.

These issues are not necessarily related to questions about territory, although territorial politics is one important aspect of the attempt to retrieve democracy. Afro-American movements for example are not territorially defined but seek self-determination through challenging negative images and cultural impediments. Black nationhood, as the author of a study of identity amongst Afro-Americans states, is 'not rooted in territoriality so much as it is in the profound belief in the fitness of core black culture and in the solidarity born of a transgenerational detestation of our subordination.'[19] Indeed, as another author notes, 'migration out of the rural South was seen by thousands of Afro-Americans as the only way to achieve individual or collective advancement and self-determination.'[20] The women's movement is another example, and the weaknesses of liberal democracy have been highlighted by feminists.[21]

Amongst students of local politics, the debate focused on how to determine who governed at the local level. Similar arguments were extended to the national level though some of the most intellectually fruitful and heated exchanges related to local politics.[22] A number of pluralist writers maintained that power was fairly evenly dispersed in society with no single grouping having ultimate control over all issues, although they conceded that the system involved competing elites rather than widespread political participation by the public. Against this view, it was argued that decision-making was much more constrained than pluralists suggested and that the scope of decision-making was confined to certain 'safe' issues.

A key argument to emerge from these exchanges was the notion put forward by Bachrach and Baratz in *The Two Faces of Power*. They developed the argument that it was pointless simply to study political institutions in order to appreciate where power lay. Instead, Bachrach and Baratz argued that there was a second face of power which had not previously been recognised:

> Of course power is exercised when A participates in the making of decisions that affect B. But power is also exercised when A devotes his energies to creating or reinforcing social and political values and institutional practices that limit the scope of the political process to public consideration of only those issues which are comparatively innocuous to A. To the extent that A succeeds in doing this, B is prevented, for all practical purposes, from bringing to the fore any issues that might in their resolution be seriously detrimental to A's set of preferences.[23]

They coined the ambiguous term 'nondecision-making' to refer to this process of subverting or limiting democratic politics. If nondecision-making is more than an abstract invention of the ivory towers or the product of a conspiratorial imagination then it suggests major deficiencies in the nature of Western liberal democracy.

In a short but powerful book on American politics, the implications of which have far wider ramifications, Schattschneider put forward his 'realist's view of democracy'. Entitled *The Semi-Sovereign People*, the book argued that despite a form of pluralism existing with a range of competing interests, the political system of the United States is inherently biased: the 'heavenly chorus sings with a strong upper-class accent'.[24] The group theorists who complacently accepted that democratic politics could be defined in terms of the existence of competing interest groups were mistaken in failing to recognise that pressure group politics is a selective process, 'skewed, loaded, and unbalanced in favour of a fraction of a minority'.[25] His critique of the choices available to the electorate developed this theme. Despite elections, numerous issues and conflicts are 'displaced' from the political agenda, 'Some issues are organized into politics while others are organized out.'[26] The American people, he argued, are only semi-sovereign in the sense that politics is organised and defined in such a manner as to exclude certain issues.

The significance of these debates to discussions of self-government is the opening up of the meaning of democracy and the identification of flaws in post-war orthodoxies. The capacity for self-government in socio-economic terms and the need to clarify the identity of the self lie at the heart of these discussions. The importance of self-worth for the democratic polity is acknowledged. African-American and feminist critics have noted the centrality of negative images and cultural impediments as well as socio-economic blocks to effective participation and power, while students of local politics have noted the importance of non-institutional forces in politics.

Conditions of Democracy

A number of democratic theorists have provided lists of preconditions for democracy. Cohen and Rogers argued for a broad definition of democracy by including the absence of material deprivation, the need for workplace democracy, and public control of investment alongside certain basic conditions – the capacity for reasoned judgement, equal freedom and reasoned deliberation, manifest processes of decision-making, and the possession of autonomy and respect for others' autonomy.[27] Margolis's 'viable democracy' required that information should be accessible, the smallest unit of government possible should be responsible for policy decisions, criticism of government should be encouraged, corporations should have members of the public on their boards, and social and environmental accounting should be institutionalised.[28] Pennock's conditions included a historical identification of a people with the interests of their shared community; open-mindedness, the dispersal of power, absence of great economic inequality, respect for persons, belief in individual rights, mutual trust, tolerance, and willingness to compromise, literacy and education, commitment to democratic procedures and values, public spirit, nationalism, balances between consensus and cleavage, and institutions of political culture, such as political parties.[29] The list of requirements seems never ending and the democratic ideal less and less attainable.

Many of the conditions listed above followed from the critiques of liberal democracy cited earlier. The socio-economic conditions are now generally seen as important, with gross inequalities undermining any democratic polity. What has emerged is a more sociological definition of democracy. As Beitz has suggested, democracy can be defined in a narrow manner which considers what is the best form of government or in a broader sense by asking what is the best form of society.[30] Institutions are important but other considerations have to be taken into account. The wider, more sociological definitions demand a wider scope of politics. Democracy in this sense cannot be attained without taking account of the distribution of power in society as a whole, and power is not merely attained through the control of public institutions.

When discussing self-government there are other important conditions which need to be considered, particularly those regarding minorities. Majority rule cannot be a sufficient definition of democracy as it involves the possibility of the majority persistently over-ruling a minority, perhaps even persecuting it. Consensual politics, therefore, is essential to democracy. Consensus is not simply acquiescence; it requires continuous dialogue and readjustment. Barber distinguishes between substantive and creative consensus, the latter corresponding with the idea of consensus meant here.[31] The balance struck between creating a consensus and permitting diversity is difficult to conceptualise, but crucial.

Pennock's inclusion of a historical identification of a people with the interests of their shared community and nationalism as a condition of democracy was based on the need for some bond which would make government possible without undue use of force. A problem arises in a state when a section feels alienated, outcast and unable to affect matters. All states require a minimum degree of consensus, some means of providing unity, if they hope to exist democratically.

Five Phases of Self-Government

The development of the idea and practice of self-government has been little different from that of democracy. Just as the enfranchised minority claimed to be able to act in the interests of the disenfranchised majority, so too did imperial powers claim to be able to act in the interests of the colonies. Subject peoples this century have been in the same position as women and working men in Britain a century ago: they have been regarded as incapable of looking after themselves and of using power irresponsibly. Allowing and acknowledging distinctiveness, in the classic pluralist manner, was permitted, but this is very different from dispersing power.

Three periods in the history of the doctrine of self-government were evident to one observer at the end of the first world war.[32] The origins of the doctrine were rooted in the French Revolution of 1789 but self-government was 'utterly destroyed by the growing ambition for conquest over a world of enemies' in this period.[33] A second phase of self-government between 1848 and 1870 began with the national revolutions of 1848 and ended in political opportunism in later years. The third period began with the first world war when the doctrine became the 'symbol of regeneration for every subject nationality'.[34] This period was, however, short-lived. The application of the doctrine to only the defeated powers in the war and the reassertion of power politics soon killed off the practice of self-government in inter-war Europe.

A further phase was evident after the second world war, beginning slowly with the independence of colonies in the Far East and continuing with a succession of African states. This new phase had a great impact on contemporary Europe in challenging the legitimacy of states which had formerly been colonial powers. Not only was there a direct challenge to colonial rule outside Europe but a major element in the European states' sense of their own identity was being threatened – what had made Britain 'Great' was being undermined by nationalists in Africa and Asia and consequently

British nationalism itself was undermined. A fifth phase became evident recently beginning with the revolutions in eastern and central Europe in the late 1980s. From the Baltic to the Adriatic boundaries dissolved which had previously seemed impregnable. The rapidity with which this occurred has been followed by a slow, painful search in central and eastern Europe as to who should constitute the *self* in self-government, and a gradual disillusionment with the doctrine of self-government itself.

Each period was ushered in with high hopes and grand visions but gradually gave way to disillusionment. The expectations were not entirely false, simply too great. The movements were generally driven by social rather than intellectual forces, though ideas inevitably played their part. The relationship between the ideals of democracy and the pressures for social change was never quite the same in each phase but some common aspects are discernible. The most significant feature of each movement was a rejection of the idea that interests are best guaranteed by allowing others to look after them. However, the idea has never been fully accepted and power politics has always intervened.

Democratic Liberal Nationalism

Max Weber defined nationalism as a 'common bond of sentiment whose adequate expression would be a state of its own, and which therefore normally tends to give birth to such a state'.[35] Nationalism, in this sense, is a classic form of collectivism. The position of individuals and individual rights are commonly seen as problematic in discussions on nationalism. The argument is the same as that which applies to socialism or any programme emphasising collective entities. The individualist concern lies at the heart of many critiques of nationalism and the predominance of 'cold war liberalism',[36] which dominated post-war English-language political theory, with critiques of nationalism and revisionist views of democracy militating against any meaningful idea of self-government.[37]

Opposition to collective entities by such liberals as Popper and Hayek was in large measure shared by many who considered themselves left-wing. One notable exception was John Plamenatz who combined liberalism with nationalist sympathies. In *On Alien*

Rule and Self-Government (1960) he concluded that national independence, political democracy and individual freedom were compatible.
More recently, others have argued similarly. Barry's discussion of
Plamenatz and MacCormick's work maintains that liberalism and
nationalism are compatible.[38] Recently, the most sustained challenge
to the orthodox liberal attitude to nationalism has been presented
by Tamir.[39] She presents the idea of the 'contextual individual',
combining individuality and sociability as 'two equally genuine and
important features':

> It allows for an interpretation of liberalism that is aware of the
> binding, constitutive character of cultural and social memberships,
> together with an interpretation of nationalism that conceives of
> individuals as free and autonomous participants in a communal
> framework, who conceive of national membership in Renan's terms,
> as a daily plebiscite.[40]

The communitarian context in which the individual operates is
not exclusively national but rather is a number of contexts each
with varying degrees of importance at different times, and each
collective entity competes for the loyalty of the individual with other
collectivities. Thus, nationalism has no prior call on an individual's
loyalty. An individual does not operate in isolation but within a
'web of identities'. Individuals will identify with communities – class,
national, religious – which will affect their values and viewpoints, and
the nation is recognised and valued as one of these.

Further to this, Tamir develops the idea of the 'morality of community', the means by which an individual's thinking on moral issues
is shaped. She lists four ways in which the morality of community
deepens our thinking on moral issues. First, it encourages members
to 'develop relations based on care and cooperation'. Second, it
provides a rational basis for the emotional urge to 'favour those who
share their life with us, and about whom we care deeply'. Third,
'principles of justice' can be agreed by individuals who share common
bonds and a sense of responsibility. Fourth, this need not result in the
abnegation of responsibility to others beyond the nation. Indeed, as
Tamir notes, 'developing the morality of community leads to a much
greater commitment to global justice than that advocated by most
liberal writers'.[41] The morality of community prevents the excesses

of individualism. Only through the acceptance of an individual's place within a collective can there be any prospect of ethical relations developing. As Miller has also argued, to show that co-nationals can rightly make special claims on us does 'not suggest that these claims exhaust the ethical universe.'[42]

A similar argument was made by Rokkan and Urwin who distinguish between the rights to roots and the rights to options:

> Roots are important because they help you know who you are and whom you can trust: they are the lifeblood of cultural identity. But options are equally important. You may not want to be locked in for ever within the same community; you may wish to find a wider arena for the use of your talents. The problem is to find some acceptable fulcrum between these orientations. Domination by roots may end up in social, cultural and even economic serfdom. The multiplication of options may result in anomia: a decrease in predictability, increased irresponsibility and a heightened depersonalized anonymity.[43]

The rights to roots provide an individual with rights to belong to a community while the rights to options are concerned with individual rights. As with Tamir, a balanced response is proposed. The tension between individualism and collectivism, or the rights to roots and the rights to options, is ultimately irresolvable theoretically but must be addressed in practice.

An argument similar to that made by Tamir has recently been deployed by Ghia Nodia, a Georgian political philosopher. He notes that denunciations of nationalism made in the name of democracy are 'actually denunciations of nationalism in the name of liberalism'. The ancient but living fear of the people amongst liberals which was noted above, takes the form of aversion to nationalism. For Nodia, nationalism and democracy may be intimately connected: 'Nation is another name for "We the People".' Following Fukuyama, he argues that a distinction has to be made between two types of nationalism – 'megalothymic' and 'isothymic'. These inelegant terms have simple meanings. Isothymic nationalism would be better understood as liberal nationalism and megalothymic nationalism as imperialism when directed beyond the nation and racism when directed internally.[44] Each demands some form of recognition in the modern world: the former demands greater recognition while the latter demands equal recognition. The liberal nationalist position is inclusive and accepts other communal identities.

Defining the Self

The issue of boundaries at sea, especially relevant because of oil and fishing, is now largely resolved, although it might have proved troublesome had Scotland become independent in the 1970s. A more pressing problem, again exaggerated, has been the position of the northern isles – Shetland and Orkney. The point made by French and Gutman, quoted in the introduction to this chapter, is relevant. If the right to secede is to be granted to Scotland then should it not also be accorded to the peoples of these islands? It is in this sense that Anthony Birch, again mentioned in the introduction to this chapter, refers to self-government as an empirical question. There are no hard and fast rules that can be applied as to the size, in either population or land-mass terms, or the capacity for self-sufficiency. It would seem that a robust case for self-government in some shape or form could be made for the northern isles given their distinct cultures and economic base. Ultimately, that would be a decision which the peoples of the islands would have to make themselves. What seems undeniable is that proponents of Scottish self-government should take account of the distinctive traditions of these islands in formulating a constitutional order. Equally, the Western Isles should be accorded similar treatment. The possession of wealth should not be seen as a reason for according special treatment to the northern isles, even though it enhances their power, while denying it to the relatively poor Western Isles.

One important aspect of the geographic definition of self-government concerns the position of the rest of the United Kingdom. While a people's right to secede may seem indisputable it might have implications for others. This may necessitate finding some role in the decision-making process for these others. The right to independence may be one which should be made by the citizens within the geographical entity contemplating secession on their own but the right to devolution is another matter. A unilateral declaration of devolution is as absurd in principle as it is impractical. While devolutionists have insisted on distinguishing themselves from those who advocate independence, they have often adopted the principle underpinning the case for independence – the right to self-determination. This matter remains unresolved in the case of Scotland. Advocates of a measure of self-government short of independence almost invariably fall back on a nationalist principle in making their case for change by arguing to exclude others outwith Scotland from the decision. This is unjustified. While Scots have every right to expect to be given fair treatment they cannot expect to dictate the terms and conditions of their continued membership of the United Kingdom. As in the case of the relationship between the northern isles and Scotland, it would be both unprincipled and ultimately foolish to attempt to use temporary power and privilege for gain. This does not mean that the rest of the UK, as a larger entity than Scotland, should have the right of veto. It means that any decision to establish a Scottish Parliament within the UK should in principle be taken by the Scots but that the details of any package involving Scotland's continued membership of the UK would need to be negotiated.

The issue of who has the right to decide on Scotland's constitutional status within Scotland is also important and raises the question of citizenship: who would have rights as full citizens in an independent Scotland? These two questions are similar but not the same. It is conceivable, for example, that an independent Scotland would define citizenship in a more liberal manner to include some who would currently be excluded from a decision on whether an independent state should exist. Exclusive and inclusive definitions lie at either end of the continuum. Exclusive definitions of citizenship and nationality narrowly define those with rights. It is possible, of course, for people to be given limited citizenship rights: the right to live and work in a country but not to vote, for example. In Britain, citizenship has evolved against an imperial background which has given rise to anomalies, restrictions and lack of consistency. However inadequate and flawed such definitions of citizenship may be, it is impossible for advocates of self-government to have much impact on this prior to self-government. In other words, defining who has the right to decide on Scotland's constitutional status especially, though not necessarily only, when this will involve a measure short of political independence, is a matter on which supporters of self-government themselves will have little impact. But having established a self-governing polity, and depending on its degree of autonomy, Scots themselves will be in a stronger position to decide who has citizenship, who can join them. It is conceivable that a more liberal definition would follow, although, especially following the Maastricht Treaty on European Union, such decisions may increasingly be taken through the institutions of the European Union.[45]

Culture versus Politics?

Sir Alexander McEwen, a leading proponent of Scottish self-government in the 1930s, argued that before any system of self-government could be fully effective 'there must be a steady growth in political self-consciousness'.[46] The need to develop the sense of Scottish identity has been a central concern of elements in the movement. However, developing a sense of self-consciousness has not only been seen as a means of bringing about constitutional change but may be worthy in itself. A question of priority may arise as has been evident in the politics of Welsh nationalism, where preservation of the language has often been seen as a greater priority than the establishment of a Welsh Parliament. This was expressed in a radio broadcast by veteran Welsh nationalist Saunders Lewis in 1962:

> Perhaps the language would bring self-government in its wake – I don't know. The language is more important than self-government. In my opinion, if any kind of self-government for Wales were obtained before Welsh is admitted and used as an official language in local and national administration in the Welsh-speaking areas of our country, then the language will never achieve official status at all, and its death would be quicker than it will be under the rule of England.[47]

A frequent distinction drawn by home rulers themselves is between cultural and political/economic nationalists. The distinction may have merit as a means of distinguishing between different strategies. Cultural nationalists stress the distinctive cultural characteristics of Scotland and place less emphasis on economic arguments. Political or economic nationalists must, by defining themselves as nationalists at all, have a conception of Scotland as a distinct entity but stress the socio-economic advantages of self-government. This applies equally to those who campaign for any limited measure of home rule.

The National Party of Scotland (NPS), founded in 1928, was much more consciously aware of the cultural dimension than its successor, the Scottish National Party, has been. Early on, the south-eastern division of the NPS approached the Scottish Vernacular Society with a view to putting pressure on the BBC to broadcast Scots language programmes and promoted the idea of a chair of Scottish Literature at Edinburgh University.[48] In 1934, the newly formed Scottish National Party invited composers to provide music for a new national anthem, written by the playwright Stewart Black. Burns' poem *Scots Wha Hae* was felt inappropriate whereas Black's *God Keep Us True* was thought to convey a less strident message.[49] The composition was performed at the annual Bannockburn rally but it never replaced Burns' poem as Scotland's unofficial national anthem.

In its early years, the SNP could be characterised as having had a surfeit of poets and a lack of politicians. Conversely, the modern SNP has been accused of being philistine. Winning votes and seats is politically significant but may not excite the same interest or enthusiasm as the recovery of the Stone of Destiny discussed later in this work. Throughout the history of the modern Scottish national movement some of the most significant developments have occurred in the field of affirmative politics, that is, in affirming that Scotland exists as a distinct political entity. The very nature of identity, tapping into subliminal consciousness, makes symbolic actions politically important. It was Andrew Fletcher of Saltoun, nationalist folk-hero and defender of the old Scots Parliament, who commended the view that 'if a man were permitted to make all the ballads, he need not care who should make the laws of a nation'. Of course, not all artistic efforts to revive Scottish culture have been motivated by the desire to further constitutional change. Numerous artists will pursue their work without any interest in political questions, but their work cannot fail to have an impact on politics and society if it is widely appreciated.

The symbolic battle over the meaning of Scottishness has had a number of forms. Efforts to stimulate a sense of Scottish identity were only one part of the battle: another was to convince Scots that this identity had a positive and political meaning. Again, the tension between those who stressed the cultural approach and those who stressed the political/economic approach is evident. Opponents of home rule argued that it was possible to be culturally Scottish but politically British.

Stimulating a Sense of Scottish Identity

The importance of the cultural climate in which the movement operates is illustrated by the case of Quebec. Quebec nationalism took on a new, more confident form from the early 1960s when a marked change occurred in Quebec society – the 'Quiet Revolution'. This has been described as a revolution of symbols in which an increase in cultural activity and new institutions provided an important backdrop for the political movement which later emerged.[50] Coleman defined the Quiet Revolution:

> The concept of a quiet revolution does not refer to changes in policy *per se*; rather it describes the spirit or atmosphere in Quebec society in the early 1960s. This was a spirit of collective strength, or cooperation, of a general will to move forward together. It was a spirit of elation, of joyful outbursts, and of hope. There was a sense that the divisions in the community that had become more and more acute after 1945 could be breached.[51]

This cultural awakening had political consequences.

There have been numerous attempts over the years by home rulers to stimulate a sense of Scottish political identity. When Charles Waddie, founder of the Scottish Home Rule Association in 1886, grew disillusioned with the pressure group approach in the late 1890s he turned from this prosaic strategy and attempted to stimulate a sense of Scottish identity by writing and staging historical plays. In autumn 1899 at the Glasgow Atheneum plays with titles such as 'The Bruce' and 'Wallace' were performed at some considerable personal expense.[52] This approach was quixotic and crude but its motivation was not so very different from the far more ambitious and highly sophisticated approach of those involved in literary nationalist circles after the first world war.

Christopher Grieve, who adopted the name Hugh MacDiarmid, was the most significant figure this century to have adopted a cultural approach to self-government. John MacCormick, a major figure in nationalist politics, viewed MacDiarmid as 'politically one of the greatest handicaps with which any national movement could have been burdened'.[53] In fact, both men contributed greatly to the national movement in their different ways. From a literary perspective, MacDiarmid's contribution was monumental, influencing a significant body of subsequent writers. His association with the SNP may have damaged the cause of self-government at the time, as MacCormick charged, but from a longer-term perspective MacDiarmid played a singular part in maintaining a sense of Scottish identity amongst Scottish writers and artists. The fact that much of his work is impenetrable to most people does not negate his importance in the self-government movement. It was the self-consciously self-confident nature of his work that helped ensure the revival of a serious literary movement rooted in Scottish identity. One biographer concluded that by the time of his death in 1978 MacDiarmid had 'changed Scotland, given the nation an ideal made in his own image'.[54] It is difficult to assess the extent to which MacDiarmid's work percolated through to the level of practical politics but some of his admirers certainly believe this happened. For a self-government movement to be successful there must exist a 'self' which is worth preserving. In this, MacDiarmid and the Scottish renaissance played a considerable, if unquantifiable part not dissimilar to the changed cultural climate brought about during the Quiet Revolution in Quebec.

In an early contribution on the subject of the relationship between Scottish literature and home rule, MacDiarmid maintained that the revival of one presupposed the revival of the other.[55] He drew an analogy between Scotland's politics and its culture. At that time he was a strong critic of Robert Burns:

> The Burns cult, so far from being of any literary or political significance, is an unparalleled phenomenon of mob-consciousness, pickled in whisky – of interest only to literary pathologists. It is, in fact, a great inhibiting agency largely accountable for the paucity and poverty of contemporary Scottish literature in technique and ideation, and the creation of interest and influence; whereby the Scottish public is kept bogged in obsolete and unnatural tastes to suit soulless commercialism centralised in London. There will be no literary revival in Scotland until genuine literary criticism replaces the auto-intoxicated folly of

patriotism . . . and until Scottish national sentiments, rescued from
the present compulsion to progressive self-parody under which they
labour as the result of causes perceived by every psychologist – the
distorting consequences of the over-Anglicisation of our affairs – and
restored to their natural functions, begin to be translated into terms
of practical politics.[56]

Though he changed his mind on Burns, MacDiarmid's fire remained
consistently directed against those who, he felt, trivialised Scotland,
undermined Scottish self-confidence, and presented the future as the
captive of a debilitated past. It was not just any form of Scottish
identity which would aid the self-government movement but only
that which gave self-confidence to the people.

Individuals and bodies without an explicitly political message have
also played a part in fostering a sense of Scottish identity. The
founders of the Saltire Society included not only political nationalists
but also those who were explicitly unionist. Founded in 1936, its
constitution stated that its primary object would be to 'foster and
enrich the cultural heritage of Scotland'.[57] It was in the Saltire Society
that Billy Wolfe, later to lead the SNP, first made contact with
questions of Scottish identity.[58] Organisations such as the Saltire
Society were part of the movement which grew out of the 'quiet
revolution' deliberately fostered by MacDiarmid and others of the
Scottish literary renaissance. MacDiarmid's efforts were an attempt
not simply to stimulate a sense of Scottishness but to create a positive
image of Scotland. Part of the problem for home rulers has been the
lack of any attempt by opponents to deny the existence of Scottish
identity. Instead, opponents have countered home rulers' demands
by attempting to de-couple political and cultural identities or by
trivialising Scottish identity.

Tartanry and Negative Images of Scottishness

Home rulers were not alone in using symbols of Scottish identity for
political purposes. Opponents of home rule have been known to project negative images of Scotland and attempt to associate these with
home rule. As noted earlier in the discussion of African-American
and women's movements, social movements must battle against
negative images held by their own potential supporters. Beveridge

and Turnbull argue that the Scottish intellegentsia have embraced 'damning conceptions of national culture – in other words as an expression of inferiorism',[59] borrowing terms from Fanon's work on the strategies and effects of external control in the Third World. The notion that Scots have come to admit the inferiority of their culture is based on the view that intellectuals have presented Scotland in a negative light, as 'a country which can be exhaustively described in terms of poverty, philistinism, bigotry, repression – a land of no gods or heroes'.[60] This, they maintain, has had a debilitating effect on Scottish politics. When a society is portrayed as deeply divided or having many negative features, it is difficult to see any reason to defend it. Self-respect is an essential aspect of self-government. If the 'self' provokes shame there may be a desire to change the 'self', perhaps to choose another community. This may be a class or another national community (British instead of Scottish); most likely it will be both.

Denying divisions and stressing national cohesion and the positive aspects of Scottish culture have been part of the agenda of self-government proponents. Opponents can easily point to divisions; the response has often been to deny their existence. Geographical divisions have persistently been cited: north vs. south, east vs. west, highlands vs. lowlands, Edinburgh vs. Glasgow, Strathclyde vs. the rest. Most potent has been the Orange vs. Green division. Scotland's self-image as a society divided between local presbyterians and Irish Catholics has proved a powerful referent for opponents of self-government during much of the twentieth century. The charge that a society with two religious traditions is incapable of self-government is not caused by an inability to look beyond Scotland but by selective comparison. The parallel often drawn is with Ireland, and Northern Ireland in particular. This is understandable given the historic ties between Scotland and Ireland but it is inadequate. The image of Scotland as a society riven with sectarianism proves less convincing when the importance of religion in the politics of every European state is considered.

McCrone challenged the notion that Scottish culture itself is dominated by negative images arguing that discussion of Scottish culture has been dominated by selected and negative images.[61] As he notes, Scottish culture's diversity corresponds with that elsewhere. In addition the development of a sense of Scottish identity 'without the encumbrance of a heavy cultural baggage'[62] also makes possible a non-sectarian definition of identity. To be Scottish does not require an ability to speak a particular language or to worship a particular God, or the same God in a particular way. McCrone's observation that Scotland may be entering a post-nationalist age with nationalism as the vehicle taking it there strikes an optimistic note well in keeping with the theory of liberal nationalism discussed earlier in the work of Tamir.

In a pamphlet published shortly before the 1992 election, Alasdair Gray described the occupation of writer as 'that of a worker in one of the few Scottish trades in a healthier state (now) than at the start of the century'.[63] The cultural vitality of Scotland has been crucial. Without any sense of identity, the notion of self-government is not possible. The 'self' has survived and a confidence has developed. However, the affirmative element has not reached out to a wide public. In part this is because the Scots who have projected a confident, even strident, image of Scotland through the arts have often also been highly critical of more popular Scottish culture. MacDiarmid is the best example, but this is not to suggest that other writers and artists have been unimportant. This has not been a comprehensive account of the literary and cultural component to the home rule movement, but rather an attempt to establish the importance of this component, that cultural revival will have a political impact and may in itself be part of a wider cultural context.

Conclusion

Discussion of the Scottish self-government movement requires a consideration of both nationalism and democracy. Their changing meanings and the difficulties associated with these ideas have been discussed in this chapter. The theoretical literature leads to the conclusion that a democratic form of politics requires the abandonment of absolutes and that there is at root a continuous struggle within the movement. The threat to self-government posed by elitism is particularly striking, and the acknowledgement that democracy cannot simply be defined institutionally should be a warning to supporters of a Scottish parliament who imagine that its institution would amount to self-government. The importance of challenging negative imagery is also important. All of these points have implications for strategies for self-government.

1. Stanley French and Andres Gutman, 'The Principle of National Self-Determination', in Virginia Held, Sidney Morgenbesser and Thomas Nagal (eds.), *Philosophy, Morality and International Affairs*, Oxford, Oxford University Press, 1974, pp. 145–146.
2. Anthony H. Birch, *Nationalism and National Integration*, London, Unwin Hyman, 1989, p. 7.
3. A. Arblaster, *Democracy*, Milton Keynes, Open University Press, 1987, p. 8.
4. Frank Cunningham, *Democratic Theory and Socialism*, Cambridge, Cambridge University Press, 1987, pp. 61–62.
5. A. Arblaster, *Op. Cit.*, p. 89.
6. UNESCO, *Democracy in a World of Tensions*, 1951 quoted in Henry B. Mayo, *An Introduction to Democratic Theory*, Oxford, Oxford University Press, 1960, p. 21.
7. M. Wiener, *Between Two Worlds: the political thought of Graham Wallas*, Oxford, Oxford University Press, 1971, p. 30.
8. See Richard Krouse, 'Two Concepts of Democratic Representation: James and John Stuart Mill', *The Journal of Politics* vol. 44, 1982; Alan Ryan, 'Two Concepts of Politics and Democracy: James and John Stuart Mill' in Martin Fleisher (ed.), *Machiavelli and the Nature of Political Thought*, London, Croom Helm, 1973.
9. V. Price, *Public Opinion*, London, Sage, 1992, pp. 16–17.
10. W. Lippmann, *The Phantom Public*, New York, Harcourt Brace Jovanovich, 1925, p. 13 quoted in V. Price, *Op. Cit.*, p. 17.
11. J. Bryce, *The American Commonwealth*, vol. 3, London, Macmillan, 1888, p. 23 quoted in V. Price, *Op. Cit.*, p. 20.
12. Joseph Schumpeter, *Capitalism, Socialism and Democracy*, London, Counterpoint, 1987, ch. 21.
13. *Ibid.*, p. 269.
14. William Kornhauser, *The Politics of Mass Society*, New York, Free Press, 1959.
15. G. Almond and S. Verba, *The Civic Culture*, Boston, Little Brown 1965; Lester Milbrath, *Political Participation*, Chicago, Rand McNally, 1965; Bernard Berelson et al., *Voting*, Chicago, University of Chicago Press, 1954; Robert Dahl, *A Preface to Democratic Theory*, Chicago, University of Chicago Press, 1956.
16. Michael Margolis, 'Democracy: American style' in G. Duncan

(ed.), *Democratic Theory and Practice*, Cambridge, Cambridge University Press, 1983, p. 117.

17. *Ibid.*, p. 118.
18. Philip Green, *Retrieving Democracy*, London, Methuen, 1985; C. B. MacPherson, *Democratic Theory: Essays in Retrieval*, Oxford: Clarendon Press, 1984; Frank Cunningham, *Democratic Theory and Socialism*, Cambridge, Cambridge University Press, 1987; Benjamin Barber, *Strong Democracy*, Berkeley University of California Press, 1984: David Held and Christopher Pollitt, *New forms of Democracy*, London, Sage, 1986.
19. John L. Gwaltney, *Dryslongo: A Self Portrait of Black America*, New York, 1980 quoted in V. P. Franklin, *Black Self-Determination: A Cultural History of African-American Resistance*, New York, Lawrence Hill, 1992, p. 3.
20. V. P. Franklin, *Op. Cit.*, p. 127.
21. Anne Phillips, *Engendering Democracy*, Cambridge, Polity Press, 1991.
22. See S. Lukes, *Power: a radical view*, London, Macmillan, 1974 ff for a review of the debate and his own contribution.
23. Peter Bachrach and Morton Baratz, *Two Faces of Power* op. cit.
24. E. E. Shattschneider, *The Semi-Sovereign People*, Hinsdale, Illinois, The Dryden Press, 1975 (1960), pp. 34–35.
25. *Ibid.*, p. 35.
25. *Ibid.*, p. 69.
27. Joshua Cohen and Joel Rogers, *On Democracy: Towards a Transformation of American Society*, Harmondsworth, Penguin, 1983.
28. Michael Margolis, *Viable Democracy*, Harmondsworth, Penguin, 1979, pp. 158–179.
29. J. Roland Pennock, *Democratic Political Theory*, Princeton, Princeton University Press, 1979, ch. 6.
30. Charles Beitz, *Political Equality: an essay in democratic theory*, Princeton, Princeton University Press, 1989, p. ix.
31. Benjamin Barber, *Strong Democracy: Participatory Politics for a New Age*, Berkeley, University of California Press, 1984, p. 224.
32. Sarah Wambaugh, *A Monograph on Plebiscites*, New York, Oxford University Press, 1920, p. 1.
33. *Ibid.*.
34. *Ibid.*, p. 2.
35. Quoted in Brian Barry, 'Self-Government Revisited' in David Miller and Larry Siedentop (eds.), *The Nature of Political Theory*, Oxford, Oxford University Press, 1983, p. 136.

36. Brian Barry, *Democracy, Power and Justice: essays in political theory*, Oxford, Clarendon Press, 1989, p. 158.

37. See Karl Popper, *The Open Society and Its Enemies*, London, Routledge and Kegan Paul, 1960, in which 'tribalism' or nationalism is attacked as one of the collectivist enemies.

38. Brian Barry, 'Self-Government Revisited' in David Miller and Larry Siedentop (eds.), *The Nature of Political Theory*, Oxford, Oxford University Press, 1983; Neil MacCormick, 'Nations and nationalism' in *Legal Right and Social Democracy* Oxford, Oxford University Press, 1981 and 'Is Nationalism Philosophically Credible?' in W. Twining (ed.), *Issues of Self-Determination*, Aberdeen, Aberdeen University Press, 1991.

39. Yael Tamir, *Liberal Nationalism,* Princeton, New Jersey, Princeton University Press, 1993.

40. *Ibid.*, p. 33.

41. *Ibid.*, p. 96.

42. David Miller, 'The Ethical Significance of Nationality', *Ethics*, vol. 98, 1988, p. 647.

43. Stein Rokkan and Derek Urwin, *Economy, Territory and Identity*, London, Sage, 1983, p. 115.

44. Ghia Nodia, 'Nationalism and Democracy' in Larry Diamond and Marc F. Plattner (eds.), *Nationalism, Ethnic Conflict, and Democracy*, Baltimore, John Hopkins University Press, 1994.

45. For a discussion of debates on citizenship and the European Union see Elizabeth Meehan, *Citizenship and the European Community*, London, Sage, 1993.

46. Sir Alexander McEwen, *Towards Freedom*, London, William Hodge & Co. Ltd, 1938, p. 130.

47. Quoted in Alan Butt Philip, *The Welsh Question: Nationalism in Welsh Politics, 1945–1970*, Cardiff, University of Wales Press, 1975, p. 90.

48. NLS, Acc. 5927, F. 5, Minute book of National Party of Scotland, South-Eastern Sub-Committee, March 5, 1932; October 4, 1928.

49. *Glasgow Herald*, June 8, 1934.

50. William Coleman, *The Independence Movement in Quebec, 1945–80*, Toronto, University of Toronto Press, 1984, p. 156.

51. *Ibid.*, p. 212.

52. *Glasgow Herald*, note following Charles Waddie's obituary notice, February 9, 1912.

53. John MacCormick, *The Flag in the Wind*, London, Gollancz, 1955, p. 35.

54. Alan Bold, *MacDiarmid*, London, Grafton, 1990, p. 499.

55. C. M. Grieve, 'Scottish Literature and Home Rule', *Scottish Home Rule: monthly organ of the SHRA*, vol. 3, no. 5, November 1922.

56. *Ibid.*

57. George Bruce, '*To foster and enrich*'; *the first fifty years of the Saltire Society*, Edinburgh, Saltire Society, 1986.

58. Billy Wolfe, *Scotland Lives*, Edinburgh, Reprographia, 1973, p. 7.

59. Craig Beveridge and Ronald Turnbull, *The Eclipse of Scottish Culture*, Edinburgh, Polygon, 1989, p. 14.

60. *Ibid.*, p. 112.

61. David McCrone, *Understanding Scotland: the sociology of a stateless nation*, London, Routledge, 1992, pp. 174–175.

62. *Ibid.*, p. 196.

63. Alasdair Gray, *Why Scots Should Rule Scotland*, Edinburgh, Canongate Press, 1992, p. 60.

Britain and British Nationalism

Introduction

To make sense of any political movement it helps to understand its opponents and the context in which it campaigns. Opponents of self-government and the British context itself have both changed considerably over the course of the last century. There have been changes in the wider political economy, the changing role of the state for example. Responses from the centre to the demands for Scottish self-government have also changed and these in turn have had an impact on strategies for self-government. It has been argued that government policies may unintentionally encourage an ethnic or regional identity and thereby create difficulties for the centre.[1] Equally, policies may be designed successfully to placate and appease demands. Connor observed that ethnonationalism 'appears to feed on adversity and denial. . . It also appears to feed on concessions.'[2] The problem for supporters of the status quo is the same as that for supporters of self-government. It is difficult to know whether a policy designed to placate and appease will succeed or have the opposite effect, stimulating new and more radical demands.

Various authors have attempted to make sense of government responses to demands for self-government. Esman has suggested that a range of options are available to the political centre.[3] It may foster acculturation and eventual amalgamation or assimilation in pursuit of an homogeneous nation. Challenges to the centre, he

argues, will often be met initially by 'studied neglect', a denial of recognition which will be superseded by ridicule if neglect proves futile.
Failing these approaches, the centre may resort either to repression
or accommodation, or to some combination of the two. Esman
distinguishes between concessional and structural accommodation:
the former involves providing subsidies or financial assistance for
economic development while the latter involves a redistribution of
power within the state, such as establishing or enhancing the powers
of regional assemblies.

Another approach discussed by Esman is that of consociational
politics, the politics of elite accommodation. This may take many
forms. One of its chief advocates, Lijphart, identified four characteristics of consociational democracy: a 'grand coalition' of all groups;
mutual veto in decision-making; proportionality in the allocation of
opportunities and offices; autonomy, often in the form of federalism.[4] A criticism of consociationalism is its inherent elitism: it offers
a model for accommodating elites and not publics. Nonetheless, it
has found favour in some shape in various places at certain times.

A further way of understanding government responses has been
offered by Rudolph and Thompson.[5] They offer a continuum
from conservative to radical responses, from output concessions,
authority-focused reforms, regime/constitutional reforms, and community restructuring. Output concessions may be economic or
cultural and can be handled by existing decision-making and administrative arrangements. Authority-focused reforms involve admitting
ethnoregional spokesmen into decision-making processes, and may
be modest or extensive. Regime/constitutional reforms bring the
ethnoregional communities themselves into the decision-making
process through referendums or following regionalisation or federalism. Community restructuring involves a redistribution of power,
and might involve independence or some lesser measure of autonomy. Significantly, Rudolph and Thompson see accommodation
by the centre as largely influenced by the 'political environment in
which the ethnoterritorial communities are situated and the size,
cohesiveness, and the level of mobilization of the movements'.[6]

A combination and refinement of these different perspectives
has been offered in an unpublished thesis by Teghtsoonian.[7]
She distinguishes between three major types of response: non-

accommodative policies; accommodative policies which are centre-oriented; and region-oriented concessions. Non-accommodative policies come in a variety of forms: they may involve neglect, ridicule, denial, threat or repression. Centre-oriented accommodative policies may be symbolic, cultural, economic, political, administrative or pro-cedural/participatory. Region-oriented concession may be symbolic, cultural, economic, political administrative or procedural/partici-patory. Administrative reforms short of administrative devolution would be centre-oriented accommodative in nature, whereas home rule or federalism would be a region-oriented concession.

An additional point is worth stressing. The changing context in which demands are made and concessions considered is important. It is vital to take account not only of deliberate responses to demands for self-government but also of other factors which will inadvertently impinge on governments in their response to such demands. The nature and role of the central state will be important. The key to this is loyalty. To whom will citizens living in the territory demanding autonomy feel loyalty, and in what measure? This leads to another important strategy employed by the centre to combat demands for self-government. The centre may attempt to develop a sense of identity and loyalty to it amongst citizens in those communities demanding self-government. This loyalty may be either an alternative to or offered in combination with another identity, though the central state will always demand prime loyalty. This process of 'nation-building' is one part of the strategy employed to combat demands for self-government. Anthony Smith has noted that the resurgence of minority nationalisms 'may well provoke a renewal of the majority nationalism'.[8] British nationalism must, therefore, be considered in understanding demands and strategies for Scottish self-government.

Establishing the Union State

In 1974 John Mackintosh wrote an article on the 'new appeal of nationalism'.[9] He noted that for most people in Britain nationalism had a 'bad taste because it has been associated with authoritarian and aggressive governments and with nasty claims to racial and cultural superiority.' However, this was changing. At base was a sense of Scottish identity:

> The uniting influence of common systems of education, local govern-
> ment, law and religion have imbued all those who have been to school,
> lived and worked in the country with a sense of being Scottish; with
> perhaps an incomplete but none the less definite element of national
> identity.

Scots also felt British. The two sides of this dual identity co-existed
with changing emphasis but world events and those in the UK had
made the British side 'less and less attractive' until many had begun
to question whether it was worth preserving.

Throughout British history, special arrangements have existed to
cater for Scottish distinctiveness and the state itself has played its
part in maintaining a sense of Scottish political separation. The
arrangements for Scotland have altered over time, partly in response
to changes in society and the organisation of British government,
and partly due to pressure from Scotland. The key features of the
relationship between Scotland and England within the Union have
been amity and flexibility. Rarely, if ever, could it be said that England
attempted to wipe out all traces of Scottish distinctiveness. On those
occasions when Scots felt aggrieved it was due to English insensitivity
rather than cultural or political imperialism. The remarkable degree
to which the building of the new state of Britain permitted Scottish
distinctiveness to persist is most evident when the behaviour of
dominant cultures and communities elsewhere in Europe is considered. As far as Scotland is concerned, Britain historically was a model
of tolerance and pluralism.

Britain was established through the union of Scotland and England and has been characterised as a union state, as defined by Stein
Rokkan and Derek Urwin:

> Not the result of straightforward dynastic conquest. Incorporation of
> at least parts of its territory has been achieved through personal dynas-
> tic union, for example by treaty, marriage or inheritance. Integration
> is less than perfect. While administrative standardization prevails over
> most of the territory, the consequences of personal union entail the
> survival in some areas of pre-union rights and institutional infrastruc-
> tures which preserve some degree of regional autonomy and serve as
> agencies of indigenous elite recruitment.[10]

This is quite different from a unitary state, as these authors define it, built up around 'one unambiguous political centre' with undeviating standardization, in which all institutions are directly under the control of the centre.[11] The 'Union state' nature of Britain was maintained by distinct arrangements for governing Scotland, the operation of central administrative boards in the nineteenth century and, later, the establishment of the Scottish Office and the development of special procedures in Parliament for Scottish affairs.

The peculiar nature of the constitutional structure of the United Kingdom today, with its political centralism and cultural diversity, is a product of this historical evolution. Debate on the precise nature of Scotland's current status has been conducted around the themes of Parliamentary sovereignty and Scottish political and cultural distinctiveness. So long as the state at the centre played a limited role in the lives of its people, the impact on Scotland's political status was also limited. Much that made Scotland different institutionally in earlier centuries revolved around local politics little affected by Parliament at Westminster, but as the centre began to play a greater part in the life of the people the nature of Scotland's position was bound to change. The Royal Commission on the Constitution (Kilbrandon), reporting in 1973, described the important changes that occurred:

> The individual a hundred years ago hardly needed to know that the central government existed. His birth, marriage and death would be registered, and he might be conscious of the safeguards for his security provided by the forces of law and order and of imperial defence; but, except for the very limited provisions of the poor law and factory legislation, his welfare and progress were matters for which he alone bore the responsibility. By the turn of the century the position was not much changed. Today, however, the individual citizen submits himself to the guidance of the state at all times. His schooling is enforced; his physical well-being can be looked after in a comprehensive health service; he may be helped by government agencies to find and train for a job; he is obliged while in employment to insure against sickness, accident and unemployment; his house may be let to him by a public authority or he may be assisted in its purchase or improvement; he can avail himself of a wide range of government welfare allowances and services; and he draws a state pension in his retirement. In these and many other ways unknown to his counterpart of a century ago, he is brought into close and regular contact with government and its agencies.[12]

These changes in the role and function of the state and its relationship with the citizen necessarily affected the structure of government and the nature of democratic politics. Political and social movements emerged around issues of welfare and employment and the state responded not only with policies but with institutional apparatus to tackle new issues.

From a Scottish perspective, the most significant aspect was the extent to which Scottish distinctiveness was catered for. Local administration, in the form of a disparate and *ad hoc* structure of local authorities, continued to perform a large part of the work of government and in particular implemented central policies either in partnership with or as an agent of central government. There continued to be a distinctive Scottish pattern to this local administration in both in its organisation and in terms of policy outputs. This was hardly surprising. Change comes slowly and is incremental. The base for each new policy or administrative arrangement will be whatever existed before and furthermore this base will be the most significant element in the new policy or arrangement. Thus, the administrative apparatus and distinct local politics evident a hundred years ago and referred to by Kilbrandon provided the continuity of Scottish distinctiveness which was inherited in the twentieth century.

There was a possibility that central government arrangements might in time have swallowed up Scottish distinctiveness. This did not occur. Indeed, central government was remarkably willing to contemplate a structure of government and policies which suggested that the United Kingdom was less than unitary. In fact, the state became, perhaps unwittingly, a major transmitter of Scottish political distinctiveness. The most significant embodiment of this was the Scottish Office. Founded in 1885, it was a unique feature of liberal democratic governments. Until the establishment of the Welsh Office in 1964, the Scottish Office was the only example of what was to become known as 'administrative devolution'. It was very much a creature of its time, set up in response to complaints that Scotland was being neglected. There was little demand at the time for a Scottish legislature. Discontent was limited on the whole to a desire for Scottish distinctiveness to be acknowledged, rather than a wish to let Scotland articulate this distinctiveness through self-government. The demand and response in the last quarter of the nineteenth century related to pluralism and not democracy, but it was within the traditions of a union, not a unitary, state.

Over time the state's increasing role meant that Victorian willingness to accede to demands for pluralist styles and structures ensured the survival of a robustly distinct pattern of Scottish politics. As new functions were adopted by government and old ones extended, the precedent set by the existing Scottish apparatus was always cited as a reason for further development. Britain never was a unitary state in the strict sense of the term. What makes the Scottish Office significant is that it represented the link between the periods referred to in the passage quoted above from the Kilbrandon Report. It was, however, more in the tradition of the pre-democratic era than the practice of modern democracy. Difference was accepted without allowing for democracy.

This affirmation on the part of Westminster of the existence of a distinctive Scottish political dimension was important. Sources of discontent existed in Scotland though there was nothing comparable to the depth of feeling that existed in Ireland (nor any appreciable reason for such). The concession of the Scottish Office did not buy off Scottish demands. Causes and grievances articulated in the 1850s by the Scottish Rights Association, which did not support a Scottish Parliament, were still being voiced in the 1880s. A particular grievance was the high cost of transacting Private Bills. Complaints were often heard that Scottish business was dealt with infrequently and hurriedly in Parliament. The neglect of Scottish public buildings including castles, palaces and cathedrals seemed to symbolise London's attitude. The 'brain-tax', with many talented Scots induced to leave Scotland by the greater attractions of London, was criticised, though it was also praised by many Conservatives and Liberals who saw the Empire as offering opportunities for Scots. The absence of Government works in Scotland, such as arsenals and publicly funded harbours, was contrasted with their proliferation in England. In the late nineteenth century, Scots saw defence expenditure along the south coast as an anachronism: England was still preparing itself for a Napoleonic invasion. The financial relations between the constituent parts of the United Kingdom was a major cause of disquiet which was fuelled with the publication of Treasury returns from the late 1880s.[13] This panoply of grievances was not sufficient to cause the establishment of a Home Rule organisation but it was an important factor.

At the first annual meeting of the Scottish Home Rule Association (SHRA) in 1888, Dr W. A. Hunter, its president, argued that the Scottish Secretary should be controlled 'not by the opinion of the people of England or Wales or of Ireland, but by the opinion of the people of Scotland'. He complained that a Scottish Secretary appointed from the Lords, as was then the case, would not be answerable to the Commons.[14] The Scottish Office offered a focus for Scottish grievances as well as an example of the Scottish dimension in British politics. The concentration of power in London was a feature of the development of Britain but much continued to be done outside the centre. The extension of activities from the centre necessitated a means of implementing policy outside the centre. This took the form of functional devolution. Scotland was to be a unit of functional 'regionalism', and as was witnessed elsewhere in Europe, 'functional regionalism imposed by the centre for its own purposes, often fed political regionalism'.[15]

The need to accommodate Scottish distinctiveness ran alongside pressure for access to the political process through an extended franchise, although these two pressures did not merge until well into the twentieth century. The franchise in Scotland had been extended in 1832 and again in 1867. Agricultural labourers still had no vote after the first reform measure and this was only provided for in reforms in 1884–85. Something 'very close to universal manhood suffrage'[16] was only achieved around the time the Scottish Office was set up but women still had no vote. As state intervention increased, the nature of citizenship, the relationship between the individual and the state, altered. Marshall accounted for the development of citizenship through the development of civil, political then social rights.[17] The relationship was complex and symbiotic. So too was the position of Scotland. As citizenship rights and the state's responsibilities increased, this was bound to have implications for the relationship between the citizen and Scotland. The state was not simply represented as a centralized entity in London but for most Scots was represented by Scottish institutions. State-citizen relations were mediated through Scottish bodies.

The issue of representation was a central concern in late

nineteenth-century Britain as demands for an increased franchise were heard. 'Representing' Scotland was part of the debate but, as noted above, was quite different from the demand for the vote. The questions of *how* Scotland's interests were to be made present in British government and *who* should make them present were not connected. The answer to the first question was addressed through the institution of the Scottish Office but no serious attempt to address the second was made at that time. The second question became more pressing as the central administrative responsibilities increased. In acknowledging a political dimension to Scottish identity, Britain had provided a basis on which a demand for self-government would be made based on democratic principles.

Scotland in the Union

While much has changed since the establishment of the Scottish Office, the essentials of the Union state have remained much the same. Catering for Scottish democracy was provided for only in as much as special Parliamentary procedures for Scottish affairs have been developed. The remit of the Scottish Office has grown although its power has not grown commensurately. Periodic stock-taking exercises to consider Scotland's position in the union have been instituted by British Governments following demands for self-government or loud expressions of dissatisfaction with existing arrangements.

Parliamentary procedures dealing with Scottish affairs are probably little known and less understood in Scotland. Scottish central administration has developed in the form of the Scottish Office and attendant quangos, agencies and non-departmental public bodies.[18] Poll evidence suggests that these bodies are not well-known in Scotland though their policies are. A study commissioned by the Royal Commission on the Constitution published in 1973 found that most Scots had never heard of the Scottish Office. Twelve years later another poll, marking the centenary of the office, found that little had changed:

'Is there a special office or organisation which helps to run Scotland?'

1973 (%)		1975 (%)	
Yes	48	Yes	36
No	34	No	31
Don't know	18	Don't Know/no answer	33
The Scottish Office	18	Scottish Office	28
St Andrews House	10	St Andrews House	2
The (Scottish) Home Office	4	Scottish Home Office	1
Secretary of State for Scotland	3	Secretary of State for Scotland	3
Other answer	6	Other answer	2
Don't know what it is called	7		

Sources: Research Paper 7 'Devolution and Other Aspects of Government: An Attitudes Survey', Commission on the Constitution, London, HMSO, 1973; *The Scotsman Magazine*, vol. 6, no. 4, July 1985.

The fact that few Scots had heard of the Scottish Office and probably fewer knew about Parliamentary procedures for dealing with Scottish business does not mean that the existence of such institutions and arrangements had no effect on Scottish public perceptions of the specifically Scottish dimension offered in the union state. Distinct housing, education, agricultural, and health policies, or at least policies delivered through Scottish institutions and debated in a Scottish context through Scottish media, were the practical and visible realities of Scottish central administrative apparatus and Parliamentary procedures understood by people living in Scotland.

The Scottish Grand Committee was set up on an experimental basis in 1894. Abandoned after the Conservatives came to power, only to be re-established with the Liberal victory in 1906, it has remained in existence ever since. Its functions and operation have changed over time. Home rule agitation in the late 1940s resulted in changes instituted by Attlee's Labour Government. A cabinet memorandum from the Secretary of State for Scotland in 1947 noted this agitation and proposed changes in Parliamentary procedure.[19] The following year a white paper, 'Scottish Affairs', was published.[20] It was a brief document but its opening sentence made clear the reasons for its publication: 'His Majesty's Government are conscious of the widespread desire in Scotland that the Scottish people should have increased opportunities of dealing with affairs of purely Scottish concern.'[21]

The Government's proposals were contained under four general headings: Parliamentary Business; Economic Affairs; Machinery of

Government and Nationalised Industries; and the Question of a General Enquiry. Amendments to the Standing Orders of the House of Commons which would enhance the remit and powers of the Scottish Grand Committee. Also proposed was a Scottish Economic Conference which would meet under the chairmanship of the Secretary of State for Scotland with a range of representatives from industry, commerce, trade unions, nationalised industries, and government departments to act as a consultative body. There was a commitment to pay special attention to the machinery of government and the nationalised industries to ensure that Scottish conditions were adequately taken into account. A Royal Commission to consider Scottish affairs was rejected although an enquiry into the financial relations between the nations of the UK was later conceded.

These four headings in the 1948 document sum up well the various responses offered over the years by British governments to Scottish demands for self-government. Agitation for self-government was not alone in the background to these developments. Parties in opposition – Labour, Liberals, and Conservatives – would play the Scottish card to embarrass the governing party. Promises made in opposition were delivered only in diluted form. The incoming Conservative Government in 1951 met little pressure coming from Scotland following the demise of home rule agitation, but the commitment to set up a Royal Commission on Scottish Affairs along with a promise to enhance the position of the Scottish Office and create separate executive authorities for the nationalised industries in Scotland, had been made in a document produced by the party in 1949. The original motive had been to exploit home rule agitation to embarrass Labour, but it meant that when the Conservatives came to power they were obliged to deliver something, however limited.

The Royal Commission on Scottish Affairs which was set up by the Conservatives concluded by recommending that certain functions previously administered on a British basis should be administered in Scotland by the Scottish Office. Responsibility for Justices of the Peace was transferred, which made little discernible difference either on public opinion or on the legal system. Roads and bridges were also transferred. This may have appeared unimportant at the time, but as the era of planning emerged in the late 1950s, and particularly through the 1960s, proved an important responsibility for the Scottish Office as it attempted, perhaps with limited success, to develop comprehensive economic planning programmes. Almost imperceptibly, accretions to the responsibilities of the Scottish Office were building up, sustaining the notion of a Scottish economy while not allowing it to tackle Scotland's underlying social and economic problems. In the era of planning, the state's role was paramount. The fact that the state was to have a robust Scottish dimension was significant.

Even if demands for self-government were in abeyance, the existence of a Scottish base provided by the state itself ensured that all was not lost. The ratchet metaphor, used by right-wing thinkers, to describe the gradual increase in state responsibilities during the course of the twentieth century, has greater relevance when applied to the development of a Scottish dimension, though the two are not unrelated. There appears to have been no attempt to impose a policy of acculturation and assimilation on Scotland in the late 1950s, the post-war period when agitation for self-government was at its weakest. The reason was simple: Scottish demands did not seem threatening. But a consolidation took place of Scottish-based government activities which had been going on for many decades and which would be important in the 1960s.

The rise of the SNP in the late 1960s signalled the importance of the Scottish dimension. Ted Heath, then leader of the Conservatives, believed that Scottish nationalism posed a great threat.[22] The Labour government reaction was to establish a belated Royal Commission, on the Constitution. As an evasive device, designed 'to spend years taking minutes' in Harold Wilson's phrase about Royal Commissions, it failed. By the time it reported, with a new chairman and a report favouring home rule, the SNP was on the rise again. Both Harold Wilson as Labour Prime Minister in the late 1960s and Ted Heath, the Conservative succeeding him, used the Royal Commission as an excuse for doing nothing. Its findings had to be awaited before a response could be given. Instead, economic measures were enacted to help Scotland and reforms instituted in the central machinery of government.

The referendum on the Labour Government's proposal was, as discussed in another chapter, the initiative of opponents of self-government. It was a 'delayed-action bomb that later blew up devolution' according to George Cunningham, the Labour MP who introduced the controversial 40% rule.[24] This rule stipulated that an order repealing the devolution legislation had to be moved if fewer than 40% of the eligible electorate voted for the measure in the referendum. The 40% rule came to dominate the debate. The failure to win the required 40%, though a majority voted 'Yes', was seen as a defeat. This had been the intention all along. The anti-devolutionists had little faith in their ability to win (though this was perhaps a mistake), and changed the rules to make victory possible.

More important was the effect of the 40% rule on supporters of self-government. The failure to fight the measure, largely based on an optimistic expectation of victory, meant that a spurious legitimacy was inadvertently given to the rule. It was too late to complain after the result became known. The Scottish public saw the result as a victory for opponents of the measure. A survey conducted after the 1979 election found that 47% of Scottish voters interpreted the referendum result as meaning that Scots did not want an Assembly; 33% felt it meant they did want an Assembly, and the remainder saw it as indecisive or were themselves uncertain as to the meaning of the result. This had been a brilliant act of anti-democratic political manipulation: the people were convinced they had done something they had not. The blow to the cause of self-government could not have been more devastating.

The Conservatives had used a number of devices in reaction to demands in the late 1970s. They promised inter-party talks and a con- stitutional convention, they claimed that they were opposed to the devolution measure on offer but not to the principle itself, and they promised to build a new Scottish national football stadium. This was all part of the party playing the Scottish card while in opposition.[25] When they came to power in May 1979 there was little pressure for self-government and little needed to be done. A few minor alterations in Parliamentary procedures were instituted, including allowing the Scottish Grand Committee to meet occasionally in Edinburgh. A Select Committee on Scottish Affairs was set up alongside other departmental committees.

For most of the 1980s, however, a different and increasingly insensitive approach was adopted by Margaret Thatcher. Support for a union state interpretation of Scotland's position within the United

Kingdom was all but abandoned. The closure of the steel industry became symbolic of government attitudes towards Scotland. The nadir came with the poll tax, which was widely seen as a measure imposed on the Scots against their will by a distant, uncaring government. It provoked a strong reaction. The question of whether the Conservatives had a mandate to rule Scotland was raised, and not only by the SNP. Labour officially backed this line and prior to the 1992 election there was support for Labour seeking a 'dual mandate', a mandate to govern Britain based on a majority of seats in the Commons or failing that a mandate to govern Scotland based on winning a majority of Scottish seats. In large measure this was a reaction to the long years of Conservative rule and the perception that Margaret Thatcher was hostile to the Scottish dimension but it was also part of Labour in opposition playing the Scottish card.

The removal of Margaret Thatcher marked a shift in the style of Conservative politics. John Major appeared more conciliatory on a range of issues, including the Scottish dimension, though he opposed any measure of self-government. During the 1992 election he agreed that his government, if returned, would 'take stock'. The stock-taking was as superficial as that after 1979. A group of 'prominent Scots' were invited to a breakfast party with the Prime Minister to discuss Scottish affairs. It was a hand-picked group, unrepresentative of public opinion.

The document which was produced, 'Scotland in the Union: a partnership for good' appeared in March 1993. Delays in its publication fuelled speculation that it might propose substantial changes. Rumours that Scotland would get more Members of the European Parliament circulated. In the event, the document was the least informed and most insubstantial of government papers reacting to agitation for self-government since the war. Despite the previous Royal Commissions (on Scottish Affairs and the Constitution) and much academic and official documentation of the union state and Scotland's position within it, 'Scotland in the Union' contained a number of factual errors and many more dubious historical interpretations. A few minor adjustments were proposed in Parliamentary procedure and some additional responsibilities proposed for the Scottish Office, though some of these had been planned anyway.

It was a cosmetic exercise but it suggested that in style at least a new approach was being adopted. The language implied a return to the idea of the union state. The key passage summing up the document was in the conclusion:

> Government in Scotland must be more visible because if government is invisible the benefits of the Union may become so too. The proposals contained in this White Paper are designed to improve the visibility of government in Scotland.[26]

In practice, little changed. The closure of Rosyth naval base, which Conservative Ministers had predicted would happen if Scotland became independent, was similar to the steel industry's demise a decade before. The Government seemed at a loss to know what to do. Playing the British card was difficult when signs of British decline were evident. The closure of a naval base and disbanding of Scottish regiments, as well as the withdrawal of sterling from the European community exchange rate mechanism, were not propitious circumstances in which to assert British Nationalism.

'Ukanian' Unionism

The appeal of the British dimension has to be considered in any serious discussion of Scottish self-government. Quite clearly, a British or UK nationalism exists which, in its most extreme form, denies the legitimacy of loyalty to any authority or entity other than itself. British nationalist fundamentalism is rarely referred to as such, but it exists and has proved a most intractable and powerful force. It is possible, however, to conceive of loyalties at different levels which, while occasionally conflicting are ultimately capable of existing together. John Mackintosh was fond of referring to the 'dual nationality' of the Scots, by which he meant that Scots have loyalties to both Scottish and British identities.[27] Home rulers and nationalists who ignore the British or UK dimension ignore an extremely powerful force.

A common element in the ideology of each of the main British political parties is this rarely admitted and even more rarely defined nationalism. It is difficult even to put a label on it given the curious nature of the state it embraces. Richard Rose pointed to this when

he asked what name could be given to the nation associated with
the government of the United Kingdom: 'One thing is certain: No
one speaks of the "Ukes" as a nation.'[28] Identifying some of the
elements and symbols of this ideology help explain it. The British/
UK conundrum should be side-stepped. It is not the geographic
boundaries of the state that are of most importance but the essence
of the nationalism involved. For that reason, a more appropriate term
is Unionism, with the acknowledgment that its variants have applied
differently in the different components of the UK in keeping with
the notion of the union state.

Nairn has provided a focus in his study of the monarchy. He argues
that the monarchy fulfils a function of paramount importance:

> It binds the State together. Anyone who buys an elementary text-
> book on the British Constitution to read it (rather than pray before
> it) knows that the Crown is a crucial element in Constitution, Law
> and Government. Were it to disappear, these would require both
> theoretical and practical reconstruction, not a few adjustments with a
> spanner.[29]

The monarchy has support which transcends party. Her Majesty's
Government and Her Loyal Opposition rarely question it. Curiously
enough, from Nairn's perspective, even the Scottish National Party
supports the monarchy. It was the SNP's original response to the
separatist jibe: Scotland would be an independent member of the
Empire (later the Commonwealth) with the monarch as head of
state. But it is doubtful whether the monarchy is as central as Nairn
believes, and if it is important at all it may be more as an artifact
than the embodiment of nationalism in the UK. Only a few years ago
when the prospect of recurring hung Parliaments seemed likely there
was concern that the 'Crown could be placed in an uncomfortable
position, and the use of her prerogative powers could become
the subject of controversy.'[30] Attempts were made to protect the
monarchy by drawing up ground rules to avoid such controversy.[31]
In a sense, this would have involved an erosion of the monarchical
state and a move towards a republican constitution, but it was not an
attack on the monarchy but rather an attempt to prevent instability
and crisis and to protect the monarchy.

The notion of the 'Crown in Parliament' is clearly a central element in Unionism but it is conceivable either that the UK could exist without its monarchy (perhaps requiring a different name), or that Unionism could end while the monarchy continued to exist, which would make the SNP appear less perverse than Nairn's position suggests. Both of these suppositions rest on an argument that there is more to Unionism than the monarchy. It would surely not be beyond the imagination of a twenty-first century Dicey to dream up some device to replace the idea of the 'Crown in Parliament' to maintain the absence of popular sovereignty. Popular sovereignty may be what Unionism is not about but this tells us very little. It does not mean that support for popular sovereignty necessarily entails the break-up of Britain.

It is not the monarchy so much as the 'Crown in Parliament' that has become a central component of Unionism. The monarch's place in the idea of Parliamentary sovereignty has declined in significance and it is not difficult to imagine a conception of Parliamentary sovereignty entirely divorced from the Crown. What is central is the conception of sovereignty itself. The sovereign is that person (or persons) who receives habitual obedience. Dicey's mark on Unionism has a special place with its contribution to thinking on the internal order of the state. His book *England's Case Against Home Rule* was published in 1886 at the height of the controversy over Gladstone's Irish home rule bill. It has dominated Unionist thinking on home rule ever since, whether applied to Ireland or Scotland. Dicey's presence was felt in the Commons in the late 1970s as much as it had been ninety years before.

It would appear that the changes permitted within the Unionist tradition are severely limited. The 'unwritten constitution', with its supposed flexibility, is extremely inflexible. Despite experience to the contrary, the assumption is that the constitution will break if bent. It is a curious constitutional conception: Unionism asserts that changing any part of the constitutional order may bring the Houses down. This is the mirror image of Nairn's view of the monarchy's central, binding position. For Nairn, the removal of the monarchy will have revolutionary consequences. For Dicey and modern Diceyians, abandoning the fiction of Parliamentary sovereignty will have revolutionary consequences. The ideology of Unionism is nebulous and has many layers of myths. For supporters of self-government it is difficult to identify the essence of the ideology and to know at what target to aim.

A Common Past

Experience of a common past is important to any national identity. Not all Unionists will agree on those things which make them feel proud, just as Scottish home rulers will argue over the kind of Scotland they seek. Unionists will differ over the kind of country they want through their differing interpretations of history. Empire and success in two world wars are important twentieth-century components of this common past shared by each of the constituent parts of the UK but there is another element which should not be neglected: the development of the welfare state is as much part of the common past as the Empire and war-time experiences. Looking at its achievements both without and within its bounds, there has been much that sets the state apart from other European countries.

The Empire is as often celebrated in the works of Scottish as well as English writers. Margaret Thatcher's favourite poet, Rudyard Kipling, was English, John Buchan was Scottish, but both were British and the Empire played a major part in their political identities. The British Empire was very important in offering a support system for this sense of a common past. Notably, even some home rulers supported the British Empire. Finlay divides home rulers into three broad groups: those who argued that the Empire and imperial system of government were fundamentally wrong and hostile to Scottish interests; those who wanted Scotland to take its place alongside the other self-governing dominion nations in the Commonwealth while maintaining close links with England; and those who advocated Scottish nationalism primarily to complement a wider and more all-embracing British nationalism.[32] Scottishness was also catered for in the British army with Scottish regiments. Threats to 'the Argylls' in the 1960s and the amalgamation or winding up of regiments following the end of the Cold War in the 1990s provoked Scottish defence of these British institutions.

The experience of war is important for the sense of a shared past. War acts as a 'mobilizer of ethnic sentiments and national consciousness, a centralizing force in the life of the community and a provider of myths and memories for future generations'.[33] This, however, assumes victory. Defeat can lead to the disintegration of a state, as happened elsewhere in Europe after the first world war and, according to Robbins, could have happened in Britain.[34] War and 'imperial destiny'created a British identity which reached its 'apogee around the First World War'.[35] Yet, a home rule movement in Scotland developed after this. The ambiguities of national identity are evident here, and as Robbins notes were exemplified by the Archbishop of Canterbury, a Scotsman, who wrote to the Prime Minister, a Welshman, rejoicing in the victory of England in the war.[36]

The second world war's great moral achievement, according to William Beveridge, founder of the welfare state, was 'national unity',[37] but war promoted fragmentation as well as cohesion.[38] According to Morgan, the pride in being British recorded in opinion polls relied increasingly on the 'subsidy or charity of the United States'. Few other nations showed both acute dissatisfaction at the 'trials of their daily lives' alongside a 'fundamental pride' in their state.[39] Victory in war could encourage a sense of greatness but this could hide the dissatisfaction with everyday concerns. Pride in being British might prove temporary while the great upheavals which were to follow, especially in a rapidly changing international environment, exposed weaknesses in the state's coherence.

The left's sense of a common past is found in the history of the labour movement. Great successes for the movement have often been British successes. Keir Hardie, the 'apostle of British socialism',[40] was the first Labour Parliamentary candidate, standing in Mid-Lanark before being elected for West Ham, London and later for Merthyr Tydfil in Wales. The Attlee Government instituted a British welfare state and a British nationalisation programme. That the welfare state could not have been inaugurated without the support of US loans has not diminished the perception of this great social advance as a truly British achievement.[41] Bevan, one of its chief progenitors, was at best cool towards Welsh claims of distinctiveness and saw himself as a British politician. The national aspect to the health service was British, and its supporters thereby encouraged to identify themselves with Britain.[42] Conversely, the perception that the Conservatives under Margaret Thatcher were attacking the welfare state might have played its part in fostering support for Scottish nationalism. Defence of the welfare state had priority and nationalism is contingent, hence many Scots in the 1980s argued that the best way of defending this great British institution was by destroying Britain.

Beyond this common past there must also be a sense of common destiny. The UK or Britain is often seen as having a particular role in the world. This has affected the country in its international relations. Late entry into the European Community, the reluctant acceptance of the decline of Empire, the continuing pretence of a 'special relationship' with the United States, and the desire to retain a defence role far surpassing the state's needs, all arise from this view of the UK's place in world politics. Stephen George has argued that Britain's conception of its role was defined in 'rather broader terms than were the national interests of some other Western European states', leading it to take an anti-EEC stance early on.[43] Churchill's view that the UK in the post-1945 world operated in three orbits – the Atlantic and the 'special relationship' with United States, the Commonwealth, and Europe (in that order) – was shared across the parties. In the crucial immediate post-war years Britain saw a future for itself in a new European order but it was a Western Europe 'as a middle kingdom under British, rather than Soviet or American, leadership.'[44] The Butskellite consensus which emerged included a view of Britain's place in the world which was very much influenced by its perceived imperial grandeur. Even in decline there was a determination to cling to a sense of 'Greatness'. Britain had, it was felt, fought and won two world wars while the Americans, with all their wealth, came into the battle after it was all but won. These sentiments have more than a popular appeal. They are as likely to be heard in an Oxford senior common room as in the proverbial working-man's pub, perhaps more so.

British greatness even has a radical form. Support for nuclear disarmament was occasionally articulated in terms of Britain's limited role in the world requiring a modest, non-nuclear defence policy. At least as often, however, came the moral rallying call for Britain to lead the world in abandoning the bomb. This was the other side of the same bombastic self-image which saw the UK as a world power requiring a world power's arsenal. Michael Foot's speech in the special Saturday morning Commons debate at the start of the South Atlantic Conflict, the 'most jingoistic speech of the morning',[45] demonstrated this radical British nationalism in its most absurd form when Foot declared Britain's role as 'defender of people's freedom throughout the world'.[46] It sounded more like a British version of the Truman doctrine than the words of an old pacifist.

Margaret Thatcher's appeal had much to do with her image as a British Bulldog 'putting the Great back into Britain'. In an adulatory magazine marking ten years of Conservative rule, Sir Geoffrey Howe stated:

> Our status within the international community has been transformed within just ten years of Conservative Government from that of a middling – and declining – world power into that of a major influence upon international affairs. Britain is leading events once more again, and helping to shape the international agenda.[47]

Even an advertisement for British Airways on the back of the publication took up the theme, asking 'Ten years on, have you noticed how everyone looks up to the British?' Enhanced self-confidence was being confused with greater influence. It was a potent political force, at least in parts of Britain. In Scotland, where an alternative national identity existed, it was easier to question the substance of British greatness.

A British Common Market

The principal economic consequence of the Anglo-Scottish union was referred to in Article 4 of the Treaty of Union:

> That all the subjects of the United Kingdom of Great Britain shall, from and after the union, have full freedom and intercourse of trade and navigation, to and from any port or place within the said United Kingdom, and the dominions and plantations thereunto belonging, and that there be a communication of all other rights, privileges, and advantages, which do or may belong to the subjects of either kingdom, except where it is otherwise expressly agreed in these articles.[48]

In essence, the Union offered Scots and English a common market. It is comparable to some of the principles set out in Article 3 of the Treaty of Rome which established the European Economic

Community in 1958, listing the elimination of customs duties and restrictions on trade and the abolition of obstacles to freedom of movement of persons, services and capital. While the 1707 treaty was more comprehensive, it has many similarities with the Treaty of Rome. One clear difference is that it was not found necessary, nor would it have been possible, to create a new state in Europe in 1958 in order to facilitate the creation of increased trade, though debate rages on the future of the relationship between economic and political union in Europe.

The economic case for the Union has long been seen as the most potent. The assumption long existed that however appealing the democratic case for self-government might be, the economic realities were overwhelmingly against it. Essentially, the case for the Union has rested on the economic case against self-government. This was based on two premises: first, that the larger economic entity of Britain is mutually advantageous to the Scots and English, and second, that Scotland is subsidised by other parts of Britain. The first argument is more convincing than the latter which remains unproven. Significantly, this conforms with an argument made in 1969 by Gavin McCrone, who later became chief economic adviser to the Secretary of State for Scotland.[49] Debate on the economic aspects of the home rule question has largely focused on the implications of independence.[50] There have been few economic analyses of the implications of devolution though that is largely due to the imprecise nature of proposals on offer.[51]

The discussion of Scotland's position *vis-à-vis* the rest of the UK should not obscure the extra-UK dimension. The European Community has become increasingly important in the economic life of the UK. This common market is seen by many as a superstate in the making. To a large extent the arguments surrounding Europe's future reflect arguments on Scotland's position in the UK. Does an economic entity require also to be a political entity and, if so, what form should it take? How is union achieved without eradicating its distinct component parts? What is clear is that as the European market supersedes the UK market, Britain is becoming redundant, at least as a common market. Indeed the danger exists of Scotland becoming peripheralised by being part of Britain. Unlike in the British Common Market, where it has had direct representation in important decision-making forums including a Minister in the Cabinet over the last century, Scotland has no direct representation in the European Union.

Public Subsidies and Dependency

The other more contentious aspect of the economic debate concerns the territorial distribution of public subsidies. Nigel Lawson, as chancellor of the Exchequer, in November 1987 said that large areas of Scottish life were 'sheltered from market forces and exhibit a culture of dependence rather than of enterprise'.[52] Margaret Thatcher described the Scots as 'privileged', subsidised by the 'marvellously tolerant English'.[53] Scotland, it is claimed, is literally dependent on the South. This notion of dependence, expressed in language more extreme than any used before, has proved one of the most potent arguments against self-government. The terms of debate have been skewed to the advantage of supporters of the status quo, and proponents of self-government have had difficulty confronting this.

In the preface to his study of British regional policy, Parsons argues that problems arise in a 'context composed of historical circumstances and intellectual or ideological predispositions and preoccupations'.[54] The context in which British regional policy, and the Scottish dimension particularly, developed was the economic slump of the 1930s and the *ad hoc* measures taken to tackle the severe malaise which afflicted certain parts of the country.[55] A new vocabulary of orthodox economic terms was begun with 'special areas' and 'distressed areas', which later developed to include 'growth points' and 'regionalism'. A consensus based upon these ideas was accepted across the parties. But it was a consensus which could not last beyond the 'good times'. Indeed it made sense to have an active regional policy in times of relative prosperity. As Gavin McCrone pointed out in 1969:

> The Midlands and the South of England can only be said to be subsidising Scotland, or Wales for that matter, if the public expenditure diverted to the latter could be released in the South or the Midlands without producing inflationary pressure. Since the southern half of England has had consistently full employment, this is clearly not the case.[56]

A problem arises for those areas in receipt of regional aid when the economy as a whole falters. The danger of the inflationary effects of transferring resources to the previously prosperous areas diminishes. Ironically, the case for the abandonment of an active regional policy is strengthened at times of economic slumps.

Regional policy is generally defined in terms of what it sets out to do – to offset a regional imbalance in the economy or to maintain the territorial legitimacy of government – rather than in terms of why it exists at all. Yet without an appreciation of why it is necessary, the picture is incomplete. Regional imbalances occur for a number of reasons. As the previous economic vitality of cities such as Liverpool and Glasgow show, less successful parts of the UK today may not always be that way, nor need they be so now. While London and the south-east have long been dominant economically and politically, there is no reason to believe that this occurs by act of God. What is generally ignored is that the 'backwardness' which causes this might, at least in part, be due to Government policies. It might be more accurate to see regional policy as the cost to be paid by those areas which are prosperous as a consequence of Government policy. It is a small cost. Not only does it fail to offset the imbalance but it produces a psychology of dependence. Regional policy is the territorial equivalent of the pervasive attitude criticised in Robert Tressel's *Ragged Trousered Philanthropists*: the producers of wealth become grateful recipients of assistance. This was evident in the late 1980s when government economic policy was designed to tackle economic over-heating in the South-East of England with high interest rates. While this would not be described as a regional policy, it was one directed at the South-East with harmful consequences elsewhere.

The debate on dependency tends to begin and end with consideration of public expenditure, though it is rarely total public expenditure that is considered. Other aspects of public finance, revenue-raising for example, do not enter into the discussion, and even less often does consideration of public policy in its totality rate a mention. The dependency argument is narrowly focused. Only those payments which are described as 'regional aid', 'state supports' or 'welfare benefits' tend to be included. Little consideration is given as to why certain parts of the UK require these particular subsidies. What is more, state support extends far beyond these. Indeed there are expenditures that while not deliberately directed to benefit a section of the community, have inequable territorial consequences. Expenditure on defence, for example, is not intrinsically a regional policy but nevertheless has a regional impact, as noted above in the discussion of nineteenth-century Scottish grievances. In any consideration of state support it would be mistaken to leave out of account those items of expenditure and policies which, while not designated as 'regional policy', nonetheless have a regional impact.

Part of the problem for the self-government movement is that assumptions are made that certain parts of the country, including Scotland, are inevitably backward and require the assistance of prosperous areas. These assumptions are part of a powerful, if only implicit, component of Unionist ideology – the idea that Scotland depends on the rest of England to maintain its standard of living. The dependency myth is debilitating. If a people are continually told that they are dependent they are hardly likely to gain the self-confidence to govern themselves. The charge of dependency from opponents of self-government involves sapping self-confidence and developing a sense of dependence. A serious commitment to developing an enterprise culture would not involve accusing Scots of being dependent. However, arguing that Scots, collectively or individually, can be independent might have undesirable consequences for British nationalists.

The Growing Significance of Europe

The decline of Empire and loosening of Atlanticism in the post-war period threw the UK back onto the third of Churchill's 'orbits' referred to earlier. The expectation that the movement for European unity would fail was confounded by events and the UK, hesitantly, applied for membership. Enthusiasm for the goal of 'ever closer union', enshrined in the EC's founding treaty, was barely evident in its successive applications. At least from a UK perspective (though it has been argued that this was also the major consideration for the six founding members),[57] membership of the EC was a means of maintaining the authority of the 'nation state' rather than creating a new European political entity. Its merits as a trading bloc were economic but these were believed to buttress rather than diminish the authority of the existing states. Membership of the EC can therefore be seen as a continuation of the 'pursuit of greatness' policy which has characterised British foreign policy throughout the twentieth century.[58]

Opposition to EC membership has had a number of sources. Some fundamentalist nationalists – British or Scottish, left or right – felt that membership undermined 'sovereignty' and the myth of the nation created by God. Others opposed EC membership for other reasons, such as perceived links with defence matters and the fear that a distant, bureaucratic central authority would undermine democratic self-government. Amongst Scottish nationalists this latter fear was frequently expressed, and it was not without some foundation. Not all fundamentalists opposed EC membership. So long as it was simply a trading bloc many, including Margaret Thatcher, were able to support it, only when it threatened to become a super-state did it provoke their opposition.

The language used in debates was significant. The key term was sovereignty. Whether it was the UK's loss of sovereignty or the need to 'restore Scottish sovereignty', a monolithic conception of state power was involved. Power was absolute and indivisible, whether within the United Kingdom or between it and its trading partners. Debate on constitutional reform was shaped by the language in which it was conducted. This debate was at least honest as to the origins of its terms, but it was dishonest in its appreciation of the impact that economic, technological and institutional changes were having on the international political system.[59]

Conclusion

Over time opponents of self-government have adopted accommodative as well as non-accommodative policies. Neglect and ridicule were particularly in evidence early in the twentieth century, but whenever the issue of self-government has forced its way onto the political agenda more accommodative approaches have been adopted. Most notably, the establishment and development of the Scottish Office and special Scottish Parliamentary procedures have been used – centre-oriented accommodative policies in Teghtsoonian's typology discussed in the introduction. Other similar policies such as developing regional aid and special economic, cultural, and symbolic measures have also been adopted. Region-oriented concessions have been rare though from the late 1960s moves towards setting up a Scottish legislature have been given serious consideration in response to the electoral successes of the SNP.

The changing context in which the Scottish self-government movement has operated has played a crucial role both in structuring the opportunities available to the movement for pursuing its goals, and in affecting the strategies to be adopted. The extent to which the movement has defined its goals has been significantly affected by what has been happening well beyond Scotland. This dependence on the wider environment might be seen as limiting self-government in the sense that the movement's goals are to some degree externally shaped. This is correct, but no more so than for any other movement. What is significant is that there is a need to adapt to changing circumstances. These circumstances may act in the interest of the movement or against it but it would be folly to develop any strategy that failed to take account of the context in which it operates.

The economic case remains of paramount importance for those who articulate the case for the *status quo* and this has influenced the arguments deployed by those who argue for Scottish self-government. The essential argument, that self-government would be too costly, has proved the most persistent and powerful argument deployed by opponents of self-government. In important respects the British case has lost its appeal. The economic case, on which Britain is largely based, was weakened with membership of the European Community. The decline of empire and Britain's international status has removed a central plank in British national identity. British nationalism, in its more progressive form, took some knocks in the 1980s when British institutions such as the welfare state came under attack. It became clear that the welfare state was not synonymous with the British state. Indeed maintenance of the union may be seen as a threat to some of those very institutions and policies previously associated with Britain. However, innate conservatism and fear of change give a potency to British nationalism which is often understated.

In addition to the changing context, which has been outwith the control of opponents as well as advocates of self-government, counter-strategies have had to be confronted by activists for self-government. The UK has proved adept at countering demands for radical reform. The use of myths, symbols and historic events have been prominent in developing a sense of British national identity. Additionally, the pluralistic nature of the state and a willingness to cater for Scottish distinctiveness may have taken the edge off home rule campaigning, and along with the nebulous ideology of Unionism has given strength to supports of the status quo. On the other hand, concessions have fostered a sense of Scottish identity.

1. Paul Brass, 'Ethnicity and Nationality Formation', *Ethnicity*, vol. 3, No. 3, 19767; Stein Rokkan and Derek Urwin, *Economy, Territory, Identity: Politics of West European Peripheries*, London, Sage, 1983, pp. 176–179.
2. Walker Connor, 'The Politics of Ethnonationalism', *Journal of International Affairs*, vol. 27, no. 1, 1973, p. 21.
3. Milton Esman, 'Perspectives on Ethnic Conflict in Industrialized Societies' in Esman (ed.), *Ethnic Conflict in the western World*, London, Cornell University Press, 1977, pp. 380–384.
4. Arend Lijphart, *Democracy in Plural Societies*, New Haven, Yale University Press, 1977.
5. Joseph Rudolph and Robert Thompson, 'Ethnoterritorial Movements and the policy process: accommodating nationalist demands in the developed world', *Comparative Politics*, vol. 17, no. 3, 1985.
6. *Ibid.*, p. 297.
7. Katherine Anne Teghtsoonian, *Institutional Structure and Government Policy: Responding to regional nationalism in Quebec, Scotland and Wales*, Stanford University Ph.D., USA, 1987.
8. Anthony Smith, *National Identity*, London, Penguin, 1991, p. 156.
9. John P. Mackintosh, 'The New Appeal of Nationalism', *New Statesman*, September 27, 1974.
10. Stein Rokkan and Derek Urwin, 'Introduction: Centres and Peripheries in Western Europe' in Stein Rokkan and Derek Urwin (eds.), *The Politics of Territorial Identity: Studies in European Regionalism*, London, Sage, 1982, p. 11.
11. *Ibid.*
12. *Report of the Royal Commission on the Constitution* (Kilbrandon), 1973, London, HMSO, Cmnd. 5460, p. 76, para. 232.

13. For the complaints in the 1850s see William Ferguson, *Scotland: 1689 to the Present*, Edinburgh, Mercat Press, 1990, pp. 320–321; *Report of the First Meeting of the National Association for the Vindication of Scottish Rights*, held in the Music Hall, Edinburgh, November 2, 1853. For the 1880/90s see for example Scottish Home Rule Association, *Scotland's Claim for Home Rule*, 1888; Marquess of Bute, 'Parliament in Scotland', *Scottish Review*, October, 1889, pp. 400–403; W. A. Hunter, *The Financial Relations of England and Scotland*, SHRA, 1892.

14. *Glasgow Herald*, September 19, 1888.

15. Yves Mény and Vincent Wright, 'General Introduction' in Yves Mény and Vincent Wright (eds), *Centre-Periphery Relations in Western Europe*, London, Allen & Unwin, 1985, p. 3.

16. George Pryde, *Central and Local Government in Scotland Since 1707*, London, Historical Association, 1960, p. 14.

17. T. H. Marshall and Tom Bottomore, *Citizenship and Social Class*, London, Pluto Press, 1992 edition.

18. Quangos are quasi-autonomous non-(or national) government organisations. A substantial number of these and other similar bodies, such as agencies and, in modern parlance, non-departmental public bodies exist with a wide range of responsibilities. See Stuart Weir and Wendy Hall (eds.), *Ego trip: extra-governmental organisations in the United Kingdom and their accountability* London: The Democratic Audit of the United Kingdom, 1994. This publication lists 374 Scottish 'egos', the generic term they use for such bodies, with more members sitting on these bodies than there are elected councillors.

19. PRO, CAB 21/3329 'Scottish Demands for Home Rule or Devolution: Memorandum by the Secretary of State for Scotland', November 1947.

20. Scottish Home Department, 'Scottish Affairs', HMSO, 1948, Cmd. 7308.

21. *Ibid.*, p. 2, para. 1.

22. Richard Crossman, *Diaries*, vol. 2, London, Hamish Hamilton, 1977, pp. 550–551.

23. 'Scotland will win with Labour', Labour Party Manifesto for Scotland, October 1974, p. 11.

24. George Cunningham, 'Burns Night Massacre', *The Spectator*, January 18, 1989.

25. James Mitchell, *Conservatives and the Union*, Edinburgh, Edinburgh University Press, 1990, ch. 5.

26. 'Scotland in the Union: a partnership for good', March 1993, HMSO, Edinburgh, p. 39, para. 10.8.

27. John P. Mackintosh, 'The trouble with Stephen Maxwell', *Question*, April 15, 1977 reprinted in Henry Drucker (ed.), *John P. Mackintosh on Scotland*, London, Longman, 1982, pp. 147–151.

28. Richard Rose, *Understanding the United Kingdom*, London, Longman, 1982, p. 11.

29. Tom Nairn, *The Enchanted Glass: Britain and its Monarchy*, London, Radius 1988 p. 89.

30. Vernon Bogdanor, *Multi-party Politics and the Constitution*, Cambridge, Cambridge University Press, 1983, pp. 86–87.

31. *Ibid.*; David Butler, *Governing Without a Majority*, London, Collins, 1983

32. Richard Finlay, '"For or against?"': Scottish Nationalists and the British Empire, 1919–39', *The Scottish Historical Review*, vol. LXI, p. 185.

33. Anthony Smith *Op. Cit.*, p. 27.

34. Keith Robbins, *Nineteenth Century Britain: integration and diversity*, Oxford, Clarendon Press, 1988, p. 184.

35. *Ibid.*, p. 185

36. *Ibid.*, p. 182.

37. Quoted in Kenneth Morgan, *The People's Peace: British History 1945–1990*, Oxford University Press, 1992, p. 3.

38. *Ibid.*, p. 23.

39. *Ibid.*, pp. 53, 108.

40. Francis Williams, *Fifty Years' March*, London, Odhams Press Ltd, nd., description of Hardie below photograph in frontispiece.

41. Kenneth O. Morgan, *Labour in Power 1945–51*, Oxford, Oxford University Press, 1985, ch. 4.

42. Kenneth O. Morgan, *Rebirth of a Nation, Wales 1880–1980*, Oxford, Oxford University Press, 1981, pp. 376–378, 413.

43. Stephen George, *An Awkward Partner: Britain in the European Community*, Oxford, Oxford University Press, 1990, p. 12.

44. Michael J. Hogan, *The Marshall Plan: America, Britain, and the reconstruction of Western Europe, 1947–1952*, Cambridge, Cambridge University Press, 1987, p. 109.

45 Peter Jenkins, *Mrs Thatcher's Revolution*, London, Pan Books, 1988, p. 160.

46. Hansard, Commons, vol. 21, April 3, 1982, col. 639.

47. Conservative Central Office, *The First 10 Years*, London, Conservative Party, 1989, p. 31.

48. Treaty of Union, 1707, article 4.
49. Gavin McCrone, *Scotland's Future: the economics of nationalism*, Oxford, Basil Blackwell, 1969, p. 52.
50. *Ibid.*; David Simpson, 'Independence: the Economic Issues' and K. J. W. Alexander 'The Economic Case against Independence' in Neil MacCormick (ed.), *The Scottish Debate*, London, Oxford University Press, 1970; Donald McKay (ed.), *Scotland 1980: the economics of self-government*, Edinburgh, Q Press, 1977; Fraser of Allander Institute, *Scotland and Independence: an economic perspective*, Glasgow, Fraser of Allander Institute, 1989.
51. Scottish Council Research Institute, *Economic Development and Devolution*, Edinburgh, SCRI, 1974; Brian Hogwood, 'Models of Industrial Policy: The implications for devolution', *Studies in Public Policy*, Strathclyde University Centre for the Study of Public Policy, No. 5; L. C. Wright, 'Some Fiscal Problems of Devolution in Scotland', in J. N. Wolfe (ed.), *Government and Nationalism in Scotland*, Edinburgh, Edinburgh University Press, 1969; Ross Leckie, 'Implications for Industry' in Michael Fry (ed.), *Unlocking the Future*, Edinburgh, Conservative Constitutional Reform Forum, 1988.
52. *Glasgow Herald*, November 24, 1987.
53. *Daily Express*, April 25, 1990.
54. Wayne Parsons, *The Political Economy of British Regional Policy*, London, Routledge, 1988, p. vii.
55. B. W. E. Alford, *Depression and Recovery? British Economic Growth, 1918–39*, London, Macmillan, 1975, p. 69.
56. Gavin McCrone, *Scotland's future: the economics of nationalism*, Oxford, Basil Blackwell, 1969, p. 49.
57. Alan Milward, *The European Rescue of the Nation-State*, London, Routledge 1992.
58. Robert Holland, *The Pursuit of Greatness: Britain and the World Role, 1900–1970*, London, Fontana, 1991.
59. See for example Joseph Camilleri and Jim Falk, *The End of Sovereignty?*, Aldershot, Edward Elgar, 1992.

Home Rule Pressure Groups

Introduction

It is helpful to distinguish between different types of pressure groups and the different strategies of each type. Two distinctions are evident in the vast literature on pressure groups. The first is between sectional and promotional groups.[1] Other writers use different terms but make essentially the same distinction. A sectional group is one that represents the interests of a section of the population such as a trade union whereas a promotional group articulates a cause or set of values such as the Campaign for Nuclear Disarmament or Friends of the Earth. As Jordan and Richardson express it, 'in broad terms, the distinction is between groups of, versus groups for'.[2] Using this definition, it is clear that a home rule pressure group would be an example of a promotional group. Promotional groups are generally less well funded, relatively unfamiliar with internal governmental activity and likely to be media-oriented.[3] This has a number of implications especially as far as strategy is concerned as can be seen when considering the second type of distinction.

The second kind of distinction is that between insider and outsider groups.[4] Insider groups are those which have gained direct access to government. A group which has attained insider status is in the enviable position of being recognised as legitimate where it counts, by those with power. There are many reasons why a group may gain insider status. It may have the support of a substantial body of opinion, its cause or interests may be shared by those in power, or government agencies may need the group's assistance in some way. If the government is dependent on a group to some extent, for example to implement its policies or as a source of expert advice, the group will be in a far stronger position than it would with widespread public support. The tendency is for sectional groups to be more likely to have insider status and for promotional groups to be outsiders but this is not a rule, and it would be quite wrong to suggest that insider groups are always effective while outsiders are ineffective. Nonetheless, Jordan and Richardson make the point that promotional groups are 'usually too politically contentious for the civil service to allow them into bed.'[5]

Insider and outsider are, of course, ideal types, and the status of any group may vary within the insider-outsider spectrum. A change of the party in power, the increased political salience of an issue, or the precise matter on which government is making a decision may determine the extent to which a group will be an insider. Grant has distinguished between three types of outsider groups: potential insider groups; outsider groups by necessity; and ideological outsider groups.[6] Potential insiders have yet to win that status but under the right conditions may do so. Outsider groups by necessity are less politically sophisticated than potential insiders in term of their knowledge of how the political system works. Ideological outsider groups do not accept that change can be achieved through the existing political system.

Home rule groups have almost invariably been outsider groups though not always ideological outsiders. They have occasionally been received by government officials, though this need not involve gaining meaningful insider status. As Hogwood has noted, if consultation is everything then maybe it's nothing.[7] Of the three categories of outsiders referred to by Grant, they have generally fallen somewhere between outsider groups by necessity and ideological outsiders.

The strategies groups adopt will in large measure be determined by whether they are promotional or sectional and insider or outsider. An outsider, promotional group (as home rule groups have been) must first decide to whom it is addressing its case – political parties, Parliament, the civil service, the media or the public as a whole – and with what purpose. Is it attempting to affect the established institutions or, more radically, somehow find an alternative opening? A study of the effectiveness of the poverty lobby in Britain reached the conclusion that a group 'forced into undertaking public campaigns would only be advertising its impotence'.[8] Appealing to the public is, at best, an indirect approach but it may be the only one available. The right to be heard where it counts is not always conferred by the public. However, in the case of the Scottish self-government movement the appeal to the public can be seen as a central part of the movement's *raison d'être*. Popular sovereignty is the objective and public support must therefore be part of the movement's strategy.

Groups without insider status may attempt to 'piggy back' on another group and campaigns may be waged by promotional groups within other political organisations such as trade unions or political parties. Identifying a particular party or parties likely to accept the group's message might offend another party, and the party chosen may not be the one which has the best chance of power. It is always easier to 'piggy back' on a party or other group which is itself on the outside than one which is on the inside.

The study of pressure groups has tended to focus on insider and sectional groups and, indeed, those which have been successful. Little attempt has been made to understand the work of more diffuse outsider groups promoting radical change. These groups have a monumental task before them, identifying a workable strategy is a major problem. Since the political context in which a group must operate will usually be beyond its control, it is reasonable to conclude that home rule groups may have failed for reasons other than their own deficiencies. The biases in the political system, as discussed in chapter two, rather than the group's strategy, may well explain failure.

Pre-1914 Campaigning

In 1886, the Scottish Home Rule Association (SHRA) was established by Charles Waddie. It was a body on the fringe of Scottish politics and its origins were largely external to Scottish politics. Not only did the Scottish movement set out to imitate the Irish movement, Scottish home rulers were driven by a desire to accommodate Irish home rule within the United Kingdom. They argued for reforms which would avoid the anomaly of having a Parliament in only one part of the country while representatives from there would still be sent to Westminster. Dicey's case against Irish Home Rule published in 1886, *England's Case Against Home Rule*, focused on the anomalies of unilateral devolution. The SHRA's existence was contingent on solving the Irish question by means of home rule all round. William Mitchell, its treasurer, noted that the organisation had been formed in May 1886, a month after Gladstone's introduction of his Irish Home Rule Bill:

> When Mr Gladstone made it a matter of practical politics, and it became evident that sooner or later the relations of the three Home partners in the British Government must be reconsidered and read-justed, the originators of the Scottish Home Rule Association were called together by Mr Charles Waddie, and after a few preliminary meetings the Association was formed, he being its first secretary.[9]

Mitchell himself had been an active Liberal in Midlothian, Gladstone's constituency and had organised a Scottish home rule meeting in April 1886, nine days after the introduction of the first Irish Home Rule Bill, having concluded that the solution to Gladstone's di-lemma regarding the position of Irish representation at Westminster was the extension of home rule to Scotland, England and perhaps Wales.[10]

Waddie also explicitly tied the SHRA to demands for Irish home rule. He claimed to be the author of the phrase 'home rule all round' and maintained throughout his life that home rule for only one part of the UK would be calamitous. In a letter to the *Scotsman* a week before he died in 1912, he warned against the repetition of the 'blunder' of 'taking up home rule for Ireland first and only'.[11] To some extent the early SHRA was a pressure group which acted to influence the Liberal leadership. Only occasionally is there evidence that its members saw much point in trying to influence Conservatives. At its fifth annual conference in 1892, a suggestion was made that a deputation visit Gladstone in Midlothian. Keir Hardie, founder of the Labour Party, argued that a deputation should also be sent to see Lord Salisbury, the Conservative leader.[12]

The objectives of the early SHRA were to support the main-tenance of the British Empire, to secure Scotland's voice in the Imperial Parliament, to establish a Scottish legislature 'with full

control over all purely Scottish questions, and with an Executive
Government responsible to it and the Crown', to secure control of
the Scottish civil service and judiciary, and to 'foster the national
sentiment of Scotland and maintain her national rights and honour'.
Problems associated with using the term home rule, given the Irish
situation, were acknowledged in SHRA publications but they maintained that the 'national aspirations of the Irish people were identical
with their own' and that the term:

> expressed more shortly and clearly than any other words that could
> be used the idea of a National Legislature and Executive responsible
> to it for the management of those affairs which belonged exclusively
> to each of the four countries composing the United Kingdom.[13]

The federalist leanings of the SHRA may not have been obvious
from the organisation's name but were evident in its publications. An
article which appeared in *Scottish Review* in July 1886 entitled 'Home
Rule for Scotland' discussed the principle and practice of federalism
elsewhere in the world and concluded that changes throughout the
Empire were leading ineluctably to federalism:

> Some such arrangement is one to which we are gradually if not rapidly
> hastening. It points the way to the grandest ideal in modern politics,
> the union of the mother country with the colonies in one real United
> Empire, the United States of Greater Britain.[14]

Defining 'purely Scottish questions' proved as difficult for the
early SHRA as for later devolutionist bodies. Waddie had set out
a list in a pamphlet originally published before the SHRA was set
up. It covered a range of issues including reform of the poor law,
reform of crofting, game laws, regulation and encouragement of the
fishing industry, and passing private bill legislation.[15] His list was not
exhaustive, as he made clear, but was designed to show that there
would be no lack of work for a Scottish Parliament. It indicated too
the reformist intentions of Waddie which were generally shared by
others in the SHRA.

Another theme which was evident in the early SHRA was the
need to lighten Westminster's workload. Parliamentary obstruction
by Parnellite Irish nationalists had added to the difficulties of passing

legislation through the Commons, and the devolutionist proposals were presented as a means of improving the government of the United Kingdom. Further evidence of the early SHRA's limited goal was its insistence that 'Parliament is and must remain sovereign and supreme', that it 'must not be fettered by any written constitution' but that the Scottish Parliament would 'exercise delegated power' and that Parliament 'must necessarily exercise a real and not a sham veto upon national legislation'.[16]

While there may have been a broad consensus on the need for change, problems arose over how to achieve it and electoral politics could not be avoided. Canvassing the views of candidates in elections and backing particular candidates caused problems for the group. In his first report as secretary of the SHRA, Waddie annoyed some members when he argued that SHRA backing for Keir Hardie in the Mid-Lanark by-election had been a mistake. This was challenged by Hardie, who pointed out that if the SHRA felt that it had made a mistake every time a candidate it had backed lost it would never make any progress. He could see no mistake in the SHRA giving him support against 'two English barristers'. Waddie argued that Hardie and the SHRA had been deceived into believing that Mid-Lanark could be won, but agreed to delete the offending passage from his report.[17] It was an early example of the difficult party balance required in a cross-party home rule pressure group.

By its fifth annual conference in 1892, the SHRA had made little progress. Waddie's report noted that 'very few references were made to Scottish Home Rule by speakers at public meetings, and none that were satisfactory, members of Cabinet rank being particularly reticent'.[18] Later, in moving a resolution to authorise the issue of a manifesto, he attacked the Radical Liberals for their 'deception' over the previous six years and identified a number of prominent Liberals, Lords Elgin and Rosebery in particular, for 'standing between Scotland and her national rights'.[19] The seconder of the resolution drew back from Waddie's comments arguing that Gladstone and Rosebery had said that Scotland would get what Scotland wanted but the difficulty was knowing exactly what that was. It was, thus, their 'immediate duty to hold a Scottish national conference to ascertain the opinion of the country upon this question before the general election'. How this was to be done was not decided. Waddie may have been correct but in a cross-party pressure group his comments had not been politically sensible.

A series of publications listing Scottish grievances, outlining schemes of home rule all round, endorsing candidates, and canvassing support had little impact. Ridiculed by the leaders of the Liberal and Conservative Parties, the SHRA faded out though some of those involved never lost faith in the goal of self-government but turned to other approaches. In 1899 Waddie staged a series of historical plays in an attempt to stimulate Scottish patriotism.[20]

The significance of the early SHRA lies in the reasons for its foundation, the difficulties it had in developing a clear strategy and its place in the development of the national movement. The distinctive aspects of politics in Scotland and a multitude of perceived grievances were not in themselves sufficient to provoke the establishment of a home rule organisation. The Irish question was central. To a greater extent than any similar organisations later, the early SHRA was a unionist body with its *raison d'être* the preservation of the union as much as the establishment of a Scottish Parliament. Had this remained the only basis of support for Scottish home rule then the movement would have disappeared with the demise of the Irish question. However, home rule became linked to progressive politics in the period before 1914, when support for reforms in Scotland were seen to require support for a parliament. This explains the radical Liberal support for home rule before the first world war and the support of Labour afterwards. The translation of home rule's meaning around this time was crucial in the development of the movement.

The Young Scots Society (YSS) emerged within the Scottish Liberal Party in 1900 and became a home rule pressure group. Its origins lay in the election defeat that year and initially it campaigned against the Boer war. Following the war it concentrated on campaigning for free trade and was credited with helping the Liberals achieve their landslide victory in 1906 in Scotland. From 1907 it placed greater emphasis on home rule. In a manifesto published in 1911, devolution was described as the 'most urgent reform of the time' after the abolition of the Lords' veto.[21] This was linked with progressive issues such as land reform, temperance, house-letting, education and poor-law reform. But its members were 'Party Liberals first, Scottish nationalists second' as Roland Muirhead, a member of YSS, noted. There were threats that it might contest elections with its own candidates against Liberals opposed to its policies and that it might become a 'Scottish National Party'. It succeeded in pushing the issue within the party and even having candidates dropped and replaced, but little else.

What was achieved was a link between socio-economic issues and those of constitutional reform. The 'New Liberalism' in its Scottish context assumed the existence of a Scottish Parliament in order to bring about a reform programme. But YSS was more a faction within a party than a pressure group. The close association of Scottish home rule with the Liberals disappeared with the rise of the Labour Party and the home rule mantle passed to Labour. Though the Liberals never introduced a measure of Scottish home rule, the pre-1914 agitation and the party's close association with the cause established a historic tradition to which it referred for many years. That the party failed to implement a home rule scheme when it had the opportunity tends to be overlooked.

Inter-War Campaigns: International Appeals

A foretaste of the inter-war home rule activities emerged just before the outbreak of the first world war. The International Scots Home Rule League (ISHRL) was formed in June 1913 aiming to unite Scots of all parties and none. The intention was to set up a network of supporters abroad, presumably based on the activities of other European nationalist organisations. The League attempted to put pressure on the Liberal Government to ensure that its commitment to deliver home rule would be honoured. To this end, its secretary visited Canada and the United States and claimed to have travelled 13,000 miles, addressed 10,000 people, and distributed over 15,000 Scots home rule leaflets. The League had also been active in by-elections in Wick and South Lanark in December 1913. A monthly newspaper was launched in November 1913 called *The Scottish Nation*.[22] By June 1922 the League boasted an impressive list of honorary presidents under its new name, the International Scots Self Government League. The Marquess of Graham held the presidency and some distinguished Scots accepted honorary positions.[23] At a

public meeting addressed by Graham in October 1922 it was made
clear that the League did not see itself as opposed to any other home
rule organisation nor did it see itself as a party.[24] It was a body with
no clear strategy. Through its distinguished line-up it may have lent
some credibility to the cause but otherwise it was an ineffective body.

The situation at the end of the war differed markedly from that at
the outset. The Irish question resurfaced on the British political agenda following the Easter Rising in 1916. Promises and concessions
were made by Prime Minister Lloyd George, including a Speaker's
Conference on Devolution. Also, US President Woodrow Wilson's
belief in the right to self-determination provided an important
backdrop to the peace conferences which met after the war. Scottish
home rulers, along with supporters of self-government elsewhere
in Europe, saw the announcement of the Wilsonian doctrine as an
opportunity. But, as Wambaugh noted, Wilson's 'repeated refusals
to favour the petitions from subject nationalities which poured in
on him' as the war was ending show that the President did not fully
endorse the right of secession.[25] Scots were amongst those whose
petitioning was met with a presidential refusal. As Wilson explained
in a speech in September 1919:

> It was not within the privilege of the conference of peace to act upon
> the right of self-determination of any peoples except those which had
> been included in the territories of the defeated empires.[26]

In October 1918 a provisional council of a renewed Scottish
Home Rule Association was formed. The new body was to be
'representative of all shades of political opinion and every phase of
industrial and social activity'. This body drew heavily on the labour
movement, unlike the first SHRA which had been dominated by
Liberals.[27] At Christmas 1918 the executive of the SHRA sent a letter
to President Wilson, 'in the name of the Scottish people', urging
him to support Scottish self-determination.[28] Forty-three Scottish
candidates who contested the 1918 election, including five who were
returned, sent the *Pétition Nationale de l'Ecosse pour obtenir sa Representation au Congrès de la Paix*. The petition, written in French, gave a potted
version of Scottish history focusing particularly on the union.

Though the signatories included some who had opposed the war,
such as James Maxton and John Maclean, the petition claimed that

the German attack on Belgium and France had 'strongly touched the heart of the Scottish nation which found a marked resemblance in these events to the loss of her own independence.' This had been why all classes of young Scots had enthusiastically signed up and 'bravely shed their blood in defence of international law and liberty'.[29] It was an avowedly nationalist document. The experience of Versailles taught the movement that the high ideals of international law were not matched by the reality of international power politics. Scottish home rulers had little to gain from appeals to an authority beyond the state. Appeals to international bodies and foreign statesmen were repeatedly made during the twentieth century but were usually half-hearted attempts to seek publicity rather than serious strategies for self-government.

SHRA, Electoral Politics and Putting Pressure on MPs

An immediate objective of the SHRA had been to influence the election of 1918. To this end all candidates contesting Scottish constituencies were sent a letter asking if they would use their influence in promoting the cause of self-government. Favourable replies were received from 25 Liberals, 17 Labour and 16 Unionists candidates. Only one candidate replied negatively – Col. A. T. H. Buchanan, Unionist MP for Coatbridge. The following year Scottish MPs were approached to ascertain their position on home rule. Nine MPs responded favourably: three non-Coalition Liberals, two labour two Coalition Liberals, one ILP and one Unionist. A further ten MPs acknowledged receipt of the letter but did not commit themselves.[30] The Unionist who had responded favourably was F. C. Thomson. His reply was clear:

> I am in favour of Devolution of Scottish affairs. I supported both by speech and vote the motion for a Committee to consider the question of federal devolution. I think exclusively Scottish affairs should be dealt with by an Assembly in Scotland.[31]

Thomson's position was to change. At that point in time the Irish Question was still being dealt with and, while the second SHRA was not so tied to the issue as its predecessor, for some politicians the solution to the Irish problem lay in a federal United Kingdom.

Scottish home rule was still becoming an issue in itself but in the process it was to lose the support of Unionists such as Thomson.

Only six MPs attended a meeting called in September 1922 with the SHRA.[32] Two referred to the widespread indifference to home rule in Scotland. Another's view was that this was the result of it having become a non-party question, of the change in attitude amongst Unionists, who felt that the Irish question had been solved, and of the 'intimate relations between Scottish and English Trade Unions in the Labour Party'.[33] The meeting ended with an agreement that they should meet again in London shortly after the opening session of Parliament with the aim of gaining support from more MPs. The election in November, which saw Labour's share of Scottish seats rise from 7 to 29, including a group of radical Clydesiders whose views were essentially nationalist, forced the second meeting back to February 1923.

A discussion on strategy took place at this better attended meeting: eighteen MPs were present – one National Liberal, one Liberal and sixteen Labour MPs. A further ten MPs sent their apologies and good wishes – four Liberals, one National Liberal, four Labour MPs and Edwin Scrymgeour, the Independent Prohibitionist MP for Dundee. It was suggested that MPs should call on the Government to summon a convention of delegates from representative bodies in Scotland and that, if the government refused, they should join with the SHRA in calling an informal convention to draft a home rule scheme to be presented to the Commons. Outside Parliament, each Scottish MP was to call a constituency conference on home rule to prepare a campaign. Tom Johnston pointed out that a home rule amendment to the King's Speech had been tabled but had not been discussed. He also agreed with J. M. Hogge, a long-standing radical Liberal supporter of home rule, who had argued for the Scottish MPs to form themselves into a group to press for a Scottish Parliament at the earliest possible moment, but the aim that emerged most clearly from this meeting, and gained support generally, was for a constitutional convention.[34]

In 1924 a letter was again sent to candidates standing for Parliament by the SHRA. Three questions were asked of each candidate: whether their election address contained a commitment to a Scottish Parliament; whether they favoured summoning a national convention to frame a scheme of home rule; and whether they would cooperate in summoning a convention if Parliament refused to do so.[35] This was to be the most significant strategic development of the SHRA and the national movement up to that time. The subsequent constitutional convention was to play a significant part in the development of ideas about how self-government might be attained. The demise of the SHRA, largely caused by the failure of the convention, allowed the idea of a national party to develop. The response to the letter was generally favourable. Of the 108 replies, 89 supported home rule and 30 either opposed or gave no opinion. Of those elected, 49 had declared themselves to be in favour of home rule.[36]

Relations With the Political Parties and Agreeing a Scheme of Devolution

A recurring issue in the SHRA was its relations with the political parties. The early SHRA had been a largely Liberal body. Roland Muirhead, despite his own Labour background, was determined that the reconstituted SHRA should not be seen as a Labour Party front and elicited the support of Henry Keith, a prominent local authority Tory from Hamilton. The Labour leadership in Scotland tried to discourage their members from joining the SHRA, fearing that inter-party cooperation would cause difficulties at elections. In 1919 James Maxton and miners' leader Robert Smillie were criticised and asked to withdraw from the SHRA by the Scottish Council of the Labour Party.[37] Nonetheless, the perception that the SHRA was a left-wing front persisted. In 1922, the Marquess of Graham, one of the few Conservatives associated with home rule, wrote to Muirhead telling him that he would not take part in a public meeting organised by the SHRA as it was not 'fully representative of all political parties in the country':

> I find that the platform party and speakers are almost all recognised leaders of the Socialist, Communist, and Bolshevist Party, with the principles of which I am in entire disagreement. . . I object to approval being exclusively expressed in favour of the Free State of Ireland, for there are many who, like myself, prefer the dominion status of Ulster, and therefore I consider partiality should be avoided.[38]

The platform party was indeed fairly left-wing but the SHRA replied that Graham's 'labelling of them as Communists and Bolshevists is both untrue and ungenerous'.[39] It transpired, as Graham explained in a letter to Muirhead, that he had been misled and 'confused some of the gentlemen with others of similar name and who are well-known Communist and Bolshevist leaders'.[40] Graham's fears were, however, not entirely without foundation. Andrew Fisher, Scots-born former Labour Prime Minister of Australia, declared at the meeting that he was a socialist and perhaps a Bolshevik.[41]

Public meetings were held frequently and often addressed by significant political figures. Commemorative demonstrations marked the death of William Wallace. A demonstration in 1923 at Glasgow Green addressed by Labour MPs urged the members of the crowd to put their hands up for home rule; the resulting famous photograph is often found in nationalist and labour movement histories. At this meeting James Maxton attacked the 'colossal impertinence' of English people in 'dominating for hundreds of years people like those of India and Ireland, not to speak of Scotland'.[42] A cartoon in the *Glasgow Evening Times* showed a tartan-clad Graham on bended knee offering David Kirkwood a crown with Maclean and Maxton standing in the background holding lions rampant with kilted angels in the top corner.[43] This was the tenor of the opposition response to the movement, and reflects the ease with which it could be lightly dismissed, aided by the colourful and exaggerated rhetoric of the Clydesiders.

By summer 1924, according to Finlay, the 'Labour grip on the Association was absolute, and blatant attempts were made to eschew all other political elements'.[44] Muirhead's concern was that the attitude adopted by some Labour elements was chasing away potential supporters in other parties, thus preventing the SHRA from becoming a genuinely cross-party body. The membership of the SHRA reflected this left-wing bias. By June 1919, 700 individuals had joined and over 100 organisations had affiliated. Growth continued and by late 1923 it claimed to have 272 affiliated organisations. By the end of 1928 over 300 organisations had affiliated to the SHRA.[45] Most of these were trade unions. However, while the SHRA may have been dominated by Labour Party supporters, Labour's leadership was unwilling to be associated with the organisation. In 1925, shortly after the failure of Buchanan's Private Member's bill on home rule,

Ramsay MacDonald, who had been an early advocate of Scottish home rule, refused to meet members of the SHRA when he visited Glasgow to receive the freedom of the city.[46] The SHRA was having the worst of both worlds: failing to win over Labour's leadership while losing support from other parties.

Agreeing a scheme of devolution was of less importance to the SHRA than promoting its cause. Schemes were devised but it is not clear whether they were to be seen as serious blueprints or as a means of gaining publicity. When the report of the Speaker's Conference on devolution was published along with the MacDonald minority report in 1920, composed in the context of solving the Irish Question, the SHRA expressed its opposition to both reports and instructed its executive to draw up a detailed scheme.[47] In December, the general council of the SHRA approved a scheme for a single-chamber Scottish Parliament having a wide range of responsibilities, leaving the Imperial Parliament responsible for the Crown and succession, foreign and colonial policy, the navy, army and air force, the currency, and weights and measures. Taxes levied in Scotland would be paid to a Scottish Treasury which would arrange with the Imperial Treasury the payments to be made for Imperial purposes. It was also decided to hold a national convention to determine along what lines self-government should be enacted.[48]

A draft bill was prepared under the auspices of the SHRA general council four years later, though it was not official policy. It recommended a Scottish Parliament with 148 members, 2 members for each of the existing Westminster constituencies. No member would be required to take the oath of allegiance. The Parliament would have the power to alter its constitution and set up a second chamber. No Scottish constituency would be represented in the English Parliament but a joint council would be set up to confer on matters of joint interest such as defence and foreign affairs, which would meet as was deemed necessary. If Ireland or Wales acquired Parliaments they too would be accommodated in the Joint Council. The Scottish Treasury would assume responsibility for 11/80ths of the existing national debt, the Goschen proportion, and would recover possession of some proportion of the assets of the UK.

At a meeting of the SHRA general council in March 1924, George Buchanan, ILP MP for Glasgow Gorbals, said it would be inadvisable to leave the working out of a bill to a convention. He had drafted a bill which he was confident would gain a majority in the Commons at its second reading.[49] Buchanan's bill was a more modest proposal than that being considered by the SHRA. It proposed a quasi-federal solution with Scottish MPs continuing to sit at Westminster until home rule all round was achieved. It was defeated in the Commons in May after the Labour Government refused to grant a second day for discussion, amidst the kind of chaos which earned the Clydesiders their radical reputation.[50]

The reaction to this failure was important in the development of the movement. At a general council meeting in June 1924 the idea of Parliamentary obstruction was proposed and a resolution was passed:

> That Scottish Members of Parliament supporting Home Rule for Scotland should combine to devise a policy, whether that of deciding that no Bill applying to Scotland should be permitted to take precedence of a satisfactory Home Rule Act or other policy, which would induce the Government to give immediate attention to the demand of Scotland for self-government through a Scottish Parliament.[51]

Maxton, although supporting the resolution, made it clear that he was not committing himself to a policy of obstruction. The key problem for the SHRA was that the movement's rhetoric did not match its practice. The next stage of the SHRA's activities saw the development of the constitutional convention, into which the SHRA threw itself almost to the exclusion of all else. Occasional forays into other activities occurred, including the Ayr by-election in 1925 when none of the candidates were deemed to have given a satisfactory reply to SHRA enquiries, and Patrick Dollan, the Labour candidate, refused to place home rule on his programme.[52]

The gradual realisation that the convention could not succeed in applying pressure created further disillusionment within the SHRA. Discussions on the formation of a National Party became increasingly frequent. A lengthy debate took place on the issue at a general council of the SHRA in December 1925.[53] The following year it was debated again. Those in favour focused on the need to put pressure on MPs.[54] A key individual involved in these debates was Roland Muirhead, who provided both enthusiasm and drive in his role as secretary as well as finance for the SHRA. In May 1926 his increasing despair was evident:

> The SHRA has now been in existence for seven years, and Scotland is still ruled from London. It is time to take stock of our progress, with a view to finding out whether further activity on the lines on which we have been and are now working is well directed and likely to secure Scottish self-government at the earliest possible date, and whether some change of policy or method is not required.[55]

In August, Robert Muirhead, Roland's brother, questioned Labour's commitment to home rule and suggested that the 'most effective' way of getting Labour or any other party to take up home rule was to 'show it votes will be lost if neglected'.[56] It was only a matter of time before Roland Muirhead was to take his money and dedicated campaigning out of the SHRA and into a new political party.

Whether intentionally or not, the strategy of the SHRA had focused on the Labour Party. No serious effort was made to convert the Unionists, though they formed or participated in government for most of the period of the second SHRA's existence. Labour may have given some support, but it was patchy and its leaders proved suspicious of any cross-party organisation. Indeed, before the SHRA could hope to make progress it had to satisfy the party's leadership by demonstrating Labour domination of the organisation, thus negating the cross-party nature from which it had derived its appeal.

The Scottish National League and Scottish National Movement

Other nationalist and home rule organisations not affiliated to any party were active just after the first world war. The most significant of these were the Scottish National League (SNL) and its offshoot the Scottish National Movement (SNM). According to Finlay, the Scottish National League was the 'most important of all inter-war nationalist groups' before the National Party of Scotland.[57] It played an important part in the establishment of an independent national party but its role is more usually seen as less significant than the SHRA. It achieved far less publicity than the SHRA during its existence and it failed to attract a significant body of followers. Its concern with a wide range of issues and its function as a forum for debating strategy were significant: economic and social programmes were devised, a

newspaper was launched, the cultural dimension was emphasised
and fierce debate took place on forging a non-Parliamentary route
to self-government. However, its often outlandish style, romantic
celticism and extreme language meant it was often treated as part of
the lunatic fringe. By 1927 it had nonetheless set the agenda for the
future strategy of the movement.

The date of the League's foundation is variously described as
1919 and 1920. It was initially closely associated with a variety of
Gaelic and celtic bodies and ideas. Sympathy with the Irish cause was
evident in its early days; even at this late stage the Irish influence on
the Scottish national movement still existed. Figures such as William
Gillies and Ruaraidh Erskine of Mar were to provide the SNL with
its chief assets – drive and determination – and its chief weaknesses
– anglophobic rhetoric and dreamy mysticism. They established the
Scots Independent in 1926, now the longest running Scottish political
newspaper. Significant contributions to debate in the national movement are to be found in its pages well into the 1950s. The weaknesses
of the SNL were encapsulated in Erskine's 'celtic communism' which
argued that a collectivist ethos in the celtic past had been undermined
by Anglo-Saxon values of greed and selfishness. The mythology of
clan solidarity and celtic moral superiority was probably picked up
from the Brighton-born aristocrat's Lewis nanny, from whom he also
learnt Gaelic.[58] Despite an intense anglophobia, William Gillies spent
most of his adult life in London where he operated on the fringes
of Irish nationalist bodies and involved himself in Gaelic and celtic
revivalism. It may be significant that this body, prone to anglophobic
denunciations, included so many Scots who lived in London. The
approach adopted by the SNL was unconventional. It hoped to
revive an old spirit in Scotland to lift the nation out of subservience.
In 1922 it issued a manifesto which declared that sending Scots to
the English Parliament was futile:

> The Scottish National League has an alternative – namely, that the
> men and women of Scotland abstain from voting at the elections
> ordered to be held in Scotland by the English Government; that the
> men and women of Scotland working towards the League objective of
> a great and democratic national convention at which Scotland's inde-
> feasible rights to complete national independence shall be reaffirmed
> and re-established; that the Scottish people take into their own hands

all the public powers of the country and administer them for, and in behalf of, the Scottish nation.[59]

This did not, of course, mean that the SNL had any time for the SHRA's convention. Its relationship with the SHRA was always difficult. In 1926 at a rally near the Wallace Memorial, W. MacLaren, the secretary of the SNL, criticised the SHRA for seeking a remedy for Scotland's grievances from the 'enemy', the English-dominated Parliament. MacLaren stated that it was not within the province of England to give Scotland a Parliament. Home rule bills had been presented and failed. Scottish MPs should pledge not to cross the border at all but to remain in Scotland and legislate for Scotland.[60]

The SNL's call for independence found articulation in two related but different ways: independence from other parties and organisations, and independence for Scotland. It compared Scotland to other small European states such as Norway, Belgium and Switzerland and urged Scots to follow their example. This purist approach made it difficult to cooperate with other bodies. Anything less than independence was seen as a sell-out and therefore to be opposed. If the SHRA exemplified the weaknesses of the gradualist approach, the SNL exemplified the weaknesses of the fundamentalist approach. Factionalism was rife and had three main sources: debates on strategy, objectives and personality clashes. These differences often surfaced in other contexts. At a public meeting in March 1923 members from the Edinburgh branch of the SNL criticised the weakness of the organisation in Glasgow, pointing out that branches had been established in Dunfermline, Arbroath, Aberdeen and elsewhere 'through no help from Glasgow'.[61] Tom Gibson, who joined the SNL from the SHRA, following the failure of Buchanan's home rule bill, showed the enthusiasm of the convert when he attacked Erskine of Mar, president of the SNL, for agreeing to speak on an SHRA platform. For Gibson and others, the SHRA had proved not only unable to deliver home rule, but to contain a sizeable element whose sincerity for the cause they doubted.[62]

A more serious split occurred in 1926. This seems to have originated in personality clashes focusing on Lewis Spence, an Edinburgh journalist. The resulting Scottish National Movement

(SNM), with Spence as its president, consisted of a large section of
the Edinburgh and Dunfermline branches of the SNL. The SNM
placed advertisements in the press, including that of the British
dominions and the USA, which brought in new members and
supporters. Establishing 'flying squads' of activists, holding public
meetings, producing literature and establishing branches of supporters was the stuff of SNM activity. It saw its role as both advocating
constitutional change and encouraging awareness of Scottish cultural
identity. Speakers addressed the need for a Scottish Parliament
alongside talks on 'Burns, the Patriot' or 'The Decadence and Revival
of Edinburgh'. Curiously, within months of its establishment, Spence
held discussions on the possibility of merging with the SHRA and
SNL: these were informal discussions which did not lead very far
but presaged later developments.[63] The SNM sent delegates to the
SHRA- sponsored constitutional convention but submitted its view
that this approach was not likely to succeed. The question was
raised within the SNM as to whether it should support bills put
forward by the SHRA. Spence's view, which appears to have been
the only one that counted, was that the SNM should support any
measure directed towards obtaining home rule.[64] It was therefore
more willing to cooperate with other bodies than the SNL but it was
hampered by anglophobia, especially Spence's own. It suffered from
having no clear strategy and no view as to how its various activities
should cohere into a successful campaign for self-government, and
in August 1924 some concern was expressed that it was 'going
backwards'. This coincided with discussions going on elsewhere in
the national movement on the way forward. Overtures from those
considering establishing a national party were forthcoming and were
welcomed. The SNL and SNM had many unpalatable features and
no more offered a way forward than did the SHRA. What they
did provide was a critique, though expressed incoherently and in
exaggerated form, of the SHRA and the established political parties.
Out of this was to emerge the idea of a separate political party.
They were not the only forums in which this idea took shape but
they were significant ones. The most important contribution of the
SNL and SNM was probably their ability to ask awkward questions. Their weakness was that they could not provide the answers
themselves.

War-Time Agitation

The SNP had been set up in 1934 but divisions within it were never far below the surface. Differences reached a head at the 1942 annual conference when a split occurred and a section of the party led by John MacCormick walked out and held a meeting of its own. They resolved that a new body – initially called Scottish Union but later changed to Scottish Convention – should be set up which would not stand candidates at elections but would rather seek to influence all political parties and cultural organisations. As a leaflet explained, the name was chosen 'because the word convention signifies the act of a people coming together in unity of purpose'.[65] Membership was recorded after its first annual general meeting at 540.[66] By December 1944, it had risen to 3,271. The membership was located in branches, including one with 15 members in Leeds. The largest branch, with 235 members, was in Edinburgh.[67] By June 1946 total membership stood at 4,773.[68] Its view of Scotland's constitutional position was that:

> the old incorporating Union, which has so seriously handicapped Scotland in the past, should be transformed into a federal union in which England, Scotland and Wales will be self-governing units within the federated whole.[69]

There was little attempt by Scottish Convention to provide much detail or to work out how federalism would operate in other parts of the UK. It was more a rallying organisation than one offering a detailed scheme. In fact, there was little that could be done while the war continued, although a full-time organiser was appointed in January 1943, advertisements were placed in the press, pamphlets written, and public meetings were held.

Much of the activity was a prelude to Scottish Convention's main strategy: the revival of the idea of a constitutional convention. This could not be launched until the war was over. In the meantime, the objective was to keep interest in home rule alive for the day when a representative assembly could meet. It was successful in gaining access to Tom Johnston, the Secretary of State for Scotland, who had been a long-standing home ruler. Accompanied by Joe Westwood, his Under Secretary, and David Milne, a senior civil servant,[70] Johnston pointed out that many of their proposals were out of the question in the circumstances of the war.[71] The report of the deputation to Scottish Convention's national committee stated that the Scottish Secretary had 'unmistakeably shown his sympathy with our aims and his approval of our organisation which apparently wielded an even greater influence than we ourselves supposed'.[72] In her diary, Naomi Mitchison, who was part of the delegation, recorded her views of the meeting:

> T. J. very friendly and anxious to talk off the record, but won't do anything political during the coalition. Emphasised all the economic things he had done, and the machinery for progress which he had produced, the Grand Council etc. The difficulty is it may all be swept away by his successor and he doesn't seem to want to stand again which is an awful pity.[73]

Mitchison's fears were justified. After standing down as Scottish Secretary at the end of the war Johnston declined an invitation to join Scottish Convention, although he expressed his gratitude to them for advancing the cause.[74]

Another cross-party initiative was launched during the war which attempted to build support for a Scottish Parliament and was aligned with Scottish Convention. William Leonard, Labour MP for Glasgow St. Rollox, initiated a 'Declaration on Scottish Affairs' which was signed by a wide range of public figures. The Leonard Declaration, as it came to be known, was the result of private non-party meetings addressing the prospect of a changed international order at the end of the war. Its origins were broadly similar to the Versailles Petition after the first world war. Following meetings between President Roosevelt and Winston Churchill in August 1941 a statement of principles, the Atlantic Charter, was endorsed by fifteen states fighting on the Allied side in the war. Amongst these principles was the right of peoples to choose their own form of government. This provided an important backdrop for the Leonard Declaration, which argued for a Scottish Parliament, warned of the dangers of an economic depression following the war, made clear its opposition to a customs barrier at the border between Scotland and England, and argued that defence needed to be maintained on a unified basis. A Scottish Parliament dealing with domestic affairs while retaining Scottish representation at Westminster was advocated. The balance of revenue raised in Scotland after making an 'appropriate contribution to United Kingdom and Imperial expenditure' would be at the 'free and unfettered disposal of a Scottish Government and Parliament'. A range of subjects was listed as falling within the scope of the Parliament, with others such as transport, labour and location of industry requiring close cooperation with Westminster.[75]

Discussions had been going on for two years prior to the launch of the Leonard Declaration. Invitations had gone out to potential signatories but the response had been disappointing 'both as to numbers and in that no influential Unionist signatures were obtained'. Amongst those who had been approached but doubted that a Scottish Parliament was the right solution was the Tory playwright James Bridie.[76] This meant that the declaration did not have the desired non-party character. Additional problems arose when someone listed as a signatory denied he was a supporter. Sir Henry Keith, then aged 90, was a former prominent Tory in Scottish local government who had previously indicated support for a Scottish Parliament. In a letter to the *Glasgow Herald*, Sir Henry denied signing the declaration. Confusion had arisen over the interpretation of Sir Henry's ambiguous reply but it proved an embarrassing moment at the launch of the declaration.[77] There was a minor flurry of publicity surrounding the launch. The Secretary of Scottish Convention, who was involved, reported that other than 'routine enquiries' a copy had been requested by the Ministry of Information in Glasgow and, curiously, by the authorities in New South Wales.[78] But, as he pointed out in a letter to the Duke of Montrose, it was 'difficult to see what action could be taken to follow up at the present time, apart from canvassing for individual signatures'.[79]

The Post-War Activities of Scottish Convention

Scottish Convention adopted two main strategies after the war: a revised constitutional convention approach and, later, a massive petition leading to demands for a national plebiscite. The details of these are dealt with in other chapters but their importance here cannot be ignored; they dominated the thinking of Scottish Convention, and the failure of each approach proved influential in the development not only of Scottish Convention but the wider movement. Some general features are raised here including the nature of Scottish Convention and its relations with other organisations, particularly political parties.

The danger of being seen to be too close to any one party was recognised, and in October 1944, Scottish Convention decided not to meet the Scottish Trades Union Congress and Labour Party as proposed by the Glasgow Trades Council. The feeling was that Scottish Convention should preserve its own identity.[80] An invitation to all Scottish MPs to meet a delegation from Scottish Convention was proposed in January 1946.[81] At the meeting with the Labour MPs, MacCormick spoke of the uniqueness of the occasion for him; it was the first time he had addressed a meeting with the power to do something. If Scottish Labour MPs lived up to their election pledge then self-government would be introduced during the lifetime of the Parliament. Two MPs, Jean Mann and Gilbert McAllister, expressed disagreement with the Scottish Convention delegation, stressing instead the priority they attached to economic and security matters. Half of Labour's Scottish MPs had attended the meeting. Neil Maclean, chairman of the British Labour Party, expressed his support for the cause.[82] The meeting with the Scottish Secretary, Joe Westwood was similar. Westwood made it clear that he was not opposed to self-government and his Under Secretary, Tom Fraser, was reportedly 'very sympathetic'.[83]

The meeting with the Unionist MPs did not take place until later. The delegation was surprised at the 'friendliness' of its reception and though the party was officially opposed to home rule the delegation formed the opinion that a 'considerable number' of Scottish Unionist MPs were favourably disposed and 'ready to throw in their lot with legislative devolution'.[84] However, the Conservatives were merely playing the Scottish card in an attempt to embarrass the Labour Government and had no intention of delivering any form of home rule.

An attempt to meet Prime Minister Attlee the following year, however, was unsuccessful. The rebuff in October 1947 was sharp. Not only did it suggest that they should meet the Scottish Secretary instead, but Downing Street remarked that Westwood's programme was 'heavy for the next month or six weeks' and suggested that a convenient date be arranged through the Scottish Office.[85] As Westwood was replaced as Scottish Secretary by Arthur Woodburn only a few days after Attlee had written to MacCormick, the reply was interpreted as a further slight on the grounds that Attlee must have written in the knowledge that Westwood would no longer be Scottish Secretary.[86] The Scottish Liberals' general council, confirming Labour suspicions that Scottish Convention had deliberately attempted to embarrass the Government, passed a resolution critical of Attlee's refusal to meet Scottish Convention.[87]

In January 1948, a meeting was arranged with Woodburn at an inauspicious time. MacCormick had been adopted as Liberal candidate to contest a by-election in Paisley with Unionist support. Only days after coming forward to fight the Labour seat, he led a delegation to meet the Scottish Secretary. The same day, Woodburn met a deputation from the executive of the Scottish Parliamentary Labour Party and the party's Scottish Council who suggested some minor improvements in the machinery for conducting Scottish affairs.[88] There was never any doubt which deputation Woodburn listened to. A meeting was eventually arranged with his successor, Hector McNeil, who became Scottish Secretary in February 1950. With his Parliamentary Under Secretaries, Tom Fraser and Margaret Herbison, and senior officials Sir David Milne and Charles Cunningham, McNeil met a group led by Cllr Robert Gray of Glasgow which included Michael Byrne of the Transport and General Workers Union. But consultation of this sort did not mean that the idea was being given serious attention in government. It was only the appearance of insider status.

Electoral Politics

At the 1945 general election every candidate was asked by Scottish Convention whether they would support a self-government bill and whether they would give priority to the issue within their party.[89] This was a fairly weak attempt to put pressure on the parties, as had been confirmed in the inter-war period, but short of contesting elections there was little else that could be done. By early July, it had received 119 replies, 73 of which supported self-government.[90]

A by-election for the Scottish Universities seat shortly before the general election in 1945 was contested by Sir John Boyd Orr. Boyd

Orr was a distinguished scientist, soon to become director of the United Nations Food and Agriculture Organisation, and stood as an Independent with the support of Scottish Convention. Although not actively involved he had lent his name to the cause and attended a meeting of the national executive of Scottish Convention shortly before the by-election.[91] He was successful but due to his other commitments stood down in October 1946, causing a further by-election. Once more, Scottish Convention sought the views of the candidates. John Bannerman of the Liberal Party, actively involved with Scottish Convention, was deemed to have supplied the most satisfactory reply[92] but the victor was Walter Elliot, the former Tory Scottish Secretary who had lost his Kelvingrove seat at the previous year's general election and was hostile to home rule.

Initially, MacCormick did not want Scottish Convention to fight elections though he had personal Parliamentary ambitions. In 1945 he contested Inverness for the Liberals and three years later he committed what is generally seen as his greatest political blunder. He had already been chosen as Liberal candidate in Paisley when a by-election was called. This would have been delicate enough given his prominent role in Scottish Convention which was then trying to convince the Labour Government to set up a Scottish Parliament. Indeed, it was only days after his official adoption as candidate, that MacCormick led the delegation to meet Arthur Woodburn, the Scottish Secretary, mentioned above. More controversially, however, a deal was struck with the local Tories to allow him a free run against Labour in the by-election. Many Liberals were outraged and Labour saw this as evidence that Scottish Convention was little more than a Tory plot to attack the Government.

A joint declaration with the Tories included a commitment to devolution but also attacked what they described as the Attlee Government's use of controls and compulsory direction of labour. It argued for a free economy, profit-sharing in industry, and a reduction in public expenditure and taxes. The section on devolution had all the hallmarks of MacCormick's influence:

> We recognise that there are differing opinions as to the extent to which such a measure (devolution) is immediately practicable, but we urge that all parties in Scotland should seek to reach agreement on this question and that it should not be made an issue in party politics.[93]

It was a hotch-pot of Liberal-Tory measures not all of which MacCormick could possibly have felt comfortable with. His willingness to cooperate with others in pursuit of a gradualist approach appeared to know no bounds. His eve-of-poll meeting was addressed by a curious range of speakers: Malcolm McCorquodale, Conservative MP for Epsom in Surrey; Major Guy Lloyd, Unionist MP for East Renfrewshire; John Bannerman of the Scottish Liberal Executive, and William Power of Scottish Convention.[94] During the campaign Walter Elliot shared a platform with MacCormick, yet two years before in the Scottish Universities by-election Elliot's views on home rule had been deemed inadequate by Scottish Convention's national committee.

MacCormick's election address concluded with his views on home rule. The concession to the Unionists was considerable:

> I recognise, however, that Scottish opinion has not yet fully crystallised in this important matter, and that, while all are agreed on the necessity of reform, there are differing opinions as to the extent of reform which is immediately practicable. The task which, therefore, lies before us is to ascertain the highest common factor of agreement among all parties, and to secure by our unity that this measure of agreement is translated into action forthwith.[95]

This statement came close to dismissing much of the work of Scottish Convention. The national assemblies sponsored by Scottish Convention had already been meeting and had made progress, alluded to by MacCormick. If the national assemblies had been about anything they were about reaching agreement on a scheme of home rule.

It had been a major gamble. Had MacCormick won it would have given him a platform on which he would most likely have distanced himself from the Unionists and made strenuous efforts to gain home rule. His defeat, however, soured the already poor relations between the national and labour movements. Douglas Johnston, who had been Solicitor-General from October 1947, was elected Paisley's MP by 6,545 votes. The perennial strategic problem confronting the Liberal Party, caught between the two major parties, was thought to have been exacerbated by MacCormick. The party could not afford to be seen as too close to Labour or the Tories. The Liberal chairman noted that Labour had scored its best result ever in Paisley, and that the only way to defeat the Attlee Government was through the Liberals acting as a progressive party winning over radical support.[96] Shortly afterwards MacCormick stood down as vice-president of the Scottish Liberals after being attacked for his approach in Paisley, though he remained a member.[97] Labour set its face against home rule.

The pact appears to have been locally inspired. Unionist Party President Lord Dunglass (Sir Alec Douglas-Home) admitted that it was a complete surprise to him when asked. Liberal leaders in London were unenthusiastic.[98] Lady Glen-Coats, Liberal candidate in Paisley at the previous general election, attacked the decision to unite with the Tories and along with Naomi Mitchison, a Labour Party member, resigned from the national committee of Scottish Convention.[99] There had been some anxiety in Unionist circles at the start of the campaign too. The local Unionist organiser had resigned, pointing out that at the general election the Liberals had won only 4,532 votes against the Unionists' 14,826.[100] The stakes had been high and the cost to the national movement was the wrath of the Labour Party without any compensating support from the Unionists.

There was some talk of contesting a by-election in the Gorbals in 1948, but it had been discovered in Paisley that by-elections offered dangers as well as opportunities. The Newton Mearns branch of Scottish Convention moved an emergency resolution at its annual meeting suggesting that Boyd Orr should be sponsored to stand with home rule 'on the Ulster model' as his main plank but MacCormick, in the chair, ruled the resolution out of order.[101] The national committee considered a proposal to form an all-party committee consisting of Scottish Convention leader who would invite Boyd Orr to stand in a personal capacity, but John MacCormick spoke of his recent experiences and argued against the proposal. The danger to the unity of the movement and the dilemma in which members would find themselves if called upon to support a Convention candidate against their own party was noted. It was agreed that nothing should be done.[102]

At Scotstoun in October 1950 a mini-referendum was held while a by-election was being fought. But this was a side-show which irritated rather than put pressure on the Labour Party. Scottish Convention insisted that it did not intend to become a political party but at its annual meeting later that year MacCormick stated that they had to 'build up something which is on a parallel with the parties' to show them that they could not ignore popular opinion. It was a thinly veiled threat:

> We shall exhaust every approach of persuasion and argument, but if in the end our reasonableness is met with complete obstruction we shall devise the means to overcome it.[103]

The difficulties were leading to tensions in the organisation. In January 1951 a group of five members of the Scottish Covenant Committee was set up to prepare a statement on strategy. It was publicly acknowledged that some differences of opinion had emerged.[104] A demand for a Royal Commission was made but this glossed over their problems. By March, the threat to contest elections was becoming more explicit. Scottish MPs were to be asked to sign a pledge that if re-elected they would press for Scottish home rule with the possibility that those who refused would find themselves opposed by a Covenant candidate.[105] MacCormick claimed that the Covenant had candidates primed to fight each of Scotland's 72 seats.[106] This coincided with a decision to create a permanent Scottish Covenant Association. As the radical newspaper *Forward* commented, the new body would assume the form, if not the substance of a political party:

> This is the latest development in a movement which has bewildered the man in the street with the variety of its different labels – National Assembly, Scottish Convention, National Covenant Committee, and so on.[107]

A game of brinkmanship was being played, and played badly. That same month, the National Covenant Association announced that it would ask MPs to pledge themselves to work for the establishment of a Royal Commission to investigate the demand for self-government.[108] It was a curious demand to make at a time when more direct pressure was being applied through the threat to contest elections. The re-launch of the movement at the official inauguration of the Scottish Covenant Association (SCA) attracted about 1,000 people to Edinburgh's Usher Hall.[109] MacCormick toyed with the idea of standing candidates but would not commit himself. All of this simply annoyed the Labour Party. At a meeting of the Scottish Parliamentary Labour Party a resolution was passed attacking the letter asking for a commitment to press for a Royal Commission. All but 4 of the 31 Scottish Labour MPs felt the letter was a form of blackmail.[110] McGovern was to be the only Labour MP to accept the pledge to 'work, vote, and speak, irrespective of party differences, for a Royal Commission on the question of Scottish home rule', but even he disapproved of the wording.[111] The Scottish Unionists were less perturbed since their party was already committed to a Royal Commission, though not to consider home rule, but even some of them indicated their irritation at the threatening tone of the letter.[112]

Maintaining the pressure, the SCA passed a resolution moved by Andrew Dewar Gibb to set up constituency associations with the prospect of fielding candidates. This was bound to irritate the nationalists too. Mary Dott, SNP Secretary, argued that there was no need to start another party as the SNP already existed. In September, the Association contested a local by-election in Airdrie. Its candidate came last in a three-way fight, though he won a respectable 21% of the vote in an area where third parties traditionally had great difficulty breaking through the polarised Catholic-Labour/Protestant-Unionist politics. His platform had in-cluded an attack on the existing local government structure, housing issues and rising levels of tuberculosis as well as making the case for a Scottish Parliament.[113]

Later that month MacCormick announced that no candidates would stand for the Association in the general election. Another appeal for public signatures was made along the lines of the Scottish Covenant. This time signatories would pledge to withhold support from any government that failed to take steps to establish a Scottish Parliament.[114] It might have been a better idea to have included such a sanction in the earlier covenant but it was now too late. At its Scottish conference in North Berwick, Labour voted in support of the establishment of a Royal Commission on self-government, and when the election was called, the party's national executive included a commitment to consider establishing a Royal Commission on the administration of Scottish affairs after the Catto report on the financial relations between Scotland and England was published. After the variety of initiatives and hard work all that could be claimed was a belated concession by Labour and Conservatives to establish a Royal Commission.

In 1952 a memorandum was prepared by the national committee recommending that the Association organise its members in each constituency in order to influence the parties at elections. The issue confronting it was 'how to translate the general public sympathy for a measure of self-government into an active force capable of bringing effective influence to bear on the major political parties'. The idea of contesting elections was ruled out because of the difficulties of building up a political machine to compete with the major parties, and as this would involve turning the association into a party. It was optimistically anticipated that Association candidates would receive 15–20% of the vote in any constituency and it was this hard core that should be targeted. It was proposed that voters in each constituency should be invited to pledge their support in whatever way was most likely to advance the cause of self-government: our aim would be to create a pressure group sufficiently strong effectively to alter the representation of parties in Scotland'.[115] They estimated that there were about 20 seats in which a turnover of 2,000 or 3,000 would make a difference. Naively, they believed there was no reason why this approach should 'destroy the all-party nature of the Covenant Association'.[116]

At a Covenant's national committee meeting to discuss the memorandum, MacCormick pointed out that even had five million people signed the Covenant the parties could still ignore it, claiming that people's preference for Labour or Tory outweighed that for home rule. The Association had to compel the parties by organising as a 'political force'.[117] The committee agreed to the proposal in principle but there appears to have been little enthusiasm. Speaking in Dumfries shortly afterwards, MacCormick reviewed the history of the movement. He noted the hurdles that had been overcome but argued that the established parties always found some reason to resist the demand for change. Since the establishment of the Scottish Covenant Association a year before, through 'quiet and careful organisation', a hard core of enthusiasts in 62 of Scotland's 71 constituencies had been built up.[118] This was a gross exaggeration of the strength of the association. The idea of contesting elections had not disappeared and two years later a resolution was passed urging the association to reconsider this course. By that time committees had been formed covering 25 constituencies with local committees covering part of 7 more constituencies and individual contacts established in a further 7. This left 32 constituencies with no Scottish Covenant Association presence.[119]

In early 1954, in order to test the likely consequence of contesting elections, the Dumfries committee approached the British Institute of Public Opinion who recommended a small test sample. A poll of 240 people in different parts of Scotland was conducted in the first week of March. Three questions were asked:

1. Have you heard of the Scottish Covenant Association?
2. Can you tell me any differences between Scottish Covenant policies and Scottish Nationalist policies?
3. If you had a Scottish Covenant candidate in the next General Election, would you be likely to vote for him?

One-third of respondents had not heard of the association. Of the 160 who claimed to have heard of it, 99 did not know the difference between it and the SNP, 48 gave answers which suggested to the Association that they had no knowledge of the differences, 9 gave answers which revealed a partial knowledge, and only 4 indicated that they had an accurate idea of the basic differences between the Association and the SNP. Of the 160 who had heard of the association, only 17 stated they would certainly vote for a Covenant candidate, 28 thought they might; 67 would not, and 48 did not know.[120] It was not a promising response.

As the 1955 general election approached the association was still uncertain. At a meeting of the national committee in February 1955 frustration and uncertainty were evident. Something novel had to be attempted but no agreement could be reached on what this should be. A by-election in North Edinburgh had occurred in January 1955 and it was agreed not to contest the seat. Instead, a questionnaire was sent to the two candidates and a decision taken that regardless of the response 'we do everything possible to harass the Tory candidate'. Members in the constituency received a letter asking them to abstain, spoil their papers or vote Labour.[121] Contesting elections, reaching an understanding with the SNP, threatening to stand candidates against Tory leaders, carrying on 'much more militantly', playing a more active part in elections were all suggested. But the fear of losing its responsible image and its all-party nature prevented the association doing anything it had not done before.

Disillusionment, Pessimism and the 'End of Another Auld Sang'

At the general election in 1955, the Association sent out a questionnaire to seek candidates' views on self-government and their willingness to support a referendum as well as various other issues. This was a tried, tested and failed approach. It was the nadir for the home rule movement. The Conservatives made much of British achievements. The coronation of Queen Elizabeth, the end of the Korean War and the conquest of Everest (by climbers from Nepal and New Zealand) all served to make the 1955 election a very British affair. The election was disappointing though the association took some comfort from the result in Inverness where John Bannerman had narrowly missed taking the seat for the Liberals and in Perth and East Perthshire where Robert McIntyre pushed the SNP into second place for the first time. The Inverness committee of the Association had given their full backing to Bannerman and it was claimed that he would have come bottom of the poll but for their efforts.[122]

The idea of a pact of some sorts with the SNP and Liberals was considered during the 1955–59 Parliament. In 1956 the Association's national committee minutes report that little progress had been made on negotiations with the parties. A pact with the Liberal Party found support only at constituency level. By the end of the year MacCormick reported to the annual general meeting that little of concrete value would be gained by pursuing SNP-Covenant-Liberal cooperation.[123]

In 1959 it was decided that a questionnaire would be issued at the general election, carefully framed 'so as to be acceptable to Labour candidates', and that the Association would try to organise a 'coherent disciplined wing of home rulers among Labour MPs in the next House of Commons, prepared to work with Liberals in advancing claims to self-government and in particular, campaigning for a Government sponsored plebiscite'.[124]

As the 1950s progressed and the Tories proved to be implacable opponents of home rule, the Scottish Covenant Association had drawn closer to Labour, a change from the 1940s when the Attlee Government had been the target of its attacks. It reflected the gradual realization that the Tories had been using the home rule movement for their own ends. The only consistent aspect of its approach was that the Association had attacked the party in government and given conditional support to parties in opposition. Even after Labour abandoned its official commitment to home rule in 1957, the Association continued to make overtures and give it support.

By the early 1960s there appeared little reason for optimism within the Association. A major blow in October 1961 was the death of John MacCormick at the age of 56. MacCormick had been the driving force of the Association and a central figure in home rule politics for over 30 years. The Association's decline had been largely due to its failure to find a strategy but in part was attributable to MacCormick's deteriorating health and the consequent lack of drive and initiative. By 1963 the Association had exhausted itself. In May, James Porteous, Secretary of the Association, stated that he was reluctantly coming to the conclusion that it was:

> no use pretending we exist as an active body any longer. Perhaps we should, like the Scottish Parliament, adjourn *sine die*, and our members can support the SNP or the Liberals as they feel disposed. It will be the end of another auld sang, but in this case we may perhaps sing a new one.[125]

Porteous himself felt that neither Labour or the Tories were any nearer to supporting home rule and the prospect of a Liberal Government was remote. There was, he felt, a possibility at a future election of an arrangement between the Conservatives and Liberals but 'it is doubtful if it would advance our cause'.[126] He felt that the differences between the SNP and the association had lost much of their force due to the 'world environment':

> Defence is very much a matter of NATO; Customs of GATT, EFTA, and perhaps the Common Market, with any other Commonwealth or international arrangements that may be made in the future. Foreign policy – well, why not? Myself, nothing would please me more than a fully independent Scotland, so long as England played fair on Customs and revenue-as-contributed. I should think this is the

feeling of us all, and what has divided us from the SNP hitherto
has been differences of opinion on the best line of approach to
self-government.[127]

Porteous felt that the prospect of getting SNP MPs elected was no
longer remote. Like many others, he was to join the SNP shortly
afterwards.

The search for a credible strategy had proved tortuous and painful
for the post-war home rulers. The belief that a changed environment
made their efforts more likely to succeed was shattered when the
Attlee Government showed little sympathy for the cause, despite
Labour's 1945 manifesto commitment to a Scottish Parliament. The
excitement of the National Assemblies and Covenant could not hide
the enormous hurdles which existed. By the late 1950s the combination of a series of failed approaches and a fairly hostile ideological
context pushed the issue to the margins of Scottish politics. This
was reflected in the organisation and strategic convolutions of the
home rulers.

The Campaign for a Scottish Assembly

The most significant aspect of the period between the demise of the
Scottish Covenant Association and the late 1970s was the absence
of a cross-party campaigning organisation. A few bodies such as
Wendy Wood's Scottish Patriots and the 1320 Club existed but these
were on the fringe of a fringe. This void was filled by the Scottish
National Party. The idea that a party might somehow embody the
entire national movement acquired a legitimacy in the absence of any
serious alternative home rule organisation. The failure of previous
attempts to achieve self-government through pressure group politics
played a part in stimulating distrust of such approaches. The electoral
breakthrough of the SNP and the clear message which this sent to
the established parties suggested that a more exciting and apparently
effective force existed. For many SNP activists, aware of the history
of the movement, the SNP was the logical development in the
campaign for self-government. This crude whiggish interpretation
had some merit but it failed to appreciate the convolutions of the
movement.

There were occasions in the late 1970s when a broad-based

national movement was canvassed. Jenny Chapman, Strathclyde University political scientist and active Liberal, was instrumental in launching a cross-party body arguing for an alternative voting system for elections to the Scottish Assembly in 1977 but hers was a fairly lonely voice arguing for cross-party cooperation around this time. Another voice which was raised in favour of a broad home rule front was Chapman's former academic colleague, Labour MP John Mackintosh. In a speech in March 1977 to the Andrew Fletcher Society, an SNP ginger group, Mackintosh urged the SNP not to campaign for total independence but to join a common battle for a quasi-federal Scotland. He drew an analogy with a two-stage rocket: 'We all go up together as far as home rule within the UK, and you can then drop the booster and try for independence if you feel like it later.'[128] It was, however, not the best moment to appeal to the SNP to adopt such a strategy. Labour MPs had effectively killed their own Government's devolution proposals a week before and a poll in the *Sunday Mail* the day before Mackintosh's speech gave the SNP 36% of the vote compared with Labour's 28% and the Conservatives' 27%, suggesting that the SNP would be close to winning a majority of Scottish seats. Support for independence was recorded at an all-time high at 31%, over 10% higher than earlier polls suggested. There may have been much merit in Mackintosh's idea but his timing could not have been worse.

The absence of a cross-party group became most obvious in the lead-up to the 1979 referendum. The need for cohesion in the national movement was paramount at that stage but no body existed to facilitate it. Instead, supporters of change campaigned against each other as much as in favour of the measure on offer, allowing the opponents of change to rally round their simple and clear objective of maintaining the status quo. An *ad hoc* pressure group, Yes for Scotland (YfS), was set up for the purpose of the referendum but its resources were limited and, for the most part, the loyalties of those involved ultimately lay outside the body. No significant political figure emerged to bridge the divide within it. The death of John Mackintosh in July 1978 robbed the movement of someone who might have been able to do so. YfS was launched in January 1978, chaired by Lord Kilbrandon, with a distinguished platform of supporters but none able to give it political leadership.[129]

Some means of bringing together not only the SNP, Labour and Liberal but also Tory supporters of home rule was required but was not found at that moment. Towards the end of the year, YfS appeared to be an SNP-front largely due to the inactivity of home rulers in other parties. Kilbrandon's view that the provision on offer did not go far enough and known sympathy for independence suggested that nationalists were running the show, and this was seen by home rulers in other parties as playing into the hands of supporters of the status quo. In November it was announced that an organisation would be launched called Alliance for an Assembly. The SNP would be excluded; it would include Alick Buchanan-Smith, Tory devolutionist MP, Russell Johnston, Liberal MP and STUC general secretary and Communist party member, Jimmy Milne.[130] In the context of home rule, it was safer for a Tory to share a platform with a Communist than a Nationalist. However, Alliance for an Assembly barely existed as a campaigning organisation.

In the post-mortem following the referendum, it was clear that a central reason for the failure of the Yes side had been its divisions. Like the League of Nations, the Campaign for a Scottish Assembly (CSA) seems to have been established to prevent a disaster which had just occurred rather than to meet the challenge of a new era. There was, however, more to the CSA than this. Those involved in the CSA's establishment saw the immediate reaction of recriminations and disillusionment as inevitable but damaging. Some means of keeping the idea of home rule alive and limiting the damage had to be found. Founded by Jack Brand, Strathclyde University political scientist and author of an authoritative history of the national movement, the CSA managed to win the approval of most of the Scottish press. It was officially launched on 1 March 1980, the first anniversary of the referendum on home rule. Its stated object was the 'creation of a directly elected legislative Assembly or Parliament for Scotland with such powers as may be desired by the people of Scotland'.[131] Brand declared that the CSA was an organisation from all parts of the political spectrum 'but we are not a political party, we are a movement for Scotland'.[132] All of Scotland's main parties were represented at the first meeting though the Conservative representative, Helen Millar was very much on the fringe of the party and gradually opted out of active politics. Significantly, the speech made by Dennis

Canavan, Labour MP, which included an attack on the Conservative Government's programme of public spending cuts, was 'drowned in a chorus of demands that he stop making political speeches and stick to devolution'.[133] Within a few years, linking constitutional reform with aspects of social and economic policy in the manner of Canavan's 1980 speech became acceptable, indeed expected, in contributions to CSA debates. Another significant aspect of the founding rally in 1980 was a commitment to arrange a convention drawn from all aspects of Scottish life to consider detailed proposals for setting up an Assembly. As Brand stated, it was intended that the convention would meet a year later and its proposals be presented to Parliament in the form of a new devolution bill. It was, however, to be almost a decade before the convention was to meet.

With its membership open to all individuals and organisations the CSA defined itself as an 'all-party, non-party organisation, independent of all political parties and other organisations'.[134] It never attracted a large membership, although affiliations with trade unions, branches of political parties and local authorities gradually built up. An idea to establish CSA groups along professional lines such as Teachers for a Scottish Assembly, borrowed from the Campaign for Nuclear Disarmament, had limited success.

In the early years the main aims were to keep the idea of self-government alive and prevent the Labour Party abandoning its commitment. Brand was explicit in seeing the Labour Party as the target of CSA activities.[135] No attempt was made to prepare a detailed scheme of home rule. Brand's view was that getting into more detail entailed getting into more controversy.[136] Support came from parts of the SNP, Liberal and Labour Parties as well as the trade unions. Few Conservatives lent their support, although one Conservative constituency association was reported to have affiliated for a period in the CSA's early days.[137] Malcolm Rifkind, as a junior Scottish Office Minister, admitted that he was still sympathetic to the idea of a Scottish Assembly within a reformed UK but denied press reports that he had told the CSA he would campaign on the issue.[138] The only senior Tory to be associated with the CSA was Iain Lawson who had been a prominent opponent of devolution in the 1970s. Lawson's conversion to constitutional change occurred as he grew increasingly disillusioned with the Conservatives, particularly over their handling of the steel industry in the mid-1980s. In 1986, the Conservative group on East Lothian District Council was reported to have voiced support for the CSA. Local government was one of the few areas where Tories who had any sympathy for a Scottish Assembly were to be found in the 1980s.

Successive Conservative Scottish Secretaries dismissed the CSA. George Younger's attitude was that the issue was a 'dead duck'.[139] Malcolm Rifkind agreed to meet the CSA in March 1986 (the idea of approaching the Secretary of State had originally been made by an SNP member at a fringe meeting at the Scottish Liberal Party conference).[140] The meeting may have been cordial but it was not very constructive. Mr. Rifkind's successor, Ian Lang, was more combative, largely because the issue emerged with greater force in Scottish politics during his time as Scottish Secretary.

One of the difficulties the CSA experienced was maintaining a balance across the parties. In the early years there appeared to be a preponderance of SNP members, provoking John Maxton, chairman of Scottish Labour MPs, to threaten to pull Labour representatives out of the organisation. Maxton insisted that the CSA had to decide whether it was campaigning for a devolved Assembly or an independent Scotland and warned of it becoming a 'front for pseudo-nationalism'.[141] Later it was to be the SNP's turn to be suspicious of Labour dominance within the CSA.

A number of important developments occurred in which the CSA was centrally involved. Labour local authority councillors had been amongst the most outspoken opponents of devolution in the 1970s but by the mid 1980s a change of attitude was discernible. A conference called by the CSA in late 1984 had set out to remove suspicions that a Scottish Assembly would try to take powers away from local authorities, or that conflict would inevitably ensue in relations between the two tiers. Fewer than a third of Scottish local authorities sent delegates or observers. Charles Gray and Mark Lazarowicz, later to be leaders of Labour-controlled Strathclyde Region and Edinburgh District respectively, told the CSA that they ought to support the local authorities in their fight against the Conservative Government if they expected to win support for home rule.[142] Within a few years Scottish local government was overwhelmingly behind the demand for a Scottish Parliament. In October 1986, the Convention of Scottish Local Authorities (COSLA), representing all Scottish local authorities, gave its backing to the idea of a Scottish Assembly for the first time by 89 votes to 20. A COSLA sub-committee was set up to investigate the implications for local government.[143] The conversion was largely due to Scottish Office attacks on local government. Nonetheless, the CSA had played a part in converting opposition to the Conservative Government into support for wider constitutional change.

The CSA was also involved in a number of symbolic demonstrations. On the fifth anniversary of the referendum, a giant key was carried to the gates of the building that was to have been the Scottish Assembly as members of the CSA hammered on the gates.[144] The key became the CSA's symbol signifying its desire to 'unlock the gates to Scottish democracy'. Later that year in conjunction with the magazine *Radical Scotland* (which effectively became the house journal of the CSA), an opinion poll was commissioned. Few polls had been conducted on the constitutional question following the referendum. The poll found that 54% of respondents thought the need for a Scottish Assembly was greater than it had been five years before, 15% about the same and 14% less. When asked which functions the Assembly should have responsibility for, there was an absolute majority for job training, the health service, energy, social security, taxation policy, the future of nuclear bases, police powers, and negotiations with the EEC.[145] The poll was widely interpreted in the press as another piece of evidence that the question of constitutional change was not dead.

Another problem identified from the 1970s was the hostility or indifference of English politicians to the idea of a Scottish Parliament. The CSA was rather slow in responding to this and generally campaigned within Scotland. In July 1985, senior officers of the CSA met officials of the North of England Trades Union Congress.[146] Dispelling fears that an Assembly would disadvantage the North of England was certainly easier in the 1980s, when a shared perception existed that people on either side of the border were suffering at the hands of the Conservative Government in London. Whether enough work was done by the CSA would only become known in the event of a Government attempting to legislate for the establishment of a Scottish Assembly.

In November 1986, the CSA held its first press conference in London for the English media. Jim Boyack, national convener of CSA, stated that it was important that people in the south did not later claim that demands for an Assembly were a surprise and they knew nothing about it.[147] It was a rather half-hearted effort but this was understandable; the effort involved in gaining the interest of the London media was enormous and could only be maintained at the cost of other activities.

The main idea which the CSA pursued was that of a constitutional convention. The idea was given support by the CSA in 1985 but it was only after the 1987 general election that it was properly launched.[148] As with previous bodies, problems set in for the CSA when its ambitions grew. It had been far easier working to keep the broad principle of home rule alive, or even attempting to tackle some of the difficulties encountered in the 1970s, than trying to reach agreement over a detailed scheme, and far more difficult to try to bring an assembly into being.

Conclusion

Cross- and non-party campaigns have come in different forms with different short- and long-term aims. They may have the task of keeping the idea alive, placing it on the agenda of the media or political parties, building up popular support for change, attempting to reach broad agreement on a constitutional settlement, drawing up a bill, or working towards the implementation of an agreed scheme. These at least will be the stated aims of the people involved. They may have alternative or additional reasons for participation: opposition politicians may find such a body a convenient platform for attacking the party in government, it may offer a means of tapping into national sentiment for electoral purposes, or it may be a means of defusing a growing demand for action either within the ranks of the party or in Scotland generally. It would be extremely naive to imagine that the aims of all those participating in such a forum would be identical or even compatible. All too often, the lack of any sanction has meant that the relationship between groups and parties was based on good faith and much hope.

Not only establishing a Parliament but even bringing the issue onto the political agenda has proved difficult. As a memorandum prepared for the national committee of the Scottish Convention in the early 1950s remarked, the problem was 'how to translate the general public sympathy for a measure of self-government into an active force capable of bringing effective influence to bear on the major political parties'.[149] A common remark of opponents of self-government has been that support for the movement is shallow or merely an ephemeral protest. Proving otherwise has never been easy.

Home rule pressure groups have always conformed to the outsider, promotional type of group identified in the introduction to this chapter. The strategies adopted reflected this. They have attempted to pressurise or 'piggy-back' on existing political parties and other institutions, to increase public support and mobilize public opinion, and ultimately to gain insider status. The lack of any sanction and the difficulties of generating public sympathy meant that the temptation to contest elections, to become a political party, was always present. At times the succession of home rule pressure groups adopted naive strategies which appeared to assume that existing public support would be sufficient in itself for them to gain insider status. On discovering that this was not enough, they invariably ran into difficulties. Disputes over strategy followed – should the organisation focus its attention on the public, Parliament, the media or the political parties? The relationships which were built up with political parties were often difficult. Association with any single party could be divisive but an even-handed approach could dissipate energy and prove pointless.

As each pressure group strategy failed, a crisis within the movement followed which led either to a new strategy and often to the birth of a new organisation or to a period of disillusionment. The failure to gain a Parliament through a constitutional convention in the 1920s led to the demise of the SHRA and the creation of an independent political party. The failure of the 1940s convention led to the Covenant which, in turn, failed and led to disillusionment. Remarkably little evidence exists of the movement learning lessons from the past. Repeated errors leading to disillusionment and internal divisions have marked the pressure group strategy.

The key problem for the group strategy was how to apply pressure in promotion of an idea with diffuse, wide-spread public support. The one role of the pressure group which has proved fruitful is that of facilitating cooperation across parties. This may be a limited role but it has proved useful. At certain times a facilitating role might have made a difference, as for example in the late 1970s.

1. A. Potter, *Organised Groups in British National Politics*, London, Faber, 1961.
2. A. G. Jordan and J. J. Richardson, *Government and Pressure Groups in Britain*, Oxford, Clarendon Press, 1987, p. 20.
3. *Ibid.*, p. 21
4. B. G. Peters, 'Insiders and Outsiders: the politics of pressure groups influence on bureaucracy', *Administration and Society*, vol. 9, no. 2, pp.191–218.
5. A. G. Jordan and J. J. Richardson, *Op. Cit.*, p. 33.
6. Wyn Grant, *Pressure Groups, Politics and Democracy in Britain*, Hemel Hempstead, Philip Allan, 1989, p. 17.
7. B. Hogwood, 'If consultation is everything then maybe it's nothing. . .', *Strathclyde Papers on Politics and Government*, 44, 1986.
8. P. Whiteley and S. Winyard, 'Influencing Social Policy: the effectiveness of the poverty lobby in Britain', *Journal of Social Policy*, vol. 12, 1983.
9. W. Mitchell, *Home Rule for Scotland and Imperial Federation*, Edinburgh, SHRA, 1892, p. 8.
10. William Mitchell, *Home Rule All Round: or Federal Union. Letter to the Right Hon. H. H. Asquith*, SHRA, 1893, p. 10.
11. Letter to *Scotsman*, January 26, 1912
12. *Scotsman*, June 4, 1892.
13. W. Mitchell, *Is Scotland to be sold again? Home Rule for Scotland SHRA*, 1892, p. 9.
14. Anon., 'Home Rule for Scotland', *Scottish Review*, July 1886, p. 20.
15. Charles Waddie, *An Inquiry Into the Principles of National and Local Self Government*, 2nd ed., SHRA, 1892, pp. 9–10.
16. Speech by Dr W. A. Hunter, President of SHRA, at first annual conference, *Glasgow Herald*, September 19, 1888.
17. *Glasgow Herald*, September 19, 1888.
18. *Ibid.*, June 4, 1892.
19. *Ibid.*, June 4, 1892.
20. See Waddie's obituary and subsequent note, *Glasgow Herald*, February 6, 1912; February 9, 1912.

21. NLS, acc. 3721, box 146.

22. *Glasgow Herald*, June 16, 1913, January 26, 1914; January 29, 1914.

23. These included Sir Daniel Stevenson, former Lord Provost of Glasgow and future Chancellor of Glasgow University who played a significant part in the development of international academic contacts and research; Sir Malcolm Smith, Liberal MP for Orkney and Shetland; Sir Robert Lockhart, former President of Young Scots; and Sir Henry Ballantyne, Chairman of Royal Commission on Housing in Scotland which reported in 1917.

24. *Glasgow Herald*, 30 June 1922, 20 October 1922.

25. Sarah Wambaugh, *Plebiscites Since The World War*, vol. 1, Washington, Carnegie Centre for International Peace, p. 4.

26. Quoted in Alfred Cobban, *The Nation State and National Self-Determination*, London, Collins, 1969, p. 66.

27. Amongst these were Robert Allan, Secretary of the Scottish Trades Union Congress (STUC), William Shaw, Secretary of the Glasgow Trades Council, William Gallacher, of the Scottish Wholesale Cooperative Society, Peter Fyfe, Chief Sanitary Engineeer for Glasgow who played a significant role in public health developments, the Rev. James Barr, Miss C. B. Cameron of the Highland Land League, Tom Johnston, editor of the radical paper *Forward*, and Roland Muirhead, NLS, Acc. 3721, Box 123/1.

28. *Glasgow Herald*, December 26, 1918.

29. *Pétition Nationale de l'Ecosse* in *Scottish Review*, Vol. 42, Spring 1919, p. 22: translation by author.

30. NLS, Acc. 3721, Box 41.

31. *Ibid.*

32. D. M. Cowan, J. M. Hogge and Joseph Johnstone (Liberals), Rear Admiral Adair and Robert McLaren (Coalition Unionists), and Duncan Graham (Labour).

33. NLS, Acc. 3721, Box 186/2.

34. *Ibid.*, Box 186/3.

35. *Ibid.*, Box 84/23.

36. *Ibid.*, Box 123/1.

37. Michael Keating and David Bleiman, *Labour and Scottish Nationalism*, London, Macmillan, 1979, pp. 62–63.

38. Letter from Marquess of Graham, *Glasgow Evening Times*, March 15, 1922.

39. NLS, Acc. 3721, Box 123/1.

40. *Glasgow Herald*, March 21, 1922.

41. *Forward*, April 1, 1922.
42. *Glasgow Evening Times*, August 27, 1923.
43. *Ibid.*, August 25,1923.
44. Richard Finlay, *Independent and Free, Scottish Politics and the Origins of the Scottish National Party, 1918–1945*, Edinburgh, John Donald, 1994, p. 10.
45. *Ibid.*, August 25, 1923.
46. Richard Finlay, *Op. Cit.*, p. 12.
47. NLS, Acc. 3721, Box 123/1.
48. *Ibid.*
49. *Ibid.; Daily Record, Glasgow Herald*, March 10, 1924.
50. Hansard, Commons, vol. 173, May 9, 1924, cols. 868–874.
51. NLS, Acc. 3721, Box 123/1.
52. *Glasgow Herald*, June 8, 1925.
53. *Scotsman*, December 8, 1925.
54. *Glasgow Herald*, June 28, 1926.
55. Quoted in Richard Finlay, *Op. Cit.*, p. 15.
56. Quoted in *Ibid.*, p. 16.
57. *Ibid.*, p. 29.
58. *Ibid.*, p. 31.
59. *Glasgow Herald*, October 27, 1922.
60. *Ibid.*, August 9, 1926.
61. *Ibid.*, March 1, 1923.
62. Richard Finlay, *Op. Cit.*, p. 50.
63. NLS Acc. 5927, Scottish National Movement Minute book, November 29, 1926.
64. *Ibid.*, May 21, 1927.
65. NLS Acc. 7505, no. 20.
66. NLS, Acc. 7295(4), Minute Book of National Committee of Scottish Convention, November 7, 1942.
67. *Ibid.*, December 2, 1944.
68. *Ibid.*, 22 June 1946.
69. NLS Acc. 7505, no. 20.
70. Milne was then Secretary of the Scottish Home Department and later became Permanent Under Secretary. He was a staunch opponent of Scottish self-government.
71. *Glasgow Herald*, November 11, 1944.
72. NLS, Acc. 7295 (4), Minute Book of National Committee of Scottish Convention, December 2, 1944.
73. Naomi Mitchison, *Among You Taking Notes. . . The Wartime Diary of Naomi Mitchison, 1939–1945*, Oxford, Oxford University

Press, 1986, p. 300, entry for Friday, November 10, 1944.

74. NLS, Acc. 7295(4), Minute Book of National Committee of
    Scottish Convention, September 1, 1945.
75. NLS, Acc. 5978, Box 1 F. 2 Declaration on Scottish Affairs.
76. *Ibid.*, Letter from Bridie (Dr. O. H. Mavor) to Porteous, 14
    August 1943
77. *Ibid.*
78. *Ibid.*, Letter to Porteous from B. Petrie, Secretary of Scottish
    Convention, 5 June, 1944
79. *Ibid.*, Letter to Duke of Montrose from Porteous, 6 June 1944.
80. NLS, Acc. 7295(4), Minute Book of National Committee of
    Scottish Convention, October 7, 1944.
81. *Ibid.*, January 5, 1946.
82. *Glasgow Herald,* January 31, 1946; NLS, Acc. 7295(4), Minute Book
    of National Committee of Scottish Convention, March 2, 1946.
83. NLS, Acc.7295(4), Minute Book of National Committee of
    Scottish Convention, March 2, 1946.
84. *Ibid.*, June 22, 1946.
85. *Glasgow Herald,* October 3, 1947.
86. *Ibid.*, 1947.
87. *Ibid.*, October 18, 1947.
88. *Ibid.*, January 10, 1948.
89. *Ibid.*, June 25, 1945.
90. *Ibid.*, July 4 and 9, 1945.
91. NLS, Acc. 7295(4), Minute Book of National Committee of
    Scottish Convention, March 3, 1945.
92. NLS, Acc. 5978, Minutes of meeting of National Committee
    of Scottish Convention, November 23, 1946.
93. *Glasgow Herald,* January 6, 1948.
94. *Scotsman,* February 18, 1948.
95. *Glasgow Herald,* February 7, 1948.
96. *Ibid.*, February 20, 1948.
97. *Ibid.*, March 9, 1948.
98. *Ibid.*, January 6, 1948.
99. NLS, Acc. 7295(5), Minutes of National Committee of Scottish
    Convention, May 1, 1948.
100. *Scotsman,* January 7, 1948.
101. *Glasgow Herald,* June 28, 1948.
102. NLS, Acc. 7295(5), Minutes of National Committee of Scottish
     Convention, July 8, 1948.
103. *Glasgow Herald,* October 2, 1950.

104. *Ibid.*, January 24, 1951.
105. *Ibid.*, March 19, 1951.
106. *Daily Express*, May 18, 1951.
107. "What Lies Behind Dr John MacCormick's Latest Move?" *Forward*, May 19, 1951.
108. *Glasgow Herald*, May 14, 1951.
109. *Ibid.*, May 16, 1951.
110. Alex Anderson, John McGovern, John Rankin, and Agnes Cullen.
111. *Glasgow Herald*, June 1, 1951
112. *Ibid.*, May 31, 1951.
113. *Airdrie and Coatbridge Advertiser*, September 1 and 8, 1951.
114. *Glasgow Herald*, October 27, November 8, 1952.
115. NLS, Acc. 7505, Scottish Covenant Association, undated memorandum.
116. *Ibid.*
117. NLS, Acc. 7505, No. 20, Scottish Covenant Association, Minutes of National Covenant Committee, September 13, 1952.
118. *Dumfries Standard*, October 18, 1952.
119. NLS, Acc. 7505, No. 20, Minutes of meeting of National Committee of Scottish Covenant Association, March 1, 1954.
120. *Ibid.*, April 3, 1954.
121. *Ibid.*, February 12, 1955.
122. *Ibid.*, June 4, 1955.
123. *Scottish Covenant Association News Sheet*, December 1956.
124. NLS, Acc. 5978, Letter to James Porteous from J. MacDonald, March 1, 1959.
125. *Ibid.*, Letter from Porteous to Angus (Gunn), May 26, 1963.
126. *Ibid.*
127. *Ibid.*
128. Neal Ascherson, 'The Strange Death of Devolution', *Scotsman*, March 4, 1977.
129. Lord Kilbrandon (Chairman of the Royal Commission on the Constitution which had reported in favour of constitutional change in 1973) was joined by Donald MacKay (economics professor), Farquhar Mackintosh (leading educationist), Ludovic Kennedy (writer and broadcaster) and Dr David Steel (former Church of Scotland Moderator and father of then Liberal leader). *Scotsman*, January 27, 1978.
130. *Scotsman*, November 28, 1978.
131. The Campaign for a Scottish Assembly Constitution, clause 2.
132. *Scotsman*, March 3, 1980.

133. *Ibid.*, March 3, 1980.
134. The Campaign for a Scottish Assembly Constitution, clause 3.
135. Jack Brand, 'A National Assembly', *Crann Tara*, No. 13, Spring 1981, p. 15.
136. *Scotsman*, January 23, 1981.
137. *Ibid.*, November 4, 1985.
138. *Ibid.*, March 1, 1983.
139. *Ibid.*, October 12, 1985.
140. *Ibid.*, March 25, 1986.
141. *Ibid.*, January 18, 1984.
142. *Ibid.*, November 26, 1984.
143. *Ibid.*, March 2, 1986.
144. *Ibid.*, March 2, 1984.
145. *Glasgow Herald*, November 30, 1984.
146. *Scotsman*, July 10, 1985.
147. *Glasgow Herald*, November 26, 1986.
148. *Scotsman*, March 1, 1985.
149. NLS, Porteous Papers, Acc. 7505, Porteous Papers: Annual and Committee Meetings 1942–55.

Constitutional Conventions

Introduction

Constitutional conventions are representative bodies 'chosen for the purpose of considering and either adopting or proposing a new constitution or changes in an existing constitution'[1] The constitutional convention is usually associated with American politics, although conventions and constituent assemblies were used during the French revolution and in framing post-1945 European constitutions. The convention is a manifestation of social contract theory. The idea is that the public ought to be brought into the process of determining the structure of government. Related to this is the notion that after a convention has reached agreement, the public should have a direct voice through a referendum to accept or reject what has been agreed by their representatives.

The history of the US states indicates the extent to which these ideas played a part in forging their constitutions. In the late 1770s concern in certain American states was expressed when the public was excluded from or given a limited role in the process of constitution-building. Massachusetts was the first state to frame its constitution through an authoritative convention and formally submit it to the people. The constitution of the US was developed through a constitutional convention, although it was not actually known as such at the time and subsequent amendments to the constitution have not required such an institution.[2]

A constitutional convention derives its authority from the people. Its value is most obvious following a revolutionary situation when an entirely new state or political order has come into existence. Its limits become clear when amendments to an existing constitution is required. If the 'constitutional defect' which requires to be addressed is the under-representation of a particular minority then the convention will ordinarily be ineffective: 'like the legislature it will reflect the interests of the groups that are overrepresented'.[3] US conventions were never entirely free of partisan interests, although less so than legislatures, and it is doubtful whether they could or should be. So long as the public can identify constitutional schemes with particular parties there is a strong likelihood of partisan influence in conventions. The key question is whether public opinion is reflected in conventions through the range of parties.

The UK has had little experience of constitutional conventions though their use has facilitated change elsewhere under UK protection, such as in Newfoundland after the last war. The most notable recent experience was in Northern Ireland in the early 1970s following the imposition of direct rule from Westminster after the Northern Irish Parliament at Stormont was prorogued. The Government in London announced in a white paper in July 1974 that it intended to establish a constitutional convention to consider 'what provisions for the government of Northern Ireland would be likely to command the most widespread acceptance throughout the community there.'[4] The subsequent Act provided for the election of a convention with 78 members elected by single transferable vote. The elections were held in May 1975 and a block of 47 Unionist members, under the United Ulster Unionist Coalition, was returned, opposed to power-sharing with the Catholic community and against any institutional association with the Irish Republic. This made any prospect of a consensus within the convention impossible. The majority report which was presented to Merlyn Rees, Secretary of State for Northern Ireland, was rejected on the grounds that it did not, in Rees's words, 'command sufficiently widespread acceptance throughout the community to provide stable and effective government'.[5] Attempts to revive the convention in order to reach agreement across the parties failed. Significantly, the initiative had come from Westminster where ultimate power still remained, and this power was used to veto the convention's majority report. Interestingly, no proposal was made by the Government at the time to institute a similar body for Scotland, where agitation for home rule was evident and the prospect of a consensus being reached was far greater.

The constitutional conventions described above were Government initiated and therefore derived their authority from that source. Those discussed in this chapter associated with the self-government movement originated from within the movement and derived any authority they had from it. This inevitably raised doubts as to the authority and legitimacy of these conventions, and proved their greatest weakness. For such unofficial conventions to challenge the authority of the state, which they would have to do in order to be effective, they required at least as legitimate a base as official conventions.

A convention is a unique political body. It is not a pressure group in the normal sense of that term, neither is it a form of direct democracy. Its representativeness, aims and objectives, sanctions, and ability to effect change are matters which have to be confronted by supporters. All too often conventions have failed because of an unwillingness to confront difficult questions, and supporters often seem naive, believing that their aims will be achieved through the power of their argument. One of the strategies which has periodically been proposed, it has often arisen in times of optimism but always concluded in despair when it became clear that a constitutional convention in itself can achieve little. The significance of conventions within the history of the national movement has often been as a forum in which debate on strategy has taken place and where new departures in strategy have begun, but ultimately conventions have been blind alleys which have diverted the force of the movement at crucial moments.

Conventions and the Early Scottish Home Rule Movement

The idea of a convention to determine Scotland's constitutional status dates from the time of the first Scottish Home Rule Association (SHRA). The idea continued to find support over the next thirty years before any serious attempt was made to establish an unofficial convention. It was proposed at the SHRA's fifth annual conference in 1892. A resolution was moved by William Mitchell, SHRA treasurer, urging the Government to submit to the House of Commons resolution:

> i.   specifying the legislative and administrative functions with the domestic affairs of the four divisions of the United Kingdom, which it is proposed to devolve on a Legislature for each; and
> ii. remitting to a convention, representative of each division, to consider and report to Parliament for its sanction, so far as approved, such constitution as the convention may consider most suitable for the Legislature of its own division.[6]

An amendment to delete the second clause was successfully moved by Keir Hardie.[7] Hardie argued that the SHRA should ensure that the issue was considered at the following election and that instead of a convention, Scottish MPs should decide on Scotland's constitutional future.[8]

Only six months after its foundation in 1918 the revived SHRA proposed that a scheme of district conferences should be held culminating in a national convention to formulate a demand for home rule which would be presented to Parliament.[9] Over a year later, the general council of the SHRA decided that a convention should be held after a 'huge demonstration' was organised.[10] This had been Roland Muirhead's idea. Muirhead distrusted Westminster and saw a body representative of Scottish opinion as more likely to influence the Government than Scottish MPs. At its annual Scottish conference in 1921, the Independent Labour Part (ILP) unanimously passed a resolution demanding the establishment of a 'Constituent Assembly so that the Scottish Nation may themselves determine upon a scheme of Self-Government suited to their own needs'.[11]

A joint conference of the SHRA and Scottish MPs in February 1923 called on the Government to summon a Scottish National Convention composed of delegates from town and county councils, education authorities, trades and labour councils, the STUC, chambers of commerce, political organisations, the Convention of Royal Burghs, and the Scottish Peers. Sixteen Scottish Labour MPs, one National Liberal, and one Liberal attended the conference and four Labour MPs sent their apologies with good wishes as did four Liberals, one National Liberal and E. Scrymgeour, Prohibitionist MP for Dundee. The conference resolved that if the Government failed to act, then the SHRA in cooperation with other bodies should call 'an informal National Convention for the purpose of drafting a scheme of Scottish Self-Government for submission to the House of Commons'.[12] It was felt that this would save Parliamentary time. The meeting strongly favoured cross-party cooperation. Tom Johnston, Labour MP, agreed with the Liberal J. M. Hogge that Scottish MPs should form themselves into a group to press for a Scottish Parliament at the earliest possible moment, but little came of this idea.

The question of support for a convention was raised during the course of the election in 1924. Each candidate in Scotland was asked by the SHRA whether establishing a Scottish Parliament would be given prominence in his or her election address and whether he or she would be willing to attend a national convention:

> It is proposed to call a National Convention in Scotland of the Scottish Members of Parliament and representatives of bodies affiliated to the Scottish Home Rule Association for the purpose of framing a scheme of self-government to be presented to the British House of Commons. The Convention has been fixed for Saturday, 15 November 1924 immediately before the meeting of the new Parliament.[13]

Of the 71 Scottish MPs who were returned to Parliament, 34 had signalled their willingness to participate in a convention: 25 Labour MPs, 3 Unionists, 3 Liberals, and 1 Independent Prohibitionist MP.

1924 Election candidates willing to attend National Convention

	Labour	Unionist	Liberal	Prohibitionist
Elected	25	3	3	1
Defeated	33	0	11	0
Total	58	3	14	1

Sources: *Glasgow Herald* 28 October 1924; Dod's Parliamentary Companion 1925 (London: Dod)

Meetings of the Convention were held and the nature and aims emerged. Of 26 Labour MPs elected in Scotland, 7 attended the first convention meeting. Opponents of home rule made much of the

influence of these members and in a commentary typical of the time
one newspaper questioned the representativeness of the convention
and played to popular prejudices:

> The Convention was dominated by seven Socialist MPs, most of
> them representing constituencies in the West of Scotland, and it is
> significant that the centre of gravity of the movement must nowadays
> be sought in that quarter. . .the Irish vote in these districts goes
> almost solidly in support of the socialist candidates. . . .If they are to
> turn native minorities into majorities as they do now it will not be
> Scottish Home Rule, but Irish rule of Scotland.[14]

It had been decided that the Scottish National Convention should
consist of Scottish MPs, representatives from town, parish and
county councils, and education authorities 'as well as other Scottish
National Bodies, including the general Council of the Scottish Home
Rule Association'.[15]A Convention leaflet claimed that it was 'more
widely representative of the various shades of Scottish opinion than
any that has hitherto been brought together'.[16]

The second meeting of the Convention was held on 30 October
1926. More detail exists on the composition of this meeting. Two
days prior to the meeting the replies to invitations gave an indication
of the nature of the body:

Scottish National Convention Invitations at 28 October 1926

Acceptances:		Replies pending	
Town Councils	10	Town Councils	34
Parish Councils	8	Parish Councils	10
		Education Authorities	13
Refusals:			
Town Councils	13		
Parish Councils	18		
County Councils	3		
Education Authorities	7		

Source: NLS, Acc. 3721 box 80/17

Willie Graham, Labour MP for Central Edinburgh, felt that there
was a need for the SHRA to bring into the convention organisations
'representing business, professional and Church people in Scotland
in order to give a more representative character to the Convention'.[17]

This concern explains the constant, though largely futile, attempts to recruit representatives of all shades of opinion to conventions.

The perennial issue of representativeness continued to be a problem throughout the Convention's existence. At a meeting in February 1928 it was reported that 3,790 individuals and public bodies had been contacted but that only a 'very small percentage of these agreed to receive deputations or had passed resolutions in support of Home Rule or indeed had even acknowledged receiving communication.'[18] This gave rise to debate on the purpose of the Convention. One speaker argued that the Convention had two objectives, keeping in touch with public bodies and propagating the case for a Parliament, and that these ought to be separated. Councils should be left alone and only asked to attend meetings once a year. The fact that an independent party had already been set up and had adopted Roland Muirhead to stand in a by-election no doubt played a part in forcing the Convention to attempt to rethink its strategy.

The main aim of the Convention had been to draft a bill because, as one member put it, one of the 'chief criticisms offered by the English Members of Parliament has been that the Scots MPs did not seem to be agreed amongst themselves as to the exact type of Home Rule measure that should be passed'.[19] The detailed work of preparing the bill was done in committee. A National Convention Committee was established which had a 'pretty free hand in approaching likely names'.[20] In 1924, in a candid comment, Muirhead conceded that it was impossible to get national representation when plans were being devised for the National Convention Committee.[21]

In 1926, the home rule bill drawn up by the Convention was widely assumed to be a Labour Party measure as it was presented in the Commons by Labour MPs. One of the few Unionist politicians who was sympathetic to the Convention, Col. Chichester Crookshank, wrote to Roland Muirhead, the Convention secretary on the subject. In response, Muirhead explained that copies of a draft bill prepared by the Convention had been sent to MPs for comments and amendments. These comments were being discussed within the Convention when the original draft was introduced in the Commons by Labour Members. 'This was done quite independently of the Committee of Convention', Muirhead explained.[22] In similar vein, Muirhead explained to another home ruler what had happened:

The Bill was drafted by a few who for the most part are not members
of any party, as far as I am aware, but the fact that the Scottish Labour
Members made use of this Draft Bill to introduce it into the House
of Commons, as their Bill, last July does not surely necessarily make
it a partisan measure.[23]

Even more irritating for Muirhead was a *Scotsman* editorial five
months later attacking the measure as a 'Socialist Bill' of partisan
origin.[24] The danger of being seen to be controlled by one party was
a persistent problem.

The bill was eventually presented in the Commons and duly
rejected causing considerable disillusionment amongst home rulers.
This disillusionment compounded earlier disappointment with the
inaction of the Labour Government of 1924. There seems, from
statements made at the time, to have been a genuine belief amongst
home rulers that drawing up a bill was all that was required for
self-government to be attained. Part of the explanation may lie in
the lack of overt opposition to home rule at the time. It must be
remembered that Labour and the Liberals had been committed to
a measure of home rule for many years and the Conservatives had
appeared, at worst, uninterested rather than antagonistic towards the
idea; only a few years earlier some Tories had been toying with the
idea of federal home rule within the empire as a means of keeping
Ireland in the Union. What became clear in the 1920s, as Scottish
home rule became an issue in its own right, was that there was deep
hostility towards the idea in certain quarters in and beyond Scotland.
One of the consequences of the Convention raising the issue on the
political agenda was that it aroused opposition which had previously
lain dormant.

A consequence of this experience was the growing realization
amongst home rulers in the 1920s that simply drawing up a measure
and presenting it to Parliament would not work. By 1927 a new
role appeared to be emerging for the Convention, as a forum for
discussing strategies for self-government. A debate emerged, more
intense and more ably articulated than at any time before or since,
on the strategies for gaining self-government. The frankness of the
debate is striking, and what makes it particularly interesting is not
only that it appears never to have been repeated in so open a
manner but that it is possible to trace the way in which certain key

individuals developed their thinking on how Scotland should attain self-government. People such as Roland Muirhead, Secretary to the SHRA and the Convention, were initially opposed to a National Party but gradually came round to the view that fielding candidates with a primary commitment to home rule was necessary.

The future strategy of the movement was the central issue discussed in the final meetings of the Convention's national committee. A motion was presented at meetings in late 1927:

> That this meeting of the Scottish National Convention believes that the passing into law of the Bill for the better Government of Scotland depends upon the creation of a National Party and decides forthwith to consider how best to create such a Party.[25]

This provoked an amendment:

> That this meeting of the Scottish National Convention believes that the passing into law of the Bill for the better Government of Scotland depends upon the support of the existing political parties and decides forthwith to enlist their services with a view to making Self-Government for Scotland the foremost plank on their programmes at the next General Election.[26]

An attempt to have the initial motion ruled out of order was turned down and complaints by the mover of the resolution that he had been interrupted by the chairman were received. In the event the amendment was carried by 57 votes to 34. This did not really resolve anything, least of all the confusion within the Convention on strategy. Indeed, a motion passed later at the same meeting urged the appointment of a committee to draft a petition for presentation to the League of Nations asking for an enquiry into the operation of the Treaty of Union between Scotland and England.[27]

The SNP Initiatives in 1939 and 1940

The establishment of the National Party of Scotland (NPS) in 1928 was the principal consequence of the failure of the Convention. A 'moderate' Scottish Party was set up in 1932 which merged with the more hardline NPS in 1934 to form the Scottish National Party. The

SNP, under the influence of John MacCormick, tried to institute a Scottish national convention in 1939. Invitations to the convention did not even mention the issue of self-government. The SNP were summoning a convention,

> for the purpose of discussing the grave social and economic problems which confront our nation today. It is our hope that by such discussion it may be possible to formulate a programme of immediate reforms which will command the support of the vast majority of the Scottish people.[28]

Two lengthy resolutions were to be debated. The first dealt with social and economic issues. The second dealt with self-government and began by stating that the Scottish people 'must realise that to achieve the economic and social aims set out in the convention resolutions, drastic changes are necessary in the legislative and administrative machine.'[29] Nothing came of this convention though considerable effort appears to have gone into its preparation. A body of sponsors had been drawn up which consisted largely but not exclusively of Nationalists.[30] However, war broke out and prevented this experiment getting off the ground.

In May 1940, Tom Johnston, then the Civil Commissioner for Defence in Scotland, had urged the necessity of preparing for the aftermath of war. A resolution submitted to the SNP National Council in December by Muirhead took note of this and proposed that a convention be set up to do just that. This convention would not include MPs and, he argued, at the end of the war it would act as a 'provisional body to deal with the practical affairs of Scotland until a permanent body was established'.[31] This was extremely ambitious and amounted to the establishment of a provisional government. The usual list of bodies was to be contacted. Muirhead was fairly clear of the SNP's role:

> At a preliminary meeting of the Convention the Scottish National Party should prepare the Agenda and so far as possible see that its members occupy as many as possible of the official positions in the Convention.[32]

It was unrealistic and nothing appears to have come of it. A much more cynical and far less serious affair than that proposed the previous year, it represents a common theme of conventions – the desire of parties to use them for their own ends.

Scottish Convention and the Assemblies in the 1940s

A split at the 1942 SNP conference was caused by a variety of internal divisions. The origins of the pressure group Scottish Convention (as distinct from the representative assemblies it set up) were explained in one of its publications:

> Scottish Convention was founded in June, 1942 by a group of people who came out of the Scottish National Party in the belief that that body had become too narrow and exclusive and too divorced from reality to form a rallying point for Scottish opinion.[33]

This is a highly partisan interpretation of events but it gives some idea of the intention of MacCormick and his followers who set up Scottish Convention. It was felt that a 'fundamental unity of purpose underlying all differences of opinion and partisan divisions' made a convention necessary. They aimed for a federal union between England, Scotland and Wales.

With the election of the Labour Government after the war, a more hopeful situation was envisaged. At Scottish Convention's annual meeting in June 1946 the national committee resolved to organise a National Assembly to demonstrate:

> the serious concern which is generally felt in Scotland about the future prospects of Scottish trade and industry, and to examine the possibility of stating an agreed measure of reform in Scottish Government which the assembly will place before the Government.[34]

The following March the first Scottish National Assembly met. The SNP decided to boycott it. A leaflet produced by the SNP for distribution to those attending the 1947 Assembly declared that 'Scotland Demands Full Control'. The SNP argued that the proposals to be submitted at the meeting were 'so ineffectual that their only result could be that Scotland's position would be worsened. . . Half-measures will not do'.[35] However, the SNP did allow individual members to attend.[36] Invitations to attend the 1947 National Assembly were accepted by 4 Scottish peers, 8 MPs (5 Unionists, 2 Labour and 1 Communist), 36 town councils, 16 district or county councils, and a range of other bodies.[37] The convention claimed that this was 'probably the most widely representative gathering ever brought together in Scotland',[38] a claim similar to that made in 1924 and less accurate.

In October 1947 Arthur Woodburn became Secretary of State. He was more hostile to the idea of self-government than his predecessor had been. The following April, speaking to the Scottish TUC, Woodburn said that when people were asked what they meant when they talked about home rule the answer was 'very vague and only in general terms'.[39] Any illusion still held by home rulers that all that would be necessary was the presentation of a scheme of devolution was shattered. A great deal of publicity was being generated but they were no nearer their goal of Scottish self-government.

In February 1949 a leading supporter of the convention privately conceded to John MacCormick that Douglas Young, his old adversary in the home rule movement, was right in saying that the 'steam has gone out of the assembly, and there is very little steam in the Convention'.[40] This was really an admission of defeat but not one which could be publicly voiced without causing disillusionment. At the fourth national assembly in 1950 the loudest applause was given to the speaker who warned that if Government and Opposition leaders refused to see representatives from the Assembly, it should consider its next step 'in a very different mood'.[41] But this was just rhetoric with nothing to back it up.

To all intents and purposes the early 1950s brought this episode of the convention idea to an end. Meetings of Scottish Convention continued to be held but with very little impact. There was no immediate transfer of enthusiasm or personnel to a new or existing political party as had happened at the demise of the inter-war convention, although the Scottish Covenant Association of 1951 can be seen as an attempt to keep the issue alive through a new organisation. More publicity was generated in this phase than previously, but the national assemblies were middle-class affairs with little popular support. The greatest success was the Covenant which gathered over two million signatures, but this only confirmed the existence of support for self-government, something which was already widely known. How this support could be harnessed to force implementation of a scheme of home rule remained unclear.

During the next phase, there was little support for a convention in the national movement. A striking feature of the national movement in the 1960s and 1970s was the dominance of the Scottish National Party. No other body articulating the case for self-government had much popular support, or was even widely known to exist. There were small fringe groups such as the Scottish Patriots, around the colourful figure of Wendy Wood and the 1320 Club, which was never as sinister as its members wanted people to believe. There was no equivalent during this period of the SHRA or Scottish Convention. There were no attempts to bring together a group of representative Scots, as the conventions had done from 1924 through to the late 1950s, to draw up a scheme of devolution, although Scottish Assemblies were held to discuss the Scottish economy and unemployment, most notably in February 1972 and January 1973. The issue of home rule spilled over into debates on unemployment on these occasions and James Jack of the STUC, which sponsored the assemblies, accused the SNP of attempting to hi-jack the assemblies.

The Conservatives' Convention in the 1970s

The idea of a convention only re-emerged in the late 1970s but in a different form and context and from quite different sources. The SNP and the Conservatives advocated a convention. The SNP came up with the idea in February 1977, when Donald Bain, SNP research officer, proposed the establishment of a convention in response to the failure of the Scotland and Wales Bill. It was a wholly different proposal to that made by Francis Pym, Conservative Devolution Spokesman. Bain's proposal involved a short Act of Parliament establishing an elected assembly which would determine and negotiate its own powers with Westminster. However, the launch of the idea by Billy Wolfe and Donald Stewart MP suggested they had a different idea. They saw the constituent assembly as a means of negotiating independence. As a proposal, it was a constructive response from the SNP at a difficult time, but it was given little serious attention in Westminster where it was inevitably seen as a radical challenge to Parliamentary sovereignty.

In a major speech in February 1977, Pym argued the case for a convention. While Tory pro- and anti-devolutionists argued for their respective positions, the party was generally quite happy to go along with the obfuscation and prevarication of Pym's proposal. During this period there was considerable tension within the Conservative Party, and by advocating a convention the Tories were avoiding taking a stance on the issue. The best illustration of the nature of the convention proposal became evident at the May 1977 Scottish Conservative conference when staunch devolutionists and anti-devolutionists joined together, without success, to vote against the measure. As far as both sections were concerned the convention was a fudge.[42]

Pym had called for an all-party conference which would meet for up to six months. The idea was being proposed by the Liberals around this time also. The precise timing of Pym's proposal is significant: it occurred only days before the guillotine vote on the Scotland and Wales Bill and it was interpreted as an attempt to woo the Liberals into voting against the guillotine in exchange for the prospect of a wider debate which would include federalism, as Pym explicitly made clear. The Liberals fell for it. That the Tories were utterly insincere was made clear within days when Teddy Taylor, their Scottish Affairs spokesman, stated that he was 'hugely relieved' that the nation had been saved from the 'costly, bureaucratic, divisive constitutional monstrosity of devolution'.[43]

There was a great deal of inconsistency in the details of Pym's idea. In February 1977 when he was wooing the Liberals he stated that it would be legitimate to discuss federalism, but independence could not be discussed. A year later, Pym stated that there were four basic choices which could be considered by an all-party conference – the status quo, an inquisitorial and scrutinising assembly, a quasi-federal system, and independence.[44] On this occasion, Pym told the press that the procedure might take 'up to three years'.[45] By June, the options had been reduced to three: strengthening the committee system in Parliament, an elected assembly with scrutinising powers able to call UK Ministers before it, and a quasi-federal system.[46] A Select Committee would consider the convention's proposals in detail before any measure went through Parliament 'in the normal way'.[47] In September he produced his lengthiest statement on the subject. He outlined the four options which an all-party conference could consider: a change in the procedures of Parliament; an inquisitorial

Assembly; a scheme of executive and legislative devolution; and a quasi-federal system.[48] A common complaint he made throughout that year was that matters should not be hurried as people were not quite clear what they wanted. This was certainly the case with Tories. They were not even sure what they were unsure about.

The Conservatives' all-party conference or convention never took place. The idea had been a convenient means of appearing to take the Scottish question seriously while maintaining a unionist position. Little was made of the Tories' somersaults on the convention by the other parties largely because they were embroiled in the debate on the Labour Government's measures.

The Constitutional Convention of the Late 1980s

The first move towards establishing a constitutional convention in the 1980s came from SNP chairman Gordon Wilson in a bill presented in Parliament in March 1980. On that occasion only 4 Labour MPs supported the idea, 1 voted against with the remaining 39 abstaining. Initially his proposal was rejected by the SNP executive but through persistent advocacy Wilson won his party over to the idea at its conference in September 1984 with strong support from Jim Sillars. The idea was taken up by the CSA and particularly by *Radical Scotland*, a journal founded in the 1980s articulating a broadly left-of-centre nationalist view and closely associated with the Campaign for a Scottish Assembly (CSA).

The 1987 election spurred matters on. The 'doomsday scenario', the re-election of a Thatcher Government while Scotland voted against the Tories, occurred (once more), but the predicted 'constitutional crisis' did not materialise. The national question was however once more firmly on the agenda of the Scottish political parties and media. The CSA set up a committee of 'prominent Scots' to draw up plans for a constitutional convention under the chairmanship of Sir Robert Grieve, a distinguished retired public servant, with Jim Ross, the retired civil servant who had been in charge of devolution in the Scottish Office in the 1970s, as secretary. How this collection of Scots was chosen is uncertain but all favoured some measure of home rule. They reported in July 1988 with the 'Claim of Right for Scotland'.

Initially, the document was hardly noticed. Its title drew historical parallels, the 'Claim of Right' invoking popular sovereignty in the demand for self-government. The basis of a convention was discussed. A directly elected Convention was dismissed as problematic despite its obvious appeal. An elected member-based convention and a delegate Convention were considered. While the 'primary responsibility for taking the lead' in forming a Convention rested on Scottish MPs, it was felt that a Convention would be more authoritative 'if supplemented'.[49] Local councillors were seen as important and it was suggested that the Convention 'should be supplemented by members nominated by or on behalf of Parties so as to address some of the Party imbalance resulting from the 1987 election'.[50] It warned that the addition of 'nominally-non-Party Members' should not give the Convention 'a Party balance out of accord with electoral voting'.[51] In the event, the convention failed to meet the standards set out in the Claim of Right.

The aim was to ensure maximum participation and in particular to encourage Labour involvement. To combat potential hostility within the Labour Party to involvement in a Convention the Claim of Right offered terms which Labour would find attractive but, as it turned out, which made the Convention unattractive to the SNP. In effect, Labour would be in overall control. After initial hesitation and a few dismissive reactions, Labour decided to participate. In a speech at Stirling University in October 1988, Shadow Scottish Secretary Donald Dewar agreed that the party would get involved. Labour had done its sums and knew that there was little for it to fear; it would dominate the Convention through the proposed structure.

In November, Jim Sillars won the Govan by-election for the SNP on a platform stressing Scottish political consensus which the CSA favoured. However, any prospect of a working arrangement with Labour was short-lived as the political battle heated up. It has been suggested that the high ratings of the SNP in opinion polls in the aftermath of Govan (System Three for the *Glasgow Herald* January 1989 showed SNP at 32%, only 4% behind Labour) 'went to the nationalists' heads'.[52] There is something in this but it is by no means the full explanation. The SNP realised that it would be in a minority, an extremely weak minority at that, in the convention and argued for greater representation. The SNP feared that Labour would use the Convention as a platform to attack it in the lead up to the European elections in June 1989. Additionally, some believed that going along with the Convention would simply side-track the party when there appeared to be a growing demand for independence. Labour's support for a Convention after earlier hostility also fuelled SNP suspicions.

The manner in which the SNP decided not to participate was bungled. Over the course of a weekend, party members found that they were suddenly opposed to something they thought they were supposed to be enthusiastic about. Nonetheless, the party overwhelmingly accepted the decision not to participate in the convention at one of its best-attended National Council meetings, the decision-making body between annual conferences. But much of the enthusiasm which had charged it in the aftermath of Govan was lost. Party unity after the by-election disappeared as bitter attacks were made on supporters of participation in the convention. Immediately after Govan, the SNP had exploited divisions within the Labour Party on the constitutional question. It was soon Labour who, united behind involvement in the convention, was able to exploit the divisions within the SNP. Labour had outmanoeuvred the SNP, recaptured the mantle of 'Scotland's national party' lost only three months before, exploited divisions within the SNP, and was able to present the Nationalists as sectarian to the public. Labour politicians could not believe how easy it had been.

A remarkable convolution occurred within the SNP. Its original opposition to the convention on offer extended gradually to conventions in principle. While a gradualist position could have been sustained while opposing involvement in the CSA's Convention, the mishandling of the decision to withdraw allowed the fundamentalist wing to grasp the opportunity and, with the assistance of former gradualists, push the party into a uncompromising stance. The fundamentalist position was asserted as the SNP abandoned any support for what still remained its policy – an elected constitutional convention. Gradualists who opposed involvement in the CSA's Convention became trapped by their exaggerated rhetoric. Opposition to the Convention became a touchstone of nationalist virility. To mention the constitutional Convention in public, even to criticise it, was interpreted as being 'soft'.

One consequence of SNP non-participation was that those who did participate were determined to reach agreement if only to high-light what they saw as the SNP's sectarianism. For the most part, the Convention's plenary sessions were devoid of serious debate but issues of importance were raised. Financing a Scottish Parliament, the electoral system, women's representation in the Parliament, and powers and responsibilities were discussed in committees. This resembled previous conventions. Almost entirely absent from debate was the action the convention would take once it reached agreement. Nothing approaching the level of debate which was witnessed in the 1920s developed. At the fifth Convention only one speaker contributed to a debate on what should happen next. Liberal Democrat Cllr. Chris Mason pointed out that the convention had made little impact on the public and argued for a referendum. The elite preoccupations of the Convention, which Mason referred to, again mirrored previous Conventions.

The Convention appears to have been more successful than its predecessors in two important respects. The number of MPs and the proportion of local authorities in attendance surpassed earlier conventions. About 80% of Scotland's MPs and MEPs attended meetings and 59 of Scotland's 65 local authorities, including all Regional and Island Councils, nominated representatives to attend. It also claimed to have faced up to certain key weaknesses in the 1978 Scotland Act. Two important areas were discussed: finance, and the voting system for a Scottish Parliament. On finance, the convention reached agreement that

a)   there should be the assignation of Scottish income tax to the Scottish Parliament and if possible the assignation of Scottish VAT and if this is not possible the best possible estimate of Scottish VAT should be found and that should be assigned

b)   the power to vary the income tax rate but some range should be defined so that the variation in income tax up or down cannot be misunderstood as being an especially wide margin

c)   equalisation to continue to be based on needs assessment starting from the present position

d)   review of the scheme to take place on a regular basis.[53]

Though an advance on the Scotland Act, 1978, it was nonetheless a fairly vague statement leaving important questions unanswered. The Convention's acceptance of a voting system other than first-past-the-post was a significant development. The fear that a Scottish Parliament would be dominated by either an ideological or geo-graphical minority, or a combination of the two, had been a reason for the high 'No' vote in areas such as Grampian and the Borders in 1979.

However, not all difficult matters had been confronted. The 'West Lothian Question' – Scots MPs at Westminster able to vote on ex-clusively English matters while equivalent Scottish matters would be the responsibility of the Scottish Assembly – remained unresolved.[54] There could be no doubt that in the event of devolution again being seriously considered by the House of Commons this question would be raised, and not only by Tories. No concession had been made by the Convention for Scotland's representation in the Commons to be cut. Given the central part the issue had played in debates in the 1970s, this was a serious omission from the work of the Convention.

By far the most difficult question, which has always eluded past attempts to gain self-government through a convention, remained unresolved: how to ensure that any agreed scheme would be put into effect. Considerable applause greeted the rhetoric of one participant at the Convention's sixth meeting who said that if Margaret Thatcher said no then 'this time we will not take no for an answer'. As on previous occasions, such rhetoric may have warmed the hearts of participants but it was empty. Related to this was the question of legitimacy. While the Convention claimed to be more representative than previous ones it was difficult to see how it could claim to speak for Scotland. Some means of lending the proposals legitimacy remained to be found.

The Convention gained the financial support of the Joseph Rowntree Reform Trust and appointed Harry Conroy, former gener-al secretary of the National Union of Journalists, as campaign director in September 1990. A strategy was launched on 30 November, St Andrew's Day. It had three parts: a media campaign to gain publicity for the convention and its objective; a Parliamentary campaign to put pressure on the Government to accept its proposals; and a grass-roots campaign to inform the Scottish public about the proposals and seek their support.[55] The strategy was almost an admission that it had failed. The rhetoric – 'We say Yes and we are the people' – of earlier meetings sat uneasily with its strategy. The Convention's supporters had no idea how its policy would be put into effect.

Conclusion

A convention truly representative of Scottish opinion has the potential advantage of claiming to speak for Scotland in a unique manner. This legitimacy in itself would make it worthwhile for politicians to participate and to reach agreement through compromise. Withdrawal from such a convention would result in the non-participant losing influence where it counts. However, all of this rests on two crucial assumptions: first, that the convention is truly representative of the Scottish people, and second, that the scheme can and will be implemented when agreement is reached. Without these the legitimacy and value of a convention is diminished. None of the attempts to achieve self-government this century through conventions has confronted these facts.

Without the prospect that an agreed scheme will be implemented there might still be some point in holding a convention. In the past it has certainly served to focus attention on the constitutional question and place it on the Scottish and, to some extent, the British political agenda. A further reason for holding a convention is to reach agreement amongst the self-government forces in Scotland as to what precisely is desired but this has the danger of dividing opinion rather than developing a consensus on the need for some sort of Parliament.

A further danger confronting conventions has always been the possibility of hi-jack by some party or section of Scottish opinion to further its own ends. This was evident in the 1920s, the 1940s, and the 1980s, first the Labour Party, next the Conservatives and then Labour again. In each case, the objective was to present the party as pro-Scottish and their opponents in Government as unsympathetic to Scottish demands. The most recent convention was a platform to attack both the Conservatives and the SNP at least as much as an attempt to further the case of self-government. Indeed, the motivations behind involvement have always been confused and sometimes contradictory. Are conventions supposed to publicise the case for a Scottish Parliament, agree a scheme of home rule, negotiate an agreed scheme or find a means of bringing about home rule against the wishes of Westminster?

At times, conventions saw themselves as embodying Scottish popular will. But if this was the case, critics asked, why should they need to ask Westminster to give its final blessing to whatever was decided? Conventions require authority and can only gain it from the public. Conventions are, in this sense, social contracts. A fundamental weakness of the conventions which have deliberated on Scotland's constitutional status this century is that there has been little evidence of this social contract. For a movement with the objective of self-government and which bases its case on public support, this has been a fundamental and, ultimately, fatal weakness. Rather than democratic self-government, conventions have embodied the very principles the movement opposes – unrepresentative, lacking legitimacy and without an explicit Scottish mandate. Each convention has, predictably, led up a blind alley.[56]

1. Walter F. Dodd, 'Constitutional Conventions', in Edwin R. A. Silgman (ed.), *Encyclopaedia of the Social Sciences*, vol. 3, New York, Macmillan, 1962, p. 244.
2. Bill Bryson, *Made in America*, London: Secker and Warburg, 1994, p. 59.
3. Walter F. Dodd, Op. cit, p. 246.
4. Brigid Hadfield, *The Constitution of Northern Ireland*, Belfast: SLS Legal Publications, 1989, pp. 125–6.
5. *Ibid.*, p. 128.
6. *Dumfries and Galloway Standard*, June 4, 1892.
7. *Ibid.*
8. *Ibid.*
9. *Glasgow Herald*, April 25, 1919.
10. NLS, Acc. 3721, box 123/1, SHRA General Council 1918–27.
11. *Scottish Home Rule Association News Sheet*, Vol. 1, no. 7, January 1921.
12. NLS, Acc. 3721, Box 186/3, special conference with MPs February 2, 1923.
13. Thurso Papers, THRS I 8/5, Churchill College Archives' Centre, Cambridge.
14. *Dundee Advertiser*, editorial November 17, 1924.
15. NLS, Acc. 3721, Box 80/17, The Scottish National Convention.
16. *Ibid.*

17. NLS, Acc. 3721, Box 81/2, Informal meeting of the nucleus of the Committee of Convention with Scots MPs January 30, 1926,
18. *Ibid.*, Box 80/17.
19. *Ibid.*
20. *Ibid.*, Box 81/2.
21. *Ibid.*
22. *Ibid.*, Box 80/17. Letter to Col. Crookshank MP from R. E. Muirhead November 9, 1926.
23. *Ibid.*, Box 84/25, Letter to Lewis Spence from Muirhead, November 29, 1926.
24. *Scotsman*, April 7, 1927; Letter to editor of the *Scotsman* from Muirhead, April 8, 1927.
25. NLS, Acc. 3721, Box 83/19.
26. *Ibid.*
27. *Ibid.*
28. *Ibid.*, Box 66/493. Letter from John MacCormick, Hon. Secy. SNP, undated.
29. *Ibid.*, Box 80/17.
30. Lady Glen-Coats of the Liberals; Rev. James Barr, the Labour MP for Coatbridge; Willie Gallacher, the Communist MP for west Fife; and two trade unionists – James McKendrick, General Secretary of the Lanarkshire Miners' Union, and John McBain, Scottish Organiser of the Foundry Workers' Union.
31. NLS, Acc. 3721 Box 66/493, 'Scottish National Convention 1941' submitted to SNP Council 21/12/40 by R. E. Muirhead.
32. *Ibid.*
33. NLS, Acc. 7505 No. 20, *Scottish Convention – What it is and What it stands for.*
34. NLS, Acc. 7295(4), Minute Book of National Committee, Scottish Convention
35. NLS, Acc. 3721 Box 74/661.
36. *Ibid.*, Letter from Mary Dott, SNP National Secretary.
37. These included eight Church of Scotland presbyteries, representatives of the Liberal Party, Communist Party, the Scottish Horse & Motormen's Association, the Sheet Iron & Light Plate Workers' Society, the Scottish Schoolmasters' Association, The Association of Scientific Workers, the Association of Building Technicians, five cooperative societies, the Saltire Society, the Scottish Reconstruction Committee, the Clan Campbell Society, three local branches of political parties, and the Milngavie Citizens' Association. NLS, Acc. 5978, Box 1, F3.

38. *Ibid.*
39. *Ibid.*, Scottish Convention 1945–49.
40. *Ibid.*, Letter from James Porteous to John MacCormick, February 1, 1949.
41. 'Will Scotland achieve self-government?', *Picture Post* May 6, 1950.
42. *Scotsman*, May 11, 1977.
43. *Ibid.*, February 25, 1977.
44. Conservative Central Office News Release, February 6, 1978.
45. *Scotsman*, February 7, 1978.
46. *Ibid.*, June 1, 1978.
47. *Ibid.*
48. Conservative Central Office News Release, September 10, 1978.
49. *Claim of Right*, 11.4.2; 11.4.6.
50. *Ibid.*, 11.4.8.
51. *Ibid.*, 11.4.9.
52. Iain Macwhirter, 'After Doomsday. . .The Convention And Scotland's Constitutional Crisis', *Scottish Government Yearbook 1990*, p. 26.
53. Letter to author from Secretary to Constitutional Convention. August 22, 1990.
54. It was called the 'West Lothian Question' because Tam Dalyell, Labour MP for West Lothian, had articulated it with most frequency and force in debates in the 1970s.
55. Harry Conroy, 'Constitutional Convention's Campaign' *The Scottish Government Yearbook*, 1992.
56. For my own predictions on the course of the CSA-inspired Convention see James Mitchell 'Constitutional Conventions and the Scottish National Movement: Origins, Agendas and Outcomes', *Strathclyde Papers on Government and Politics* No. 78, 1991.

Referendums, Plebiscites and Petitions

Introduction

This chapter is concerned with attempts to institute direct democracy in the cause of Scottish self-government. Direct democracy simply means directly involving the public at large in politics, not just their elected representatives. There are a number of ways of doing this. Referendums, plebiscites and petitions are examples, and general points on these are followed by a discussion of the debate on the use of such devices within the self-government movement. The terms referendum and plebiscite have been used interchangeably, particularly earlier this century, though the former has in recent times been used more. The plebiscite was used in the French Revolution as a logical extension of the doctrine of popular sovereignty.[1] A plebiscite has come to acquire a more precise meaning and is concerned with questions of sovereignty. The use of plebiscites to determine the government of disputed territories has been evident since the end of the eighteenth century. After the first world war, its use was tied to the doctrine of self-determination associated with US President Woodrow Wilson and the League of Nations. Numerous examples of the successful use of plebiscites have been listed in works by Sarah Wambaugh, an official of the League.[2] Those held in the period before the first world war included formal and informal plebiscites, with or without agreement between any two parties involved in a disputed area, and even occasionally under international supervision.

Translating the idea of direct democracy into a practical scheme, especially if the government opposed it, has proved difficult, which explains why the demand for a plebiscite has been heard less often than might have been expected. However, at various times, different organisations advocated the use of a referendum to determine the views of the Scottish people on constitutional reform. The question or questions posed by a referendum have differed over the years but generally a fairly straightforward choice between the status quo and a vaguely worded alternative, usually open to interpretation as independence or devolution, has been proposed by proponents of change while their opponents have usually suggested a choice between the status quo and independence. The choice of more than two options has been proposed infrequently.

Reasons for Holding a Referendum

Certain countries have constitutional requirements to hold referendums when, for example, a constitutional amendment is proposed or when a stated number of voters has demanded one on some issue. Alternatively, governments may find a referendum useful in order to legitimize a decision – the government would have to be fairly confident of success or open-minded as to the result if it decided to conduct a referendum which it was not legally bound to. The French referendum on Maastricht in 1992 is an example of a legitimizing referendum which was not required, but which nearly backfired on the Mitterrand Government when only a narrow majority voted in favour of the measure. A government may decide to hold a referendum because of internal divisions within the government, legislature or party. The 1975 British referendum on continued membership of the European Community is an example. The 1979 devolution referendums in Wales and Scotland were proposed in response to divisions within the Parliamentary Labour Party. The only means by which the government could expect to get the devolution legislation on the statute books was by conceding a referendum to opponents of devolution.

Support for a referendum may be the result of frustration caused by the failure or perceived futility of working through existing or other channels. There is evidence that referendums are institutions of last resort, after all else has failed. Referendums have been seen as inadequate as decision-making institutions or as a means of resolving conflict. This is often because as last resort institutions to deal with intractable problems they merely follow the failure of all other methods.

A number of problems can arise during the conduct of a referendum. While in theory a referendum separates an issue from all others and provides the electorate with a clear choice, this does not happen in practice. A referendum on a vaguely-worded question would have the merit of allowing a wide range of views to come together in making the case for change. The weakness is that in this disparate group, supporters of the status quo will attempt to identify all those arguing for change with the least popular or most extreme position amongst them. Even when the option for change is clearly spelled out, the fact that it remains the only option other than the status quo does not prevent opponents of change equating it with support for other, more extreme or unpopular, measures – including measures and issues which may not be directly related to the issue being considered.

The motivation behind holding or advocating a referendum varies. In its most genuine form, support for a referendum is based on a desire to find a means of ascertaining public opinion or resolving a political difference. Justification for this when elections exist must be found. Unless there is some constitutional provision for use of a referendum or some precedent, some other justification for the use of the referendum has to be found.

Another motiviation has been a desire to find some means of reaching over established decision-making processes and institutions, including Parliament and the political parties, directly to the public. The problem with this is that by-passing Parliament and political parties may not be feasible if the referendum is to have official status. An unofficial referendum runs the risk of being treated as illegitimate not only by Government but also by the public and may result in a low turnout, making it easier for Government to ignore the result. The nature of the referendum, whether consultative or binding, is important. The result of a consultative referendum may be ignored, or at least play only a limited part in determining the course of action of a government.

Support for a referendum on an issue may be a challenge to opponents or an attempt to embarrass them. Challenging opponents to let the people decide has the advantage of implicitly claiming public support and forcing opponents on to the defensive. In that sense, it is a campaigning technique associated less with the referendum *per se* than as an appeal for public sympathy. In the case of referendums offering more than two choices, the motivation may be to allow for a wide degree of consensus while permitting diversity of opinion. For advocates of change the multi-option referendum combats the problems associated with lumping together a disparate group, hence preventing supporters of the status quo the opportunity to equate a change with any particular, unpopular form of change. But some means of ensuring that a definite conclusion is reached is required, to avoid a stalemate with no single option commanding majority support.

In addition to referendums, petitions allow mass participation in the political process. Petitions carry less authority and are less ambitious in scale and intention. Petitions are a common feature of local pressure group activity but less so at a national level. The Chartists presented their demands for extending democracy to Parliament accompanied by petitions in 1839, 1842 and 1848. It was claimed that the final petition had 5.7 million signatures. A Commons committee studied it with a view to finding flaws and claimed that it actually contained fewer than 2 million signatures, including those of 'Mr Punch' and 'Queen Victoria'.[3] Even this lower estimate was impressive but, as a strategy, it was inadequate. The Chartists had to pursue their goal in other ways, a task made difficult by the fact that the Charter's objectives involved changing the political system itself.

The UK Experience of Referendums

There is no provision in constitutional law in the UK for holding a referendum. The doctrine of Parliamentary sovereignty has ensured that any alternative source of political authority, including the people, has found little favour amongst constitutional purists. However, expediency has occasionally forced even the most ardent upholders of the faith to abandon their opposition to extra-Parliamentary sources of authority. Dicey is the most notable example. He had been the nineteenth century's greatest advocate of the doctrine of Parliamentary sovereignty, largely to combat Irish home rule. His support for a referendum undermined the doctrine he was closely associated with but was consistent in its intention of blocking Irish home rule.

Dicey was concerned in 1890 that the Liberal Party, which he had supported until four years earlier, was likely to be returned to power at some stage and would pursue a policy of home rule without popular support. It was for this reason that he asked, 'Ought the referendum to be introduced into England?'[4] The idea found favour amongst some Conservative politicians at various stages in the twentieth century but its actual introduction in practice has been the result of the 'vicissitudes of party politics'.[5]

The idea of a Government-sponsored referendum only took form in the 1970s. The precedents of the referendum on Northern Ireland and European Community membership were important in the context of the self-government movement. Though the rules set for these differed markedly from that on devolution. The late 1960s saw a revival of interest in the use of referendums in Britain. European Community (EC) membership and the intractable problems of Northern Ireland were raised as issues which should be dealt with by referendum. The Liberals, with their staunch commitment to EC membership, were the first party to advocate a referendum, voting for one at their 1969 conference.[6] The Liberal view was that this would be the only way to resolve the question of membership decisively given the divisions in the country and within the Labour and Conservative Parties on the issue.

The UK only held a referendum on EC membership after Labour 'renegotiated' the terms of entry. Harold Wilson found the referendum a useful tool. With it he could maintain a semblance of party unity by allowing each side to agree to disagree. Additionally, he could play the populist card. Labour's renegotiation of the terms of the UK's membership of the EC was little more than window dressing but Wilson claimed that he had won a better deal and could now recommend that voters support continued membership.

Five main problem areas existed for the Government regarding the conduct of the referendum in 1975: counting the vote; broadcasting arrangement; control of expenditure; wording the question; and government information policy. There was no standard reference to consult. Counting proved the most 'vexatious of the issues', according to a study of the 1975 referendum.[7] The question of which units should be used in the count had to be confronted. A proposal that results should be declared by constituency was defeated. In Scotland the new regions established under the reformed structure of local government were used. Broadcasting followed the pattern of general elections with the 'umbrella organisations' set up for each side given equal access and each given four broadcasts in the style of party political broadcasts. Control of spending amounted to the publication of receipts and expenses of each of the organisations with a grant equivalent to the cost of a full-page advertisement in every Sunday and daily newspaper awarded as an incentive to comply.[8] The actual wording of the question in the referendum was subjected to much scrutiny and a polling organisation was commissioned to test for bias. In the event a compromise was found which allowed both the terms 'European Community' and 'Common Market' to be used. The Government agreed to distribute literature throughout the country, with leaflets giving the case for both sides. In addition, a unit was established to answer questions from the public within the Central Office of Information. Complaints from opponents of the EC that the unit was biased led to an anti-Market information office being set up.[9]

The referendum in 1975 was a lesson in how the views of the electorate can change. There was speculation that the Scots might vote against membership while the rest of Britain voted in favour. Polls in Scotland in the early part of 1975 suggested this might happen. In January, only 29% of Scots were in favour of continued membership while 45% were against but on polling day, 33% of the Scottish electorate voted to remain in while 25% voted for withdrawal and 41% did not vote.[10] As Harvie has pointed out, Labour and SNP anti-EC campaigners could not mobilise their vote, which was to be an encouraging sign for Tories who were considering a referendum on devolution.[11]

The 'Troubles' in Northern Ireland found Westminster caught off guard with the Government struggling to find some means of bringing an end to the violence. The prorogue of Stormont and imposition of direct rule in 1972 solved certain problems but created others.

Under the Ireland Act, 1949, it had been affirmed that Northern Ireland would not cease to be part of the UK without the consent of Stormont. Without Stormont, some other means of determining the views of the people had to be found. The Conservative Government made clear its intention to hold a referendum though Labour had doubts. Merlyn Rees, Shadow Northern Ireland Secretary, warned that such a poll would 'only polarise views and tell us what we know' though he saw a possibility of holding a plebiscite after an all-party conference to lend legitimacy to any recommendations that emerged.[12]

In 1973 a 'border poll' was conducted in which two questions were asked: 'Do you want Northern Ireland to remain a part of the United Kingdom?' and 'Do you want Northern Ireland to be joined with the Irish Republic outside the United Kingdom?' Other options, such as being part of neither the Irish Republic nor the United Kingdom or becoming part of the republic only after the free consent of those living in Northern Ireland, were not offered. The latter option was, in fact, the policy of the Social Democratic and Labour Party (SDLP), the largest opposition party in Northern Ireland.[13] Predictably, the poll resulted in a low turnout, 58.6%, with a tiny fraction, 0.6% of the electorate, voting to join the Republic after the SDLP, amongst others, urged voters to boycott the referendum. The fact that there was no agreement on the 'rules of the game' meant that the initiative failed to resolve what many believed to be an intractable problem.

Tentative Moves Before the War

Referendums on constitutional reform were frequently called for during the inter-war period. Little strategic thinking seems to have gone into developing strategies for self-government in this period, with a range of approaches being adopted simultaneously. The referendum was simply one amongst many. In the late 1920s, Lewis Spence's Scottish National Movement (SNM) supported a referendum and proposed this in a letter to the Scottish National Convention (SNC) then meeting. The SNM believed that as efforts to secure self-government 'through the medium of the British House of Commons have proved ineffectual, continued effort in that direction appears to them altogether purposeless.' A referendum, they maintained, would 'not only stimulate the interest of the Scottish people in the subject, but, if it proved to be in favour of such a policy, would have the effect of disarming present opposition in the House of Commons and elsewhere, and vindicate once and for all Scottish predilections in this respect.'[14] In his reply, the Secretary of the Convention stated that 'when four out of five of the Scottish Members of Parliament vote in favour of Self-Government there is a sufficiently clear indication that the majority of the people are anxious for a National Parliament in Scotland.'[15] The Convention's supporters appear to have wanted to avoid this proposal. At the second meeting of the Convention, the letter from the SNM was read expressing its 'feeling of fraternal work', but omitting the section implicitly critical of the Convention's approach and the SNM support for a referendum. As frustration grew within the Convention in the late 1920s the case for a referendum was heard again. At a meeting of the national committee of the Convention in June 1927 the idea of taking a plebiscite of the Scottish people was suggested but was only one amongst a number of proposals and appears to have been given little serious consideration.[16] A meeting of the Convention in December 1927 discussed a resolution proposing that the 'rights and liberties of the people of Scotland can only be safeguarded by attacking the Referendum Vote to the proposed Scottish Parliamentary Constitution.' It was defeated by 39 votes to 15.[17]

The National Party of Scotland called on the Government to hold a plebiscite in 1931. John MacCormick, NPS secretary, wrote to the Prime Minister:

> We require that the plebiscite should take the simplest form possible – for or against complete self-government, and that in the event of a majority supporting our claim a constituent assembly, representative of the Scottish people, should be established with full powers to determine the future constitution of Scotland and to arrange for her relationship with England.[18]

The only logical reason for the NPS's support for a referendum at that time was the need to generate publicity for the cause. Occasional references to referendums were made by the SNP and in particular its gradualist wing in the 1930s. At its annual conference in 1935,

Sir Alexander MacEwen stated that the SNP had invited the Conservative, Liberal and Socialist Parties to join with it in organising a Scottish national ballot on the question of self-government.[19] At its 1939 conference the party affirmed its commitment to a national plebiscite on the question of self-government.[20] Under MacCormick's influence, proposals for a plebiscite and Convention were being debated but were foiled by the advent of war.[21] This early period was one when the movement's strategy was unclear. Amongst the elements in this blunderbuss approach was advocacy of a plebiscite but it was never carefully thought through. This reflected the general confusion over strategy marking this period. Advocating a referendum was about generating publicity for the cause or the party.

The Covenant

The first serious attempt to involve the public directly in the movement, beyond electoral politics, came after the war. This grew out of disillusionment with the failure of the National Assemblies of Scottish Convention. It was felt that something needed to be done to demonstrate the existence of overwhelming popular support for self-government. What was proposed was a giant petition or, as it was called, Covenant. There had been an earlier proposal for a covenant in 1930 launched by the National Party of Scotland in which supporters pledged themselves to 'do everything in our power to restore the independent national status of Scotland' but which had come to nothing.[22] After its launch in 1949 at the third National Assembly, the Covenant quickly gained a substantial number of signatures. It was partly an attempt to translate existing support into an effective force for change and partly an attempt to find a strategy to fill the void created by the failure of the National Assembly meetings. It gained considerable media attention but had little impact.

The idea emerged at a meeting in the Inchrie Hotel in Aberfoyle, later renamed the Covenanters' Inn.[23] The Covenant was a broad statement of principle to allow as many people as possible to sign:

> We, the people of Scotland who subscribe to this engagement, declare our belief that reform in the constitution of our country is necessary to secure good government in accordance with our Scottish traditions and to promote the spiritual and economic welfare of our nation.

We affirm that the desire for such reform is both deep and widespread through the whole community, transcending all political differences and sectional interests and we undertake to continue united in purpose for its achievement.

With that end in view we solemnly enter into this Covenant whereby we pledge ourselves in all loyalty to the Crown and within the framework of the United Kingdom, to do everything in our power to secure for Scotland a Parliament with adequate legislative authority in Scottish affairs.[24]

The number of people who signed the Covenant was disputed. It was never possible to ascertain the validity of each signature but the fact that several 'Donald Ducks' had solemnly signed the Covenant and a number of home rulers admitted later to having signed on a number of occasions undermined the exercise. MacCormick claimed in December 1949 that an index system was used in order to check each signature against the electoral register for each constituency.[25] Had this actually been done, it would have given the home rulers a means of putting pressure on individual MPs but MacCormick's claims proved unfounded. It would, of course, have been a huge task, probably beyond the limited resources of the movement.

While there may be room for doubting the precise figure of those who signed the Covenant, there is little doubt that a considerable number of Scots signed. Within a fortnight it was claimed that over 100,000 Scots had signed.[26] As each month passed the list of claimed signatures grew: over 400,000 in December 1949; 700,000 by January 1950; 900,000 in February 1950.[27] By September 1950 the figure claimed stood at 1,700,000.[28] Attempts were made to use town halls as venues for collecting signatures but with limited success. Glasgow Corporation, for example, decided against giving the National Covenant Committee use of its municipal buildings.[29] By December 1949, about 75 town councils had agreed and 20 refused to put premises at the disposal of the organisers.[30]

The figure aimed at was high and, indeed, was never achieved even accepting the movement's own claims. According to MacCormick:

We want first to show that the majority of the people in Scotland want this reform. Until we have got our 3,000,000 signatures we shall not have shown that. When we obtain the signatures we shall take steps to present our claim to the political parties.[31]

Whether this figure had been planned from the outset or emerged from MacCormnick's rhetoric is uncertain. It was an almost impossible target. At the 1950 election the total Scottish electorate was only 3,370,190 and 2,726,684 electors voted.

One difficulty was in getting MPs to sign. Two MPs were early signatories: John McGovern, Labour MP for Shettleston, and Willie Gallacher, Communist MP for West Fife.[32] Herbert Morrison, Leader of the Commons, had previously warned Labour MPs not to make pledges of support to any or commit themselves to work for any policy not officially endorsed by the Government. Morrison, like Attlee, was 'sternly centralist';[33] even a whiff of rebellion could result in a Labour MP being left out in the cold, and on an issue on which the Government was so cool this was certain.

After gathering the signatures, the question was what should be done next. In themselves the signatures could not bring about a Scottish Parliament. At a meeting of the National Covenant Committee in January 1950, MacCormick explained the steps planned in the event of gathering a sufficient number of signatures. A National Assembly, representative of Scottish opinion, would be called which would instruct the national committee to approach all parties in order to negotiate on the basis of proposals for a Parliament. If this was refused then it was probable, he claimed, that a further meeting of the Assembly would be called at which commissioners would be appointed to enlist the support of every Dominion Government and to take 'whatever further steps then became necessary.' This, he felt, would keep the issue well clear of party dispute.[34] This hypothetical scenario was highly improbable and could only have heartened the opponents of change. There was, in fact, no clear idea as to what should be done next. A number of years later, the novelist Nigel Tranter, who had been involved with the Covenant, noted the naivety of the project and suggested that the politicians were ready for real concessions. The Covenant's supporters had erred in failing to add a 'sanction clause' at the end of the Covenant, saying that signatories would vote against politicians who failed to endorse home rule.[35] Another view shared by SNP members and opponents of any measure of home rule was expressed in an editorial in the *Glasgow Herald*:

If and when 36 or more of the Scottish MPs were to be pledged to securing a Parliament for Scotland, then there would be unquestionable grounds for action by a Government. . .They must in the end either put up candidates of their own or obtain pledges from MPs of the major parties.[36]

Reaction to Pressure

The Covenant provided a temporary fillip for the Convention by generating publicity and keeping the issue before the public. It did cause some anxiety in the government as witnessed by the reaction of Scottish Secretary Arthur Woodburn. Woodburn was the least sympathetic to home rule of the three Scottish Secretaries who served under Attlee. In response to a call for an inquiry into home rule in November 1949, he suggested that MacCormick had stated that the only way in which Scotland would get justice was for someone to throw a bomb at Downing Street.[37] It was a dishonest statement. MacCormick demanded an apology and retraction but Woodburn, accompanied his two most senior civil servants, Sir David Milne and Charles Cunningham, repeated his accusation brandishing a newspaper cutting reporting a speech MacCormick had made to the General Council of the Scottish Liberal Party in October 1947. The report quoted MacCormick saying in response to Attlee's refusal to meet a delegation of home rulers:

> Why is it that Mr Attlee can consider so important a matter – the most pressing in Scotland – so lightly? It is simply because we in Scotland have been so well behaved. If some young enthusiast for Scottish Home Rule were to throw a bomb in the region of Downing Street the question of Scottish self-government would leap into the headlines and become a matter of national urgency.[38]

MacCormick denied that this was meant to be taken as a call to arms but he had been as naive in making the speech as Woodburn had been dishonest in misrepresenting it.

In November 1949, The Unionists issued their manifesto 'Scottish Control of Scottish Affairs' which argued for an increase in Scottish Office responsibilities.[39] The Covenant was having some impact and one Unionist MP, Col. Sir Alan Gomme-Duncan representing Perth, was involved with Scottish Convention. The Unionists could see value in associating themselves with the cause so long as they did not need to promise anything. As they were in opposition, this proved simple. Woodburn sent a memorandum to the Cabinet on 'Scottish Affairs' in December 1949 in which he stated that he felt it right to let them know that home rulers were 'very active' in Scotland but that 'no further action by the Government is called for' at that time.[40] He expected that the Covenant would be presented in due course and those involved would 'seek to time this so as to cause the maximum embarrassment before the General Election.'[41] He explained that while Labour had contested the 1945 Election in Scotland on a platform of home rule he had since argued that it was not opportune for it to be considered and that he had resisted a demand for an enquiry into Scotland's financial relations with England. He informed his colleagues that the issue was 'bound to be widely canvassed' at the forthcoming election and while Labour MPs had agreed to concentrate on other issues, 'I must report that in some cases I have persuaded them against their will and that some are genuinely apprehensive of this campaign.' It was, however, his expectation that the publication of the Tory manifesto would result in the Scottish press moderating its 'plugging' of devolution.[42] He conceded to his Cabinet colleagues something he never dared say in public:

> These campaigns obtain their success because interest in the subject in Scotland is always present, widespread and sincere. It is accordingly essential that every support should be given to the great body of reasonable opinion in Scotland which does not support drastic changes but which is liable to be shaken by any action which can be represented as imposing on Scotland decisions in the making of which she appears to have had no real voice, or as being designed primarily to meet conditions south of the Border.[43]

The Cabinet endorsed Woodburn's views.[44]

Local Plebiscites and the Failure of Alternatives

In March 1947, the Scottish Convention's Assembly discussed three resolutions. The first stated the minimum demand of the Scottish people, that the Scottish Grand Committee should be reformed to give it legislative powers, and was carried by 98 votes to 13. The second gave support to the Leonard Declaration in favour of self-government and was passed by 216 votes to 2. The third, a call for a referendum on self-government, was rejected unanimously by the Assembly.[45] However, the success of a local plebiscite allied with the failure of the National Assemblies to have much impact changed attitudes on holding a referendum. In January 1949 the Scottish Plebiscite Society conducted a poll in Kirriemuir in Angus. The Society had been formed in 1946 by Peter Thomson, an Edinburgh advocate, as secretary.

Kirriemuir was ideal for this first venture as the local provost agreed to supervise the count and, if subsequent electoral history is any guide, it was fertile ground for nationalist politics. The town had an electorate of 2715 and 2310 (85%) voted in the ballot. Three choices were presented to the voters:

1)   I am in favour of an independent Scottish Parliament;
2)   I am in favour of a Scottish Parliament which will deal with purely Scottish affairs similar to the Parliament of Northern Ireland;
3)   I am not in favour of a Scottish Parliament of any kind.

The results showed overwhelming support for change:

Option 1	539 (23%)
Option 2	1595 (69%)
Option 3	122 (5%)
Spoiled papers	54 (2%)

Thomson became a sheriff in 1962 and continued to support a referendum. His active support for a referendum in the 1970s led to his dismissal from the bench in December 1977, the first sheriff to be sacked for political activities in seventy years. Disillusioned with the plebiscite and referendum approach he advocated support for the SNP in the 1980s. In an advertisement he paid for himself in the London *Times* in February 1982, coinciding with the first meeting in 40 years of the Scottish Grand Committee in Edinburgh, Thomson addressed himself to all electors in Scotland: 'If you want any reform – however slight– you have no alternative but to vote Nationalist' as this was the only way to ensure that constitutional reform was taken seriously, 'Any political party which pretends to be able to deliver reform in face of a low Nationalist vote is misleading itself and the

electors.'[46] Almost 40 years after the establishment of the Plebiscite
Society, and having consistently supported this approach for most of
the period, he had come to see its deficiencies.

The national committee of Scottish Convention wrote to
Thomson congratulating him on the plebiscite and agreed also to
send a letter to the Government calling for a national plebiscite.[47]
Once more, frustration with other methods led to support for a
referendum. The failure of the Scottish National Assemblies and
Covenant forced home rulers to consider alternative campaigning
strategies. But the SNP at its annual conference later that year voted
by 57 to 9 against asking the Government to hold a 'plebiscite to
ascertain the wishes of the people in the matter of self-government'.
The *Scots Independent* reported that the conference was 'impatient
with any suggestion that any effort should be diverted from winning
Parliamentary and Local Authority elections even for the purpose of
pressing the London Government to take a plebiscite'.[48] The view in
the party was that the quick fixes associated with John MacCormick
were proving futile and that a long slow haul was the only way
forward.

At a meeting in May 1950, the National Covenant Committee
decided to send a questionnaire to all Scottish MPs. The purpose
was to reach agreement on the means of resolving the constitutional
question. MPs were asked how Scots could have their desire for a
Parliament realised, if not by signing the Covenant or through a plebiscite.[49] Few MPs bothered to respond. Only four (Labour MPs John
Rankin and John McGovern and Liberal MPs A. J. F. MacDonald
and Jo Grimond) accepted without reservation that the Covenant, if
signed by a majority of electors in Scotland, was sufficient evidence
that a majority desired a Parliament to be set up. Sir William Darling
(Unionist) thought that the Covenant was inadequate, but supported
a plebiscite. Liberal MP John McLeod thought a Royal Commission
should be held first, while Labour MP David Pryde merely confirmed his support for a Scottish Parliament and Unionist MP Col.
Gomme-Duncan asserted that his party's policy was correct.[50] The
questionnaire had attempted to force MPs into a corner, to state on
record whether they accepted the Scottish people's right to determine
the constitutional status of Scotland and, if they did, how this could
be done. It was, therefore, not surprising that so few MPs replied.

Support for a plebiscite was voiced by home rulers in Parliament. In May 1950, the Earl of Mansfield, on the Conservative benches, unsuccessfully urged the Government to hold a plebiscite. Lord Morrison, for the Government, argued that, principled objections aside, the issue was too complicated to be dealt with by means of a plebiscite.[51] The unionist *Glasgow Herald* in an editorial three months later expressed its opposition in terms similar to the Government:

> The practical political problem is not whether the Scottish electorate like the idea of a Parliament in Edinburgh but whether they want one at once and consider the question should have priority over other matters. The simple test is whether they will return Parliamentary candidates pledged accordingly. A plebiscite could not be phrased so as to provide a clear answer. And even if that difficulty could be overcome the result might still be ambiguous.[52]

Hector McNeil, Secretary of State for Scotland, argued that the issue was too complex to be dealt with by a plebiscite and that constitutional change must be considered and settled by the process of Parliamentary democracy.[53]

A by-election in Glasgow Scotstoun provided an opportunity to influence events and it was decided to hold a plebiscite on self-government on the same lines as that held in Kirriemuir. Scotstoun was highly marginal. At the previous general election, the Unionists won the seat with a majority of 239 over Labour. MacCormick told the press that prominent opponents of self-government, including local authority figures such as Victor Warren and Sir Patrick Dollan of Glasgow and Arthur Woodburn MP, would be invited to speak in the constituency as well as supporters of change. The possibility of standing a candidate had been considered but the plebiscite idea was believed to allow unity across the parties.[54] Meetings were held during the course of the by-election. A letter in the form of an election address was sent to all voters giving a brief history of the movement, and claiming that 1,600,000 signatures to the Covenant had been collected. A card was provided on which voters could record their views on the desirability or otherwise of a Scottish Parliament. The question was put to the electors:

Are you in favour of the setting up as soon as possible of a

Scottish Parliament to deal with Scottish affairs, it being understood that matters relating to the Crown, defence, foreign and imperial policy, customs and excise, will remain under the control of the UK Parliament in which Scotland will still have its members?[55]

The problem of credibility arose with this approach as it would be very difficult to check whether each card returned came from a *bone fide* voter. MacCormick conceded that there was no reliable method of checking each returned card:

We are appealing, as it were, to the honour of the electors to treat this seriously, and I think that, while we will not be able to guarantee the result 100 per cent, we will be able to say that it is, by and large, a genuine inquiry.[56]

Inevitably, the Labour candidate in the by-election questioned the authenticity of the result of the plebiscite, claiming to have heard of a person who did not live in Scotstoun getting two copies of the voting paper from the office of Scottish Convention. The more honest approach, he argued, would have been for the Covenant Committee to have nominated a candidate.[57] The Unionists held Scotstoun with a majority of 1,319 over Labour. The plebiscite resulted in an overwhelming majority in favour of a Scottish Parliament: 20,800 for and 4,227 against with 57 spoiled papers, and with 69% of cards returned.[58]

In August 1950, the executive of the Covenant had decided to develop the demand for a national plebiscite by inviting all local authorities to lend their support to the idea.[59] They were to be asked to adopt a resolution pressing the Government to hold a national plebiscite which would be organised in the same way as elections. MacCormick's view was that if the local authorities supported the idea and the Government rejected it then the Covenant Committee should ask the local authorities to hold their own plebiscites.[60] The resolution submitted to each local authority in Scotland recommended that a plebiscite be held and that if two-thirds of voters supported a Parliament then a Royal Commission should be established to recommend the best means of implementing Scottish home rule. It was a fairly convoluted route but the most difficult task would be to convince the local authorities to pass the resolution. From late November into the new year, local authorities throughout Scotland considered this request. Edinburgh Town Council responded quickly

but refused to accede to the Covenant Committee's request.[61]
Glasgow Corporation voted 72 to 24 against with only 2 of the 30
Labour members on the Corporation and 22 of the 56 Progressives
supporting it. Cllr. Robert Gray, a prominent figure in the national
movement and Progressive (Conservative) member, moved the
resolution.[62]

By mid-January 1951, the Covenant Committee claimed that 30
Town Councils had forwarded resolutions to the Prime Minister
and Secretary of State asking for an official plebiscite while 26 had
refused and 7 decided to take no action.[63] These claims were dubious
in two ways. The list provided did not include all local authorities
which had voiced opposition to the resolution or decided to take
no action. Even ignoring the omissions, which included Edinburgh,
Lanark, Greenock, Wigtown and Kilsyth, in terms of total population
the opponents outstripped the supporters: using figures from the
1951 census, the total population of those authorities supporting the
resolution totalled 168,845 while those opposing it totalled 1,559,162
with 147,903 taking no action.[64] There were 196 town councils in
Scotland in total at the time. The main problem was that most local
authorities had simply failed to respond.

The Relaunch of the Movement

The failure of this venture forced the Committee to consider an
alternative course and later that month five leading members were
appointed to prepare a statement outlining future strategy. It was
publicly admitted that some differences in approach had emerged.
A few weeks later the new course which was emerging provoked a
Glasgow Herald editorial:

> The twisting and turning of the covenant movement grows increas-
> ingly eel-like. The Scotstoun plebiscite failed to show the desired
> result in spite of the use of pre-paid 'ballot-forms'. Little more is likely
> to be heard of the attempt to canvass local authorities' support for a
> national plebiscite. Now agitation is to start, according to the latest
> recommendations of the Scottish National Covenant Committee, for
> the setting up of a Royal Commission charged, apparently, with the
> task of making the same kind of half-baked investigations as the
> committee have themselves been conducting.'[65]

Not for the first time, the *Herald* argued that 'popular desire' for home rule could only be claimed when a majority of Scottish MPs pledged in its favour were returned.

The idea of a plebiscite was pushed to the back-burner for a period but not entirely forgotten. It was clear that the issue was causing tension in the organisation. A month before the 1951 general election, the Covenant Association asked the Government to establish a Scottish Parliament or else hold a plebiscite. They threatened, unconvincingly, to conduct a plebiscite themselves if the answer they received was unsatisfactory and pointed to the constituency organisations they were establishing as evidence of their intention.[66] Following the election, yet another revival of the organisation was staged. An 'inaugural' meeting of the 'new' Scottish Covenant Association was held in Glasgow at which Ian Hamilton, of Stone of Destiny fame, moved a resolution urging constituency committees to prepare local machinery for a plebiscite before the end of 1952. Others felt this was impractical. It was pointed out that the cost of sending out 3.5m letters would be in excess of £20,000 in postage alone while envelopes and literature would easily double the cost. In support of the resolution, MacCormick argued that the collection of 2m signatures for the Covenant had confounded the prophets of doom and that 'if we go boldly to the people we can create such a storm and excitement in Scotland that the plebiscite machinery will prepare itself'.[67] It was too ambitious an idea for the Covenant Association in the wake of the setbacks of the previous years.

Periodic requests for a plebiscite were heard during the 1950s. In April 1955, a new organisation was launched, the Nationalist Society of Loyal Scots, with the aim of ascertaining the 'national will' by means of a plebiscite. Two conditions were regarded as essential: that the plebiscite should take place only after a six month period in order for a reasoned debate to occur, and that it should not be held immediately before or during a General Election or when one or other of the major parties had raised an issue of major importance.[68] This was, however, an organisation which was on the fringe of the national movement, which meant it was barely visible in Scottish politics generally and, as with so many similar bodies, it fizzled out.

At the 1955 election, the Covenant Association decided to ask candidates their views on self-government and whether they supported a plebiscite.[69] However, this was the high point of unionism in post-1945 Scotland. A request sent to Anthony Eden to hold a plebiscite was turned down in 1956. The government did not consider that the 'complex issues involved in the consideration of the case for a Scottish parliament can be dealt with by means of a plebiscite'.[70] In March 1957, it was suggested at the National Committee of the Covenant Association that pressure be put on the Government to hold a plebiscite. Others believed that the priority ought to be getting MacCormick elected to Parliament.[71] At its 1958 conference the SNP approved a resolution calling for a national plebiscite, an idea it had rejected in 1949. The national movement looked and sounded tired, with no new initiative to capture the imagination. The plebiscite idea was advanced more as a means of attempting to keep the issue of home rule on the political agenda than as a serious strategy.

In June 1959, the 4080 voters in the Borders town of Peebles received ballot papers from the Scottish Plebiscite Society. As with the Kirriemuir plebiscite held a decade before, the Peebles plebiscite was given some credibility by the involvement of the local provost as returning officer. A high turnout of 75.4% was recorded which the organisers compared with the 43.1% turnout at the previous municipal elections. Support for independence was at 16%; those against any form of Scottish Parliament at 12% and those in favour of a Scottish Parliament to deal with domestic affairs at 66%.[72] Once more, the apparent success of a local plebiscite encouraged the view that this might be the way forward.

The Plebiscite Appeal Fund

The launch of a new 'non-party, independent body' to conduct a national plebiscite in Scotland on St Andrew's Day, 1961 marked the beginning of the most ambitious project to hold an unofficial plebiscite. In a letter to the press, a number of prominent figures urged their fellow Scots to contribute money to the project. The *Scottish Daily Mail* gave the appeal front-page status under the headline '£100,000 CRUSADE'.[73] A fund of not less than £100,000 was the target. The fifteen signatories covered an impressive range of public life in Scotland.[74] It was intended that the plebiscite would be conducted by the Scottish Plebiscite Society by postal ballot under the supervision of a distinguished British and Commonwealth board.

In June 1962, the questions to be asked in the plebiscite were spelt out. There were to be four choices. The first would ask whether the elector wanted to retain the present system or adopt a measure of devolution. Those who voted for change would be asked to record on the reverse side of the voting paper their preference for one of three possible options:

> (a)   a Scottish Parliament on the lines of the Northern Ireland Parliament, (b)   a Scottish Parliament to handle all Scotland's internal affairs, or (c)   a totally independent Scottish Parliament as the legislature of a quite separate state which might or might not wish to opt out of the Commonwealth.

It was felt that 75% of the electorate would have to vote in the plebiscite for credibility. Later that year, the novelist Nigel Tranter expressed his concern that the question posed might be too complex and called for simple, brief and clear-cut wording.[75]

Money was slow to come into the fund and the Appeal Committee avoided discussing its progress.[76] At the launch of the Glasgow appeal in June, £39 was raised from an audience of about 300. Amongst those on the platform at the launch of the Glasgow appeal were Dr John Highet, John Bannerman, Michael Byrne, and Cllr. Teddy Taylor, who was later to advocate referendums on hanging and the European Union as a Conservative MP.[77] That month it was decided to appoint a full-time organiser for the fund. Claims that the appeal had raised a substantial sum were designed to maintain what little momentum there was in the campaign. In July, Major F. A. C. Boothby was appointed chief organiser of the Appeal with a headquarters in St Vincent Crescent, Glasgow. Additionally, an organiser for the North of Scotland was based in Banff. Following the appointment of the two organisers the sum raised had increased by £1,100. Salaries for the organisers, a typist and expenses had amounted to £2,704. It was decided to dispense with the services of the organisers, who were told that they would no longer be needed after only three months in post.[78] In February 1963 the services of professional fund raisers were sought but by the end of 1963, only £3,000 had been raised. The Appeal Fund was wound up in February

1964. The assets amounted to £1,000 – only 1% of the sum originally targeted. This was transferred to the Scottish Plebiscite Society.[79]

It had been a highly ambitious project. Even had it succeeded in raising the required amount it would have been a major gamble. In June 1962, the *Economist* had asked a question which the Appeal Fund never had to face: could any plebiscite have validity if it was not accompanied by a political argument over the consequences of any decision?[80] The fact that the Appeal failed to raise anything like the sum required testified either to a lack of public interest or a perception that an unofficial plebiscite would simply be dismissed. Gathering signatures demanding a Scottish Parliament had proved far easier than gathering money to fund a plebiscite to ascertain the wishes of the Scottish people on constitutional reform.

This did not dampen the enthusiasm of a few stalwarts determined to conduct local plebiscites. Even as it was becoming evident that the appeal was failing, a plebiscite was held in Jedburgh. With an electorate the same size as Peebles, which had been polled in June 1959, it offered the opportunity of keeping alive the idea of a national plebiscite. The organiser of the poll and of the Appeal Fund in the Borders was the redoubtable Anthony J. C. Kerr. The Jedburgh plebiscite showed overwhelming support for change. Of the 1064 votes cast, only 130 were against a Scottish Parliament, 919 wanted change with 15 spoiled papers. Of the 919 who wanted change, 149 wanted a Scottish provincial Parliament with limited powers, 419 were for a Scottish Parliament able to deal with all Scottish affairs, and 298 supported an independent Scottish Parliament with its own Foreign Office and Armed Services, while 53 papers did not specify which type of Parliament Scotland should have.[81]

The Liberals' Multi-Option Referendum

The rise of the SNP in the late 1960s triggered yet another discussion of a referendum. In 1968, James Davidson, Liberal MP for West Aberdeenshire, introduced a Private Member's Bill to 'authorise referenda in Scotland and in Wales to enable the Scottish and Welsh people respectively to indicate their views in regard to the future government of their countries'. It was to be a consultative, not a binding, referendum.[82] Davidson could claim consistency having been an early advocate of a referendum for Gibralter in 1966 – a measure initially rejected by the Government but later accepted.[83] His bill failed at second reading in the Commons in February 1969, but received strong support from the *Scotsman*. In January 1969, the paper carried an article by Davidson setting out the case for a referendum in which he rehearsed arguments he was to put to the Commons a month later.[84] Alongside the article, the *Scotsman* carried a questionnaire which it invited its readers to complete and return. Readers were asked to express their views on Scotland's constitutional status in order of preference. Four options were offered:

1.   Should the existing system of government continue unchanged?
2.   Should the Secretary of State and the Scottish Grand Committee be given more power and more functions?
3.   Should a domestic Parliament be established in Scotland with jurisdiction over all internal affairs, and with federal status within the United Kingdom?
4.   Or, should Scotland have complete independence within the Commonwealth including sovereign control over foreign and Commonwealth relations, defence, and Customs and Excise?[85]

To add to the confusion, a fifth question was listed immediately below these options, 'Should there be a referendum?'

Analysis of the returned questionnaires was provided by an Edinburgh University academic a week before the second reading of Davidson's Bill.[86] 1,382 replies had been returned, under 3% of the paper's readership. Of these, 88% favoured a referendum. Of the first preferences, the most favoured option was independence:

Question	First Choice	Percentage
1	59	4.5
2	64	4.9
3	478	36.6
4	706	54.0

A method was then used to weight the preferences in order to reach an outcome in keeping with the *Scotsman's* viewpoint. A single point was attached to every last preference, two points were awarded for every third preference, three points for every second preference and four points for every first preference. The justification behind this

method was that while one choice might be popular as a first preference for one respondent, it might be unpopular enough with all other
respondents to render it less politically attractive or feasible than it
first seemed. The absurdity of the system used and the departure
from the standard preferential system in counting the results was
striking. This resulted in a different outcome:

Question	Points	Percentage
1	1574	12.8
2	2739	22.3
3	4095	33.4
4	3887	31.5

A further alternative method of calculation was considered. This
attempted to work out the most frequent of possible combinations.
The three most common were:

	Choice	Percentage
4321	Independence as first choice, status quo last	50.0
3412	Federalism as first choice, independence second	16.5
3214	Federalism as first choice, independence last	12.5
Total		79.0

This demonstrated how simple it is to manipulate statistical results
through sophistry, and the importance of setting ground rules from
the start.

On the day of the second reading, the *Scotsman* carried an editorial
arguing that a referendum would be fair and that the major parties
would 'earn more respect if they showed that they have as much confidence in the will of the people as the supporters of self-government
have'.[87] It was ignored. The bill was defeated by 81 votes to 13. Apart
from the Liberals, support for the bill came from Winnie Ewing of
the SNP, Gwynfor Evans of Plaid Cymru, Willie Baxter and Emrys
Hughes of the Labour Party and Teddy Taylor of the Conservatives.
Merlyn Rees, for the Labour Government, argued that four choices
confused the matter and suggested that only one choice should be
offered – 'Do you want complete independence, or do you want
association inside the United Kingdom?'[88] A further criticism voiced
by Rees was that the English were being left out.[89] Many of the

contributions in the debate from opponents of the bill were notable for their irrelevance. Supporters pointed to precedents, including Gibralter and Newfoundland, but their relevance was denied or the arguments deflected.

The Devolution Referendum as a Stalling Device

The perception that the national movement had been halted in its tracks at the 1970 general election removed the issue of constitutional change from the agenda of politics for a time. The revival of the movement signalled by the SNP electoral breakthrough in 1974 forced the issue to the fore once more. Initially, the Labour Government refused to consider a referendum. In July 1974, Harold Wilson stated that a referendum was a 'wholly exceptional procedure'.[90] Following the 1975 European Community referendum Wilson was pressed by Willie Hamilton, anti-devolutionist Labour MP for Central Fife, on holding a 'separate and distinct referendum in Scotland, among the Scottish electorate, on the question whether they want complete separation, as advocated by the SNP'. Wilson's view was that there would be:

> great opposition in this House to a devolution referendum held purely in Scotland. Certainly such a referendum would have to cover Wales and England as well. Everyone in the United Kingdom has the right to be represented.[91]

Wilson had answered a different question: Hamilton had asked for a referendum on 'separatism', though there was a logic in Wilson's position, as devolution to Scotland would have implications for the rest of the UK. Initial support for a consultative referendum came from politicians who wanted to block devolution. Others argued for a referendum on 'separatism': the terminology indicated the views of those who took this line. In late 1976, Ted Heath called for a referendum on Scottish independence while supporting legislative devolution. His analogy was with the border poll for Northern Ireland conducted at the time he had been Prime Minister.[92]

The introduction of a referendum clause to the Scotland and Wales Bill in 1977 was a clear reversal of Government policy. It was forced on the Government by backbench hostility to devolution. Michael

Foot, in charge of the legislation, admitted that this was the case. At least 140 MPs had signed a motion urging that there should be a referendum and stating that they were not prepared to give their assent to the bill without this provision.[93] Considerable procedural wrangling accompanied the Government's introduction of the new referendum clause in the bill. Objections were raised to such a fundamental change being introduced at committee stage. Prescient comments were made by John Mackintosh. He had opposed a referendum on European Community membership and was equally opposed to a referendum on devolution. His view was that if opponents of the Bill found it unacceptable then their 'moral obligation' was to vote against it. Though an advocate of devolution for the previous twenty years, Mackintosh wished the Commons to have the 'courage of its convictions and reject the Bill'.[94] As events subsequently showed, he was correct to fear that:

> Sensible schemes for revenue allocation to an independent Assembly, sensible schemes of representation, and sensible schemes for easing the relationship between Edinburgh and Westminster and Cardiff and Westminster will be debated with the overhanging thought in people's minds: 'Will this help us to defeat or to carry this proposal at the referendum?'[95]

The referendum campaign began at committee stage of the Scotland and Wales bills. Clause 1 of the Scotland Bill, a general declaration that changes proposed in the bill did not affect the unity of the UK or supreme authority of Parliament, was defeated on the first day in November 1977.[96] Nationalist MPs had, of course, voted for this but it was anti-devolution MPs voting with an eye to the referendum who wanted the removal of this clause as it would make it easier to sustain the argument that devolution was the 'slippery slope to separatism'.

Norman Buchan argued that the Government had made a 'disastrous error' in proposing only one question. He argued that it was necessary to distinguish between support for devolution and for independence. Otherwise, any Scottish Assembly would be challenged from its first day of existence by the SNP demanding to move on towards independence. A question on independence would clarify matters and give the Assembly a 'breathing space'.[97] He argued that there was a qualitative difference between issues such as government intervention in industry, the national health service, comprehensive education and constitutional reform. General election results showing support for the SNP did not necessarily reflect support for independence. SNP support was based on a number of things as well – 'the question of not liking Strathclyde, the question of the kind of school one's kid goes to, the state of the roads'.[98] Lord Home argued in the Lords for a second question on separatism in March 1978:

> First, Parliament would be able to see what is the real opinion in Scotland about separation. Secondly, any Scottish Nationalists elected to the Assembly would be given notice that they should not abuse the terms of whatever devolution Bill is passed into law.[99]

The 40% rule which had been introduced into the legislation at committee stage in the Commons proved a major stumbling block. This had laid down the provision that if less than 40% of persons entitled to vote actually voted 'Yes', the Secretary of State would move the repeal of the Act in Parliament. No such clause had been attached to the EC referendum in 1975. In fact, the Government's position regarding the EC referendum had been set out in a white paper in early 1975 when it had been asserted that 'a simple majority' was all that was required.[100] An attempt by Conservative MP Peter Emery to introduce a qualified majority provision did not even lead to a vote. Supporters of qualified majority voting three years later when the devolution bill was being considered were anti-devolutionists from both the Labour and Conservative parties who privately worked together to ensure its passage. Recognising that such a measure had a better chance of being passed if moved by a Labour MP, Tory anti-devolutionists stood back to let London Labour MP George Cunningham move it in the Commons. The interpretation of the measure as meaning that abstainers belonged to the 'No' camp was deliberately fostered. The democratic right to abstain was being removed – a different matter from compulsory voting which at least did not preclude the right to spoil the ballot paper.

The Scottish vote in the EC referendum in 1975 would not have met the 40% provision. In fact, the lack of precision in the electoral register would have made it impossible under a range of outcomes to determine whether 40% of electors had voted 'Yes'. In 1975, the question of a recount had exercised the minds of

Government and the president of the Royal Statistical Society had suggested that anything less than a 150,000 majority for either side would have to result in a recount. If that was the case with a simple majority referendum, the prospect of dubiety in the result of a referendum with a 40% clause, especially using a register riddled with inaccuracies, ought to have caused greater anxiety than it did. The clause introduced confusion, was anti-democratic, broke with precedent, and was impossible to implement with precision; it was simply a wrecking device. In 1975, the official Conservative position had been to oppose the principle of a referendum but otherwise do what they could to speed up the passage of the EC referendum legislation because they supported continued membership. Their position with the devolution legislation was exactly the opposite – they supported the principle of a referendum and allied clauses but did everything possible to damage the devolution legislation and undermine the prospect of home rule.

Supporters of home rule were divided while opponents presented a more united facade during the campaign. There was a stark contrast with 1975 when two distinct 'umbrella' organisations had come into being which could be dealt with for purposes of broadcasting, expenditure, and Government-supported leaflets. This was not to be the case in 1979 largely due to the official Labour policy. Helen Liddell the party's general secretary, stated that Labour would not be 'soiling our hands by joining any umbrella Yes group'.[101] This proved disastrous for the 'Yes' side. The official Labour and SNP campaigns seemed at times to have an eye on the first elections to the Assembly rather than winning the argument in the referendum itself. Divisions in the 'Yes' camp appeared almost as great as those between them and opponents of home rule. The context was also important, with the Labour Government unpopular following the 'Winter of Discontent'. These factors and the inability of the supporters of change to find a means by which they could articulate distinctive but coordinated positions worked to the advantage of unionists.

The 'No' side was much better funded, better coordinated, more clearly targeted and more professional. The simplicity of the 'No' message contrasted with the confusion of messages and divisions within the 'Yes' side. A deliberate effort was made by Conservatives to dilute the Tory image of the 'No' campaign. The Conservatives alone of the major parties refrained from launching their own campaign, preferring instead to channel efforts through 'Scotland Says No' (SSN).[102] The anti-devolution campaign set out to capture not only the support of hardline unionists but also those who might oppose the particular measure on offer. Throughout the campaign, it was stressed that a 'No' vote would not be interpreted as a vote against the principle of devolution. Francis Pym, Conservative devolution spokesman, stated that the 'status quo is not an option'.[103] He promised a devolution bill within three years of the Tories coming to power.[104] Lord Home's intervention a fortnight before polling was devastating, especially as it came from someone long associated with support for a limited measure of home rule. His call for a much improved measure – with tax-raising powers and proportional representation – and insistence that a 'No vote need not imply any disloyalty to the principle of devolution' was the single most important speech made during the campaign proper.[105] Margaret Thatcher's message on the eve of poll that a 'No' vote would not mean that devolution would be buried confirmed Home's position.[106] At the same time, Teddy Taylor was running a vehemently unionist campaign in typically populist manner arguing that devolution meant higher taxes, more bureaucracy and left-wing extremism. The 'Yes' side mistakenly responded, denying these accusations; but in doing so they merely accepted the agenda set by their opponents and were placed on the defensive.

Support for a referendum on home rule in the 1970s had been initiated by opponents of change and was not a genuine attempt to allow the people a direct say in how Scotland should be governed. It was deliberately manipulated in favour of those whose idea it had been. Yet, even with the changes in the 'rules of the game' and the divisions in the 'Yes' camp, the Scots voted for change.

Do you want the provisions of the Scotland Act 1978 to be put into effect?

Yes	1,230,937 (51.6%)
No	1,153,502 (48.4%)
Rejected Ballot papers	3,133
Turnout	63.7%

This constituted only 32.9% of the electorate voting Yes under the terms of the Scotland Act, according to the calculations circulated by the Government to take account of registration inaccuracies, with a 63.7% turnout. It was, however, seen as a defeat.

The Emergence of the Multi-Option Referendum

The idea of a referendum was viewed with suspicion in the national movement following the 1979 experience, especially by those who had also found themselves on the losing side in the 1975 referendum. There was little prospect of another Government-sponsored referendum, or any action on home rule, under the Conservatives. Whether an incoming Labour Government would need to hold a referendum before embarking on the establishment of a Scottish Assembly was occasionally debated in the early 1980s, though it was generally agreed within the movement that this would be unnecessary. As the pressure for change built up after the 1987 election the referendum, amongst other ideas, re-emerged. John Maxton, Labour's front bench Scottish affairs spokesman, urged the Government to hold a referendum to settle the question 'once and for all' in September 1987.[107] This was a break with Labour policy for much of the 1980s and signified the growing confidence of home rulers. The movement was at last regaining confidence that there was widespread support for change which would be demonstrated in a referendum. Two significant aspects to the idea of a referendum were evident: the desire to return the debate on Scotland's constitutional status to Scotland, and the emergence of an attempt to find a *modus vivendi* between the parties.

In March 1988 Margaret Ewing, SNP Parliamentary group leader, moved a referendum bill with four options: no change; devolution; federalism; and independence. A referendum had been one of the demands made by SNP leader Gordon Wilson in negotiations establishing the constitutional convention in 1989. It was around this time that the idea was also taken up on the nationalist wing of the Labour Party and the gradualist wing of the SNP. A new internal pressure group, Scottish Labour Action, discussed the idea, and one of its founders, Jack McConnell, canvassed the idea of running an unofficial referendum alongside regional council elections.[108] McConnell abandoned such notions, along with much of his radicalism, on his appointment as the Labour Party's Scottish general secretary. Within the SNP, a referendum had the support of deputy leader Alex Salmond. In February 1990 he launched an initiative to back a multi-option referendum which would include the status quo, the Convention's scheme once it had been decided, and the SNP policy of independence in Europe. However, the SNP executive rejected the idea.

The most significant supporter of a referendum to emerge at this time was Charles Gray, leader of Strathclyde Regional Council. He advocated three options though he recognised the hurdles in running a referendum.[109] The SNP officially came round to supporting the idea in October 1990 following Alex Salmond's victory in the SNP leadership contest.[110] As an election was imminent, the prospect of the idea making much progress was limited. Opposition to a referendum was forcefully expressed by members of the Labour and Liberal Democrat leadership, although Malcolm Bruce of the Liberal Democrats, one of the most vehement opponents of a multi-option referendum, was defeated by his executive who voted in favour of it in late 1990.[111] However, at its annual conference in 1991 his party backed him and rejected a multi-option referendum.[112] A poll of Scottish MPs conducted by *Scotland on Sunday* found little support for a multi-option referendum.[113] Divisions over a referendum within the Convention led the Greens to withdraw from the body in November 1990. Other supporters of a referendum in the convention existed but they held their fire until the election was over, fearing that to raise the question would only lead to rifts which would help the Government. No serious work was done to prepare for the eventual possibility of running a referendum in the event of a fourth Conservative victory. The idea had gained widespread currency by early 1992 as a possible strategy, but beyond that no real progress was made.

Conclusion

The experience of the 1979 referendum on home rule left a bitter taste in the national movement. The prospect of Parliament conceding a referendum while remaining hostile to home rule would be highly unlikely unless it were designed to achieve a unionist result. The idea of an unofficial referendum has a long pedigree in the national movement but it has rarely been taken seriously. The financial, logistical, and political difficulties in bringing one about have proved enormous. The costs involved in running an unofficial referendum are considerable even if a postal referendum were used. Organisations which might be willing to help out are bodies which themselves run on a tight financial basis and could not afford to divert resources from raising money for their own purposes to a referendum appeal. Logistical questions are also considerable. Without some semi-official status or use of public institutions, notably local authorities, it would be difficult to conduct a referendum, to ensure it was fairly policed and that a count could take place efficiently. The principle of equal opportunity for every voter to cast his or her vote might be facilitated by a postal ballot but that would bring its own difficulties including increasing the possibility of vote-rigging.

The most significant set of problems have been political. Legitimacy is of greatest importance. The level of legitimacy accorded to a referendum is determined by the level of participation. A high turnout lends it moral force which might overwhelm any other difficulties. The gamble involved in running an unofficial referendum has prevented it from making much progress. In the final analysis, referendums – whether official or unofficial – are often institutions of last resort. They are used when all else has failed. This has been true of their use by Governments as well as their advocacy by sections of the self-government movement.

1. Sarah Wambaugh, 'Plebiscite', *Encyclopedia of the Social Sciences*, New York, Macmillan, 1943, p. 163.
2. Sarah Wambaugh, *A Monograph on Plebiscites*, London, Oxford University Press, 1920; *Plebiscites since the World War*, vols. I & II, Washington, Carnegie Endowment for International Peace, 1933.
3. W. A. Speck, *A Concise History of Britain, 1707–1975*, Cambridge, Cambridge University Press, 1993, p. 80.
4. A. V. Dicey, 'Ought the referendum to be introduced into England?', *Contemporary Review*, April 1890.
5. Vernon Bogdanor, *The People and the Party System: the referendum and electoral reform in British politics*, Cambridge, Cambridge University Press, 1981, p. 66.

6. *Ibid.*, p. 39.
7. David Butler and Uwe Kitzinger, *The 1975 Referendum*, London, Macmillan, 1976, p. 55.
8. *Ibid.*, p. 57.
9. *Ibid.*, p. 163.
10. *Ibid.*, p. 151.
11. Christopher Harvie, *No Gods and Precious Few Heroes*, London, Edward Arnold, 1981, p. 162.
12. Hansard, Commons, vol. 842, August 3, 1972, col. 941.
13. Vernon Bogdanor, *Op. Cit.*, pp. 63–5.
14. Acc. 3721, Box 80/17, Letter from Spence to R. E. Muirhead, October 29, 1926.
15. *Ibid.*, Reply to Spence from R. E. Muirhead, November 5, 1926.
16. *Ibid.*, Box 81/2, Committee of Scottish National Convention, June 11, 1927.
17. *Ibid.*, Box 83/19, Note of meeting of Convention, December 13, 1927.
18. *Glasgow Herald*, May 19, 1931.
19. *Ibid.*, May 13, 1935.
20. *Ibid.*, May 29, 1939.
21. J. Haworth, *The National Party of Scotland and the Scottish Self-Government Movement: 1928–1939*, Syracuse D.SS. 1968, p. 85.
22. *Glasgow Herald*, June 14, 1930.
23. *Ibid.*, November 2, 1949.
24. Scottish Covenant, National Library of Scotland.
25. *Glasgow Herald*, December 19, 1949.
26. *Ibid.*, November 23, 1949.
27. *Ibid.*, December 8, 1949; January 7, 1950; February 20, 1950.
28. *Ibid.*, September 28, 1949.
29. *Ibid.*, December 7, 1949.
30. *Ibid.*, December 19, 1949.
31. *Ibid.*, December 19, 1949
32. *Ibid.*, November 9, 1949.
33. Kenneth Morgan, *Labour in Power*, 1945–51, Oxford, Oxford University Press, 1985, p. 306.
34. *Glasgow Herald*, January 9, 1950.
35. *Observer*, 'Nationalism in Britain' August 2, 1959.
36. *Glasgow Herald*, January 9, 1950.
37. Hansard, Commons, vol. 469, November 16, 1949, col. 2097.
38. *Glasgow Herald*, November 21, 1949.
39. *Ibid.*, November 29, 1949

40. PRO, Cabinet Papers, CP (40) 251, December 12, 1949, 'Scottish Affairs' by Secretary of State for Scotland.

41. *Ibid.*

42. *Ibid.*

43. *Ibid.*

44. PRO, Cabinet Conclusions, CC72 (49) 6, December 15, 1949,

45. *Glasgow Herald*, March 24, 1947.

46. *Times*, February 16, 1982.

47. Acc. 7295(5) Minutes of National Committee of Scottish Convention, 5 February 1949.

48. *Scots Independent*, November 1949.

49. *Glasgow Herald*, May 31, 1950.

50. *Ibid.*, July 28, 1950.

51. Hansard, vol. 167, Lords, May 17, 1950, col. 380.

52. *Glasgow Herald* editorial, 'Plebiscite and Parliament', August 18, 1950.

53. *Ibid.*, July 13, 1950.

54. *Ibid.*, September 4, 1950.

55. *Ibid.*, October 27, 1950.

56. *Ibid.*, October 12, 1950.

57. *Ibid.*, October 18, 1950.

58. *Ibid.*, October 27, 1950.

59. *Ibid.*, August 23, 1950.

60. *Ibid.*, October 30, 1950.

61. *Ibid.*, November 30, 1050.

62. *Ibid.*, December 8, 1950.

63. *Ibid.*, January 13, 1951.

64. *Ibid.*, January 13, 1951 and *Census Scotland, 1951, Vol. II, Population of Towns and Larger Villages and of Urban and Rural Scotland.*

65. *Glasgow Herald*, February 17, 1951.

66. *Ibid.*, September 24, 1951.

67. *Ibid.*, October 29, 1951.

68. *Scots Independent*, April 23, 1955.

69. *Glasgow Herald*, April 26, 1955.

70. Acc. 5978, Scottish Covenant Association, Box 2, F. 3, Letter from Prime Minister's Office, June 6, 1956.

71. *Ibid.*, Minutes of National Committee of Scottish Covenant Association, March 2, 1957.

72. *Glasgow Herald*, June 8, 1959.

73. *Scottish Daily Mail*, December 2, 1961.

74. Lord Airlie (Scottish representative peer and Governor of

the British Linen Bank) John Bannerman (chairman of
the Scottish Liberal Party), Lord Boyd Orr (Chancellor of
Glasgow University and Director of the Clydesdale and North
of Scotland Bank), Michael Byrne (general secretary of the
Scottish Transport and General Workers Union), W. Hope
Collins (managing director of William Collins, publisher and
president of Glasgow Chamber of Commerce), Lawrence Daly
(Communist Fife County Councillor and prominent National
Union of Mineworkers official), the Countess of Erroll (Lord
High Constable of Scotland), Dr Leonard Gray (former president
of Edinburgh Chamber of Commerce), Tom Johnston (former
Secretary of State for Scotland), Sir Gordon Letham (former
governor of British Guiana), Sir Ian Moncrieffe (Albany Herald
of Scotland), Sir John Ure Primrose (former chairman of the
Convention of Royal Burghs and Provost of Perth), John
Rankin (Labour MP for Govan), J. Rollo (chairman of the
Highland Fund and managing director of Rollo Industries),
and Sir Thomas Taylor (Principal of Aberdeen University).
Glasgow Herald, December 2, 1961.

75. *Glasgow Herald*, November 20, 1962.
76. *Economist*, June 9, 1962.
77. *Glasgow Herald*, June 27, 1962.
78. *Ibid.*, January 4, 1963.
79. *Ibid.*, February 29, 1964.
80. *Economist*, June 9, 1962.
81. *Glasgow Herald*, February 4, 1963.
82. Bill 26, ordered to be printed by the House of Commons,
     November 27, 1968.
83. Hansard, Commons, vol. 733, August 4, 1966, col. 157.
84. *Scotsman*, January 18, 1969.
85. *Ibid.*, January 18, 1969.
86. *Ibid.*, February 6, 1969.
87. *Ibid.*, February 14, 1969.
88. Hansard, Commons, February 14, 1969, vol. 777, col. 1736.
89. *Ibid.*, col. 1745.
90. *Ibid.*, vol. 877, July 23, 1974, col. 1291.
91. *Ibid.*, vol. 901, December 4, 1975, col. 1929.
92. *Scotsman*, September 14, 1976.
93. Hansard, Commons, vol. 925, February 10, 1977, col. 1750.
94. *Ibid.*, col. 1716.
95. *Ibid.*, col. 1719.

96. *Ibid.*, vol. 939, November 22, 1977, cols. 1323–1409.
97. *Glasgow Herald*, February 11, 1977.
98. Hansard, Commons, vol. 925, February 1, 1977, col. 281.
99. Hansard, Lords, vol. 389, March 14, 1978, col. 1217.
100. Cmnd. 5925, January 23, 1975, para. 3.
101. John Bochel, David Denver and Allan Macartney (eds.), *The Referendum Experience: Scotland 1979*, Aberdeen, Aberdeen University Press, 1981, p. 17.
102. *Scotsman*, November 29, 1978.
103. *Ibid.*, December 6, 1978.
104. *Ibid.*, January 15, 1979.
105. *Ibid.*, February 15, 1979.
106. *Ibid.*, February 28, 1979.
107. *Ibid.*, September 9, 1987.
108. *Observer Scotland*, July 9, 1989.
109. *Scotsman*, October 1, 1990.
110. *Scotland on Sunday*, October 14, 1990.
111. *Glasgow Herald*, October 18, 1990.
112. *Scotsman*, April 8, 1991.
113. *Scotland on Sunday*, October 21, 1990.

The Party Strategy

Introduction

The birth of the Scottish National Party was described by the *Scots Independent* as like the birth of a child: 'its significance and potentialities are only realised by those closely associated with it.'[1] It was to be forty years before any signs justifying this faith were shown. During most of this period it was on the fringe of Scottish politics. However, in order to understand the *raison d'être* of the party and contemporary debates on strategy it is necessary to consider the earlier period of its history. In large measure, the issues confronting the modern SNP have not changed since its foundation though debates on strategy are less divisive than in earlier times. In part this is because a considerable degree of consensus exists within the SNP today, compared at least with its formative years.

The history of the SNP in the development of the national movement is of greater importance than any other organisation. The party has been at the sharp end of politics, confronting and challenging other parties. Additionally, its support is the yardstick by which popular support for constitutional change is generally measured, particularly amongst opponents of home rule and outside Scotland itself. However frustrating it may be for supporters of constitutional change in other parties, it has consistently been the level of SNP support that has been watched with most interest. This places the party in an ambiguous position within the movement. Non-party members and supporters who want to see constitutional change need the SNP while the SNP, despite its rhetoric about seeking a mandate for independence, seeks to influence other parties that it challenges directly in the electoral arena.

A number of conflicts have been evident during the history of the party similar to those outlined in the theoretical literature on parties, and these are explored in this chapter. These conflicts have erupted with different levels of intensity at different times and it is helpful to consider them in context. The most significant tension within the SNP has concerned strategy: between fundamentalists who seek to isolate and give priority to independence and pragmatists or gradualists who see measures short of it as at least a step in the right direction. Related to this tension are attitudes towards social and economic issues. Fundamentalists tend to be wary of involvement in socio-economic debate, fearing that this might dissipate energy and resources unless the issue is directly linked to the constitutional question. Pragmatists tend to see social and economic issues inextricably tied up with constitutional change, although amongst pragmatists there are those who fear that divisions on socio-economic change will lead to factionalism. There is no direct link between the fundamentalist position and opposition to developing socio-economic policies, or between the pragmatic position and support for developing a socio-economic position. Fundamentalists will welcome the opportunity to demonstrate that some public policy discriminates against Scotland. Pragmatists may find that pragmatic compromise makes the development of a coherent socio-economic position, if not particular policies, difficult.

Key junctures mark off periods in the history of the party. Though these are inevitably artificial, they are useful in an attempt to make sense of the many years that the National Party has existed. The first period to be considered is that leading up to the formation of the National Party of Scotland in 1928. This was a period of disillusionment with other strategies, and high hopes for the direct challenge that an independent political party offered. The second period is that between 1928 and 1942 when many of the assumptions of activists regarding the nature of the party and its prospects were shattered. Sharp internal conflict and considerable disillusionment marked this period. The next period, between 1942 and 1967, is a neglected one in the history of the party yet it was important. A quiet time, marked by sober assessment of the party's potential, it was the necessary prelude to the breakthrough which was suggested in the electoral contests of the latter part of the period. If this was the party's sober era, the period from 1967 to 1979 was the SNP's drunk period. Electoral successes and a rapid rise in membership fuelled the expectations of activists only to be dramatically cut short in 1979. The final period, from 1979, is the most difficult to assess because of the confusion of strategies, the enormous shadow cast over the party following the defeats of 1979, and its historical proximity. What emerges from each period is the importance of strategy in internal debates and the impact of external factors in determining the course of action adopted.

The political identity of any part will undergo changes, often dramatic, but a core set of values and a basic approach to politics is necessary in order to maintain continuity of membership and electoral appeal. When parties contest elections they require stability of support otherwise they must approach the electorate afresh at the start of each election campaign. Two factors are required for the creation of a base of support: an ideology or set of principles which can be readily identified by the electorate, and a stable group of supporters who will normally vote for it because they agree with this ideology.[2] The relationship between a party and the electorate is one of three important sets of relationships with potential for tension identified by Mény.[3] The others are the relations between the party apparatus and the 'party in office', and relations within the apparatus of the party itself. A fourth and quite distinct relationship has to be considered in the case of the Scottish National Party: relations between the party and the wider national movement.

A further set of questions concerns the institutionalisation of a party – the way the party 'solidifies'.[4] Janda's account of party institutionalisation stresses three aspects: the age of the party, the depersonalisation of its organisation, and its organisational differentiation. His study of a range of parties in different countries concluded that those which have made the transfer from charismatic leadership to develop tight organisations were more likely to have a future than those based solely on charismatic leadership and personalities.[5] The difficulties in setting up and building support for a new party are considerable. Established parties jealously guard their electoral territory and established opponents will tacitly combine to fend off any new challenger. Some diluted form of the programme being propagated by the new party may be incorporated into those of the established parties. An example of this in recent years is evident in environmental politics and the responses of established parties to the potential threat posed by Green parties. Non-major parties need not win support to influence the composition, leadership and doctrines of the major parties.[6]

Another difficulty new parties may face includes an electoral system which discriminates against them. In the UK, the first-past-the-post voting system has long conspired to maintain a two-party system, although at times, such as in the inter-war period, more than two parties have existed as the system undergoes transition with one major party being replaced by another. The lack of state support for political parties has further strengthened the position of the two main players with their corporate sponsors. The resources involved in establishing and running a political party are considerable and without assistance, either from the state or corporate supporters, even popular support is ineffective. The Labour and Conservative parties are two of the most institutionalised parties in Western Europe. Both have been sufficiently flexible to incorporate emerging challenges into their programmes. Of all West European party systems, the United Kingdom's has proved the most resilient to change and the least likely to witness the rise of new parties. Even the Social Democratic Party, with considerable media support, a substantial array of established political figures, and the grassroots backing of the Liberals, failed to establish itself in the 1980s.

The SNP is by no means unique. Its experiences have a striking resemblance to those of the Quebec nationalist party, the *Parti Québécois* (PQ). The process of developing a political identity and the debates between the visionaries who stressed independence and those who wanted a more pragmatic approach and focused on the need to articulate social and economic policies were common to both parties.[7] The pragmatist-fundamentalist tension has also been evident in PQ from its inception,[8] and differences between the party apparatus and its publicly elected representatives have caused problems.[9] Even PQ's attempts to articulate a coherent ideology show some similarity with the SNP experience. An unwillingness to accept the socialist label while attempting to project a left-of-centre position has been common to both parties. Jacques Parizeau, PQ's current leader, declared his position in language similar to that which Gordon Wilson used in the 1980s: 'I am centre-left; socialist no.'[10] Writing of the PQ convention in 1981, following defeat in the constitutional referendum in May 1980 and exclusion of Quebec from discussions on the Canadian constitution, the Canadian journalist Graham Fraser could easily have been describing a scene from the SNP around that time. He wrote that the Convention stood as a 'testimony, not only to the rage and humiliation that seemed to be felt by the whole nationalist community in Quebec, but to its loss of judgement, restraint, and equilibrium – personal and collective.'[11]

THE FOUNDATION YEARS, TO 1928

Accounts of the formation of the National Party of Scotland have generally followed the personal and highly subjective account offered by John MacCormick in *The Flag in the Wind* (1955). The role of Glasgow University Scottish Nationalist Association (GUSNA) is given prominence in these accounts. An alternative, and more accurate, account was offered in a review of MacCormick's book which appeared in the *Scots Independent* (SI).[12] Debate on the idea of an independent party had been taking place within the constitutional convention and in the various nationalist bodies which existed in the 1920s. According to the SI account, Arthur Henry of the SHRA was the prime mover, along with Tom Gibson of the Scots National League and Henry Balderstone of the Scottish National Movement. Omitted from both accounts, however, is a convincing explanation as to why the party was established at all.[13]

As disillusionment built up within the SHRA and the constitutional convention, a view developed that a more direct approach was required. Not only had the pressure group approach failed, but working through the Labour Party was also seen to be futile. Calls for an independent national party were being made in 1925 in the SHRA. At its general council meeting in December that year there was a lengthy discussion of the topic and it was agreed to ask delegates to discuss the question with their sponsoring organisations. Additionally, disillusionment with the course the constitutional convention was taking was increasingly being voiced, and calls for an alternative strategy were made. The idea of a party was only one of many suggestions which included demanding a Royal Commission, working through the local authorities to petition the King and Prime Minister, holding a referendum, and engaging in acts of civil disobedience.

In June 1927, at a meeting of the national committee of the convention, a resolution was moved to set up a Scottish National Party. From subsequent correspondence it would appear to have been a lively debate.[14] The resolution was defeated by 18 votes to 8, but this did not kill the idea off. Roland Muirhead, a prime mover in the convention's establishment and a major financier of the home rule cause, opposed the move but admitted that he was 'fast coming to the conclusion that there does not seem to be any other likely way to get self-government'; he felt however that the moment was not opportune.[15] Supporters of an independent party believed that a 'few meetings' amongst home rulers were required to establish how an independent party would operate. By the end of 1927 a group had been formed within the convention which was explicitly advocating the establishment of a party.

The secretary of the Scottish Nationalist Party Group was Arthur Henry. A report of a meeting in November 1927 records that eight people were present, none from Glasgow University Scottish Nationalist Association (GUSNA). The issue of a party had been discussed in the SI and within the small circle which produced the paper. The SI had been set up in 1926 as the organ of the Scots National League and was radical in its politics; at times it sought to counter the Celtic romanticism which pervaded that organisation. The main contributor in its early years was Iain Gillies, joint editor with his father William, who as early as February 1926 was of the opinion that a National Party was required.[16] In 'Scotland's need: a national party', which appeared in the paper in September 1927, Gillies argued his case. He identified the SNL and SHRA as the most notable home rule bodies. The former laid the basis for a 'democratic, progressive and radical-minded' party; the question was whether the Association would accept this policy and join with the League in 'putting forward and securing the return of National candidates'.[17]

The culmination of this activity came early in 1928. Roland Muirhead announced his intention to stand as an independent home rule candidate. His disillusionment with the Labour Party and SHRA had reached the point when he felt he could no longer give them his support. Muirhead's departure from the SHRA removed an important source of finance for the organisation. In April, he wrote an article in the SI in which he recounted both his personal political progress and that of the movement. The failure of a home rule bill moved in the House of Commons and the lack of any commitment to home rule in the manifestoes of any of the major parties in 1924 had marked the end of his hope that they would deliver. Home rule had been in the 'background' at previous elections and this would remain the case 'until an independent Scottish National Party arrives'.[18]

It had not been an easy decision for Muirhead, who had devoted considerable energy and money to Labour politics over a long number of years. The reaction to the idea of a National Party from Labour was predictable. In the words of one Labour home ruler, it was tantamount to a declaration of war against the socialist movement.[19] Making the break with Labour was bound to be difficult, but it was felt necessary. The ambiguity in attitudes towards other parties, particularly Labour, amongst members of the independent party was evident from the outset. Labour still retained much respect amongst defectors and there was still some hope that it might deliver home rule, indeed one aspect of the strategy was that it might provoke Labour into action. However, the ambiguity was one-sided – Labour members were unambiguously hostile to the new party.

GUSNA played a more significant role in the mechanics of setting up the new party. MacCormick, GUSNA's secretary, sent letters to various organisations in January inviting them to discuss the idea of a National Party. Meetings were arranged at which representatives from four organisations were present: GUSNA, the SNL, SNM and the SHRA. The formal adoption of a resolution setting up the party was passed in March 1928 but the critical part was winning support from the existing home rule bodies. GUSNA and the SNL had already effectively decided to support the idea. Lewis Spence, president of the SNM, wrote to members of his organisation in March informing them of the formation of the party and asking them to vote on the matter. The SHRA, with its large Labour Party membership, witnessed the most heated debate.

A resolution passed in February by the committee of the constitutional convention stated that the passage of a home rule bill 'depends on the support of the existing political parties'. This proved embarrassing for Muirhead, the convention's secretary, who offered to resign but agreed to stay on until someone could be found to replace him.[20] As an election drew nearer and as debate intensified on the case for an independent party, the convention and the SHRA were becoming forums for debating strategy rather than organisations pressing the case for self-government.

At its annual meeting in 1928, the SHRA debated a resolution moved by Muirhead urging the organisation to recommend that its members should join the National Party of Scotland (NPS). Opposition to the resolution came from trade unionists, who defended the Labour Party, arguing that it had been in power for only nine months in 1924 with minority support in the Commons. They pointed out that the previous five home rule bills had been presented by Labour MPs, and that the party's chairman and chief whip had indicated support for home rule in letters sent in the previous three weeks. The SHRA was largely made up of Labour members and the resolution was seen as a direct appeal to them. One Labour Party member backing the resolution observed that Labour itself did not even have home rule and that the party could not appoint an organiser without the permission of London headquarters, a point which was to be repeated over sixty years later by home rulers within the party. No resolution of the question was reached but the fate of the SHRA was sealed. Without the support and membership of Muirhead and others who went off to found the NPS, the SHRA was crippled.

From these discussions it is clear that some saw the value of an independent party as its ability to put pressure on existing parties rather than winning outright support for itself. In late 1927, one speaker at a convention meeting drew an analogy with the party established by Parnell 'which led to the conversion of Mr Gladstone and induced him to support a principle which he had formerly opposed.'[21] At an earlier meeting, however, a more direct role for a Scottish National Party had been articulated. It was suggested that any Member of Parliament representing the new party would 'undertake' to put the question of Home Rule for Scotland in the first place and give it precedence to all other Parliamentary questions that should arise.'[22]

THE FORMATIVE YEARS, 1928–42

In this second phase, the party faced a number of difficult questions. Internal tensions afflicted it as did the issue of its relations with other parts of the home rule movement, in particular with home rulers in other political parties. Debates within the party were largely about the precise definition of self-government and the strategy to be adopted to achieve it. Policies on specific issues appear to have been less divisive than defining a working ideology, although on occasion policy matters produced splits. Added to this was the personalities factor. Much of the rancour in the internal debates was probably due to differing perceptions of what the party stood for and how it should proceed. These were affected by the different experiences of its leading members. The slow institutionalisation of the party, as these different experiences converged within the party, eventually resulted in the emergence of a distinct political outlook, but there was little evidence of this process during the period before the second world war. It was a painful experience but, although it seemed likely at times, the party did not destroy itself through internal squabbles. Coming as they did from a range of different political backgrounds with little in common other than the goal of self-government (which itself was often defined in very different ways), the members of the new party would require many years of working together before they could forge a coherent party.

Even before the party had been established, there had been differences amongst the founding groups over the meaning of self-government. The SNL had been more hard-line than the SHRA in its definition. Similarly, the SNL tended to be more hard-line in its relations with other parties and organisations. This was reflected in discussions regarding the merger with the Scottish Party, which had been set up in 1932. The most outstanding feature of the Scottish Party was that it consisted of some minor figures from the Scottish establishment. It had been founded as a moderate home rule party – its members often styled themselves 'Moderates'. Moderate it may have been in respect to the Scottish question, but it included members with extreme right-wing views. A leading founding figure was Andrew Dewar Gibb, an academic lawyer at Glasgow University who harboured crypto-fascist views. Gibb, along with journalist George Malcolm Thomson, had set about establishing a right-wing pressure group partly in reaction to the radicalism of the NPS, and stressed that a Scottish Parliament could be set up while maintaining and strengthening the unity of Britain and the Empire. In the words of Thomson, they sought to offer nationalism for Tories – 'a synthesis of Toryism (real Toryism) and nationalism'.[23] A strong element of anti-Catholic bigotry and anti-Irish racism was also evident. The nationalism espoused by Gibb and Thomson was wholly different from that of most members of the NPS, where Pan-Celtic cultural sympathies and radical social and economic policies were often combined. The initial intention of Gibb and Thomson had been to join the NPS with some others and take it over but their obvious, major differences had soon deterred them from forging links with the party. Other right-wing and Liberal activists were coincidentally concluding that there was a need for a new organisation to campaign for self-government. An activist in Cathcart Unionist Association, Kevan McDowell, found support when he argued that Scottish self-government was not only compatible with British imperialism but was a necessary corollary of maintaining the Empire. Sir Alexander MacEwen, Provost of Inverness, published *The Thistle and the Rose* in 1932 arguing the case for a moderate measure of self-government.

The Scottish Party was launched in December 1932 with a number of prominent figures present – the Duke of Montrose was elected president, Sir Alexander MacEwen chairman, and McDowell secretary and treasurer – and an executive was elected which included Sir Henry Keith and Sir W. E. Whyte, two of the most prominent figures in Scottish local government, Sir D. M. Stevenson, soon to become Chancellor of Glasgow University, Sheriff J. R. N. Macphail, and an assortment of academics and other figures. It was a loose coalition of Liberals and Tories brought together by support for a moderate measure of home rule and a distaste for the NPS. At least one speaker at the launch wanted an explicit statement dissociating the new party from the NPS.[24] For many of those involved, home rule would be presented not as a challenge to the British Empire but as a means of strengthening it. This basic tension in the movement was to recur. In effect, it was a tension between respectability and radicalism. The NPS was more independent and critical of the London-based parties than was the more pragmatic Scottish Party.

The tensions between the National Party and the Scottish Party did not prevent some supporters from recognising the common ground that existed between them and working towards a merger. John MacCormick, secretary of the NPS, was convinced that his party needed some prominent Scots in its membership. His approach to politics was elitist and involved appeals to establishment figures, often with more regard for their social standing than their political viewpoint. He hoped that the Scottish establishment would be converted to the cause and saw a link with the more respectable Scottish Party as helpful. MacCormick's attempts to attract prominent figures to the NPS were fruitless prior to the merger.

The process of merger was facilitated by the joint candidacy of Sir Alexander MacEwen at a by-election in Kilmarnock in 1933. The differences between the parties had been overcome by the simple expedient of stressing their joint commitment to Scottish self-determination – the Scottish people would determine Scotland's precise constitutional status and the policies to be pursued by a Scottish Parliament. This irritated a number of NPS members who objected to the passage in MacEwen's election address which referred to any future 'modification or revision of the Act of Union'.[25] Though last in the poll, MacEwen's 17% was respectable and encouraged support for the merger.

In early 1934 the process of merging proceeded. Agreement was reached in January on a resolution between representatives of both parties which was to be put to conferences of each. It involved considerable concessions to moderate opinion:

(1)   The establishment of a Parliament in Scotland which shall be the final authority on all Scottish affairs, including taxation and finance;
(2)   Scotland shall share with England the rights and responsibilities they, as mother nations, have jointly created and incurred within the British Empire;
(3)   Scotland and England shall set up machinery to deal jointly with these responsibilities, and in particular to deal with such matters as defence, foreign policy, and customs;

(4)   It is believed that these principles can be realised only by a
Scottish National Party independent of all other political parties.[26]

The resolution was approved by the NPS in late February and by
the Scottish Party in early March. Some hardliners had left the party,
allowing the debate on merger to proceed in relative tranquillity. The
launch of the newly constituted Scottish National Party took place at
a conference on April 7, 1934.

The terms of the merger could only paper over the differences
within the party. Differences existed over ideology, goals and
policies, tactics and strategy, and personalities. The complexity of
divisions within the party was underscored by the shifting positions
of a number of key figures. The early years were experimental, with
individuals switching allegiances and changing opinions on strategy
and tactics. The external environment and the party's experiences
in this period were important factors in the shifting lines of
division. Ultimately, the high expectations of a breakthrough led to
introspection and internal feuding. It was to be a decade before the
party settled down and a further two decades before this process
began to bear fruit. What is most remarkable is that the party
survived at all.

Policies and Ideology

The definition of the party's goal was deliberately kept vague in order
to bridge the divide between the moderate aspirations of those who
wanted a Scottish Parliament with the United Kingdom and those
who sought to sever all political links with England. Expressions of
opposition to devolution had different sources. Compton Mackenzie
represented the hardline romantic position condemning 'devilution',
as he described it.[27] Others believed that devolution might be
offered to Scotland to appease nationalist sympathies and thereby
halt progress to independence, leaving Scotland in a provincial
relationship with London.[28] For some, devolution was an attractive
first step, and if the party succeeded in forcing other parties to
move towards its objectives it would have achieved a degree of
success.

It was not just the relationship with England which divided the
party but Scotland's position within the British empire. The empire

was a source of pride across the political spectrum, and many Scots had made a career out of it, or had family who had. Support for the empire was electorally expedient, it chimed with moderate opinion within the movement, and it provided an answer to opponents who charged that Scotland would be dangerously exposed as an independent state. The Cathcart Unionists were passionate supporters of the empire. For them, self-government for its constituent units was a means of saving the empire – self-government was the expedient, the empire their primary concern. Their attitude towards self-government and empire was the reverse of that of many NPS members.

Within a year of the merger, the first major split occurred. McDowell, who had been made overseas secretary of the SNP, expressed strong support for the empire, designed to encourage Conservatives to join the party. This annoyed the party's more radical elements and irritated those who saw this as opening divisions which, at least implicitly, it had been agreed at the time of merger should be avoided. Not only did McDowell raise the question of empire he argued that Scotland would continue to have representation at Westminster, the Imperial Parliament. Though McDowell was in a minority and found few allies amongst other former senior members of the Scottish Party, the row was well aired in the press and McDowell continued to berate the SNP for its 'Sinn Fein, Free State, separatist, disruptive propaganda' for many years. His preferred slogan was 'For Scotland, King and Empire'.[29] The defeat of a resolution attempting to change the party's constitution failed in 1935 and McDowell resigned along with a few others. Many members of the party shared his views, though in less extreme form and with less conviction, maintaining a level of dissent in the party even after the resignations.

A related issue which divided the party at the end of the decade was its position on the war and conscription. The party had a strong pacifist wing. Allied with this, there were those who felt that Scotland paid a higher price than other parts of Britain in war casualties, a view fuelled by the experience of the first world war. In late 1938, with signs of impending war, the party issued a manifesto in which the Government was criticised for abandoning the collective security policy of the League of Nations but which drew back from outright condemnation of war. Scotsmen, it insisted, would fight 'in collaboration with England and the British Commonwealth' in a just war for the principle of collective security and a responsibility to small nations. It criticised the 'game of power politics' which was suicidal to small nations.[30] The manifesto was similar to the original agreement which had established the SNP. It papered over differences within the party in the hope that nothing would happen which might bring the issue to a head.

In circumstances of peace it had been possible to face both ways at the same time but that was impossible when war finally broke out. The outbreak of war provoked a major row and ultimately the most significant split in the party's history. It brought differences to a head and prompted a section of the party to leave and attempt to achieve their goal through the medium of a pressure group. The war situation was to be a severe test of the SNP's durability. War apart, the party was not in particularly good health. As Finlay states, it had an 'uninspiring leadership, poor discipline, low morale, declining branch activity, increasing financial pressures, and last, but not least, the stigma of being nothing more than an inconsequential fringe group in Scottish politics'.[31] Divisions which had lain just below the surface emerged at this most testing time. The international situation and the party's attitude towards the war assumed greater importance than any other matters. Alliances within the party were formed which in other circumstances would have been unlikely, and strong disagreements on this key question divided many of those who in other circumstances might have been expected to agree. The significance of the political context overtook all other considerations in determining the internal dynamics of the party. Unusually for the SNP, strategy was less important than policy at this crucial juncture in its history, although it was involved in as much as the question of the party's image was a major consideration for those who supported full backing of the war effort.

After war broke out, the party initially offered to place its offices at the Government's disposal and to give it full support. In order to placate the pacifists in the party, a request was made for a clearer definition of war aims from the Government and the need for 'those principles of self-government for which it is supposed to be fighting' to be put into practice in Scotland. This evoked memories of the demands made by home rulers at the time of the Versailles Treaty which were rebuffed. Once more, the Government simply ignored the nationalists, and the party's national council withdrew its offer of cooperation.[32] The SNP could be largely ignored as a threat to the state during the 1930s but during wartime any organisation, however small, which appeared to be set on disrupting the war effort was bound to be the subject of close scrutiny by the security services and a target of enemy propagandists. The policy of non-cooperation was reversed and members of the party's executive did their best to project the party as patriotic, but more trouble was to come.

The question of conscientious objection to the war was to be the issue on which the party divided. At its 1940 conference, the SNP had urged the government to widen its definition of conscientious objection to include 'profound political conviction'.[33] The more radical elements wanted not only to express their conscientious objection to the war but to challenge the legitimacy of the declaration of war as far as Scotland was concerned. It was argued that Westminster could not declare war on behalf of the Scottish people. The unlikely figure of Douglas Young, a classics scholar and poet, became the hero of the anti-war faction while MacCormick led the pro-war faction. On almost any other matter which divided the party, most notably regarding attitudes to other parties, Young was far closer to MacCormick than to most of those with whom he found company at that time. He was to leave the SNP a few years later over his refusal to quit the Labour Party (dual party membership was permitted until the late 1940s). MacCormick was at that time involved in trying to establish a cross-party front in favour of home rule and this probably increased opposition to him. The perception that the party was making little progress was only enhanced by the unpropitious circumstances of war. The existing leadership, power-less to do anything, came in for sharp criticism from elements in the party.

The anti-war arguments were abstruse, a mixture of convoluted legal thinking and a dubious moral code, and it is difficult to imagine that they alone won Young the chairmanship in 1942. He had been found guilty of refusing to be conscripted in April 1942. Personalities were no doubt crucial in explaining the defeat of William Power,

MacCormick's candidate,[34] but circumstances were at least as important. MacCormick's domineering style would have been acceptable, as it had been in the past, in the right circumstances. Young had gained considerable publicity during his trial and within sections of the party this gave him a status approaching martyrdom. In large measure, the candidates stood as proxies: Power for MacCormick and, in a more complex manner, Young for a battery of sometimes contradictory opinions.

Tactics and Strategy

There were two aspects to the debate on strategy within the SNP in its formative years. The first concerned elections to public office and the second relations with other organisations, including political parties. MacCormick had noted in discussions preceding the foundation of the NPS that little consideration had been given to questions of strategy. The prime motivation was to create a 'united front' which would act as a focus for the movement. There was a tendency to ignore difficult strategic questions by adopting unrealistic plans. In 1932 the NPS adopted a three-stage plan involving the establishment of a Scottish National Convention leading to a Scottish National Constituent Assembly, which would then result in a Scottish National Parliament. The party's executive was 'confident that Scottish National Self-Government can be won by intensive effort in three years'.[35] It was always easy to avoid difficult questions by adopting such a 'strategy', especially when critics within the party could be accused of lacking faith if they dared to object.

Often a number of strategies ran in tandem, partly due to the lack of a coherent plan and partly because the diffuse nature of the organisation allowed different individuals with their pet theories to speak on behalf of the party. A plebiscite, a Covenant, a convention, and the contesting of local and Parliamentary elections were all official policies of the NPS in its short history before the merger with the Scottish Party.[36] The assumption that the party would contest elections existed from the outset, though the implications in terms of relations with other parties, particularly over dual membership of parties, was not addressed. The narrow defeat of Cunninghame Graham in the Glasgow University rectorial election in October 1928 may have played a part in fomenting a desire to contest elections[37] but the idea was already well-rooted. If those forming the party had any notion of what a political party was, as distinct from any other type of political organisation, it was in terms of contesting elections as an independent body. Even this most basic assumption came under scrutiny when the party's forays into electoral politics proved unsuccessful. Debates over dual membership of political parties and contesting elections were essentially about the nature of the National Party. Should it be a truly independent party or should it act as a pressure group?

When the idea of a separate party had been mooted in 1926 it was suggested that even if it failed on its own to bring about home rule, its existence might prove the 'stimulus required to make the Labour Party move'.[38] However, a direct challenge to Labour was just as likely to result in it abandoning home rule as making it a priority. Having originated as a reaction to the failure of Labour to deliver home rule, the National Party had Labour in its sights from the outset. Its relationship with Labour, and to a lesser extent with the Liberals, proved far more complex and difficult than its relationship with the Unionist Party which was seen by most (though not all) as implacably opposed to any measure of self-government. The closeness to Labour and the hope that it might be provoked into action did not, however, mean that a clear strategy was developed. The first electoral contest engaged in by the NPS was a by-election in Midlothian in 1929, when Lewis Spence was the candidate. The party was initially cautious about contesting the by-election but when Spence declared his intention to stand all caution was cast aside. The party even appointed a paid professional organiser for the by-election who was, by MacCormick's account, an unmitigated disaster. Spence proved equally awful as a candidate. His eve-of-poll speech, during the Burns season, consisted of a lengthy Burns oration in verse in Middle Scots.[39] It was easy for the party to dismiss its poor showing as a result of inexperience, a bad campaign and an eccentric candidate.

The party tended to set its hopes too high. It had initially intended to contest seven seats in the 1929 general election but in the event only two were contested. At subsequent by-elections its share of the vote rose to over 10% – 10.1% in Shettleston in June 1930,

13% in East Renfrewshire in November 1930 – keeping alive faith in the electoral strategy. The 1931 general election saw five NPS candidates in the field with a commendable result in Inverness where MacCormick won 13%, joining two others in saving his deposit. Again, by-elections in 1932 saw the party poll respectably in Montrose (13.5%) and Dumbartonshire (11.7%). The Unionist candidate held Dumbartonshire against a strong challenge from Tom Johnston for Labour, with the NPS candidate winning more votes than the margin between the other two. Both Labour and the Nationalists interpreted the NPS vote as having robbed Johnston of a seat in Parliament. Johnston had been committed to home rule, and continued to argue for it afterwards, but he recognised the dangers in the NPS strategy for Labour. At this stage, the NPS may have been strong enough to deprive Labour of a seat but it was not sufficiently strong to exert pressure to make home rule a priority.

The question of dual membership of parties was to prove highly divisive in the formative years. The long association with other parties of many of those who joined the NPS, Scottish Party and SNP could not be dismissed lightly. Personal contacts had been built up, and continued to be maintained. Roland Muirhead continued to communicate with his erstwhile colleagues in the ILP who attempted to bring him back to the fold. The NPS and Scottish Party differed on this issue with the latter largely accepting dual membership. The issue had been fudged at the time of merger and it appears that many members of the SNP did not realise the extent of dual membership within the hierarchy of the party. A decision had been made not to tolerate dual membership at the party's executive in December 1934,[40] and it was only when the Duke of Montrose, SNP President, resigned the Tory whip in the House of Lords the following year that many party members realised he had ignored the policy. The party debated the issue at its annual conference that month. Sir Alexander MacEwen spoke against the attempt to prevent dual membership, arguing that although the party was independent of all other parties it had never insisted that membership of other parties should be prohibited. A compromise proposed by MacCormick was accepted which stated that the party 'expects no office-bearer of the Scottish National Party will take part in the work of an English-controlled party'.[41] The issue continued to haunt the party, with supporters of dual membership, such as Sir Alexander MacEwen, concerned that 'exclusiveness' was damaging the cause. Others wanted to purge the party of dual members as they saw this as encouraging equivocation and strategic dissipation.

By the outbreak of war the main question dividing the SNP concerned its relations with other parties. This was expressed partly in debates on dual membership, but also on whether the party should work alongside other parties and organisations for a measure of self-government, especially if this meant something less than independence. This key division had been evident from the start and was to recur with unceasing regularity throughout the history of the party.

FORGING A POLITICAL IDENTITY, 1942–67

It would be tempting to describe the two decades after 1942 as barren in the history of the SNP. It might be equally tempting to present it as a period when right-wing fundamentalists and *poujadists* were in the ascendant. This is entirely wrong; the party was more disciplined, more confident and more genuinely independent but also more consistently willing to cooperate with others than ever before. It recorded few successes and failed to make much of an impact during this period but many of the tensions which had previously afflicted it were either resolved or else some *modus vivendi* was achieved which allowed the various viewpoints to co-exist. The party grew more self-assured and during this period the foundations were laid for the breakthrough which was to come in the late 1960s and 1970s. Other important factors included the external environment and the activities of other organisations that were part of the national movement.

The departure of many of the key figures of the inter-war period – through expulsion, resignation or boredom – left the SNP with a new leadership as the war drew to a close. The generation which came to the fore during the war was to dominate the party for the following twenty years. These were not the colourful characters who had made their mark in the 1930s but a more unassuming and patient generation. The SNP was growing out of its heavy reliance on personalities. The continuity of leadership and greater discipline meant that the party was able to forge a more coherent political identity. It was moving from 'charismatic leadership' based on a few key personalities to a tighter organisational structure. Overall, it was more the external environment rather than anything the SNP did or did not do that explains its apparent failure to make progress.

Policies and Ideology

Despite the intensity of wartime propaganda attempting to instil British patriotism, the SNP had some good results during the war. This was largely thanks to the war-time pact between the major parties: by-elections were to be contested only by the party which had previously held the seat. This agreement had not included minor parties such as the SNP or Commonwealth. The latter, founded in 1942 by Sir Richard Acland, contested seats where a 'progressive' candidate was absent. It won three by-elections during the war but held only one at the 1945 general election (Chelmsford, which Labour failed to contest). Commonwealth and Nationalists cooperated over the contesting of by-elections. From the late 1941 many candidates who stood for these parties or as independents did well in by-elections. The success of the SNP during the war has to be placed in context: voters may well have been voting SNP in protest against the lack of choice resulting from the wartime deal between the major parties.

Scottish resentment at aspects of wartime policy further aided the SNP. In April 1940, William Power contested Argyll winning 37% of the vote having made rural depopulation and economic decline themes in his campaign. The unpopularity of Neville Chamberlain may also have been a factor. Some electors probably voted SNP as a means of expressing their British nationalist concerns regarding the acceptability of the Prime Minister. In 1944, Douglas Young won 44% of the vote in Kirkcaldy and in 1945 Robert McIntyre won Motherwell for the SNP. Motherwell was lost at the general election only twelve weeks later, after McIntyre had served only twenty-one days in Parliament.

McIntyre had been organiser and then secretary of the party and from 1947 to 1956 he was its chairman. He was steeped in Scottish Presbyterianism: his father was a radical United Free Church minister and both his grandfathers had been ministers. Educated at Daniel Stewart's College and Edinburgh University, he had a medical training, specialising in respiratory illnesses with his early work amongst tuberculosis sufferers. He was to be the main influence on the party in this period of its history. In 1944, he wrote 'Some Principles for Scottish Reconstruction', which was adopted by the party. It was a blend of economic radicalism and social conservatism much in keeping with its author's background. While suspicious of the powers of the state, stressing that Scotland was 'dependent for its existence on the home and the individual, rather than on the State', he argued for radical measures of state intervention in the fields of housing, industry, fishing and land ownership. Deliberately attempting to avoid too statist an approach, he stressed decentralisation and community control. As a set of principles it was not concerned with the detail of how these should be effected. It was, in essence, a revival of the old radical, decentralist, participatory tradition which had been swallowed up by the Fabian approach within the Labour Party.

At its 1946 conference, the party endorsed a policy statement which fleshed out some of the principles which McIntyre had listed. This statement was to remain the basis of SNP policy into the 1960s. It was a progressive document. Local government was given a major place in Scotland, it noted that a 'particularly intimate relationship' would always exist with other parts of the British Isles. Economic planning at different levels was advocated, including a Scottish regional tier, and economic power, particularly control of land, was to be diffused in order to 'safeguard democracy'. Scotland's major natural resources were given consideration. Social services were proposed along fairly radical lines. The programme was solid and the lack of any extreme or quirky aspects appears to have irritated some later commentators. Hanham, for example, dismissed the SNP in this period as 'emphatically the party of the little man' and its philosophy as designed to make a 'direct appeal to the ordinary man in the street who has never taken an interest in politics'. He was equally contemptuous about its stress on participation: 'the television maintenance man and the fitter snatched away from their workshops are no substitute for an experienced local leadership'.[42] The whole point of the programme and McIntyre's outlook was precisely democratic self-government founded in a distaste for elitist styles and attitudes. Cultural matters were largely ignored and the emphasis was on 'bread and butter' issues.

In his chairman's address to the 1948 party conference, McIntyre's message was not too different from that of mainstream social democrats in the 1990s – recognising the dangers of creating massive state bureaucracies through nationalisation programmes which served neither those who worked in them nor the community as a whole and striving for an alternative way to combine social justice with economic efficiency:

> The problem is how to make the State and industry the complete servant of a living and thriving community, responsive to human needs, both material and spiritual; and the struggle is that of the community to maintain its freedom against any who would control them through control of the industrial machine.[43]

The 1948 party conference also passed a policy by 57 votes to 33 supporting European unity. Mary Dott had attended the Hague Congress on behalf of the SNP, at which Churchill had made his famous speech referring to the need to create a 'kind of United States of Europe' and which saw the foundation of the European Movement. Dott seconded the motion calling for direct Scottish representation in a European Federation at the SNP conference while the pacifist activist Archie Lamont, suspended from membership later that day, opposed it.[44] Pro-European sympathies were also finding expression in the Scottish Convention at that time.[45] Occasional references to Europe can be found in contemporary nationalist literature. Europe was replacing the Empire as the wider stage on which an independent Scotland would play its part.

In the mid-1950s, support for European integration was being voiced again. An article in the *Scots Independent* confronted the obvious criticism of integration, that it would involve 'exchanging one controlling authority for that of a whole set of nations'. It argued that European integration was wholly different in that the relationship with a whole group of nations was 'very different from that of subjection to a single and much greater nation'.[46] A year later

George Dott was arguing for a policy which could be presented as an alternative to the 'vacillations of Eden's policy':

> We are a European people, and instinct and interest alike should align us with our European kindred . . . Let us stand by the folk with whom we have a genuine common interest – let us create a European authority.[47]

But difficulties also arose from developments in international politics. Old divisions over pacifism were in danger of being resurrected with the decision to base US troops on Scottish soil and then to site a US nuclear base in Scotland. The party objected to Scotland serving as a base for training foreign troops at its conference in 1960, with only four delegates disagreeing.[48] At the next year's conference the party strenuously opposed the Government's decision to allow a Polaris base to be built in Scotland, while reaffirming support for membership of the North Atlantic Treaty Organisation (NATO). This was to be a key issue over the next few years, attracting into the party a new breed of nationalists and making unilateral disarmament one of the key policy stances of the party. These new members, often ex-Labour Party, were to be significant in the development of the SNP in the next stage of its history. This new generation hardened the party's opposition to nuclear weapons, although the 1963 conference only narrowly, by 45 votes to 43, called for an end to the manufacture, testing and stockpiling of nuclear weapons.[49] The party's stance on Europe was also affected by this new breed of members. Suspicious of anything in any way associated with the Cold War, the 1962 conference had unanimously supported a resolution deploring Government policy supporting European integration.[50]

These new members, particularly Billy Wolfe, were keen to update the 1946 policy statement and work on detailed policies began. The first major statement was on the coal industry in 1963. In 1966 the party published a short pamphlet, 'The SNP and You', which set out its policies and broad ideology. The ideal of increased citizen participation in politics which was emerging on university campuses in the 1960s was reflected in SNP thinking. Developments in the international environment and reaction to the policy of the government of the day also played a part in SNP policy-making. Carving out a distinct political identity had been achieved, although from the

1960s the desire to be something other than Labour or Unionist was as much evident as genuine independent thinking.

Tactics and Strategy

In his opening remarks to the SNP conference in 1946 the party chairman, Dr Bruce Watson, warned that attempting to win self-government through British parties involved 'wasteful, exhausting, maddening processions of deputations, prayers, appeals, protests, agitations, and so on, followed inevitably by a series of promises, assurances, safeguards, and sometimes cynical rebuffs, with frustration, futility, and miserable compromise at the very most.'[51] Though this was the dominant view in the SNP in this period, it did not preclude cooperation with other bodies. The question of dual membership was ultimately confronted and a decision taken against it in 1948. One of those affected by the decision was Douglas Young, who resigned from the party over it. Young remained committed to self-government, though he was always more in favour of devolution than independence. Far from becoming a loyal Labour Party member he criticised Labour for abandoning a clear commitment to home rule in favour of a pledge to establish a Royal Commission later that year.[52] Once the decision had been taken to outlaw dual membership the question was effectively closed.

Relations with other parts of the national movement proved, as ever, more difficult than with the established political parties, especially after Labour dropped its commitment to home rule. The split in the SNP in 1942, which saw the formation of Scottish Convention, was a source of tension but the dual membership policy did not prohibit SNP members from joining the Convention and many did. Indeed, the Scottish Covenant Association relied heavily on SNP members gathering signatures. The party decided not to participate in the Scottish National Assembly organised by the Convention in 1947 because the agenda did not include discussion of 'self-government with full control over financial and economic affairs'.[53] At its National Assembly in November 1949, the SNP decided that branches should take no official action and that it should be left to individual members to do as they pleased.[54] This was not much of a problem for MacCormick and other leading figures in Scottish Convention who did not want their organisation tainted by association with the SNP. The other theme developed by the SNP was that the Assemblies had no sanction: if the Government ignored its demands there was little Scottish Convention could do. The argument was articulated by opponents of the movement as well as by the SNP. In 1950, an editorial in the *Glasgow Herald*, a newspaper which strongly opposed any measure of self-government, argued that the national movement must 'put up candidates of their own or obtain pledges from MPs of the major parties'.[55]

Meetings with Scottish Convention were occasionally held on an informal basis. One such meeting took place after the 1945 election to discuss the tactics most likely to lead to the Labour Government fulfilling its manifesto commitment to establish a Scottish Parliament. It was agreed that the Convention was 'constitutionally best fitted' to draw up a home rule bill which would be based on the Leonard Declaration, a home rule blueprint drawn up by Labour MP William Leonard during the war, and that MPs Willie Gallacher and Neil MacLean should be approached to introduce it.[56] Some efforts were made to build a common public front but these do not appear to have been welcomed by the leadership of either the Convention or the SNP. It was far better that each organisation knew its part and kept to it, preventing opponents from accusing the more moderate Convention of harbouring 'extremist' elements. But the SNP was more openly supportive of the Covenant and McIntyre was one of the signatories at its public launch. Further evidence of tacit cooperation emerged when the SNP decided not to contest the Paisley by-election when John MacCormick stood as a 'National' candidate with Liberal and even Unionist support.[57]

It was only with the decline of the Covenant movement that more open cooperation could take place. In the mid-1950s there was some talk of creating a 'home rule front' consisting of the Liberals, the SNP, and the Scottish Covenant Association. The Liberal Party had its worst post-war election in 1955, winning only 1.9% of the vote with Jo Grimond elected as its only Scottish MP. In July, the *Scots Independent* carried a letter signed by some leading figures arguing for the merger of the SNP and the Covenant Association.[58] The terms of the proposal were that the Association should accept that the new body would contest every by-election it could fight, that the SNP would withdraw its requirement that all members should formally declare that they belonged to no other party, that the National Covenant of 1949–50 should be introduced again with an additional clause binding the signatory to vote for the new party in any by-election, and that the SNP should accept the Covenant's home rule demands as the basis of the new movement's policy.[59] The idea was explored at an SNP National Council. McIntyre made it clear that he saw scope for cooperation between members of the SNP and the Covenant, particularly in fighting elections. James Porteous of the Covenant Association maintained that the matter was too important for any hasty decision to be made. Given past experience it was hardly surprising that nothing came of the proposal. There were those in the SNP who did not want to abandon support for independence. The idea that the SNP would contest only by-elections was a compromise. However, as MacCormick's candidacy in Paisley had shown, bitterness occurred when a home rule candidate posed a serious threat to an established party. The idea was an honest but flawed attempt to find a means of uniting the movement and applying effective pressure.

A sign of frustration emerged within the SNP in 1950 when Roland Muirhead founded the Scottish National Congress. Muirhead had been involved in the movement for as long as any other leading figure and had seen its ups and downs at first hand. For him, McIntyre's defeat in 1945 signalled the failure of the electoral route to self-government. Some new course would have to be found. His radicalism and strong sympathies with anti-colonial struggles led him to see the Indian National Congress as the model. The 'Gandhi method of non cooperation and civil disobedience' was to be his new approach though little evidence of such tactics being put into effect ever emerged.

In 1958 a row erupted in the SNP after Ian Howard, a party member, acted as election agent for a Liberal candidate in a by-election in Glasgow Kelvingrove at which there was no SNP candidate. He was expelled along with three other members. This led to the setting up of a new body, Scottish Alliance, claiming to have members from every party but, like so many fringe bodies, it could find no distinct role for itself within the movement and soon disappeared.[60] It was evident that there remained a tension on the question, if not of dual membership, then of relations with the Liberals. The party leadership felt obliged to issue a statement on 'Unity in the National Movement' which stated that the SNP, Covenant Association and Scottish National Congress maintained their separate identity because their separate methods required it but, in general, they remained on good terms. In a reference to Scottish Alliance, the party maintained that there were no other significant bodies although occasionally 'one-man parties' arose appealing for a common front, which were simply cheap self-advertisements.[61]

In July 1959, the *Glasgow Herald* carried two articles on the theme of the decline of Scottish nationalism.[62] The gradual withering of the Covenant Association and the SNP's lamentable performance at the election three months later seemed to confirm its conclusions. However, the early 1960s saw life breathed back into the movement through a series of good by-election results. This was partly facilitated by the decline of the Covenant Association, which allowed the SNP to argue that an electoral strategy was the only credible approach. The influx of new members had been aided by a feeling that Labour could not win an election again. Internal battles within the Labour Party had resulted in unilateralism being adopted in 1960 only to be reversed in 1961. The Labour movement was experiencing a crisis in its debate over strategy. This uncertainty and division amongst Labour activists proved fertile ground for the SNP but it was only after Labour was returned to power that the SNP was able to take full advantage of disillusionment amongst that party's supporters.

The first major breakthrough came in Bridgeton in Glasgow in 1961 when the SNP candidate Ian MacDonald won 18.7% of the vote. MacDonald's talents as an organiser and his enthusiasm for the cause have been noted as major factors in allowing the SNP to take advantage of propitious circumstances.[63] Following Bridgeton, he sold his farm in Ayrshire and acted as the party's first full-time official in almost thirty years. The West Lothian by-election in 1962 gave Billy Wolfe, SNP candidate, his first taste of politics. Government fiscal policy was hitting the shale oil industry, which directly employed over 1,000 people in the constituency. Wolfe's background as a chartered accountant gave him the ability as well as the status to challenge the economic logic of the policy and cast doubt on suggestions that Scotland was too poor to govern itself. Another theme was the issue of membership of the European Economic Community. Wolfe was part of the new breed of nationalists who were hostile to EEC membership. The by-election saw the SNP launch one of its most successful slogans, 'Put Scotland First'. George Dott had adopted the slogan when he stood for Kilmarnock in a by-election in 1946, but not in the systematic manner practised during and after the West Lothian by-election.[64] The SNP came a good second with 23% of the vote in a seat it had not previously contested and the Conservatives lost their deposit for the first time in Scotland in 42 years. What had emerged in both by-elections was a new style of politics. The vibrancy and relevance of the campaigns were conveyed through a well-organised machine and model candidates.

Another feature of the SNP in this period associated with West Lothian was the adoption of the party symbol. The Campaign for Nuclear Disarmament (CND), from which the SNP drew members and ideas, had adopted a Greek symbol for peace as its own. In 1963 the idea of finding a similar symbol which would become 'instantly recognisable' as the SNP's was adopted initially by Wolfe's West Lothian constituency party and later by the party as a whole.[65] It was to become the party's trademark. Its success can be measured by the refusal of many cartoonists and SNP supporters to accept alterations to the basic design in the 1980s, including Jim Sillars in the 1988 Govan by-election, who continued to use the 1963 symbol.

However, by-election results were not always as good as in West Lothian. The following year a string of by-elections saw the SNP vote slip back. The party polled under 10% in Kinross & West Perthshire, Dundee West, and Dumfriesshire. The view that the SNP should hold back from contesting Dumfriesshire had been overruled by the leadership. Some party members believed that the SNP did less well when the Liberals were contesting a seat and this provoked a debate on a pact. When the question of a Liberal-SNP pact was raised in 1964 by Billy Wolfe it was ruled out. The SNP decided that it would not countenance a pact unless certain conditions were met: that the Liberals put self-government at the head of their electoral pro-gramme, that they pledge themselves to demanding self-government if and when a majority of seats was won by SNP or Liberal MPs, and that their MPs would return to Scotland if the Government refused to pass the necessary legislation.[66] John Bannerman, chairman of the

Scottish Liberals, insisted that the SNP abandon independence and support federalism as a condition for a pact.[67] Given the demands of each party, there was little prospect of an agreement. There was some sympathy for the idea within the Liberal Party. Michael Starforth, Liberal treasurer, supported the idea and a few years later defected to the SNP.

Gaining access to the media was recognised to be important not only as a means of getting the party's message across but also gaining status as a serious political force. In 1964 Anthony Wedgewood Benn, as Postmaster General, refused to allow separate party political broadcasts for Scotland and Wales and refused to meet a delegation from the SNP or Plaid Cymru, but after much pressure, the SNP had its first broadcast.[68] In it, Billy Wolfe argued that Scotland was directly subsidising England and not, as was generally claimed, the reverse. Over 500 requests for more information came into SNP headquarters in the next two days.[69] Arguing for fair access to the broadcast media was to be a major element in SNP campaigns in the 1960s and, indeed, ever since.[70]

In 1966 the SNP conference was attended by 600 delegates, double the number of the previous year, and the party was claiming a growth in membership from 2,000 to 30,000 in four years with the number of branches having grown from 20 to over 200. It was going to be far less easy for the other parties to ignore the SNP. The pressure of increased membership had led to a major overhaul of the party's organisation. This task was undertaken by Gordon Wilson, the SNP's assistant national secretary, in 1964. The structure of the SNP drawn up by Wilson has remained largely intact since, despite minor alterations such as increasing the number of vice-conveners.[71] A key feature of the structure of the party is its openness, with many opportunities for ordinary members to participate in debates. Additionally, the party gives activists ample opportunities to hold some kind of office. While entirely compatible with the SNP's self-governing ethos, this has resulted in an appearance of anarchy and greater division than would have occurred with a more streamlined and centralized structure.

The electoral strategy came to be the central component of the SNP approach. Lack of resources meant that it was not always possible to contest every by-election, and hopes of fielding a large body of candidates usually proved too ambitious. But gradually a profile was built up in a few seats which helped the party in later years. Contesting local elections was part of this approach. This was in part a response to a jibe by Secretary of State Michael Noble that the SNP 'couldn't run a toffee shop'.[72] In Stirling, the SNP became the largest party in 1967. McIntyre was elected to the local council and served as provost for a number of years. Other nationalists were being elected to local government posts elsewhere in Scotland. In Angus, Arthur Donaldson had been finance convener in the mid-1950s. Experience in local government was likely to teach party members that politics was the art of the possible as well as forcing them to develop policies. However, it was not until 1965 that the SNP issued a manifesto specifically for municipal elections in Glasgow. Amongst other things, it called for a Government Minister to be appointed with responsibility for Glasgow's housing – a proposal repeated by the SNP shortly before the 1992 general election.[73]

Splits and Factions

Some of the earlier antagonisms continued to fester for a number of years. At the party's 1948 conference, Robert McIntyre as chairman had attempted to bring the proceedings to a close while a number of resolutions remained on the agenda. Amongst these was one on Scottish neutrality in the event of a future war between the superpowers. This had provoked Archie Lamont, a strong supporter of Scottish neutrality, to accuse McIntyre of being a traitor. McIntyre treated Lamont's suspension as a matter of confidence in his chairmanship, ensuring an emphatic vote against Lamont.[74] This was an extreme but not untypical example of the new disciplined leadership style. The party could not afford to rip itself apart debating hypothetical situations such as Lamont had wanted. Policy-making focused on the 'bread and butter' issues of everyday life which McIntyre felt were essential in developing the party's image.

The party's slow progress was a source of frustration which spilled over into internal debates. The 1955 election had seen the Unionists achieve their best result, winning 50.1% of votes cast in Scotland, an unparalleled achievement this century for any party in Scotland. It was a very poor election for the SNP. Only two seats were contested, bringing the party 0.5% of the Scottish vote, although McIntyre came second in Perth and East Perthshire. The '1955 Group' was set up to challenge the existing leadership and two days after the election it expressed dissatisfaction with the failure of the party to 'show results after thirty-seven years' and criticised the 'dictatorial' leadership.[75] A more sinister threat, again caused by frustration, emerged later that year.

McIntyre had been intent on projecting an image of the SNP as responsible and mature, but extreme and anti-English speeches of some members was making this difficult. This had provoked the leadership to circulate the party's branches with a warning that violence and violent propaganda would not be tolerated. The trouble focused particularly on two branches, both established within the previous year, in Renfrew and Edinburgh South. Moves to expel those involved were set in train and Douglas Henderson, an Edinburgh University student, was informed that he had forfeited his right to SNP membership for contravening the terms of a resolution which emphasised that no racial hatred or violent action or its encouragement would be permitted. In a move intended to pre-empt expulsion, seven party members resigned in October 1955 complaining that there had been 'nothing but talk for twenty years'.[76] Rumours began to circulate that a large scale split was imminent. McIntyre and others in the leadership were determined to stand firm, and attacked the 'Teddy boys' who were causing the problem. A breakaway eventually came at the end of October when the Nationalist Party of Scotland was formed. As with the NPS in 1928, students played a part in its foundation. The interim secretary was Henderson, one of those who had resigned to pre-empt expulsion. He attacked the SNP for its 'negative and pro-English policies' and criticised the 'dictatorial attitude' of its leadership, particularly McIntyre.[77]

Henderson's message and ability as a speaker made him a potentially dangerous figure for the national movement. McIntyre's pragmatic approach based on developing an independent, responsible profile for the cause was bound to be endangered. The only course open to the SNP was outright condemnation of the new party. This became urgent following the first meeting of the new Nationalist Party, when Henderson told his audience that any English people in the hall who had sense should 'get out of Scotland now while the

going is still good . . . while they are still in one piece'. He alluded
to the activities of nationalists in Cyprus, where a series of British
government blunders had provoked a militant reaction that April.
The new party was not only tarnishing the positive message which
McIntyre hoped to convey, Henderson's anglophobia was causing
deep offence within the SNP. The new party claimed to have taken
a third of the SNP's 1,350 members within a week. The SNP maintained that around 70 members had been lost to the new party, and
that these had been concentrated in a few recently formed branches.
The leadership felt that many of those involved in the new party had
deliberately engaged in entryism with a view to taking over the SNP,
and that when this had failed they had broken away attempting to
perpetrate the maximum damage possible.

Over the course of the next few months the alternative visions
of the two parties were starkly presented at public meetings. In
November McIntyre asserted that the Scots were:

> not good haters and we do not want to make them that. Our quarrel is
> not with the ordinary person in England and we do not want to build
> up a virulent anti-English feeling in Scotland. That sort of thing would
> not go down with the Scottish people. We must maintain our own
> standards of our own self-respect. In that way we will be successful.[78]

It was as much a statement of McIntyre's personal convictions as
an attack on the new party. The links between personal, collective
and mutual self-respect within Scotland and between Scotland and
its neighbour lay at the foundation of McIntyre's political philosophy
and informed the strategy and the policies he was developing within
the SNP. The contrast with the rantings of the leaders of the new
party was stark. James Glendinning, of the Nationalist Party, declared
that the Nationalists were 'out to make trouble', maintaining that
the 'English give no indication of listening to reason'. Opposition
was to be 'crushed' and the 'so-called Scots in our midst' exposed
as the 'Quislings that they are'. Henderson managed to be even
less subtle when he spoke. If the English stayed in Scotland, he
maintained, the new party would 'not be responsible for their life
or limb'.[79]

Born out of frustration, the Nationalist Party of Scotland eventually fizzled out but it had been a serious embarrassment to the

movement at a difficult time. Henderson re-emerged in the SNP later and became MP for East Aberdeenshire, 1974–79. His speeches were less extreme but, as witnessed at the party's 1976 Motherwell conference, he could revert to form. As deputy leader after 1979 he was to face the same kind of harsh, and sometimes unfair, attacks for incompetence and indolence as he had himself made against the party leadership 25 years earlier. Once more, frustration within the party at events largely outwith its control was the cause of the resentment which focused on the leadership.

THE BOOM YEARS, 1967–79

A much more professional organisation emerged in the 1960s as more Scots, often well-educated, joined the party for the first time. This combination of expertise and political inexperience was double-edged. High expectations of victory within a short period of time and frequent political blunders went along with the production of detailed, often highly impressive policy documents. A problem for the party at this stage was that its membership fluctuated wildly, corresponding with its electoral support. Many stayed with the party but all too often members would drift out and in or, more often, just out. Building up high hopes generated excitement which could attract members but the disillusionment which followed a setback was costly. The stability of the earlier, fairly barren period contrasted with the instability of this time of great expectations.

This was the period which saw a major electoral breakthrough for the party. In 1967 the SNP managed to gain a highly respectable vote in the by-election in Glasgow Pollok despite the tightness of the contest between Labour and the Conservatives. This precursed the breakthrough later that year in Hamilton when Winnie Ewing, a charismatic young lawyer, won one of Labour's safest seats with 46% of the vote. Circumstances were on the SNP's side. Harold Wilson's Labour Government had been in disarray. Unpopular and divisive measures were being pursued by the Government – wage restraint, an application to join the European Economic Community, support for the USA in Vietnam and sterling, an important symbol of Britain's position in the world, was in crisis. Labour had taken Hamilton for granted for years and its organisation in the constituency was weak.

By contrast, Winnie Ewing personified the bright, confident future which the SNP seemed to offer.

The victory led to a massive rise in SNP membership and high hopes of a breakthrough at the subsequent general election. The 1970 election proved the SNP's best performance up to that time but, against the expectations the party set itself, it was viewed as a set-back. Hamilton was lost and only when the final result came in from the Western Isles where Donald Stewart was the candidate, did the party win its first seat at a general election. Donald Stewart's election was a fillip but it soon became clear that the former Provost of Stornoway intended to devote his attentions to his constituency. He was to play little part in running the party or indeed in travelling around Scotland making speeches as Ewing had done. An indication that all was not lost came with a by-election in 1971 in Stirling and Falkirk when Robert McIntyre won 35% of the vote.

Circumstances were to the SNP's advantage in the lead-up to the 1974 elections. In 1969, Harold Wilson's Labour Government had set up a Royal Commission on the Constitution (Kilbrandon), designed to 'spend years taking minutes', in response to Winnie Ewing's victory in 1967. This effort to 'manage' the issue backfired when the Commission's report finally appeared in late 1973 coinciding with and probably contributing to another wave of support for the SNP. Signs of a potential nationalist breakthrough had been in evidence in March when Gordon Wilson won 30% of the vote for the SNP in Dundee East. The Kilbrandon report supported a Scottish assembly and was published a week before two by-elections – in Edinburgh North and Govan. It helped place Scotland's constitutional status on the political agenda at a crucial moment. Govan was won by Margo MacDonald with 41.9% of the vote while Billy Wolfe won only 19% in Edinburgh North. The party had initially made the Edinburgh seat its priority but as the campaigns proceeded it had become clear that its best prospect was in Govan. The SNP were on the march again.

The two general elections in 1974 saw the long-awaited SNP breakthrough. Despite the tightness of the contest between Labour and the Conservatives at British level, a distinct Scottish campaign emerged. In February 1974 the SNP won seven seats, retaining the Western Isles but losing Govan. Eight months later these seven were held and a further four added. The SNP's eleven MPs were an odd assortment. Only Donald Stewart and Winnie Ewing had any Parliamentary experience and many of the others had very limited political experience. The media interest in this newly successful party meant that the party was under close scrutiny.

The main item of Scottish interest during the 1974–79 Parliament was the passage of the Labour Government's devolution legislation. When Labour lost its overall majority it became dependent on minority parties, including the SNP and Plaid Cymru, which had won three seats in October 1974, for its majority in the Commons. These were difficult times for the new MPs. With a minority government at Westminster, attention focused on their actions, and in particular how they dealt with the tricky issue of devolution. The inexperienced group were tested to the full. The electorate's verdict in 1979 was that the SNP MPs had failed.

Following the referendum in 1979 on the devolution proposals, at which a majority voted in favour of change but failed to meet the weighted majority demanded by Parliament, the group attempted to force the Government's hand by proposing a vote of no confidence. The defeat of the Government and subsequent general election saw the party lose nine of its eleven seats and its vote plummet from 30% to 17%. The return of Margaret Thatcher's Conservative Government brought an end to debates on constitutional reform for a number of years and marked the beginning of a period of introspection and internal wrangling in the SNP and the wider national movement. The high hopes which had characterised the earlier period gave way to a deep sense of disillusionment and betrayal. In part, circumstances had conspired against the SNP, but the party had failed to take advantage of opportunities and had made a series of tactical blunders.

The rise of the SNP in this period demonstrated that this was by far the most effective means of putting the issue of self-government onto the British political agenda but problems emerged in moving the issue on to implementation. In previous periods the relationship which had been the key source of conflict had been that between the party and the wider movement. In this period the relationship between the 'party in office', that is, those members elected to public office and the party apparatus, particularly the party's elected officials, became increasingly tense, not to mention the relationship between the party and the electorate.

Policies and Ideology

During 1967–79, greater emphasis was placed on the image projected by the party in the development of its policies and ideology, though little of substance changed. The criticisms that the SNP was a single-issue party – 'SNP: Still No Policies' – played its part. Following its success in Hamilton, the SNP's conference in 1968 paid considerable attention to financial and economic matters and debated a written Scottish constitution. To some extent this was part of the preparation for independence believed to be just around the corner, but also it was an attempt to increase the party's credibility. Policy-making was not entirely made secondary to strategic considerations: defence was also debated and the party's radical, and unpopular, stance re-affirmed. A key development in policy was agreed in December 1969, renouncing 'separatism and isolationism as outdated concepts' and accepting that Scotland should be part of an 'association of states of the British Isles'. Economic interdependence within the association was, in Wolfe's words, 'obviously essential'.[80] This softening of the party's policy was designed to win votes. This was aided by Billy Wolfe's successful challenge for party chairmanship against Arthur Donaldson that year. Wolfe set up a series of policy committees. However, the policies did not always give a clear indication of how SNP members elected to public office should act in council chambers or in Parliament.

In the early 1970s the work of the policy committees continued but Wolfe perceived a need to find some means of presenting the range of policies as one coherent package. Whether by accident or design, a distinct core of policies was becoming evident. James Kellas described the SNP at the 1970 election as 'something of a "Social-Democratic" party, rather more collectivist than the Liberals, yet apparently opposed to centralisation and bureaucracy'.[81] The February 1974 manifesto made explicit reference to the 'programme of social democracy which the Scottish National Party proposes for the foundations of a self-governing Scotland'.[82] Reference was made to the 'special relationship' to be established amongst the people of the British Isles, and support for a referendum on EEC membership allowed the party to tap into popular misgivings about the 'common market'. There was little difference in the party's October manifesto, 'Scotland's Future', which was published in August with a supplement added for the election.

One new aspect of SNP policy was its support for industrial cooperatives. Wolfe became involved in a cooperative in Glasgow shortly after the West Lothian by-election in 1962 where he met Isobel Lindsay, Tom McAlpine and Keith Bovey, all of whom later joined the party. The influence of the new generation, typically represented by these four, was considerable. Not only were they strong advocates of cooperatives but they were involved in the Campaign for Nuclear Disarmament. The 'new left' and counter-culture influence of the 1960s was to be significant in the party, although notably absent amongst its MPs and SNP-controlled councils.

Labour accused the SNP of being right-wing; the Tories accused it of being left-wing. The test came in the lobbies of the House of Commons. The extraordinary circumstances of the 1974–79 Parliament meant that the normal comfort of opposition was not available to the SNP. After the Labour Government lost its overall majority in November 1976, it became necessary for the new Prime Minister to cobble together agreements with minority parties including the SNP. This caused enormous difficulties for the SNP MPs, some of whom feared adverse electoral consequences of being too closely associated with Labour. The party had always attempted to place itself either midway between the two main parties or on a different plane altogether. The party's self-conscious efforts not to be seen to be in the pocket of Labour or the Tories involved calculating the number of occasions the group voted with each. Electoral success did not bring with it ideological self-confidence. If anything, the party lost its determination to carve out a new direction in the pursuit of a balanced image. Especially after Margaret Thatcher became Conservative leader in February 1975, the SNP and the Labour Government needed each other for their own purposes. Neither could acknowledge this publicly, and both walked a political tightrope for the next four years.

The most controversial action of the group, apart from its vote on the no confidence motion in 1979, was its record on the Nationalisation of Aircraft and Shipbuilding legislation. After Hamish

Watt, the party's whip, ostentatiously ripped up a telegram from shop stewards urging SNP support for the bill, the party voted against the second reading only to reverse its vote at a later stage. The message could hardly have been worse: the SNP's confused position on nationalisation was bound to irritate the maximum number of people. The affront to the trade unions would be used by Labour in its heartlands while the SNP's support for the third reading would be used by the Conservatives in theirs. It was an exceptional example of the Parliamentary group's incompetence but it was symptomatic of the desire to balance its voting behaviour rather than adopt a distinct, confident position of its own.

Tactics and Strategy

A strategy based almost exclusively on contesting Parliamentary elections came to dominate SNP thinking, yet there appears to have been little care taken to devise a coherent electoral strategy. There was no evidence of the party seriously targeting constituencies. A blunderbuss approach was adopted: the party would throw everything it had at the electorate in the hope of winning everything or at least something. It was as if each Scottish voter was as likely to be a potential SNP voter as the next: voters were 'all Nationalists under the skin'.

The SNP was confused in its understanding of who voted for it or were most likely to do so. The breakthrough in 1974 had been largely at the expense of Conservative seats and it was readily accepted that this meant the party had won over Tory voters, making a breakthrough in the central belt difficult. This was an absurd interpretation of events which the Labour Party fondly repeated to the discomfort of SNP activists in the central belt. In fact, the Conservative vote had held up fairly well in the seats won by the SNP. The interpretation of the elections provided by one analyst was that a large manual-worker component within the electorates of seats such as Argyll, Banff, Moray and Nairn had combined with a substantial small-town element to vote SNP.[83] The 'major proportion' of SNP support had come from 'natural anti-Conservatives'. Labour's unwillingness over generations to organise in such constituencies presented the SNP with an opportunity. This made the task of breaking into the

central belt easier than was suggested by those who assumed that
the SNP's 1974 support consisted largely of former Tory voters.
A similar message could be projected throughout Scotland without
the prospect of losing ground where the advance had occurred. The
failure to confront the fact that certain sections of the electorate were
more likely to vote for it than others meant that the SNP failed to
take advantage of its base of support.

The discovery of oil and gas in the North Sea in the 1960s gave
the SNP an important propaganda tool. The party was fairly slow
to develop its oil campaign but when the full-blown campaign was
launched in March 1973 it was the most sustained and powerful
in its history. 'It's Scotland's Oil' became a slogan which proved
effective in combating claims that an independent Scotland would be
economically unviable. In its sharpest form – evident in the slogan
'Rich Scots or Poor Britons?' – the campaign led to accusations that
it was selfish and caused much anxiety within the party. Supporters
of the campaign, including Margo MacDonald, felt that explaining
how the wealth generated from oil would be spent was a sufficient
response to this criticism. In time, however, the oil issue dominated
SNP campaigns and the party became repetitive. Oil had been given
such prominence that it seemed to confirm opponents claims that
without it Scotland was not economically viable.

The breakthrough achieved by the SNP in the elections in 1974
may have been aided by its oil campaign but the legacy was costly.
Attempts to revive an oil campaign in the early 1980s were half-
hearted. Where the SNP was temporarily successful was in its impact
on the other parties. By 1972, even before the launch of the main
thrust of its campaign, each of the other parties was promising that
substantial oil revenues would be channelled to Scotland and the
SNP 'seemed scarcely any more nationalist' than its opponents.[84] The
oil issue was as much a challenge as an opportunity. The staggering
wealth of the North Sea would be difficult to convey to an electorate
which was understandably sceptical of a panacea.

Similar problems were evident in local government as later became
clear in Parliament. The burst of support for the SNP following
Hamilton had brought success in the council chambers. In municipal
elections in 1968 the SNP won more votes than any other party and
held the balance of power in Glasgow. The party won 36% of the

vote in Glasgow, 35% in Edinburgh, 30% in Dundee, Paisley and Aberdeen, and 25% in Coatbridge, Clydebank and Dunfermline.[85] This breakthrough meant that the party could no longer be ignored but that was double-edged. As the *Economist* suggested, the SNP's achievement had earned it the 'right to be taken as a very serious force – politically and emotionally, if not always intellectually'.[86] Problems soon arose as councillors began to appreciate what was entailed in being elected. Political differences within groups were exposed. The chaos in the council chambers was partly blamed within the party for the subsequent disappointment at the 1970 general election. But the party failed to learn the lessons, and success in local elections in the 1970s resulted in a repetition of chaos, resignations and humiliations similar to those of a decade before.

Robert McIntyre's objective in contesting local elections had been to demonstrate that the SNP was competent. The objective in this later period was to chalk up as many victories as possible in the pursuit of an electoral breakthrough at Parliamentary level. The party was inverting its own philosophy in pursuit of strategic objectives: Westminster was taking on greater importance than local self-government in Scotland. SNP provosts in East Kilbride and Falkirk fell out with their group but could not be dismissed, leaving a running sore which was exploited by opponents. No distinct SNP approach to local government emerged, and there appears to have been little attempt to find one. On issues such as increasing rates, council house rents and sales, the party had nothing new to say. One logical extension would have been to avoid participation in local government; this was the line the SNP took in Dundee, largely at the insistence of Dundee East MP Gordon Wilson. In itself, local government featured little in the party's outlook. McIntyre's idea of creating local self-governing units which would act as examples of what could be achieved through national self-government was simply ignored.

The idea of a pact with the Liberals gained currency after Winnie Ewing's victory. Within the Liberal Party, Jo Grimond was known to view the idea favourably and at the Liberal Assembly in Edinburgh in 1968 it had been the subject of much discussion. Other Liberal MPs, particularly Russell Johnston, attacked the idea. Home rule had long been part of Liberal policy but, as Ludovic Kennedy, Liberal

Council member, remarked, it rarely received serious attention.[87] In 1967 he tabled a resolution demanding that home rule should be the 'principal aim and object of our policy' and in domestic matters that 'all other issues should be considered in relationship to it'. As he wrote in an article the following year, 'To my great astonishment this resolution was first carried unanimously, and thereafter, and equally unanimously, ignored.'[88] The next year he tabled a resolution urging the Liberal leadership to engage in talks with the SNP to arrange a temporary truce in Parliamentary elections. The resolution was not called and instead one proposed by James Davidson, MP for Aberdeenshire West, was passed stating that if the SNP approached the Liberals then discussions could take place. The problem was that by this stage the SNP had won Hamilton and was polling well. As was remarked of the Liberal Assembly in Edinburgh, the SNP could have 'rounded up in half an hour a larger and more enthusiastic attendance than the Liberals succeeded in doing after a year's preparation.'[89] Kennedy resigned from the Liberals and although he never joined the SNP spoke on its behalf, most notably for Winnie Ewing in the Hamilton by-election. There was no doubting the sincerity of individual Liberals but the strategy of forming pacts was never a starter.

The key issue on which the SNP failed to develop a coherent strategy was devolution. The prospect of a measure of self-government being legislated for brought tensions to a head. A variety of views existed in the SNP on devolution with the old pragmatist-fundamentalist tension to the fore. Some party members supported devolution and were at best lukewarm in their attitude towards independence. Others saw devolution as a stepping-stone towards independence – a concession which would lead to greater demands. Still others, the hardliners within the party, viewed devolution with suspicion, as an attempt to stall the movement. This was the mirror image of the hard-line unionist view, which saw all devolutionists as supporters of independence or 'separatism'. So long as the Government of the day refused to concede any measure of devolution the obvious strategy was to build up support for independence while leaving open any question of support for devolution.

Difficulties arose when the Government appeared willing to concede something. At one level, the party's strategy was clear: to gain the maximum level of power for an elected Scottish Parliament. However, it was never quite so simple. The party was in a position to influence matters in the early part of the 1974–79 Parliament due to the electoral threat it posed, and in the latter part due to the Government's lack of an overall majority. Bringing the Labour Government down involved a number of imponderables. The Conservatives were moving away from their commitment to devolution, always suspect anyway, so a change of Government might not mean progress even if the SNP sustained or increased its level of support, and SNP support fluctuated throughout the 1975–79 Parliament. It fell behind its October 1974 level during 1975 but was generally around 30% until 1978 when support began to slip away. Labour was internally divided on the issue and the Government had no clear strategy, making it difficult for the SNP to know how to react. The existence of a substantial body of anti-devolutionists, some sceptics, others diehards, meant that it was not clear what the outcome of key votes in the Commons might be. There were other minority parties to which the Government could appeal, leaving the SNP out in the cold. Additionally, the fundamentalist element within the SNP criticised support for devolution and was augmented at times by others who felt that a more hardline attitude ought to be adopted depending on circumstances. The external political environment kept changing, internal pressure fluctuated, and the balance of opinion in Parliament, the focus of the pressure, was an unknown quantity. Inevitably, the SNP position had to change with the circumstances.

The SNP was given a potential breathing space with the referendum on European Community membership in 1975 before the Government tackled devolution, but the changing political environment and the party's involvement in the debate on EC membership meant that a strategy on devolution was not devised. The SNP had adopted a hostile attitude towards the EC and its decision to campaign for withdrawal marked it out from other parties. The hope that Scotland would vote 'No' while the rest of Britain voted 'Yes', thus polarising opinion on a national basis, was not realized. Instead, the SNP was seen to be on the losing side. The short-term tactic was to prove costly to long-term strategic considerations. Neither were any cross-party links on the 'No' side established which might later prove useful in debates on devolution, other than those between Jim Sillars and some SNP members.

Devolution was debated at the 1975 party conference which resulted in a vaguely worded commitment to participate in a democratically elected Scottish assembly. It would have been difficult for the party, which participated in elections to the Commons, not to participate in elections to an assembly. The resolution gave no indication as to how the MPs should vote in the Commons. A more substantial debate occurred at the following year's conference when a resolution was proposed which stated that the party was 'prepared to accept an assembly with limited powers as a possible stepping stone', but asserted that 'nothing short of independence will meet the needs of the Scottish people'. An amendment to delete the passage referring to the assembly was proposed but was defeated by 594 votes to 425. From that point, many hardliners accepted the decision. While some doubts remained, it was felt that the party had to present a united front. After 1979 this was no longer to be the case.

A classic problem confronting all parties was before the SNP; the temptation to respond to the demands of activists had to be resisted in order to ensure that a modest measure would be enacted. As Wolfe told the national council in September 1976:

> We must avoid projecting an aggressive or destructive image . . . It is safer to risk provoking impatience among our dedicated supporters than to try to satisfy nationalist sentiment at the risk of alienating possible new support.[90]

The cooperative approach which was emerging in the SNP's relations with the Labour Government over devolution continued to cause anxiety, which partly explains the Parliamentary group's more hostile attitude on other issues such as nationalisation. Additionally, a clear difference in approach was opening up between sections of the party in Scotland and its MPs in Westminster. From 1976 through to Spring 1979 the SNP could hardly have been more cooperative in its relationship with the Labour Government on the issue of devolution. There were moments when this caused severe problems. In February 1977, the Scotland and Wales Bill was defeated when a Government guillotine motion was lost. The SNP view was that Labour was failing to keep its side of the bargain. Angry at the Government and buoyed up by a surge in the polls, the party wanted to bring the Government down.

However, the Callaghan Government was saved by the Liberals who feared annihilation at the polls. The voting behaviour of the Liberals during the 1974–79 Parliament proved a major problem for the SNP group whose attempts to maximise pressure on the Government on devolution and other issues were often frustrated by the Liberals' unpredictable voting behaviour. The Lib-Lab Pact gave the Government room for manoeuvre and carried with it none of the demands which SNP support would have involved. When maximum pressure was required and might have had effect, David Steel was 'more concerned with winning access to ante-rooms of power than with the changes which might flow from that power'.[91] The problem for the SNP was that it was not alone in being able to act as a pivot between Labour and the Conservatives. The Liberals' voting record made the SNP look consistent. Liberal negotiators failed to put any pressure on a Government which was, at best, lukewarm in its support for devolution.[92]

The next occasion on which SNP support for devolution was severely tested came in January 1978 when a wrecking amendment was moved by Labour MP George Cunningham. A referendum on devolution had been conceded by the Government to win the support of its own backbenchers. The amendment laid down a provision that if less than 40% of the electorate, as opposed to those who voted, voted 'Yes' then the Government would move an order in Parliament repealing the devolution legislation. Some discussion went on in the SNP as to whether the party should continue to support the measure given this provision. The consensus was that it was too late to withdraw support and that to do so would be taken as a tacit admission that support for constitutional change amongst the Scottish public was weaker than had been claimed.

The Cunningham amendment was merely the first of a series of setbacks suffered by the SNP in 1978. Remarkably, there had been no by-election in Scotland from the October 1974 election until the Garscadden by-election in April 1978. Garscadden had been one of the SNP's prime targets. By SNP standards, the campaign was a disaster. The Parliamentary group distanced themselves from the candidate's views on defence during the campaign and the election agent publicly admitted that the canvas returns showing the SNP doing spectacularly well were bogus. Additionally, Labour and Conservatives privately conspired together to damage the SNP. The SNP vote rose from its October 1974 position but, measured against expectations and what was required at the time, it was a poor result. Labour's success in holding Garscadden marked a turning point. Devolution died in the 1974–79 Parliament on the day Donald Dewar, one of Labour's most consistent and sincere home rulers, entered Parliament as Labour MP for Garscadden. Labour was no longer frightened of the SNP and its anti-devolutionist wing gained strength commensurate with the SNP's loss of influence.

In May 1978, the easing of pressure on the Government was confirmed when Margo MacDonald failed to win the second Scottish by-election of the Parliament in the symbolically important constituency of Hamilton. This time the SNP could not blame its candidate. In October, a third by-election, in Berwick and East Lothian, suggested that the SNP was a spent force. A major row over the selection of the candidate added to the impression that the SNP was in disarray. By-elections, which had proved so important in the past in pushing the issue of home rule to the fore, were having the opposite effect at the very time when one last push was required. Three successive victories for Labour, the devolutionist party, helped kill devolution and there was not much the SNP could do.

In June 1978, the SNP committed itself to campaigning for a 'Yes' vote in the referendum. That same month David Steel announced that the Liberals were withdrawing their support from the Labour Government. The problem then arose as to what the SNP should do in Parliament between then and the referendum. The Tories, baying for an election, made a commitment to hold a referendum on devolution and promised to accept the result. For some in the SNP, the temptation to bring Labour down was tempered by the SNP's poor showing in the polls and the knowledge that the Tories had all but abandoned support for devolution. For others, the sordid nature of Parliamentary deals allied with doubts about the Government's ability to muster support amongst its own backbenchers and the prospect of a referendum regardless of who won the general election made bringing down the Government attractive. Tension between the MPs and the executive increased. The dominant view on the executive was to keep Labour in power until the referendum. It was amongst the MPs, who had most to lose personally, that support for bringing down the Government was strongest.

A motion of no confidence in the Government was moved when Parliament met again after the summer recess. Callaghan had named the date of the referendum in the Queen's Speech and promised five more seats for Northern Ireland – all designed to win the support of the minority parties. Nine of the Parliamentary group ignored the instructions from the party's executive and voted against the Government but Callaghan survived. The two MPs who broke rank were criticised by their Parliamentary colleagues while the executive rebuked the group for voting against the Government. Once more, the party faced both ways at the same time. As polls showed the party slipping further, falling membership and bitterness in internal debates added to its difficulties.

In January 1979, the SNP appeared briefly to stage a minor recovery in the opinion polls but from February to the election in May the party was polling worse than at any stage during the 1974–79 Parliament. SNP members worked tirelessly for the Labour Government's devolution measure though they were often sceptical of its merits. By the time the referendum campaign had ended a perception had emerged within the SNP that devolution had been used to scupper home rule. Labour activists in Scotland were believed to have been at best indolent and at worst active in pursuit of a 'No' vote. Bitterness amongst SNP members at Labour duplicity was at an all-time high.

The result of the referendum left the SNP stunned, and disappointment turned into resentment. Support for keeping Labour in power declined. Labour was believed to have hung on to power with SNP support while having no intention of delivering devolution. Little would be gained by keeping the Government in power but much would be lost in helping to defeat it. The 40% rule stipulated that the Secretary of State had to move a repeal order on the Act, but there was nothing to prevent the Government voting against its own order. Callaghan had no intention of moving the order because he feared the divisions it would show up in his party, since many Labour backbenchers would certainly vote for repeal. Labour's Chief Whip told Callaghan that difficulties within the Labour Party were much greater than those posed by the SNP.[93] Ideally, the SNP wanted the repeal order moved. The chances of the defeat of the repeal order were slim, but greater than if the Conservatives were in power. It would also expose Labour's divisions, which might have helped in the subsequent election.

The attempt to force Callaghan's hand failed. The SNP group voted with the Conservatives and Liberals to defeat the Government three weeks after the referendum. The party in Scotland backed the Parliamentary group with a vote in favour of bringing the Government down passed by the party's quarterly national council. This time there were no abstentions amongst the MPs and this made all the difference – the motion of no confidence in the Callaghan Government was passed by 311 votes to 310 in the Commons. Hamish Watt, the SNP MP who had abstained in the November no-confidence vote, later expressed deep regret at his decision to go along with the group. The ensuing election campaign was fought with diminished resources and demoralised activists. 'British' issues such as trade union reforms and the management of the economy pushed the constitutional issue aside. With little enthusiasm, the SNP argued that a vote for it was the only way to ensure the implementation of Labour's devolution policy. Only the Western Isles and Dundee East were retained in the election which saw the SNP vote fall from 30.4% to 17.3%. The 1974–79 Parliament had offered the SNP its greatest opportunity. It was mishandled, though circumstances beyond the control of the party had made its task difficult.

During the Parliament tensions arose in each of the four sets of relationships mentioned in the introduction to this chapter. The relationship with the electorate was problematic because the party failed to project a coherent and consistent political message. It was as easy for Labour to point to the SNP's support for 'Tory policies' as it was for the Tories to point to SNP support for 'socialist causes'. The party never seemed clear whether the seats they held had been won because defecting Tories had voted SNP or, as was largely the case, because anti-Tory coalitions had been built up in previously Tory-held constituencies. The relations between the party and members elected to public office – councillors and MPs – deteriorated. The party had neither the means of controlling its MPs and councillors nor any effective lines of communication linking them to the party apparatus. Gordon Wilson had stood down as senior vice chairman (deputy leader) on his election to Parliament and has subsequently suggested that this was a mistake as it removed a potentially valuable link. The lack of a link between the MPs and the executive often led to misunderstanding, not to mention bitterness. Relations between the party and its councillors were given little serious attention. This proved a serious mistake as groups of councillors embarrassed the party throughout the period. Relations within the party were relatively good. Debates were often vigorous and there was always an outlet for ordinary party members to play a part in policy-making. Any tensions within the party reflected or were caused by problems elsewhere. Finally, relations with the wider movement were a major source of tension. The party assumed that it alone embodied the movement, and was unwilling to acknowledge the serious commitment to home rule, if not independence, of politicians in other parties. Labour MP John Mackintosh was a possible exception. Even Jim Sillars, who broke from the Labour Party to create the Scottish Labour Party (SLP), was treated with suspicion, and the SNP contested South Ayrshire in 1979 where Sillars stood as an SLP candidate against an official Labour candidate. The tragedy for the movement was that Sillars lost the seat by 1,521 votes while the SNP won 3,233 votes. Cooperation within the movement at this stage might have given it an additional, exceptionally talented MP in the early 1980s.

The conventional wisdom on the SLP is that it was founded on the ego of its leader, Jim Sillars, spurred on by a group of journalists.[94] This is far too crude. Journalists and writers played a significant part in its foundation but the SLP had deeper roots and involved great political courage on the part of those involved, particularly Sillars. The breakaway was front-page news and would have been regardless of whether a small group of journalists were sympathetic or not. Nonetheless, many journalists were guilty of exaggerating its significance. The *Glasgow Herald* was typical of this; its Scottish political correspondent wrote that the Labour party had been 'irretrievably split' with the establishment of the SLP – with its 396 members.

A profile of Sillars in 1975 noted that a man who is 'going to change his mind in the stiff orthodoxies of Scottish political life needs a bomb-proof opinion of himself'.[95] This was to be both one of his major assets and one of his major weaknesses. Sillars's defection was never forgiven by his former Labour colleagues and the bitterness had a lasting effect. His career had been one of the most promising of Scottish Labour MPs and he had turned down a junior Ministerial office, much to the surprise and dismay of Prime Minister Harold Wilson and his press secretary.[96]

The idea to set up the SLP was rooted in two events, the South Ayrshire by-election in 1970 and Britain's entry into the European Community. The by-election was a turning point for the SNP when the tremendous support which had been shown for it in Hamilton in 1967 was reversed when Sillars, as Labour candidate, demonstrated his formidable skills. Sam Purdie, the SNP candidate in South Ayrshire, was later described by Sillars as his 'political twin'.[97] In a sense, Purdie was the founder of the SLP. He was a former Ayrshire miner and election agent for Labour MP Emrys Hughes, whose death had caused the by-election. After the 1970 general election Purdie argued that Labour's victory in Scotland was no reason for rejoicing when the Tories had won in Britain. This was to haunt Sillars. Before his election to the Commons, he had been highly critical of home rule. His pamphlet, with Alex Eadie, 'Don't Butcher Scotland's Future', was the most sustained and important Labour response to the SNP in the 1960s, but his growing sympathy for self-government became evident shortly after his election to the Commons, as witnessed by his contributions to Parliamentary debates.

Membership of the European Community was crucial in this. Sillars has recorded the development of his views.[98] Less well known is how open he was about the development of these views at the time. Few of his Labour Party colleagues could have been unaware of his changing opinions. As early as June 1973, Sillars informed Tony Benn that he had become a 'convinced Scottish nationalist' and four months later he said that if Britain stayed in Europe he would 'become a Scottish nationalist member'.[99] Significantly, Sillars broke with Labour only after the referendum on continued membership of the EC. This was not the only reason for the breach with Labour. The mid-1970s was a period of great excitement in Scottish politics on the issue of constitutional change. The final spur was the Labour Government's weak measure of devolution. The behaviour of the SNP Parliamentary group made a straightforward switch very difficult, although negotiations did take place. One idea which was mooted was that Donald Stewart should stand down as SNP Parliamentary leader to be replaced by Gordon Wilson, with Sillars as deputy. Instead, the SLP maintained an independent existence.

Sillars was joined by Paisley MP John Robertson, who played a relatively minor role in the SLP and stood down at the subsequent election. The 1979 election in South Ayrshire with the long lead up to it was a bitter affair. Sillars' defeat killed off the SLP. It had failed to establish itself as a party. It had been reliant on one man and, despite his abilities, the prevailing mood acted against the party. Under first-past-the-post there was little electoral space for a further home rule party. Sillars joined the SNP in 1980, days after the party suffered heavy defeats in local elections. The SNP, he maintained, was 'now the only vehicle capable of securing home rule for Scotland'.[100]

A number of former Labour members joined the SNP via the SLP. This was not its only role. In its early articulation of independence in Europe, combined with a clear position on socio-economic issues, the SLP pre-empted the SNP of the late 1980s. There was probably more sympathy within the Labour Party for the SLP than was ever publicly evident, and had an electoral breakthrough been achieved some of Sillars's more timid colleagues might have joined him. Many SLP supporters later claimed that had the party been set up at a different time it would have been successful. External circumstances had once more proved decisive.

IN THE SHADOW OF '79

The referendum and general election in 1979 cast a long shadow which has affected SNP thinking ever since. Over the summer months of 1979 a faction emerged calling itself the '79 Group. The aptness of this name was probably not appreciated even by its own members. The '79 Group and the fundamentalist backlash were flip sides of the same coin. Both were reactions to defeat, deriving from events in the past rather than looking forward. The '79 Group's early meetings suggested that it might have become an intellectual ginger group similar to the Fabian Society in the Labour Party. Instead, it became a faction perceived by others as a threat to party unity. The party itself adopted the political equivalent of the foetal position –

turning away from the external political environment and returning to fundamentals. It was only forced out of introspection by the shock of the 1983 election result, when it held on to its two seats but saw its vote fall to 12%. The Parliament of 1983–87 witnessed a slow healing process but in 1987 both the Western Isles and Dundee East returned to Labour. Donald Stewart's vote did not transfer to the SNP candidate and local organisational weaknesses were blamed for the defeat of party leader Gordon Wilson in Dundee East. Three new gains were chalked up, however, bringing back to Parliament 'retreads' Margaret Ewing in Moray and Andrew Welsh in Angus East along with Alex Salmond in Banff and Buchan.

The 1987–92 Parliament offered opportunities for an SNP advance. Labour had been defeated for the third consecutive time and the electoral arithmetic suggested it had little chance of winning again. The Tories were reduced to a rump, defending unpopular policies, most notably the poll tax. A younger generation of SNP activists, much tougher and more sophisticated, was emerging around Alex Salmond. The party was far more confident and more prepared than before. The Govan breakthrough, when Jim Sillars took the seat from Labour in November 1988, appeared to signal the start of an advance and might have done so but for a dramatic change of strategy.

The key political divide in Scotland for most of the 1980s had been that between the Conservative minority governing Scotland and the opposition parties. A theme of Scottish politics which developed in the 1980s was the notion that the Conservatives were 'anti-Scottish'. This had been an undercurrent in SNP propaganda from the mid-1980s which was fuelled by the decline of the steel industry and the imposition of the poll tax. It was a theme which all opposition parties found attractive, though there was some disquiet within the Labour Party that this 'soft nationalist' message might help the SNP and among some hardline SNP members who felt that it failed to address Labour's weakness on the Scottish question. The portrayal of the Conservatives as 'anti-Scottish' proved one of the most potent themes of politics north of the border, and helped to undermine the position of the government and highlight the constitutional question. It also related to the SNP's changing political identity. Implicitly, the corollary of the Conservatives being anti-Scottish was that Scotland's political culture was left-wing or socialist. From early in 1989, the

Tories had a relatively easy time as the main battle became that between SNP and Labour – a battle which, ultimately, hurt them both and helped the Tories. Given the circumstances – a confident SNP and a propitious context in which an electoral advance could be achieved – the return to fundamentals in the late 1980s was unusual. The fundamentalism of the early 1980s was due to defeat but that of the late 1980s was in response to a perception of strength.

Factions and Splits

At the first formal meeting of the '79 Group a number of papers were discussed. Like the SNP generally at the time, the group's members suffered from introspection and self-justification. Many younger party members joined and the student wing of the party provided it with its most solid support. The combination of some older members with scores to settle and an irreverent youthful membership gave it a cutting edge. However, it lacked a substantial mature core able to steer a less confrontational course and avoid some of its excesses. The connotation of 'illegality, if not malevolence and pathology'[101] associated with factions in political parties was to be the group's major problem. This was heightened by the lack of experience of organised factions in the SNP, the circumstances of its establishment, and the manner in which some of its members articulated themselves.

Inevitably, the group was treated with suspicion and hostility by sections of the party. Its posturing and ill-defined socialist and republican rhetoric simply encouraged a view that it was out to cause trouble. It did, however, provide an exciting body within the SNP at a time of disillusionment, and may have played a part in keeping a number of members in the party. The group was a fairly hetero-geneous body and its public face hid the variety of views and even some sophisticated analysis which existed within it. The differences between some of its members and others in the party were not always obvious but the very existence of an organised faction created divisions. Instead of building support across the SNP, the group's existence meant that people who would ordinarily be sympathetic were often placed in the invidious position of having to take sides. Ultimately, for most SNP members outside the group this meant taking sides against it.

A crude analysis of the referendum result was offered by the '79 Group: working-class Scots had voted 'Yes'; this should be the SNP's target and a 'socialist' message was required to win over this vote. The leaps involved in the development of this position were huge but it was uncomplicated and appealing. For other members the group was simply a means of continuing a battle which had gone on at executive meetings and with the former MPs. Much of the group's time and energy was devoted to intra-party battles and any intention of contributing to the intellectual development of the SNP was never realized. Its contribution to policy development was limited. Its main area of interest was strategy.

The other major development in reaction to the events of 1979 was a fundamentalist backlash. The party conference that year took place in September in Dundee. Billy Wolfe had announced his intention to stand down as chairman. Three candidates stood for the post – Gordon Wilson, Stephen Maxwell, and Willie MacRae. Margo MacDonald was challenged in the post of senior vice chairman by defeated MP Douglas Henderson. The differences were about strategy. The '79 Group candidates attempted to present the battle as a matter of left versus right as this would have been to their advantage, but the key issues were relations with other parties and support for devolution. Wilson and Henderson were seen as supporters of a more hardline attitude while Maxwell, who had directed the SNP's 'Yes' campaign in the referendum, and MacDonald were associated with the pragmatic approach. The group became associated with this position although there were within it members who adopted a fundamentalist position. MacRae had demagogic tendencies and could rouse a nationalist audience easily. Despite the circumstances, he won only 52 votes.

Wilson had a resounding victory, winning 530 votes to Maxwell's 117. He had a number of advantages – he was better known, he had succeeded in holding Dundee East at the election when nine of the eleven MPs went down to defeat, he had a long involvement with the party, and he was not tainted by association with factionalism and, to a lesser extent, devolution, as was Maxwell, at least in the minds of SNP members. Wilson sounded like a fundamentalist at the time but he played a significant part in pulling the party back from the hard-line position over the next four years. Henderson defeated

MacDonald by 450 votes to 169. He was an unreconstructed fundamentalist with right-wing views. He had a talent as a public speaker,
as had been evident in the mid-1950s when he led a breakaway from
the SNP. He became the main enemy of the '79 Group and bitter
exchanges followed his election. Elections to other posts followed
the same pattern.

The high point for the '79 Group came at the 1981 conference in
Aberdeen. Jim Sillars had joined the party the year before, making
it clear that the '79 Group had made this possible. His intention
to be 'just a useful ordinary member'[102] was not shared by other
members of the group, and in 1981 Sillars stood successfully for vice-
chairman for policy. Two other group members were also elected
vice-chairmen. The group had identified three key resolutions at the
conference: one demanding a 'real Scottish resistance and defence
of Scottish jobs' involving direct action 'up to and including political
strikes and civil disobedience on a mass scale'; a resolution acknowledging the 'failure of the private sector in Scotland' and supporting
an enlarged public sector; and one supporting 'armed neutrality' for
an independent Scotland, reversing the policy of support for non-
nuclear membership of NATO.[103] In his first speech on the floor of
an SNP conference, Sillars argued for the civil disobedience resolution. His rhetoric was powerful: 'Sacrifices there will be. People will
be hurt . . . it will be unpopular at first . . . We have to be prepared
to accept that the cell doors will clank behind some of us.'[104] The
resolution was passed, as were the other two '79 Group targets. These
successes were interpreted as a major advance for the left.

Set in context, however, the Aberdeen conference was not a radical
break with the past. The party had a long tradition of supporting
unilateralism. The NATO decision to embark on a major programme
of siting medium-range nuclear weapons in various parts of Europe
affected progressive parties throughout Europe, and in Britain it
provoked the relaunch of the Campaign for Nuclear Disarmament
(CND). In this context the change of policy was relatively modest.
It owed more to the changing international environment and the
support of long-standing supporters of nuclear disarmament such
as Isobel Lindsay and Billy Wolfe than the '79 Group's activities.
Indeed, Sillars himself had reservations about this policy. The resolution on the public sector was simply a reaffirmation of existing

policy expressed in bolder language. Even the civil disobedience resolution was not such a break with the past as was generally assumed. The 1979 conference, interpreted by the group as involving a lurch to the right, had passed a resolution urging the executive to plan non-violent civil disobedience to prevent the dumping of foreign nuclear waste in Scotland.[105] The mover of that resolution had been Tom McAlpine and there was little evidence of '79 Group activity around it.[106] In 1981, the civil disobedience resolution was taken more seriously, largely because of Sillars's part in its success.

Support for civil disobedience had a number of sources: those who genuinely wanted a 'resistance campaign', those who saw it as a means of altering the SNP's image with the electorate, and those who were experiencing a knee-jerk reaction, if somewhat belatedly, to the events of 1979. No senior party member spoke against it though many, Wilson included, were known to be opposed. Many members who opposed the resolution regarded this as political cowardice and were further angered by Wilson's attempt to avoid the decision by announcing at the close of the conference that Sillars would be given responsibility for implementing the civil disobedience strategy. Not only had the mood of the party been misread by the Group but the mood of the electorate was not appreciated. Over the previous year, the party had organised a series of demonstrations against the rising levels of unemployment and none of these had attracted much support. One rogue poll showing SNP support rising to over 20% was grasped as evidence after the conference of public endorsement of the strategy. Other polls told a different tale. *Systems Three* for the *Glasgow Herald* showed an SNP high of 22% in March falling away to 18% in May and remaining at around that level for the rest of the year. The only other occasion that year when the SNP polled over 20% with *System Three* was in October – before the first and only civil disobedience occurred, after which SNP support fell to 17%.

Divisions over the '79 Group were acted out through the implementation of civil disobedience. The group had mistakenly assumed that the party was behind it and had allowed its most prominent member to be accountable for a strategy which had little prospect of success, not least because other senior members opposed it. Sillars was right in thinking that many senior members were attempting to sabotage the strategy and discredit the Group. The Group simply had not planned any response to such an event. The act of civil disobedience which was eventually effected was a breakin at the Royal High School in Edinburgh, which was to have been the Scottish Assembly building. Six party members, all members of the '79 Group, were arrested and charged with vandalism in October.[107] The intention had been that the Group would break in and a 'declaration' would be read out. In fact, breaking into the building proved more difficult than expected and the declaration was never actually read out. The reaction of the opposition parties was to ridicule the SNP rather than to feign outrage at something that could barely be taken seriously even by SNP supporters.

On the day of the break-in, the *Glasgow Herald* carried a front page report of a private letter purportedly written by Sillars to Dafydd Elis Thomas, Plaid Cymru MP. The letter was fairly innocuous though the tenor of secrecy caused some concern. Sillars denied having sent it and suggested that a 'dirty tricks' department was at work within the party. A plan to stage a mass demonstration the following weekend flopped when Sillars decided that mass civil disobedience might get out of hand. Added to his problems was a boycott of the demonstration by some senior office bearers, some of whom used its association with the Assembly building and devolution as an excuse to distance themselves from civil disobedience. In effect, the SNP's civil disobedience strategy collapsed because of its farcical and secretive character, the lack of will to carry it through, the undermining of Sillars by senior office-bearers, and a misunderstanding of the mood of the public and the party. The Group had been supplied with sufficient rope with which to hang itself.

As the 1982 Ayr conference drew near it was clear that a major show-down would occur. A number of senior members who had been targets of the Group organised themselves into the 'Campaign for Nationalism'. Winnie Ewing, Robert McIntyre and others launched the Campaign at the conference with the sole intention of having the '79 Group proscribed. The Campaign had quoted Sillars's own words of five years previously in its news-sheet for the conference:

Because of the underlying feeling in the hearts of so many SNP members, socialists would be doing the national movement a disservice by
trying to convert that party to our way of thinking. A positive attempt
to carry the SNP to socialism would smash that party to pieces, and
when its forward movement was gone, the Unionists would have a
field day.[108]

Wilson was left with little alternative and, staking his leadership on
the matter, moved an emergency motion that all groups be proscribed. The conference endorsed Wilson's motion by 308 votes to
188. Whether delegates voted for Wilson's resolution by conviction
or in despair is unknown. This vote no more marked an outright
victory for the hardliners than 1981 had represented a great victory
for the '79 Group. Sillars retained his post as an SNP vice-chairman,
suggesting that delegates did not entirely accept the hardliners'
views. Whatever the intentions of the delegates, the impression was
instantly created of a party at war with itself and a leadership intent on
destroying its leftwing. The '79 Group had styled itself the SNP's
left, although most party members who could be identified as socialists never joined it and many of the group's members were moderate
social democrats who used more radical rhetoric. Chris Baur of the
Scotsman penned a 'Lament to the Seventy-niners after R. Burns',
commemorating the dead at the 'Battle of Ayr, 5 June 1982':

> Scots, wha hae wi Winnie bled,
> Scots, wham Sillars ne'er has led,
> Better tae be dead than Red
> in the SNP!
> Now's the day tae grasp for powr,
> Stamp oot a' thon Left-wing showr,
> And see proud Gordon triumph owr
> Thon vile Conspiracie!
>
> Wha will find the Labour knave,
> Infiltratin' oor conclave?
> 'For God's sake, man. Come on! Behave!
> 'A socialist? No' me!'
> Tell the workers no' tae mourn;
> Freedom's cause is no forlorn!

> Maybe no' the morn's morn,
> But in Eternitie![109]

The Group was already in decline before the Ayr conference. With only 217 members at its dissolution there had even been talk of winding it up. Instead, an almighty row which was to drag on for a number of months ensued. In an attempt to get round the banning order, Group members formed the Scottish Socialist Society which included members of other parties and was therefore not an internal SNP group. The party understandably resented this move and wrote to the society's interim committee informing them that they would be expelled if they went ahead with setting it up. Margo MacDonald, a member of its interim committee, later resigned from the SNP.[110] She had joined the party in 1966 and won the Govan by-election in November 1973. Though she lost it at the general election the following February she was elected senior vice-chairman and served in that post until her defeat in 1979. Despite the executive's decision in the run-up to the 1979 election that she should not appear on television on behalf of the party, as it was felt that she lost it votes, MacDonald remained the party's best known member. A poll in February 1981 asked respondents to name the main leaders of the SNP – 28% of the electorate (29% of SNP supporters) named Margo MacDonald; 18% named Winnie Ewing (21% of SNP supporters); 12% Billy Wolfe (21% of SNP supporters) and 13% Gordon Wilson (26% of SNP supporters).[111] Her departure was a severe blow to the SNP. She only rejoined the party after the 1992 election.

Alex Salmond was amongst those who were expelled from the SNP, the sentence later being commuted to suspension, for forming the Scottish Socialist Society. The bitterness spilled over into other business. In his report to the party's national council in December 1982, Sillars accused Wilson of 'moral blackmail and unprincipled actions'.[112] The SNP was in a sorry state as the 1983 election approached. Few constituencies had candidates in place. The SNP was polling well under its 1979 level of support in the first half of 1983 and in the June election its vote fell from 17.3% to 12% and 53 out of 72 deposits were lost. The party held on to its two seats and narrowly missed winning a couple of other seats. In more propitious circumstances, it could have won Banff and Buchan, and Moray.

The '79 Group episode in the SNP's history is significant as it concerned a battle about strategy. It also highlights the difficulties which factionalism can create. One interpretation of the episode is that the party began by lurching to the right in 1979 followed by a lurch to the left in 1981 before lurching back to the right again in 1982. A generally intolerant attitude towards groups might also be an interpretation. However, this is too crude. At one level there was a considerable degree of animosity and intolerance displayed but there is ample evidence that the grass-roots non-aligned membership – which is the most significant element in the SNP as in most parties – was fairly tolerant and quite uncertain as to the direction the party should take. This tolerance was shown in its refusal on successive occasions to ban the '79 Group, despite the efforts of some senior party members. It was only in 1982, after the '79 Group was discredited for the bungled campaign of civil disobedience and with Gordon Wilson's ultimatum, that all groups were proscribed. Significantly, '79 Group members were elected to senior office throughout the period and continued to be re-elected, even at the Ayr conference in 1982. A small number of '79 Group members did fall away but, as a survey conducted in 1983 discovered, the overwhelming majority remained in the party.[113] In time, many of those who had dropped out of active politics came back again. A few stray former members finally returned to the fold in 1988 following Jim Sillars's success in Govan.

The emergence of another group in the early 1980s was symptomatic of the reaction to defeat in 1979. Siol Nan Gaidheal (SNG) advocated direct action and was active in campaigns against the dumping of nuclear waste in the Galloway hills in the early 1980s. Its members wore military-style Highland dress and carried brightly coloured banners on demonstrations. Its language was militant and its literature promised that it would take direct action 'where words go unheeded', though its activities rarely lived up to its threatening postures. At a meeting of the SNP's national council in December 1980 an attempt to have both the '79 Group and SNG proscribed failed. Supporters of both groups, together with members who were not satisfied that sufficient evidence of wrong-doing had been provided, combined to prevent proscription. This cross-factional support is not untypical in political parties; it was motivated by support for the right to organise in groups rather than specific agreement on aims or outlooks. However, the SNG became increasingly embarrassing to the SNP with its militaristic styles and disruptive behaviour. Along with all other organised groups, SNG was banned by the SNP in 1982.

Perhaps the most remarkable aspect of the period was that despite appalling public scenes of division and a disregard for its image with the electorate, the SNP managed to hold on to its two seats in 1983. A core of dependable support had been built up, but this reservoir of core supporters was nowhere near as great as the SNP assumed and 1983 was a sobering election. Stability was evident in terms of policies. Members of the '79 Group, particularly those new to the party, exaggerated the degree of change in policy which occurred. The key issue which had not really been addressed, was how an ideological consensus should be projected to the electorate, and how the ordinary members could ensure that the elected apparatus and SNP members elected to public office would abide by policies informed by that consensus.

Policy and Ideology

A number of attempts were made in the months following the 1979 election to understand what had gone wrong, but the outbreak of hostilities signalled by the establishment of the '79 Group led to heated exchanges in which there was little room for reasoned discussion. A memorandum by Billy Wolfe on the SNP results criticised the behaviour of its MPs, the abandonment of its social democratic image, the poor relations between the MPs and the party's executive, and the lasting damage done by a 'rabble-rousing speech' during the 1976 conference by Douglas Henderson:

> What I believe the Parliamentary group have wittingly or unwittingly reduced us to is a fundamentalist nationalist image. We have lost the social-democratic middle ground, and both of the main British parties can point to us and say that we are either anti-Tory or anti-Labour.
> . . . It was and is unfortunate that the MPs were reluctant to listen to criticism and comments and advice . . . the MPs did not continue to project the image of the party which had won us support throughout Scotland.[114]

Wolfe later withdrew some of these criticisms but many in the party agreed with his views as originally expressed.[115] A similar critique was offered by Tom Nairn in the *Scotsman* in July. The SNP had attempted to base its appeal on the 'hopeful myth of an inevitably resurgent, classless nationalism'. An abundance of policies developed by the party was not, in itself, sufficient. It was the 'framework, the new central outlook holding them together' which counted.[116]

The need for a party to have a clear 'political identity' has already been noted. The failure to project a clear identity allows a party's identity to be defined by its opponents. The problem with defining the SNP's identity as equidistant between Labour and the Conservatives was that this was vague and easily manipulated by its opponents. A more confident message was required. One means of changing the party's image was to alter its policies. Hence, debate on policy and ideology in the SNP in the 1980s was secondary to questions of strategy. Party image was the main concern of '79 Group members who saw changing or highlighting aspects of the party's existing programme as a means of projecting a different image to the public. One member was quoted as saying that 95% of policies were left-wing but the 'real trouble is that the party is not prepared to accept the implications of this and admit its actual political character to the outside world'.[117] There was, in fact, a remarkable degree of stability in policy terms. It was the presentation which was to change.

The degree of agreement on policy was evident at the party's 1979 conference which was otherwise a fractious affair. On the first morning of the conference a resolution was overwhelmingly passed which endorsed the primacy of the public sector in regenerating the economy and demanded that oil revenues be used to eliminate poverty rather than fund tax cuts. At the time, following an election in which even the Labour Party had promised to 'reduce the burden of income tax' if elected,[118] this was a fairly unorthodox position. There were few significant policy developments in the early 1980s suggesting a move to the left. What was changing, however, was the profile of the SNP. Ideologically, the 1980s saw a fair degree of consistency, but strategically the SNP changed direction. It was beginning to acknowledge its radicalism on social and economic issues. The label 'moderate left of centre' was adopted by Gordon Wilson towards the end of the 1979–83 Parliament as a description of the SNP's ideology. He had used the term as early as 1981 but it only came into common use as the 1983 election approached. The problem with 'moderate left of centre' was that it was a relative term and it was unclear what it related to – left of the Labour party or left of centre in Scottish politics? Additionally, 'left' and 'right' are terms used by political activists rather than the electorate. The SNP's problem, as a relatively new party in a fairly stable party system, was to find some means of identifying itself on socio-economic questions without the advantage of language readily understood by the electorate.

A more significant policy change, relating to the European Community, was occurring gradually and almost unnoticed. A major initiative was launched in August 1983 by Gordon Wilson in which he determined to reverse the anti-NATO policy, explicitly back EC membership, and move away from a hard-line fundamentalist position. He failed to have the anti-NATO policy reversed but succeeded in winning support for EC Membership. This was possible because the main divisions at that time did not correspond with divisions on European Community membership. Both Jim Sillars and Winnie Ewing were strong supporters of EC membership, though they were significant figures in opposing camps on other more divisive matters. Plaid Cymru had reversed its policy on the EC shortly before the 1983 election; farmers in rural Wales, where Plaid did well, benefited from the Common Agricultural Policy.

The policy on Europe was not widely recognised as significant until a few years later. Once again, the changing political context played the most significant part in helping the SNP. The 'Euro-sclerosis' which afflicted the European Community in the late 1970s had been followed in the early 1980s by difficulties over the Community's budget, but by the late 1980s the situation had changed. Jacques Delors's presidency of the European Commission and the launch of the 1992 programme thrust Europe onto the political agenda of all member states. At the SNP's 1988 annual conference, overwhelming support for 'Independence in Europe' was won. Opposing the resolution, Isobel Lindsay and Tom McAlpine found that they were part of a diminishing band of members who had formerly been highly influential. Lindsay's argument was that only independence outside the European Community would give Scotland the opportunity to 'pursue the same strategy as the successful small states in Europe who have remained outside the EC'.[119] Her position was weakened by the fact that her fundamentalist leanings on Europe sat uneasily with her gradualism on home rule short of independence. The coincidence of heightened interest in Europe and the priority attached within the SNP to its policy of 'Independence in Europe' proved an exciting mix. Few Scots probably appreciated the detailed arguments involved in the SNP policy but it conveyed an impression of saying something relevant, modern and linked to events in the wider politics of Europe. It also caught the other parties off guard. No meaningful alternative to independence in Europe emerged, only the vague slogan 'Europe of the Regions'.

The European policy had important implications for party strategy. Apart from contributing to enhancing the image of the party as a modern, progressive force it was also seen as providing an answer to the 'separatist jibe'. Like the inter-war policy of membership of the Empire, membership of the EC was presented as offering a stable political and economic framework for a small state. The end of the Cold War following the revolutions in eastern and central Europe also created a favourable climate in which the SNP could claim that the world was safer. Subsequent events in central and south-eastern Europe, however, with 'ethnic cleansing', violence, and instability, damaged this picture for the SNP.

Tactics and Strategy

A distinct feature of the 1980s was the way the SNP slowly began to move away from contesting Parliamentary elections as its sole political strategy, although ultimately this still dominated its thinking. The irony of a nationalist party which held Westminster in contempt placing such emphasis on Parliamentary elections appears to have been lost on most party members. The emergence of a non-Parliamentary approach was not due to any radical reappraisal of strategy but largely to the failure to make much progress in elections. This approach took two forms. The first still focused on the House of Commons but involved treating it less reverentially than in the past. The second was a move towards extra-Parliamentary activities. Neither was well coordinated but both showed the beginnings of a new style of campaigning by the SNP.

One of the '79 Group's more successful ventures had been a seminar on 'Parliamentariansism' in October 1981, and a '79 Group publication proposed options. The meeting was overshadowed by the break-in at the Scottish Assembly building the previous evening by prominent SNP members but contributions from a range of speakers including Daffyd Elis Thomas MP of Plaid Cymru made it a successful event. The Welsh Nationalists were viewed as more radical and less reverential with regard to Westminster, although by the late 1980s the situation had changed. Occasional outbursts from the public gallery by Welsh language supporters had not been unknown in the past and extra-Parliamentary campaigns by Welsh nationalists were commonplace. In 1985 a group of five SNP members was removed from the Commons for shouting 'English Tories out: give us an assembly' on the sixth anniversary of the devolution referendum.[120] As often occurs with such demonstrations, the MPs sitting in the chamber were showered with leaflets. This was, however, atypical of SNP campaigning, although it did signal the emergence within the party of a group willing to disrupt sittings of Parliament.

Prior to the 1987 election, the SNP drew up plans for Parliamentary disruption and direct trade union action in the event of the Conservatives winning again at Westminster but without a 'mandate' in Scotland. Isobel Lindsay and Alex Salmond drew up the original report and Jim Sillars and Margaret Ewing looked at options for disrupting Parliament. Related to this approach was the party's support for an elected convention and a belief that enough Labour members would support such a course of action.[121] The first indication that this approach was being put into effect came in March 1988 when Alex Salmond, by then SNP MP for Banff and Buchan, interrupted Nigel Lawson's budget speech. The disruption had been planned well in advance and timed for a moment of high drama in the Commons. But even this was not unrelated to contesting Parliamentary elections. The SNP was convinced that the increase to over 20% in its showing in the polls was largely attributable to this act. The condemnation of Salmond by Neil Kinnock caused some Labour MPs concern and Dennis Canavan, Labour MP for Falkirk West, walked out of the Commons in protest at Kinnock's reaction.

This proved an extremely useful backdrop for the SNP in launching its campaign of non-payment of the poll tax and the Govan

by-election later that year. A Commons committee debating a piece
of Scottish educational law was the next SNP target a year later.
Only one SNP MP was officially on the standing committee but two
others turned up. Labour and Tory MPs voted to report them to the
House and adjourned the committee. This had not happened since an
attempt by Labour MPs to disrupt local government reorganisation
legislation in 1973. The *Scotsman* noted the 'extraordinary level of
bitterness' felt by Labour towards the SNP.[122] Labour was in danger
of being eclipsed by the SNP in much the same way as moderate
Irish home ruler Isaac Butt had been by Charles Stewart Parnell a
century before.

A year later Jim Sillars set out to repeat Salmond's effort by
moving a writ for a by-election in Wales to prevent the budget speech
being made. This was foiled by Neil Kinnock who, as Leader of the
Opposition, was alone able to help the Chancellor of the Exchequer
by inviting him to make a statement which the Chancellor used to deliver his speech. It was a classic example of the power which could be
wielded when the two front benches colluded. Piquancy was added as
Sillars and Kinnock had been Labour colleagues some years before.
Labour was highly defensive, as indicated in a bitter attack on the
SNP by Labour's Scottish spokesman Donald Dewar in the *Glasgow
Herald*.[123] Its lack of novelty and the bitterness of exchanges between
the SNP and Labour meant that Sillars's interruption of Lawson's
speech lost much of its impact. The SNP promised further disruption
and party members called for more, but speculation that this would
be followed by further disruptive activities proved incorrect. Despite
the approval of party activists there was clearly a difficulty in the small
Parliamentary group. Margaret Ewing, the group leader, was alone
amongst her colleagues in not taking part in any disruption or 'anti-
Parliamentary' behaviour. An additional problem lay in finding some
novel method of causing havoc. The 1980s were the most disruptive
period in twentieth-century Parliamentary history as measured by the
number of occasions when MPs were suspended. Significantly, the
1970s, at the height of Nationalist presence in the Commons, had
been one of the quietest periods. No doubt reaction to Margaret
Thatcher's conviction Government played some part in this but the
SNP experience in the 1970s had brought about a rethink.

The need to make sense of the defeats in 1979 and to develop a strategy avoiding earlier errors dominated thinking immediately after the election that year. For many in the party, this meant distrusting other parties and refusing to cooperate with them in any way. As happens in parties which suffer a major setback, and as was happening in the Labour Party at this time, the SNP adopted a purist no-compromise position. The strategy of working for independence gradually was abandoned in favour of 'independence nothing less'. By a large majority, the 1979 conference voted not to 'engage in any more dealings in assemblies, devolution, or meaningful talks'.[124] It was an untenable position, but until the party began to move out of the shadow of 1979 it was to be the official line.

The 1983 election proved important and Wilson sought to bring about changes to move the party back to a more pragmatic stance. In this, he had the support of a wide cross-section of senior members. What was required was some means of maintaining the party's distinct position, support for independence, while avoiding the impression that it was 'hell-bent on an almighty leap into goodness knows where', as a *Scotsman* editorial put it.[125] The idea of a constitutional convention commended itself as it would involve elections in which SNP candidates would stand on a platform of support for independence but would accept the opinion of the electorate. In March 1980 Wilson moved a Bill in the Commons for a directly elected convention, but he had difficulty in convincing his party of its merits. The idea had been the central part of his address to conference in 1982 but the next month the SNP executive overwhelmingly rejected it.[126] Ironically, it was '79 Group members who backed Wilson. His deputy, Jim Fairlie, described the idea as 'another political blind alley'. In the lead-up to the 1983 conference Wilson made clear his support for a more pragmatic approach. Support for independence, he argued, gave the party its energy and dedication, but by appearing intransigent the SNP was not furthering the cause.[127] At the conference he described the fundamentalist position as erecting a barrier between the party and the electorate. After a two-hour debate, the SNP voted to drop support for 'independence nothing less' but also rejected the idea of a convention by 173 votes to 141.[128] The main supporter of the hardline position was Jim Fairlie who had warned against supporting devolution at the 1976 Motherwell conference. His consistent stance helped him in the mood which prevailed after 1979 and had allowed him to succeed Douglas Henderson as senior vice-chairman. As time passed and a more sober assessment of what had happened in 1979 developed he became increasingly marginalised.

The 1984 conference saw the party narrowly adopt a resolution supporting an elected constitutional convention. Jim Sillars challenged opponents of a convention to explain how independence could be achieved. It was agreed to cooperate with the Campaign for a Scottish Assembly (CSA) in working for a convention. The party was divided on the idea but it gave the SNP a more constructive image and allowed it to argue for independence while being willing to support a lesser measure simultaneously. It was a good campaigning position, but little attention was paid to how a convention would be established and what should be done in the event of one being set up which was not along the lines the SNP proposed. The fundamentalists in the party continued to growl from the side and made every effort to undermine the policy.

Following the 1987 election, the CSA set about establishing a convention and a group of 'prominent Scots' was given the task of drawing up a plan. The idea of a convention had won widespread support in the media. However, the SNP was completely unprepared for the eventual outcome of the CSA-inspired discussions. Some leading figures in the party were convinced that Labour would not accept the idea under any circumstances. The CSA was determined to bring the Labour Party on board but the cost proved to be the SNP's participation. The Govan by-election of November 1988 had intervened and the SNP victory proved a major spur for Labour. The events of 1989 can only be fully understood in this context. The question of forging links across parties and the means of articulating a case to the wider electorate were once more core questions confronting the party in this highly charged political atmosphere.

The role of Sillars in shaping the SNP's approach was considerable. After returning to active politics following a period working abroad, Sillars argued in 1984 that the Scottish left had to bury its differences. Each party should be free to pick its own tactics and methods to suit its own organisation and traditions.[129] A major theme which he developed following his membership of the SNP was that the party had frequently failed to appreciate the nature of the Labour Party. The clearest statement of this view was expressed in his book, *The Case for Optimism*:

> Generalised attacks upon the Labour Party when the target should be the Parliamentary Labour Party (by far the least popular element and most open to indictment) can too easily be taken as denigration of the whole Labour movement and its history. People will reject attempts to blacken a party if their contact with the organisation is a local person, or shop steward, all too obviously working hard for the general good of the community. Listeners to a tirade simply cannot associate the devilish targets with those they know to be good people and so you get, at best, switch-off. At worst, you get a strong hostile reaction, more particularly from activists who see and feel things in much sharper tone than does the general public.[130]

He wrote movingly about little-known figures in Labour politics in Ayrshire who had dedicated time and energy working for others, often at costs to their health. This thinking underpinned the campaign fought by the SNP in Govan in late 1988. Attacks on Labour's leadership were made but a sharp distinction was drawn between those Labour leaders who had 'sold out' and ordinary members, supporters and voters.

Immediately after the by-election, Sillars stated that he would be looking for common ground with the 'nationalist wing of the Labour Party'. His overtures were immediately and bluntly rebuffed. This did the SNP no harm. Being seen as cooperative was becoming a positive element in the make-up of the party's image. It was, however, the SNP which eventually threw the cooperative message aside. The consensual style was replaced by belligerent campaigning led by Sillars himself. Sillars carried enormous authority at the time, although his subsequent actions severely dented it. His return to Westminster probably opened old wounds. Having a 'bomb-proof opinion of himself', as Ascherson had written in 1975, was not the same as lacking sensitivity. Former Labour comrades knew how to goad him and did so unmercifully. Additionally, the underlying strength of the hardliners within the SNP was not widely appreciated. The combination of traditional hard-liners and Sillars proved a powerful force.

Another important figure was Iain Lawson, a much under-rated

SNP hardliner who had defected from the Tories over the closure of Gartcosh steel mill in the 1980s. Despite their different political backgrounds, Lawson and Sillars were similar. If Sillars was the 'Hammer of the Nats' in the late 1960s, then Lawson could claim that title in the late 1970s when he proved the most impressive campaigner in the Garscadden by-election, doing more to floor the SNP candidate than Labour's Donald Dewar. Both Sillars and Lawson were emotional politicians who used powerful rhetoric, and both had experienced the trauma of leaving a party and joining one they once loathed. Neither could be described as having the zeal of the convert: both had always approached politics zealously. A political alliance had probably been developing before Govan but the by-election cemented it. It was to prove the key alliance in the SNP in 1989.

Lawson's antipathy to cross-party campaigning was based on his experiences campaigning to save Gartcosh. His views were set out in a letter in the *Scotsman* in June 1986 in which he called for a halt to 'all-party' campaigns. He suggested that these campaigns suited the Labour Party:

> The tactics are as follows:-
> 1. Set up an all-party grouping made up of equal representation from all political parties. Top this up with representatives from all affected local authorities (usually Labour-controlled), trade union members (usually Labour members), STUC (usually Labour members), a few ministers and a few other representatives from other groups.
> 2. Have a main sub-committee made up of one representative from each group (inbuilt Labour majority).
> This ensures inbuilt Labour control. At the first and every meeting urge the need for a co-ordinated campaign with every move being made through the 'all-party' grouping. This effectively inhibits other political parties from taking separate measures which may embarrass the Labour party. Any suggestion of independent action results in accusations of 'rocking the all-party boat' to the detriment of the workers involved.[131]

Lawson's critique was not without foundation, but it denied the possibility of a genuine and potentially successful all-party campaign as, indeed, had been waged in late 1982 to prevent the closure of Ravenscraig steel mill.

Lawson's comments in 1986 about cross-party campaigning could have applied to the convention. The prospect of European elections in June 1989 and fears that the Convention would be used as a means of attacking independence in Europe concerned some SNP members. The party had legitimate and understandable fears which were all too often lost sight of as the debate on participation heated up. Even Nigel Griffiths, Labour MP for Edinburgh South, acknowledged the legitimacy of the SNP's fears that the Convention would be 'swamped by Labour'.[132] There was also a tremendous change of mood in the SNP. The most notable supporter of all-party campaigns was Isobel Lindsay. Her involvement in the CSA throughout the 1980s and on the steering committee which drew up the 'Claim of Right' testified to her commitment to this approach. By the time the party was swinging back to a more cooperative stance her own position within the party was on the wane. She remained a significant figure because of years of hard work but at the 1987 conference she was narrowly defeated by Mike Russell, an impressive but little-known candidate, for the post of vice-chairman for publicity. In part this was due to a feeling that she had mishandled the 1987 general election campaign, which she had directed. Her husband, Tom McAlpine, was equally committed to a cooperative strategy and had over many years been the SNP's steel spokesman, frequently arguing that his shoulders were 'broad enough' to take any attacks from Labour members at cross-party campaign meetings. By the late 1980s he was replaced as steel spokesman by Iain Lawson. A strange coalition emerged in the SNP which gradually pushed aside people like Lindsay and McAlpine. Their marginalisation represented the emergence within the SNP of a new breed of left-wingers and the demise of the 1960s SNP left. Not only was the new breed less inclined to support a more consensual style but it was pro-EC. External circumstances had combined with a revival of confidence to undermine the 1960s generation.

For most party members, the first serious hint that the SNP would not participate in the convention was a report in the *Glasgow Herald* in late January 1989.[133] Only a fortnight before the paper had reported progress in discussions between Labour, Liberal Democrats, and the SNP. A meeting of representatives of each of the parties was attended by Jim Sillars, Margaret Ewing and Gordon Wilson for the SNP.

Shortly after this, the SNP representatives decided that the party would not participate, after consultation with all senior members apart from Alex Salmond, who was the most significant figure likely to dissent. Wilson was a lame leader following his defeat in 1987 as MP for Dundee East and had been eclipsed by Salmond and then Sillars. Sillars had always viewed Wilson as malleable and the leader's strong anti-Labour predilections were never far below the surface. Other senior office-bearers could be relied on to do as asked or told. The one problem would have been Salmond. Wilson did attempt to contact his deputy, although Salmond supporters doubted that he tried hard. It was never clear why the decision had to be made at that time. The strategy of the Greens, who demonstrated more skill than the SNP, was probably similar to Salmond's preferred approach. The executive of the party was presented with a *fait accompli* leaving opponents little chance to demur, although Lindsay tried vainly to have the decision reversed.

Robert McIntyre's intervention is worth noting. In SNP politics in the early 1980s, McIntyre had become identified with a hard-line, right-wing viewpoint because of his opposition to the '79 Group. This reflected the mood of the times in which caricature replaced serious analysis. As was seen earlier, he had been a patient, determined and pragmatic leader who had opposed SNP participation in the Scottish Assemblies in the 1940s but was willing to work with other bodies when possible. With this background, it was hardly surprising that he wrote to executive members urging them to adopt a pragmatic approach. He argued that the SNP should only withdraw if and when the package being produced was not to its liking as the public would then understand its reasons.[134] It was wise advice which the party ignored to its cost. The SNP executive voted 22 to 1 in favour of the leadership in early February. Isobel Lindsay could not even find a seconder for her position on the executive.

The battle was then set for a national council meeting in Port Glasgow in March. In the build-up to the meeting, media pressure for the SNP to reverse its decision was intense. Opinion poll evidence showing a decline in SNP support from its post-Govan high and appeals from a range of distinguished non-party Scots were used to try to bring the party back into the fold but the poll evidence was far from conclusive. *System Three* for the *Glasgow Herald* recorded the

SNP at 32% in early January 1989, falling to 28% in late January, down to 27% in February and holding steady at that level for three months. The gradual decline from the peak was expected and the much more substantial shift only became evident from June 1989 after the more hardline, non-cooperative approach became instilled in SNP campaigning.

The array of supporters of non-participation at the national council included Wilson, Sillars, Lawson, Margaret Ewing and Salmond. The vote was 191 to 41 in support of the negotiators recommendation not to participate, but this masked an underlying mood of uncertainty. The debate was one of the most ill-tempered and tense in the SNP for years. Lindsay's speech was courageous but sounded like a grand gesture of defiance at the end of a career in SNP politics. She asked whether the party was now really saying that Jim Fairlie, the consistent hardliner presumed politically dead up to that point, had been right all along. Her audience did not want to hear that the SNP could not make it on its own. The SNP hardliners achieved within the party what they were never to achieve in the wider arena of Scottish politics – a polarisation which cut out the middle ground.

TOWARDS THE 1992 GENERAL ELECTION

A number of SNP members hoped that once the debate was over something might be recovered. Nobody expected the SNP to join the Convention but some members hoped that some *modus vivendi* might be found. The idea of a referendum emerged and was supported by Salmond and a few others but was immediately rejected by the SNP executive. It was proving difficult to move the party back from its hardline attitude. The gulf between the hardliners Sillars, Wilson and Lawson and the more pragmatic element around Salmond was growing and becoming more personal. The ultimate break came when Wilson announced his intention to stand down as leader in 1990. Once more, his deputy was not consulted, although the Sillars faction was informed of Wilson's decision in advance. Sillars considered standing and was urged to do so by his supporters, who were scouting about to see how much support existed for him before the official announcement that Wilson was retiring. Margaret Ewing was, no doubt, informed by Wilson of his intentions, although she

probably did not realize what was going on in the Sillars camp at
the time. It was clear that Sillars would be defeated if he stood
although not by the margin that soundings taken earlier in the 1980s
had suggested when he was considering challenging Wilson for the
leadership. The full force of the Sillars camp backed Margaret Ewing
against Salmond in a leadership contest, which demonstrated how
badly the hardliners had misread the party in the wake of the Port
Glasgow national council.

Margaret Ewing, as Margaret Bain, had been SNP for East
Dunbartonshire in the 1974–79 Parliament where she gained a
reputation as a left-winger and one of the most able members of
the group. The media expected her to win easily in 1990 as she
had a number of advantages. Apart from having prior knowledge
of the battle, she was an extremely well-liked party member and the
'Ewing' name was no disadvantage. She also had the support of a
wide range of senior members including Wilson, Sillars and Lawson.
What should have been a strength, the wide base of support, proved
a disadvantage. Two campaigns were waged on her behalf – one run
by her husband Fergus, son of Winnie, and another by the Sillars
camp. The latter campaign did her more harm than good. In the
style of factional politics which the SNP had little taste for, the Sillars
camp called a meeting to which the party's 'central belt activists'
were invited.[135] Those attending noted the absence of Salmond
supporters. Accounts of the meeting suggest it was an unmitigated
disaster with personal attacks on Salmond made by a few recognised
malcontents. These tactics backfired spectacularly and Ewing had
enormous difficulty reconciling her own, genuinely decent approach
to politics, with that of those who were supporting her.

The leadership contest reflected the key tensions within the party
on strategy. Though the party had voted against the Convention it had
never given its backing to the kind of fundamentalism which afflicted
the party from 1989. The massive margin for Salmond – 486 to 186
– was recognised within the Salmond camp as due in part to the
Sillars onslaught. The error of assuming that the party had returned
to fundamentalism at Port Glasgow had damaged the heir-apparent.
Salmond's campaign team was headed by Mike Russell, mistakenly
dismissed as a light-weight by the Sillars camp. Over the summer of
1990 Russell, with a small group of mainly younger members, built

up a detailed picture of the party's thinking. By the morning of the vote he was able to give a remarkably accurate forecast of the result for the leadership contest as well as the other offices.[136] There had also been the question of how the candidates chose to present themselves. Journalist Derek Bateman, who provided the most informed coverage of the contest, quoted a party member as saying that 'Maggie offered her CV. Alex offered a manifesto'.[137] Ewing had demonstrated a long-standing commitment to the party and was well liked. Salmond's victory, as he knew and could not afford to forget, was not a vote against Ewing who remained his Parliamentary group leader. Salmond would be tested on his manifesto.

Within minutes of winning the SNP leadership in Perth in 1990, Alex Salmond's opponents were talking to the media about his overthrow. His demise was predicted and hoped for by some of his erstwhile associates from the '79 Group days. His position appeared strong given the almost clean sweep of posts won by his supporters. In fact, the Lawson-Sillars axis still carried weight, and differences, often with little basis other than personalities, continued to affect the party. Sillars commanded more public attention through the media than any other figure with the possible exception of Salmond. His approach altered completely between the Govan by-election and the general election. His belligerence was no longer directed against the Conservatives but against Labour, and it was bitter and uncompromising. He had forgotten the advice he had given to the SNP in his book quoted above.

As the 1992 general election approached, the signs of an SNP advance were mixed, although on balance the most likely outcome was always that the SNP's vote would rise, perhaps considerably, without a commensurate increase in its Parliamentary representation. 'Scotland free by '93' had been the prediction Sillars made immediately after the Govan by-election, but in the circumstances this had received scant attention. It was only in 1991 when Alex Neil, an SNP vice-convener, announced to a stunned SNP conference that the party's executive had decided to adopt the slogan that it was given public prominence. Alex Salmond appeared as surprised as anyone else. In one of his best performances as Shadow Scottish Secretary, Donald Dewar ridiculed the idea at Labour's conference. The SNP was beginning to look silly, a sure sign that it was taking its own rhetoric too seriously and was not paying sufficient attention to the electorate.

On the other hand, external events were to the SNP's advantage. Not only had the victory in Govan helped electrify the atmosphere of Scottish politics, the poll tax continued to harry both the Government and the Labour Party. Dick Douglas, who had been defeated in 1974 by the SNP's George Reid in Clackmannan and East Stirlingshire, had been returned as Labour MP for Dunfermline West in 1979. His refusal to pay the poll tax was initially presented by his Labour colleagues as a gesture of defiance on an issue about which few doubted his sincerity, but he became increasingly disillusioned with Labour. His protests against the poll tax included delivering a petition to the Queen following a run from Edinburgh to London in 1988. In March 1990, he was expelled by Labour and sat as an independent. In October he joined the SNP. The Parliamentary group numbered five, two of whom were former Labour MPs. Sillars and Douglas were treated to the vilification and venom which Labour reserves for apostates. Poll tax, the election of Sillars and the defection of Douglas helped the SNP develop its image as a party of the left. Events in the 1987–92 Parliament allowed the SNP's new political image to emerge – nationalist, leftist, and European.

Three events within the space of a fortnight in January 1992 pushed the issue of home rule to the forefront of British politics. A debate in Edinburgh's Usher Hall witnessed the leaders of the four parties debating Scotland's constitutional future with Alex Salmond of the SNP easily outwitting Donald Dewar, Malcolm Bruce and Ian Lang of Labour, the Liberal Democrats and the Conservatives respectively. The next week, the *Sun* newspaper declared itself in favour of independence with a front-page banner headline 'Rise now and be a nation again'.[138] The *Sun* was in battle with the *Daily Record*, and Rupert Murdoch's News International was willing to forego support for the Conservatives in pursuit of commercial gain. History was repeating itself. In the early 1930s a circulation war had seen the *Daily Record* and Beaverbrook's *Daily Express* supporting Scottish home rule for exactly the same reason. Less than week after this an opinion poll commissioned by the *Scotsman* and Independent Television News showed support for independence at 50%.[139] Though subsequent evidence indicated that this had been a rogue poll, the SNP and most of Scotland's political commentators caught the fever. Around this time, the Conservatives changed their approach on the constitutional question. Following the demise of Margaret Thatcher there had been speculation that a softening of attitude and possibly a move towards home rule might be accommodated. The Tory response coincided with what has since become known as their 'near campaign', a dummy run for the subsequent election, in Britain as a whole. It was a period in which the Conservatives tested their tactics against the opposition, especially against Labour's tax plans. The return to a hard-line, no-compromise stance on the constitution was part of the 'near campaign'.

As the election approached, polls showed the SNP support considerably up on its 1987 showing but too low to be certain of taking any more seats. Dick Douglas decided to contest Glasgow Garscadden against Shadow Scottish Secretary Donald Dewar with little prospect of success, and retaining the Govan seat was never certain, especially given the resources Labour poured into winning it back. The most likely result was always that the SNP would see its vote rise dramatically but have fewer MPs in the new Parliament, though the prospect of picking up a few Tory seats was always possible. In the event, the party retained the three seats won in 1987, won 21.5% of vote and saved all its deposits. The loss of Govan and the failure to take any further seats combined with pre-election expectations and claims to make what should have been a solid measure of progress seem like defeat. Once more, the SNP had been defeated by its own hype.

CONCLUSION

The establishment of an independent national party grew out of disillusionment with alternative strategies. Its establishment was not as straightforward as most existing accounts suggest. Many of those involved had to break with allegiances to other parties formed over many years and did not easily conclude that an independent party was necessary. Indeed, many still clung to old loyalties until the issue of dual membership was resolved 20 years after the foundation of the National Party of Scotland. Even this did not remove the ambivalence many party members felt towards other parties, particularly towards the Labour and Liberal Parties. This contributed towards the party's many uncertainties and ambiguities which revolved around whether it was a conventional political party or something else.

The process of developing a distinct political identity which would attract active members and loyal voters was slow and uncertain. It was only after the split in 1942 and the emergence of new leaders, notably Robert McIntyre, that the party began to establish itself as a potentially serious force. The limited progress made during the 1950s was due to the external environment which was not conducive to advances, and frustrations allowed factionalism to develop. By the early 1960s the SNP had established a loosely defined political identity for itself and did not rely on charismatic leaders and personalities. This proved a solid base on which advance could be achieved in the more propitious environment of the 1960s. Despite the development of policies in the 1970s what was lacking was an obvious core. Outside observers might identify the core as social democracy, as indeed the party did in its manifestos in 1974, but the party was reluctant to give it a label. By the late 1970s the SNP appeared to model itself on US parties with a set of policies which might or might not cohere aimed at groups of Scots rather than on the West European tradition of parties with a core ideology informing policy-making. There was, nonetheless, a remarkable coherence to the party's policies. Only in the 1980s, painfully and slowly, did the SNP come to acknowledge itself as a party of the left.

Tensions within the SNP have persisted around issues evident from the outset. Primary amongst these has been the pragmatist-fundamentalist division. It concerned strategy rather than policy. This central tension affected each of the four other relationships identified in the introduction to this chapter: between the party and the electorate; between the party apparatus and those holding public office as party representatives; relations within the party; and those between the party and the wider movement. This tension has remained unresolved and is probably irresoluble. The goal of independence was the party's *raison d'être* and belief in its attainment enthused its members, but so long as there was only minority public support for independence there would have to be compromises. A balance which took account of the changing political context was required; and this could not fail to appear inconsistent and cause difficulties at times.

1. *Scots Independent*, vol. 8, No. 97; May 1934.
2. S. M. Lipset and S. E. Rokkan, 'Cleavage structures, party systems and voter alignments', in S. M. Lipset and S. E. Rokkan (eds.), *Party Systems and Voter Alignments*, New York, Free Press, 1967.
3. Yves Mény, *Government and Politics in Western Europe*, Oxford, Oxford University Press, 1991, p. 75.
4. Angelo Panebianco, *Political Parties: Organization and Power*, Cambridge, Cambridge University Press, 1988, p. 49.
5. K. Janda, *Political Parties, a cross-national survey*, New York, Free Press, 1980
6. *Ibid.*, p. 50.
7. Véra Murray, *Le Parti Québécois: de la fondation à la prise du pouvoir*, Montreal, Hurtubise, 1976.
8. Graham Fraser, *René Lévesque and the Parti Québécois in Power*, Toronto, Macmillan, 1984, p. 50.
9. *Ibid.*, p. 60.
10. *Ibid.*, p. 157.
11. Graham Fraser, *Op. Cit.*, p. 311.
12. *Scots Independent*, May 28, 1955. The account was written by Elma Gibson, wife of Tom Gibson.
13. The most detailed and informed account is found in Richard Finlay, *Independent and Free, Scottish Politics and the Origins of the Scottish National Party, 1918–1945*, Edinburgh, John Donald, 1994.
14. NLS, Acc. 3721, Box 81/2, Correspondence discussed at meeting of Committee of Scottish National Convention, November 26, 1927.
15. *Ibid.*
16. Richard Finlay, *Op. Cit.*, pp. 53–4.
17. *Scots Independent*, September 1927.
18. R. E. Muirhead, 'Towards a National Party: The Coming General Election', *Scots Independent*, April 1928.
19. Richard Finlay, *Op. Cit.*, p. 22.
20. NLS, Acc. 3721, Box 81/2, Committee of Convention, February 18, 1928.
21. *Ibid.*, Box 80/17.
22. NLS, 3721, Box 81/2.
23. Quoted in Richard Finlay, *Op. Cit.*, p. 93.

24. *Glasgow Herald*, December 2, 1932.

25. Richard Finlay, *Op. Cit.*, p. 147.

26. *Glasgow Herald*, January 31, 1934.

27. *Ibid.*, October 1, 1932.

28. *Scots Independent*, March 1931, p. 67.

29. See for example the correspondence in the *Glasgow Evening Citizen*, April 14, 21, 26, 1937.

30. *Glasgow Herald*, October 29, 1938.

31. Richard Finlay, *Op. Cit.*. p. 206.

32. *Glasgow Herald*, December 8, 1939.

33. *Ibid.*, February 27, 1940.

34. See H. J. Hanham, *Scottish Nationalism,*, London, Faber, pp. 167–9; Jack Brand, *The National Movement in Scotland*, London, Routledge and Kegan Paul, pp. 240–1.

35. *Scots Independent*, vol. 6, no. 71, September 1932.

36. A plebiscite was requested from the government in a letter to the Prime Minister, *Glasgow Herald*, May 19, 1931; for support for a covenant see *Glasgow Herald*, June 14, 1930; for a constitutional convention see *Scots Independent* vol. 6, no. 71, September 1932. The party contested various elections in this period and intended to put up 200 municipal candidates in 1932, *Glasgow Herald*, August 8, 1932.

37. Andro Linklater, *Compton Mackenzie*, London. Hogarth Press, 1992, pp. 233–4.

38. Robert F. Muirhead, *Scottish Home Rule*, August 1926, p. 17.

39. John MacCormick, *Flag in the Wind*, London, Victor Gollancz, 1955, pp.38–9.

40. Richard Finlay, *Op. Cit.*, p. 180.

41. *Glasgow Herald*, May 13, 1935.

42. H. J. Hanham, *Scottish Nationalism*, London, Faber and Faber, pp. 179–80.

43. Robert McIntyre, *The New Look in Politics*, SNP, 1948.

44. *Glasgow Herald*, May 24, 1948.

45. 'United States of Europe', Notes on Convention, November 1944; 'United States of Europe', *Forum*, vol. 1, October 1946; William Power, 'The Next Step in World Politics: A United States of Europe', in *Forum* vol. 2, No. 1, November 1947.

46. 'European integration as safeguard for small nations', *Scots Independent*, April 23, 1955.

47. George Dott, 'Towards a Better Europe', *Scots Independent*, October 13, 1956.

48. *Glasgow Herald*, June 6, 1960.
49. *Ibid.*, May 20, 1963.
50. *Ibid.*, May 28, 1962.
51. *Ibid.*, May 27, 1946.
52. *Ibid.*, December 17, 1948.
53. *Ibid.*, March 22, 1947.
54. NLS, Acc. 3721, Box 74/661, Letter from Mary C. Dott, SNP national secretary, to SNP branch secretaries.
55. *Glasgow Herald*, January 9, 1950.
56. NLS, Acc. 7295 (4), Minute book of National Committee of Scottish Convention, November 10, 1945.
57. *Glasgow Herald*, January 9, 1948.
58. Oliver Brown, Compton Mackenzie, David Rollo, John Kinloch and Moray McLaren.
59. *Scots Independent*, July 2, 1955.
60. *Glasgow Herald*, April 1, 2, 5, 1958.
61. *Ibid.*, April 14, 1958.
62. *Ibid.*, July 8, 9, 1959.
63. Jack Brand, *The National Movement in Scotland*, London, Routledge and Kegan Paul, 1978, pp. 259–60.
64. Billy Wolfe, *Scotland Lives*, Edinburgh, Reprographia, 1973, p. 14.
65. *Ibid.*, pp. 46–7.
66. *Glasgow Herald*, March 9, 1964.
67. *Ibid.*, March 10, 1964.
68. Hansard, Commons, vol. 704, December 15, 1964, cols. 49–50.
69. *Glasgow Herald*, September 30, October 2, 1965.
70. Billy Wolfe, *Op. Cit.*, 1973, pp. 71–6.
71. The term 'convener' was adopted in place of 'chairman' at the 1988 party conference. This had the merit of being a Scottish term and avoided the sexism implicit in the term 'chairman'.
72. Interview with Dr Robert McIntyre, 1992.
73. *Glasgow Herald*, April 27, 1965.
74. *Ibid.*, May 24, 1948.
75. 1955 Group information mimeo, May 28, 1955, quoted in Jack Brand, *The National Movement in Scotland*, London, Routledge & Kegan Paul, 1978, pp. 255–6.
76. *Glasgow Herald*, October 27, 1955.
77. *Ibid.*, October 29, 1955.
78. *Ibid.*, November 12, 1955.
79. *Ibid.*, November 17, 1955.
80. James G. Kellas, 'Scottish Nationalism', in David Butler and

Michael Pinto-Duschinsky, *The Brish General Election of 1970*,
London, Macmillan, 1971, p. 458.

81. *Ibid.*, p. 457.
82. SNP manifesto, February 1974, p].
83. Michael Dyer, 'Why Tory stronghld crumbled', *Scotsman*,
October 24, 1974.
84. W. Miller, J. Brand, M. Jordan, *Ohnd the Scottish voter 1974–79*,
London, Social Science Research buncil, 1980, p. 15.
85. *Economist*, May 18, 1968.
86. *Ibid.*, May 11, 1968.
87. Ludovic Kennedy, *On My Way to l Club*, London, Collins,
1989, p. 305.
88. *Ibid.*
89. *Economist*, September 21, 1968.
90. Chairman's report, SNP national ouncil, September 4, 1976.
91. Alistair Michie and Simon Hoggat *The Pact: the inside story of
the Lib-Lab government, 1977–78*, Ladon, Quarter, 1978, p. 66.
92. *Ibid.*, p. 122.
93. James Callaghan, *Time and Chance,* london, Fontana, 1988,
pp. 560.
94. Henry Drucker, *Breakaway: the Scoth Labour Party*, Edinburgh,
EUSPB, nd.
95. Neal Ascherson, 'Jim Sillars: a futte Prime Minister of Scotland',
Scotsman, November 1, 1975.
96. The author was present at an intenew conducted during the
Govan by-election in 1988 when Je Haines, Wilson's press
secretary and then working for th Mirror group of papers,
told Sillars this.
97. Jim Sillars, *Scotland: the Case for Opusism*, Edinburgh, Polygon,
1986, p. 32.
98. *Ibid.*; Jim Sillars, *Independence in Eupe*, Edinburgh SNP
publication, June 1989.
99. Tony Benn, *Against The Tide: Diari 1973–76*, London, Arrow
Books, 1989, pp. 46–73.
100. *Scotsman*, May 5, 1980.
101. Dennis Beller and Frank Belloni, 'The Study of Factions',
in Frank Belloni and Dennis Belle (eds.), *Faction Politics:
Political Parties and Factionalism in Cnparative Perspective*, Oxford,
ABC-CLIO, 1978, p. 6.
102. *Scotsman*, May 5, 1980.
103. SNP 47th annual conference, 198| resolutions 3, 17, 36.

104. *Scotsman*, May 29, 1981.
105. SNP 45th annual conference, 1979, resolution 10.
106. *Scotsman*, September 14, 1979.
107. *Ibid.*, October 17, 1981.
108. Jim Sillars quoted on news-sheet of 'Campaign for Nationalism', SNP conference, June 1982.
109. *Scotsman*, June 7, 1982.
110. *Glasgow Herald*, September 17, 1982.
111. *Scotsman*, MORI poll, March 11, 1981.
112. *Glasgow Herald*, December 2, 1982.
113. *Radical Scotland*, June/July 1983, pp. 7–9.
114. Billy Wolfe, Confidential 'Comment on SNP Results and on Matters Affecting Them', 1979.
115. William Wolfe, letter in *Scotsman*, July 12, 1979.
116. Tom Nairn, 'Decade of mistakes, scars – and hope', *Scotsman*, July 2, 1979.
117. *Scotsman*, September 18, 1979.
118. Labour Party manifesto 1979, p. 14.
119. Isobel Lindsay, 'Time to take an independent approach to Europe', *Scotsman*, November 13, 1988.
120. *Glasgow Herald*, March 2, 1985.
121. *Ibid.*, March 27, 1987.
122. *Scotsman*, March 15, 1989.
123. Donald Dewar, 'Government only victor after nationalists' day of mayhem' *Glasgow Herald*, March 17, 1989.
124. SNP Conference resolution, 1979.
125. *Scotsman*, editorial, August 30, 1983.
126. *Ibid.*, July 7, 1982.
127. *Ibid.*, September 6, 1983.
128. *Glasgow Herald*, October 1, 1983.
129. *Scotsman*, August 27, 1984.
130. Jim Sillars, *The Case for Optimism*, Edinburgh, Polygon, 1986, pp. 25–6.
131. Iain Lawson, letter in *Scotsman*, June 26, 1986.
132. N. Griffiths, 'Retrospect and Prospect', in Owen Dudley Edwards (ed.), *A Claim of Right for Scotland*, Edinburgh, Polygon, 1989, p. 59.
133. *Glasgow Herald*, January 28, 1989.
134. *Scotsman*, February 8, 1989.
135. The term 'central belt activists' seems to have been invented by supporters of Sillars and used frequently

by a *Glasgow Herald* reporter who would quote a
'central belt activist' in unattributed comments attacking
Salmond.

136. Interview with Mike Russell, September 22, 1990.
137. *Scotland on Sunday*, September 23, 1990.
138. *Sun*, January 23, 1992.
139. *Scotsman*, January 29, 1992.

Direct Action and Parliamentary Disruption

Introduction

Movements attempting to bring about radical change may feel constrained by the established political structures and choose to work outside them. Certain movements are 'excluded' from the political system and must use unconventional methods. Campaigners for the extension of the franchise, for example, had little choice other than to use unconventional methods of campaigning. Being excluded from the established political order meant that the unenfranchised would either have to rely on those with votes to act on their behalf or operate entirely outside Parliament. The early labour movement initially had little alternative but to break the law in the pursuit of the right to organise trade unions.

The Scottish national movement does not fit into this category of excluded movements, but it has had impediments in its way which have occasionally made alternative campaign techniques attractive. Gaining public support for the cause, indeed winning the support of a majority or even all of Scotland's elected representatives, might not be enough to bring about change. Home rule within the United Kingdom requires either convincing other parts of the UK of its merits or convincing them that the costs of its denial are in some sense too great. The consequence of this has been a frustration which has made the national movement appear, in a limited way, similar to excluded groups such as the early suffrage and labour movements.

National identity has an important symbolic dimension which lends itself to unconventional styles. Kellas has referred to the 'psychic income' of culture in his study of nationalism in reference to those things which 'satisfy the mental and spiritual needs of human beings" as distinct from 'material interests such as incomes and jobs'.[1] For many activists the display of symbols and affirmation of Scottish identity is an objective in itself rather than a strategy.

Revolutionaries and Resolutionaries

Temptations to blame flaws in the democratic process for the failure of the self-government movement have been great. As early as 1923, the view was being expressed that the demand for self-government was continually being refused. In a letter from the SHRA to delegates to the Imperial conference meeting in London it was pointed out that at the previous election the Tories had won only 15 seats while the opposition won 59:

> Is it because Scotland has been too constitutional in its methods of pressing for self-government that its demand has been ignored?[2]

But the movement remained constitutional to the point of respect-ability. Occasional attempts to organise revolutionary cells have proved farcical. Following the National Party of Scotland's poor showing in the 1929 election, three of its more colourful characters – Compton Mackenzie, Hugh MacDiarmid and Ruaraidh Erskine – set up Clann Albain (Scotland's Children). Its aim was to undertake illegal and politically sensitive work. It proved more active in its founders' imaginations than in reality. A desire for attention seems to have been as much a motivation as anything else. MacDiarmid was quoted in 1930 saying that the chief of Clann Albain was one of the 'most distinguished living Scotsmen' and that members did not know the names of any of the office bearers.[3] This provoked the attention of the Special Branch and led to Compton Mackenzie, himself a former secret serviceman, being interviewed. Clann Albain's plans were rumoured to include seizing the island of Rhum, occupying Edinburgh Castle, and seizing the Stone of Destiny.[4] It was not to be the last organisation which caused the movement embarrassment by indulging in threats and wild claims.

A less self-indulgent but equally ineffective organisation was set up by Roland Muirhead in 1950. Scottish National Congress had been set up because of the failure to get any independent Scottish Nationalists elected to Parliament after thirty years of effort. It supported a policy of civil disobedience and drew inspiration from the Indian National Congress. It was largely a one-man show with a membership in 1951 of around 70.[5] In 1959 Muirhead admitted that initially there had been two founders of Congress but he was by then the only one left.[6] There was disillusionment with the Parliamentary route. In 1955, Muirhead declined an invitation to stand as an independent Nationalist candidate in a by-election in Greenock on the grounds that he had 'little faith in sending Scots to the London Parliament as a means of securing Scottish self-government'.[7]

A statement issued by Congress in March 1951 promised that Scottish youth who protested against conscription would be pro-tected.[8] In the Commons, Lord Advocate John Wheatley said that it was important to distinguish between revolutionaries and resolutionaries.[9] By 1959, Congress had done little to refute Wheatley's dismissive reaction. The issue of siting Polaris on the Clyde, which played a significant part in reviving the national move-ment in the 1960s, saw Muirhead at the age of 92 taking part in direct action protests.[10] Muirhead's death in August 1964 at the age of 96 effectively killed off Congress. The desire to appear respectable led the SNP to proscribe Congress members from SNP membership in 1958, although there appears to have been little to the group beyond bluster and rhetoric.

A number of unconventional approaches were considered in the 1950s, owing to the movement's weakness at the time. Radio Free Scotland was one of these, and a number of those involved, including Gordon Wilson, were later associated with more conventional forms of politics. As a pirate radio station it had little impact, although it produced a fair number of stories which fed into nationalist mythology.

In the 1960s a secretive body, not dissimilar to Clann Albain of the 1930s, emerged, calling itself the 1320 Club. The SNP's hyper-sensitivity regarding any association with violence led it to prohibit members of the club in 1968. Once more, the 1320 Club's decision to be secretive, if ultimately harmless, was sufficiently embarrassing for conventional nationalists. One individual long associated with unconventional activities was Wendy Wood. In her autobiography, she recounts her refusal to pay national insurance as a protest at the removal of the National Insurance Board from Scotland to Newcastle, and as a means of getting sent to prison in order to publicise the ill-treatment of women prisoners.[11] She was one of the few romantic Scottish nationalists who fulfilled an ambition to be sent to prison. Campaigning for prison reform, vigorous street campaigning against Mosleyite fascists, and removing the Union Jack from Stirling Castle after a rally at Bannockburn in 1932 were among her achievements, but she provoked greater interest among the police than the public at large. Her most dangerous action was a proposed fast to death as an old woman in December 1972, in protest at the Heath Government's failure to deliver its promise of a Scottish assembly. Jim Sillars, then a Labour MP, pleaded with the Government to publish a discussion paper and pleaded with Wood to give up her fast. She did so after six days following a vague reference to a discussion paper on constitutional reform made by Gordon Campbell, Secretary of State for Scotland.[12] Wendy Wood was behind some of the more outlandish and ultimately harmful activities on the fringe of the national movement and was potentially more dangerous, if certainly more sincere, than many other figures who craved attention.

In the 1980s, a body resembling previous secret nationalist societies emerged in reaction to the 1979 defeats. Siol Nan Gaidheal (SNG) (Seed of the Gael) initially professed to be a cultural body and consequently attracted to its membership a few senior nationalist figures. SNG played an active part in opposing the dumping of nuclear waste in the Galloway hills in the early 1980s, but it is usually associated with its black and gold banners, quasi-militaristic uniforms, and extreme language. Its most significant member was Willie MacRae whose intemperate language and impatience found a welcome within SNG. His death in 1985 provided SNG and other fringe groups with the nearest thing to a martyr the movement could offer.

Occasional outbursts of violence have caught media attention over the years, for example the 'Conspiracy Trials' of the early 1950s and the Tartan Army trials the 1970s. The role of *agents provocateurs* is alluded to by many supporters of self-government who realize that violence could only damage their cause. Evidence that this is not simply paranoia was provided in the so-called 'Conspiracy Trials' in the 1950s. A series of articles written in *The People* in 1954 by one of the main witnesses noted the role played by a former personal bodyguard to the British High Commnissioner in Palestine, who instructed the conspirators in the use of firearms and cooperated with the police as an undercover agent.[13] The easiest way to discredit the national movement was to associate it with violence.

Blowing up 'EIIR' post boxes in protest at the designation of the new Queen as Elizabeth the Second caused mainstream home rulers considerable embarrassment. Interviews with figures involved in the national movement at the time confirm that those suspected of involvement were made aware of the undesirability of this course of action, and it was made equally clear that any evidence of involvement would immediately be passed on to the police. It has not always been possible to contain or control the small groups whose activities worried the national movement from the late 1960s. Disentangling fact from fantasy here is not easy, since exaggerating their effect and support is part of the tactics of such groups. It is easy to assemble various incidents over many years to suggest some coherent, systematic underworld of intrigue. There may have been 79 bombing incidents, 40 bank raids, and numerous hoaxes and bomb scares between 1968 and 1990, but this is not evidence of a 'secret war' against 'the Anglo-American state', as one book contrives to suggest.[14] The most striking features of the activities of those who have been convicted have been their counter-productive nature and their utter incompetence.

The Return of the Stone

Not all unconventional campaigning is of the sort discussed above. Much is positive and has been helpful to the national movement. An example of symbolic politics which rattled the British government occurred when the Stone of Destiny was removed from Westminster Abbey at Christmas 1950. Those involved were a group of Glasgow

University students led by Ian Hamilton who has told his story in two books.[15] The removal of the Stone provoked a storm of indignation amongst establishment figures, and considerable mirth in Scotland. It was taken far more seriously at the highest level of government than was appreciated at the time. Discussions at Cabinet level were held on the matter with the Historiographer Royal of Scotland, Dr Henry Meikle, supplying a history of the stone as an appendix to one paper presented to the Cabinet.

The Stone is part of the Coronation throne on which the British sovereign is installed as head of state. It had been in Westminster Abbey for over 650 years. By legend, it had been the biblical pillow on which Jacob had slept at Bethel and was brought to Scotland from Egypt and eventually to Scone where Kings of the Picts and, later, the Scots were crowned. According to legend, the last Scottish king to be crowned on the Stone was John Balliol in 1292. Four years later Balliol had sent it to London along with other artifacts. Following the battle of Bannockburn a treaty was negotiated at Northampton in 1328 which provided for, amongst other things, the return of the Stone to Scotland. Nothing was done until the Public Records (Scotland) Act, 1937 was passed when nine historic documents were sent by the English Master of the Rolls to Register House in Edinburgh but the Stone remained in London. *The Bulletin*, sister paper of the *Glasgow Herald* and edited by a leading nationalist, led the criticism and called for the return of the Stone. Wendy Wood protested in Edinburgh with a placard, 'England disgorges some of the loot, but where is the Stone of Destiny?'[16] Meikle's account of the story of the Stone for the Cabinet ended with the Latin prophecy which had been translated by Sir Walter Scott:

> Unless the fates are faithless found,
> And prophet's voice be vain,
> Where'er this monument is found,
> The Scottish race shall reign.[17]

In 1924 a bill had been presented in Parliament by David Kirkwood, Labour MP for Dumbarton Burghs, to remove the Stone from Westminster Abbey and place it in Holyrood Palace in Edinburgh. Kirkwood maintained that the Stone was a 'symbol of our nationhood. It is a venerable relic' [18] His appeal was based on sentiment:

> When we seek bread and shelter for our people, we also demand roses. The great spiritual, historical and sentimental bonds that bind together a race – these we cherish. The more material things of life are alone but as bread that turns to dust and ashes in the mouth. They are the materialists who jeer and sneer at the demand of a nation for the ownership and custody of the symbol of its nationhood.[19]

Lord Apsey, Conservative MP for Southampton, spoke against the bill. His motives were equally sentimental, and he quoted the Latin verse associated with the Stone.[20] The Commons voted by 201 votes to 171 against, with the Clydesiders, including Tom Johnston, supporting the measure.

The idea of removing the Stone had occurred to Hugh MacDiarmid in 1934. He planned the escapade on a trip to London on literary business but when he met up with his accomplices he had to admit to a problem: he had spent the money raised in a pub.[21] The raid which did succeed came after the war and involved MacDiarmid's foe in the national movement, John MacCormick. MacCormick was then leader of Scottish Convention, the respectable cross-party home rule pressure group. He could not, therefore, be involved directly. The removal of the Stone provoked indignant protests from the British establishment. The Dean of Westminster condemned it as an act of sacrilege and vandalism. Having returned the Stone to Scotland it was not clear what should be done next. Public opinion appeared to be sympathetic, if only because of the audacity of the act and because nobody had been hurt. With the Stone lying in hiding it was serving no real purpose, and the decision was taken on MacCormick's advice to return it. Four months after it was removed from Westminster Abbey, Hamilton and his accomplices placed the Stone in Arbroath Abbey, a historically significant place since it was here that a declaration of Scottish independence had been signed by Scottish bishops in 1320.

The reaction of the Government was interesting, demonstrating that the Stone's symbolic significance was at least as great for the British authorities as for Scottish nationalists. At a Cabinet meeting the day after its deposit in Arbroath, the Home Secretary told his colleagues that arrangements were being made to bring it back to London 'in circumstances which should obviate the danger of any demonstrations'.[22] A further Cabinet meeting was informed that the police had identified those responsible for the Stone's removal. The difficulty for the Government was deciding whether to take action against them. The Attorney-General, Sir Hartley Shawcross, recommended that no action be taken, but during the discussion it was recognised that difficulties might arise if it became known that the authorities were aware of the identity of those responsible but were not prepared to proceed against them.[23] The Cabinet invited the Lord Chancellor to arrange a meeting with the Ministers concerned to advise the Attorney General.

A subsequent cabinet meeting discussed a memorandum from the Attorney-General. In this, Shawcross pointed out that it might be problematic to prosecute the individuals concerned as it would be difficult to prove that they had intended to deprive the owner of the Stone permanently. Juries were unpredictable and, in Shawcross's estimation, a jury would 'probably not convict of the felony of larceny'.[24] Similar arguments applied to the crime of 'sacrilege', the crime of breaking and entering a Church with intent to commit a felony. A third alternative was the charge of malicious damage. The wooden throne in Westminster Abbey had been damaged in the act of removing the Stone but, as Shawcross noted, this was 'incidental and collateral to the main offence'.[25] Additionally, only one of the four had admitted to damaging it. Other difficulties had to be taken into account:

> I am satisfied that a prosecution would do no good except perhaps to the defendants to whom it would give the opportunity of being regarded as martyrs if they were convicted or as heroes if they were acquitted . . . In Scotland a prosecution would produce a very adverse reaction.[26]

At the Cabinet meeting concern was expressed about some of the Attorney-General's points. It was suggested that other nationalist movements might attempt to remove the Lane Pictures from the Tate Gallery or the Elgin Marbles from the British Museum. It was decided to avoid any suggestion that the incident had brought discredit to those who supported Scottish self-government but that the Government should condemn sensational or extreme measures in pursuit of it. The Cabinet also invited the Scottish Secretary, Hector McNeil, to submit a memorandum to the Cabinet on issues arising in connection with the future location of the Stone.[27]

The subsequent memoranda and Cabinet discussions show how close the Labour Government came to returning the Stone to Scotland. McNeil's memorandum included the appendix on the history of the Stone by the Historiographer Royal for Scotland referred to above. Meikle's view was that under the terms of the Treaty of Northampton of 1328 there was an obligation to return the Stone to Scotland. McNeil offered three alternatives: leave the Stone in Westminster Abbey; return it to Scotland for custody between coronations; and arrange for it to be displayed in various Commonwealth capitals at different times. He found the second 'attractive', with St Margaret's Chapel in Edinburgh Castle the most suitable destination. This would be seen in Scotland as a 'generous gesture'. To do otherwise would result in 'continuing agitation not only by the nationalist movement but by the Church of Scotland – which is being very vocal in the matter – and from other quarters'.[28] A memorandum by the Lord Chancellor, Lord Jowitt, disagreed with Meikle's view of the Treaty of Northampton, although this was not fully explained. The main question he dealt with concerned the custody of the Stone. He concluded that it was for the Crown on the advice of his Ministers to make a decision, although the Dean and Chapter of Westminster should be consulted.[29]

The Cabinet meeting which discussed these memoranda decided to postpone a decision for at least a year to avoid the appearance of a 'concession to the recent act of vandalism in Westminster Abbey'.[30] A problem arose a few days later when the Paymaster-General told the Lords that the Government was considering where the Stone should be placed and that consultations were in progress with the Church of Scotland.[31] This was not quite what had been agreed at the Cabinet meeting but it was decided at the next meeting that nothing should be done either to retract the Paymaster-General's statement or to raise the issue again.[32] A motion in the Lords moved by Lord Brabazon in May 1951 found some support for its return to Scotland.[33]

Any prospect of the Stone being returned to Scotland after a respectable interval of time ended when the Conservatives won the election in October 1951. The Scottish Secretary, James Stuart, and Lord Chancellor Simonds prepared a memorandum for the Cabinet in February 1952. The Dean of Westminster, who strongly opposed returning the Stone to Scotland, had approached the Government the previous December urging them to make a decision soon. Stuart and Simonds argued that the Stone should remain in Westminster Abbey.[34] At a Cabinet meeting which discussed the matter there was general agreement but it was decided to consult the Leader of the Opposition and 'certain prominent Scottish Members of the Opposition' as similar consultations had taken place previously.[35] At the subsequent Cabinet it was disclosed that the Leader of the Opposition had signalled his agreement. As a Parliamentary Question was to be asked in the Lords the following month suggesting that the Stone be placed in St Giles Cathedral, Edinburgh, it was decided to use this opportunity to state publicly that the stone would remain in Westminster Abbey.[36]

The episode had caused far more anxiety in Government circles than was probably appreciated at the time. In the conclusion to his book on the Stone, Ian Hamilton asked whether it had been worth the trouble. His answer is significant:

> Nobody sang in Scotland in the middle part of this century. To be more correct, those who sang did not derive their songs from Scotland. Their sources were foreign and what they sang was only an alien copy of other peoples' ways of life. Now everyone sings Scottish songs, and if I were a unionist politician of whatever party, but especially of the Labour Party, I would be counting the songs, rather than the votes. The people who make the songs of a country, have a habit of making the laws also.[37]

The reaction of the Attlee Government suggests that this was a view which they shared to some extent. The matter was not treated lightly but took up time at a number of meetings of the Cabinet. Cabinets had previously had placed before them memoranda which referred to the national movement, but rarely had an issue caused such consternation. This 'hunk of sandstone', as Hamilton called it,[38] was as symbolically important to those who wanted to maintain the union as it was to those who wanted it to end.

The removal of the Stone was a classic example of student politics: an irreverent gesture of defiance. This form of politics seems to have suited the national movement well but it gave the impression that it was not entirely serious. As if to confirm this, electoral success for the movement around this time was confined to winning a university rectorial contest. In 1931 the novelist Compton Mackenzie was elected by the students of Glasgow University. John MacCormick had been one of the principal backers of that campaign. In 1950, shortly before the Stone episode, MacCormick was himself returned as rector by Glasgow University students. His rectorial address in early January 1951 was made at the height of interest in the Stone and was a typically ribald student affair. MacCormick seems to have been most at ease amongst students and commanded a personal following amongst many of them, probably owing to his idealism and oratory.

The experience with the Stone made successive governments much more sensitive to symbols of identity. In 1956 the Postmaster-General submitted a memorandum to the Cabinet on 'Stamp Issues for Scotland, Northern Ireland and Wales' in which the question of producing postage stamps carrying symbols or designs appropriate to the country or area of origin was discussed. The question was by no means clear-cut:

> An objection to the proposal may be that it might encourage extreme nationalist elements. It might, on the other hand, have the opposite effect by giving satisfaction to the many who, while not holding 'nationalist' views, are warmly attached to their country of birth. The dominance of the Sovereign's head on all stamps would symbolise the unity which, combined with diversity, provides the continuing strength of the British tradition.[39]

The question was discussed at Cabinet level. The Scottish Secretary was unable to attend the meeting but had given the Home Secretary authority to express Scottish Office support for the idea of a Scottish symbol. The Chancellor of the Exchequer was concerned that this would provoke a demand for separate coinage but the balance of opinion was in favour of the proposal as a 'harmless means of giving satisfaction to national feeling in the constituent parts of the United Kingdom without serious risk of encouraging separatist movements'.[40] Two years later a similar matter arose when the Burns Federation approached the Postmaster-General with a proposal to produce a special stamp to mark the bicentenary of the birth of the Scottish poet. This was rejected on the grounds that it ran contrary to accepted practice and it was important that any 'arrangement was not associated with Scottish Nationalist sentiment'.[41] British governments have been at least as conscious of the importance of political symbols as the self-government movement.

The EIIR Case

With no prospect of a Scottish Parliament while the Conservatives were in power in the 1950s, modest victories to give heart to campaigners were the best hope for the movement. It was not that Scottish identity was threatened; in its annual report for 1951, the Church and Nation Committee of the Church of Scotland had noted the growing interest in Scottish history and tradition, and the stimulation of dramatic and musical activities which they attributed to the 'resurgence of Scottish national sentiment'.[42] Scottish cultural identity thrived alongside British political identity. This provided at least the potential for developing a Scottish political identity. In this very British era, one significant victory was achieved which has become part of the mythology of contemporary Scottish nationalism, particularly notable as it concerned a primary facet of Britishness, the monarchy. John MacCormick's legal tussle with the Lord Advocate resulted in a much-needed victory. The case had its origins in the coronation of the new Queen. Princess Elizabeth was to succeed her father on the throne and to assume the title Queen Elizabeth II under the Royal Style and Titles Act, 1953. The claim that she was the second Elizabeth offended Scots because the first Elizabeth had only been Queen of England.

The two main protagonists involved were MacCormick and Hamilton, both of whom had been involved in the Stone of Destiny episode. MacCormick and Hamilton were respectively chairman and secretary of the Scottish Covenant Association, the respectable home rule pressure group, but raised the action as private individuals with MacCormick acting for himself in the Court of Session. Hamilton was then training for the bar and his case was taken by John

Bayne, an active home ruler and advocate. The basis of the case was not simply the fact that the title was historically inaccurate but that it involved the principle of Scottish popular sovereignty and challenged Dicey's notion of Parliamentary sovereignty. Essentially, the Scottish principle maintained that the people were sovereign while that of Dicey maintained that the Crown in Parliament could not be bound by any other authority, including the people. As presented by MacCormick, the case involved a conflict between English and Scottish legal traditions. Few Scots, including Scots lawyers, were probably aware of the distinction before the Royal Titles case but it was to become a part of case law referred to in any standard work on constitutional law and a piece of nationalist mythology.

MacCormick appeared before Lord Guthrie in the Court of Session three days before the coronation of Queen Elizabeth, where his claim was dismissed on three grounds: the title was authorised by Act of Parliament and therefore not subject to a legal challenge, the Treaty of Union did not prevent any numeral to be used by a reigning monarch whether historically accurate or otherwise, and the petitioners had no title to sue as the question was one of public policy not of legal right. In finding that the 'doctrine of the sovereignty of Parliament is recognised in Scotland as a basic principle of constitutional law', Lord Guthrie refused to accept the basis of MacCormick's case.[43] However, this left open the possibility of an appeal which was pursued.

The subsequent course of the case proved fortunate for MacCormick. It was held before three judges including Lord Cooper, Lord President of the Court of Session, Scotland's most senior judge. He had been a Unionist MP in the late 1930s before his elevation to the bench but had been drawn to nationalist politics. Cooper had privately informed Sir John Reith of the BBC during the war that if he gave up being a judge, he would have returned to politics as a Nationalist.[44] Cooper overturned part of the previous judgement of Lord Guthrie. He found against MacCormick but his judgement was sufficiently ambiguous in one important respect to allow the movement to interpret it as a victory. While accepting Guthrie's second and third points, Cooper's judgement on Parliamentary sovereignty was significantly different:

The principle of the unlimited Sovereignty of Parliament is a distinctively English principle which has no counterpart in Scottish Constitutional law. It derives its origins from Coke and Blackstone, and was widely popularised during the nineteenth century by Bagehot and Dicey, the latter having stated the doctrine in its classic form in his Constitutional Law. Considering that the Union legislation extinguished the Parliaments of Scotland and England, and replaced them by a new Parliament, I have difficulty in seeing why it should have been supposed that the new Parliament of Great Britain must inherit all the peculiar characteristics of the English Parliament but none of the Scottish Parliament, as if all that happened in 1707 was that Scottish representatives were admitted to the Parliament of England. That is not what was done.[45]

The case had been rejected but it was a moral victory and provoked a reaction amongst legal thinkers on the nature of the Anglo-Scottish Union.[46] In attempting to assert the idea of Scottish politico-legal distinctiveness, at least amongst a section of society, it had proved successful. As a landmark in the history of the national movement it proved encouraging. In some ways the term had greater symbolic importance than it has had practical application but it is something which activists saw and still see as important. It is difficult to measure the importance of symbolic victories, but in a movement which had just come through a period when high hopes had been shattered it was a useful fillip.

There were however short-term costs, whatever long-term gains are now evident. The monarchy was seen as sacrosanct by many of the more 'respectable' elements in the national movement. MacCormick, Hamilton, and Bayne appear to have had no overtly republican sympathies, although targeting such a symbol of British identity as the monarchy might easily have been interpreted in such a way. The fear that challenging the Act might be seen as disloyal to the Crown had worried many of the more conventional campaigners for home rule, especially following the Stone of Destiny episode. In May, John Campbell, a prominent Glasgow solicitor, resigned from the national committee of the Covenant Association bringing to light the extent of discontent. Other prominent home rulers had already severed their links with the association including Dr Nevile Davidson of Glasgow Cathedral and John Cameron QC, Dean of the Faculty of

Advocates.[47] Other less well-known figures also drifted away, mainly due to disillusionment following the failure of the Covenant to secure a Scottish Parliament but triggered too by the more radical approach adopted by MacCormick.

Parliamentary Disruption

Parliamentary disruption had been a key weapon in the armoury of the Irish nationalists in the nineteenth century. Parnell's mastery of the technique lay in his 'iron stamina, a cool indifference to the clubman's atmosphere of the House of Commons, and his concern only for the way in which what was said there would strike people in Ireland'.[48] The Commons sat for twenty-six hours, its longest continuous session, debating a bill dealing with South Africa in July 1877 when business was disrupted. Subsequently, Parliamentary procedure was tightened to give more power to the front benches. There has never been any comparable sustained campaign in Parliament by Scottish home rulers in part because the two front benches became extremely powerful over the Commons as a whole.

Frustration at the failure of Buchanan's home rule bill led to some discussion of Parliamentary obstruction in 1924 within the SHRA. A resolution was passed at the general council of the SHRA suggesting that Scottish MPs should:

> combine to devise a policy, whether that of deciding that no Bill applying to Scotland should be permitted to take precedence of a satisfactory Home Rule or other policy, which would induce the Government to give immediate attention to the demand of Scotland for self-government through a Scottish Parliament.[49]

Amongst those who supported the resolution was James Maxton, one of the 'Red Clydesiders'. He made it clear that he did not see this as a commitment to Parliamentary disruption. He conceded that disruption might be justified and effective but argued that Labour had to be given the chance of 'restoring Scottish independence'. Labour had not been in office as often as other parties.[50]

In February 1925, Scottish Labour MPs held up Parliamentary business in a wrangle over the appointment of an English MP as

chairman of the Scottish Grand Committee (SGC), preventing business proceeding in the committee.[51] This was not the first occasion
that the committee had been chaired by an English MP; only about
18 bills out of 70 or so debated in the SGC from its inception in 1907,
had been chaired by a Scottish MP. Roland Muirhead recorded his
pleasure in a letter to Tom Johnston:

> I trust this is only a prelude to more and stiffer obstruction, and that
> Members will not desist until the Scottish claim that the Bill is a breach
> of the Treaty has been admitted.[52]

The matter was resolved when it was agreed to adjourn the business
on the understanding that the Chairman's Panel Committee would
consider the matter again. No change was proposed by the Panel. As
one newspaper headline put it, it was 'much ado about nothing'.[53]

Robert McIntyre caused irritation following his election to Parliament for the SNP in 1945 when he refused to be sponsored
by any other MP, which meant that he could not take his seat.
The custom of new members requiring two sponsors had been
introduced in 1688, prior to the Treaty of Union, as was pointed out
by a Labour MP.[54] McIntyre's disruption of proceedings happened
when the Commons had assembled for a Churchillian oration in
memory of F. D. Roosevelt who had just died. McIntyre's refusal
to accept sponsorship has not become part of nationalist folklore
despite having all the necessary ingredients. He not only succeeded
in holding up events in the Commons, but also provoked a debate
between Winston Churchill and Aneurin Bevan which focused on
the conflict between the 'privileges, usages and customs of the House
and the right of the constituents of this country to elect a person
to this House', as Bevan expressed it, or between Parliamentary and
popular sovereignty, as McIntyre might have described it.

The SNP MPs elected in 1974 showed far more respect for
the Commons than had McIntyre. No disruption of Commons
procedure was ever attempted and no debate took place at SNP
conferences on Parnellite tactics. This was probably due to the
expectation that some measure of home rule was inevitable and
would only be blocked if the SNP were to lose its image of
respectability.

Some Labour MPs talked about disrupting Parliament following the 1983 election. A group of five Scottish Labour MPs (George Foulkes, John Maxton, Dennis Canavan, John Home Robertson, and David Marshall) prepared a paper for discussion at a seminar for Scottish Labour MPs, the party's Scottish Council, the Scottish Trades Union Congress, local government representatives, and the Cooperative Party in September 1983. They noted the party's commitment at that year's conference to campaign 'all out for devolution, irrespective of which Government is in power at Westminster'. It was argued that Labour's position on devolution was stronger than on other issues as the Conservative Government had 'no mandate' to rule Scotland. In order to succeed, a range of tactics would be required:

> demonstrative action and protests will need to be backed up by Parliamentary obstruction, local authority and trade union pressure as well as possible challenges in the courts to the Secretary of State's authority.[55]

The Scottish Grand Committee was seen as an 'alternative source of authority directly challenging the Scottish Office.' As an elected body it would, they felt, be in a 'much stronger position to provoke the constitutional crisis necessary to get changes', with meetings in Edinburgh evolving into an unofficial Scottish Assembly. Local authorities and trade unions were important, but the means of putting pressure on the Government were not explained. Parliamentary action was stressed, perhaps because the authors were MPs. Packing Parliamentary committees to reflect the Scottish party balance, forcing votes, and unofficially calling meetings of the Grand Committee were all mooted alongside extra-Parliamentary activities. Nothing came of these proposals and the ideas were quietly forgotten. A few years later it was the SNP which picked up some of the ideas contained in the paper only to be condemned for doing so by some of the Labour MPs who had argued for this approach in 1983.

Non-Payment Campaigns

In 1927, Tom Johnston addressed a meeting of the Scottish National Convention. Afterwards he was asked a series of questions, including whether he would support a referendum if the Convention's home rule bill was voted down in Parliament. Johnston's reply was that he would go a 'great deal further than that':

> If I saw a big movement in Scotland having an active interest at election times, and being refused by Parliament I think the withholding of income tax by a large number of people in this country would bring Mr Winston Churchill [Chancellor of the Exchequer], who had already pledged himself in favour of the measure, to book very quickly.[56]

This was radical rhetoric, designed to win the approval of activists, rather than a serious proposal to secure a Scottish Parliament. Even Tom Johnston would indulge in this from time to time.

Not every proposal to withhold tax was so cynical. Even the Scottish Covenant Association considered civil disobedience in the early 1950s after its demands were ignored. A confidential memorandum written by Ian Hamilton, national organiser, in the early 1950s suggested a campaign focusing on transport. He noted that the Association had previously focused on 'emotional' issues at the expense of the 'practical', though his proposal on this occasion was not devoid of an emotional element itself. The case for a Forth Road Bridge and improved Highland transport would be made by a 'Motor Car Taxation strike'. The car tax fell due at the start of each year and all motorists had to pay £12.10/- within a fortnight or face a fine. Hamilton proposed that the Association enlist a body of 100 motorists who would delay payment. A document to be signed by non-payers was proposed.

Hamilton claimed that the middle-class nature of those who would be involved in the protest would add weight to the campaign:

> It is not news when avowed revolutionaries bread the law; it is news when a middle class body breaks the law. I think we would attract space in the English papers where we so badly need it. I also think we would excite sympathy throughout the world.[57]

If the campaign was successful, Hamilton envisaged it extending to other areas, including refusing to pay the television licence if the BBC 'became too unpopular'. It was a bold proposal made by a radical within a conservative organisation. It would have had a greater chance of acceptance in the more radical Scottish National Congress, but had the Covenant Association adopted this approach it would have had far greater impact. The Association was too timid and respectable to go along with Hamilton's proposal.

Poll tax and Parliamentary Disruption

Over 30 years later, the idea of a non-payment campaign was launched by the SNP. The Government abolished domestic rates, a local property tax, and introduced a flat-rate charge in the dying days of the 1983–87 Parliament. It was designed to protect the beleaguered Scottish Conservatives. However, the movement in opposition to the community charge was to prove far more dangerous to the Conservative Party than the middle-class revolt against rates which had provoked its introduction. An early symbolic victory was scored when the term 'poll tax' became almost universally used in preference to 'community charge'.[58] The fact that the legislation applied only to Scotland led to accusations that Scotland was being singled out. John Maxton, a Labour front-bench spokesman, argued in February 1987 that the poll tax had been 'imposed in Scotland by a government with no mandate to do so and one that the Scottish people had so clearly rejected'.[59] Timothy Raison, an English Conservative MP, expressed relief that Scotland was to be the 'legislative pacemaker or guinea-pig'.[60]

Opposition to the poll tax in Scotland was overwhelming, and the campaign against it offered the national movement a golden opportunity. As Barker has noted,

> If Scotland is seen as a distinct political community, either by virtue of its history and culture, or by virtue of its geographical and economic relationship with the rest of the United Kingdom, or by virtue of its voting patterns at recent general elections, then the poll tax can be presented as one foisted on a small community by its larger neighbour, voted through by English MPs against both the general and the particular wishes of the people of Scotland. As such, both the principle of nationality and the principle of democracy are affronted.[61]

The strength of the anti-poll tax movement and the potential it offered for mobilization beyond the immediate issue lay in linking the constitutional question to the most important political issue of the day. But equally it demonstrated that the Labour party's electoral strength in Scotland did not equate to political power. Labour could not stop the poll tax. The question was whether the poll tax would be used to benefit the national movement or whether it would be used in the narrower partisan interests of the SNP.

The SNP had little experience of direct action, although a number of its members had been involved in direct action anti-nuclear campaigns. The party had passed resolutions at conferences, notably in 1979 and 1981, supporting civil disobedience in campaigns against nuclear dumping, in defence of the Gaelic language, and on the issue of unemployment, but little had come of these. At its 1987 conference the SNP backed away from supporting direct action against the poll tax, although a number of members either urged the party to take such a stand or personally committed themselves to do so. The early rumblings of opposition came from outside the party. Tenants associations and other community groups were particularly active while the SNP leadership looked askance at proposals to launch a non-payment campaign. Towards the end of that year, however, the party's attitude hardened as the scale of opposition became clear.

Initially, the SNP had called for a cross-party campaign against the poll tax but this was rejected by the Labour-controlled Convention of Scottish Local Authorities and trade unions,[62] although four months later a working group was set up organised by the STUC. As had happened with the Constitutional Convention, the SNP became suspicious of cross-party campaigning. The STUC campaign document made no reference to non-payment and the SNP sought to amend it, arguing that a mass campaign of non-payment might be necessary and that it would be impossible to sustain such a campaign without early preparations.[63] The withdrawal of the SNP was condemned in the media but the party's fear that non-payment would be 'shunted into never-never land' had foundation. The SNP, having initially been rebuffed when it proposed cross-party action, was now accused of sectarianism.

Early in 1988, the party announced that it would fight local elections in May seeking a mandate to organise a mass campaign against the poll tax. If the SNP won more votes than any other party then a mass non-payment campaign would be launched. The prospect of this happening was remote. At the previous district council elections the SNP had won 11.7% of the vote behind Labour (45.7%), Conservatives (21.4) and the Alliance (12.8%). The SNP's stance was designed to put Labour, as Scotland's largest party, under pressure. However, a growing element within the SNP was coming to accept the need for a non-payment strategy in its own right. A poll in March 1988 showed that support for non-payment (42%) was about the same level as opposition to it (44%), and amongst SNP and Labour supporters there were clear majorities in favour of non-payment.[64]

Difficulties in the Labour party also played a part. Dick Douglas, Labour MP for Dunfermline West, had resigned as chairman of the backbench group of Scottish MPs and attacked his leader at the Scottish party's conference where it had been decided to postpone making a decision on how to oppose the poll tax. That same conference saw the launch of a new fringe group within the Labour party in Scotland. Scottish Labour Action prioritised home rule and called for a tougher response to the poll tax.

In March 1988, Alex Salmond interrupted the Chancellor of the Exchequer's budget speech and was suspended from the House of Commons. The reaction to the speech suggested that there was potential support for a more radical approach. The party's standing in the polls rose above 20% the following month and rarely fell below that level from then to the next election. The SNP won 21.3% of the vote at the district elections, almost double its vote four years before. Labour still had a huge lead with 42.6% of the vote but the SNP felt justified in pursuing its non-payment strategy as it had just come ahead of the Conservatives. The party officially backed non-payment at its national council meeting in June.

The final endorsement of the strategy within the SNP came later that year at the party's annual conference in Inverness. This proved to be one of the most important conferences in the SNP's history. In addition to launching its independence in Europe policy, the party supported poll tax non-payment with only one speaker opposing it. He had asked whether the party could claim to have a mandate when it had won only 21% of the vote on local elections while criticising the Conservatives, who had won 24% at the general election, for running Scotland without a mandate.[65]

The confusion over what constituted a mandate for the launch of the poll tax campaign was compounded shortly afterwards by the launch of the party's recruitment of an 'army' of non-payers. Initially the party intended that these should be people who could afford to pay the tax: 'Can Pay, Won't Pay' was to be its slogan and a target of 100,000 was set. This represented 2.6% of Scots liable to pay the poll tax, and would have reduced local authorities' income by less than 1%. But the figure owed more to rhetorical flourish than calculation. No thought went into how the party would cope with collecting such a vast list of names and it came under pressure from opponents and the media for evidence of its list. Over time, the SNP's strategy changed. Under the direction of Kenny MacAskill, poll tax spokesman, the aim seemed to be to gather together as many non-payers and play down the 'Can Pay, Won't Pay' strategy. There had been little thought at the outset on the long-term tactics of the campaign.

However, the SNP's difficulties were nothing compared to Labour's. Before Labour's recall conference to discuss the poll tax, Dennis Canavan, Labour MP for Falkirk West, argued that if Scots were constantly denied their legitimate demands as expressed at the ballot box then the Treaty of Union was a 'Treaty of Treachery which no Labour politician should defend'.[66] However, the conference met in Govan and voted against non-payment. This was the prelude to the Govan by-election. SNP candidate Jim Sillars made non-payment a central part of his successful return to full-time politics. Govan ended any doubts that non-payment had popular appeal. Following the by-election, Sillars promised a programme of 'carefully chosen' disruption of Parliament and maintained that there was a need to find common ground in Scottish politics.[67] These objectives proved incompatible.

The bitterness between Labour and the SNP was at its height around this time. Polls in early 1989 showed the gap between the parties narrowing. Labour hatred of apostates, especially those who became troublemakers, was vicious. There was little prospect of the Labour leadership seeking common ground with the SNP in normal circumstances and Labour's electoral strategy from the mid-1980s dictated that it appear respectable in order to win Conservative votes in the south of England. Sillars' intended disruption of the 1989 budget, following the success of his colleague Alex Salmond the year before, was foiled by Neil Kinnock when the Labour leader went beyond the call of duty in helping the Government present its budget statement in the Commons, to the SNP's fury. Dick Douglas's disillusion with Labour over the poll tax grew. In early 1990, he decided to stand as an independent Labour anti-poll tax candidate in the regional council elections and was finally expelled from the party after 42 years as a member.[68] In October he joined the SNP to become the fifth member of its Parliamentary group. His gradual move towards the SNP only soured the already poor relations between the two parties.

Winding up the non-payment campaign was not without difficulty. The Government's abandonment of the poll tax in 1991 was not retrospective. Bills still had to be paid and the SNP had paid little attention to this. Its initial 'Can Pay, Won't Pay' campaign would have been easier to wind up because those who had been encouraged to withhold payment would have been in a position to pay up when the campaign was over. However, little effort had been made to encourage supporters to prepare for the eventual success of the campaign and pay the poll tax. Neither was it clear what the party should do to protect those who fell into the 'Can't Pay, Won't Pay' category. Non-payers had been swelled by vast numbers of those who realised that local authorities did not have the resources to chase them, and it was possible to avoid payment on purely selfish grounds.

The timing of the Government's *volte face* on the poll tax was potentially to the SNP's advantage. It had organised a special conference to debate Europe and this could have been used to celebrate the victory over the Government. Instead, the lack of clarity in the SNP's poll tax strategy meant that a heated debate was held on whether the party had scored a victory and whether to end non-payment. By 244 votes to 132, the party voted to end its 'Can Pay, Won't Pay' campaign. Over a third of delegates did not think there was a victory to celebrate. The campaign ended in confusion, as it had begun. Its objectives had been defined in broad terms: to defeat the poll tax and strengthen the case for self-government. In reality, another objective had intruded, and embarrassing the Labour Party came to dominate the SNP's non-payment campaign. In part, this was a reaction to the conservative response to the poll tax of Scotland's Labour establishment, who in their turn wanted to undermine the SNP more than the tax. The anti-poll tax movement could have been a much more serious challenge to the legitimacy of Conservative rule in Scotland, mobilizing the national and labour movements. Divisions within and between the two most significant progressive movements in Scottish politics meant that its victory was limited. The poll tax was defeated but little emerged from the debris. The lesson appeared to be that direct action could be divisive and dangerous as well as foster self-confidence.

The Government's decision to abandon the poll tax may have owed as much to its inherent impracticability as to non-payment, but non-payment played a part in highlighting its deficiencies and the outrage it provoked. It marked a victory for the non-payers rather than the official Labour opposition. Labour's 'Stop It' campaign was cosmetic. In terms of creating an episode in radical history, this was one in which the national movement had played a more concerted and proud part than the official labour movement, although it was where these two movements met that the most interesting developments occurred. It proved that the combination of the labour and self-government movements could be a very powerful political force. Equally, it showed that more radical campaigning could stir up party political enmities even more than conventional styles of campaigning.

Conclusion

For the most part, the movement for Scottish self-government has been highly conventional and respectable. On those few occasions that direct action and Parliamentary disruption have been proposed, there has been at least a minority within the movement who have opposed its use. Even those cases which have become part of nationalist folklore, such as the removal of the Stone of Destiny, were at the time frowned upon by leading figures in the movement. Another striking feature of the movement has been the extent to which leading figures have promised radical action but failed to deliver. The radical rhetoric of the Scottish self-government movement has generally been just that. From promises to disrupt Parliament in the 1920s to Labour home rulers' talk of challenging the Conservatives' 'mandate to rule Scotland' in the 1980s, there have been numerous examples.

of movement activists being led up the radical path only to discover it leads to a comfortable and conservative career at Westminster.

Paradoxically, the movement has shown remarkable reverence for Parliamentary proceedings, given that central to the movement's objectives is a belief that Westminster's importance should be limited. Home rulers contradict themselves and undermine their cause by treating Westminster with reverence. It would be wrong, however, to ignore those many occasions and individuals offering a different perspective. A genuinely radical tradition exists which acknowledges in action the need to employ a strategy with less importance attached to elections to Westminster and which is less in awe of Parliament. The 1980s suggested that the more radical tradition was being rediscovered.

1. James G. Kellas, *The Politics of Nationalism and Ethnicity*, Basingstoke, Macmillan, 1991, pp. 61–62.
2. *Glasgow Herald*, November 1, 1923.
3. Alan Bold, *MacDiarmid*, London, Paladin, 1990, p. 282.
4. Andro Linklater, *Compton Mackenzie*, London, Hogarth Press, 1992, p. 234.
5. *Glasgow Herald*, March 19, 1951.
6. *Observer*, August 2, 1959.
7. NLS, Acc 3721, Box 49/167, Letter to Capt. Pape from R. E. Muirhead, November 14, 1955.
8. *Glasgow Herald*, March 19, 1951.
9. Hansard, Commons, vol. 486, April 3, 1951, col. 17.
10. *Observer*, February 19, 1961.
11. Wendy Wood, *Yours Sincerely for Scotland*, London, Arthur Barker, 1970, pp. 79–82.
12. *Scotsman*, December 7–14, 1972.
13. *The People*, October 10, 17, 31, 1954.
14. Andrew Murray Scott and Iain Macleay, *Britain's Secret War: Tartan Terrorism and the Anglo-American State*, Edinburgh, Mainstream, 1990.
15. Ian Hamilton, *A Touch of Treason*, Moffat, Lochar Publishing Ltd, 1990; *The Taking of the Stone of Destiny*, Moffat, Lochar Publishing, 1991.
16. Ian Hamilton, *Op. Cit.*, 1990, p. 48.
17. PRO, Cabinet Papers, CP(51) 117, April 26, 1951.
18. Hansard, Commons, July 15, 1924, vol. 176, col. 217.

19. *Ibid.*, col. 217–8.
20. *Ibid.*, col. 220.
21. Alan Bold, *MacDiarmid*, London, Paladin, 1990, pp. 362–7.
22. PRO, Cabinet Minutes, CM27(51)6, April 12, 1951.
23. *Ibid.*, April 16, 1951.
24. PRO, Cabinet Papers, CP(51)111, April 17, 1951.
25. *Ibid.*
26. *Ibid.*
27. PRO, Cabinet Minutes, CM29(51)4, April, 19, 1951.
28. PRO, Cabinet Papers, CP(51)117, April 26, 1951, 'The Stone of Scone' Hector McNeil.
29. *Ibid.*, CP(51)120, March 30, 1951.
30. PRO, Cabinet Minutes, CM34(51)3, May 10, 1951.
31. Hansard, Lords, vol. 171, May 9, 1951 col. 855.
32. PRO, Cabinet Minutes, CM35(51)3, May 10, 1951.
33. Hansard, Lords, vol. 171, May 9, 1951, colc. 829–58.
34. PRO, Cabinet Papers, C(52)26, February 8, 1952.
35. PRO, Cabinet Minutes, 15(52)2, February 11, 1952.
36. *Ibid.*, CC20(52)7, February 1952.
37. Ian Hamilton *Op.Cit.*, 1991, p. 203..
38. Ian Hamilton *Op. Cit.*, 1990, p. 62.
39. PRO, Cabinet Papers, CP(56) 148, Memo. by Paymaster-General, June 15, 1956.
40. PRO, Cabinet Conclusions, CM(56) 44(9), June 19, 1956.
41. *Ibid.*, CM(58)45(5) May 22, 1958.
42. *Glasgow Herald*, May 4, 1951.
43. *Session Cases*, 1953.
44. Christopher Harvie, *No Gods and Precious Few Heroes*, London, Edward Arnold, 1981, p. 103.
45. Quoted in appendix to John MacCormick, *Flag in the Wind*, London, Victor Gollancz, p. 216.
46. See for example K. W. B. Middleton, 'New Thoughts on the Union Between England and Scotland', *Juridical Review* vol. 76, 1954.
47. *Glasgow Herald*, May 5, 1952.
48. Robert Kee, *The Green Flag: a history of Irish Nationalism*, London, Weidenfeld and Nicolson, 1972, p. 364.
49. *Glasgow Evening Citizen/Glasgow Herald*, June 16, 1924.
50. *Glasgow Herald*, June 16, 1924.
51. *Ibid.*, February 27, 1925.
52. NLS, Acc. 3721, Box 83/18, Letter to Tom Johnston MP from Roland Muirhead, February 27, 1925.

53. *Daily Record and Mail,* February 27, 1925.
54. Hansard, Commons, vol. 410, April 17, 1945, cols. 34–48.
55. George Foulkes, John Maxton, Dennis Canavan, John Home Robertson, David Marshall, *Defending Scotland Against Thatcher: An action plan for the Labour Movement* n.d.
56. NLS, Acc. 3721, Meeting of the Scottish National Convention, McLellan Galleries, Glasgow, January 28, 1927.
57. NLS, Acc. 7505, No. 20, Ian Hamilton, 'Confidential' memorandum on proposed resolution on policy for forthcoming annual general meeting.
58. David Deacon and Peter Goulding, 'When Ideology Fails: The Flagship of Thatcherism and the British National and Local Media', *European Journal of Communication*, vol. 6, 1991, pp. 291–332, referred to in Rodney Barker, 'Legitimacy in the United Kingdom: Scotland and the Poll Tax' *British Journal of Political Science*, vol. 22, 1992, p. 521.
59. *Glasgow Herald*, February 13, 1987.
60. *Guardian*, November 28, 1986.
61. Rodney Barker, 'Legitimacy in the United Kingdom: Scotland and the Poll Tax', *British Journal of Political Science*, vol. 22, 1992, pp. 530–1.
62. *Glasgow Herald*, November 13, 1987.
63. *Scotsman*, April 11, 1988.
64. *Ibid.*, March 11, 1988.
65. *Ibid.*, September 16, 1988.
66. *Glasgow Herald*, September 16, 1988.
67. *Scotsman*, November 12, 1988.
68. *Glasgow Herald*, 17 April, 1990.

Conclusion

Hope and Hopelessness

Previous chapters have focused on each of the different strategies deployed by the national movement this century. In this concluding chapter, the different approaches adopted or proposed since 1992 are considered. The most striking feature of this period has been the repetition of past experiences with little appreciation of what had gone before. No period in the twentieth-century history of the national movement can be described as typical but few periods compare with that since 1992, except perhaps the late 1920s, in the intensity of debate and diversity of strategies considered. One theme of this book has been the importance of context and here again the period discussed in this chapter brings this out.

In an article discussing the prospects for reform of the communist social system, the noted Polish commentator Leszek Kolakowski described the hope and hopelessness of the reformers.[1] Despite the obvious differences between Scotland's predicament and that of Poland, there are similarities. The tendency to veer from extremes of optimism to extremes of pessimism, from believing that reform within the basic structure is possible to believing that the system is unreformable, have been as evident in the Scottish home rule movement this century as they were in reform movements in Eastern and Central Europe prior to 1989. What often went unnoticed in Eastern Europe were the slow undercurrents of change. Equally significant were those changes which manifested themselves spectacularly but which were often misinterpreted.

This has also been true in Scotland. The gradual decline of Britain has altered the context in which debates on Scottish self-government take place. On the other hand, by-election victories for the SNP, for example, have often been misinterpreted as signalling the imminence of independence. Equally, the failure to make the much heralded breakthrough in a general election, though electoral progress is achieved, is often interpreted as a major setback. The hope and hopelessness of the predicament of the self-government movement is as evident today as it has been throughout the century.

The period since 1992 has witnessed surges of pessimism and optimism which resemble the twentieth-century history of the movement telescoped in time. Jim Sillars was defeated in Govan and commented that there were 'too many ninety-minute patriots' in Scotland; he suggested that Margaret Thatcher had been right all along in believing that the Scots would 'bottle out'.[2] At the 1992 SNP conference Alex Salmond and Winnie Ewing adopted a less pessimistic line and warned the party against blaming the people. Muriel Gray articulated the feeling of many home rulers immediately after the 1992 general election in an acerbic commentary on the results:

> We messed up. Split our vote. . . Unfortunately, we're all going down with the ship, and I have no fear in repeating that it is the people's fault and nobody else.[3]

Joyce McMillan, Gray's fellow columnist, compared Scots to those whose self-esteem is so low that they tend to react to stress 'not by lashing out at others but by physically hacking away at their own bodies, lacerating, cutting, hurting', and argued that Scots must 'learn to meet our national setbacks with determination, a touch of mature equanimity, and a firm setting of the face towards better days.'[4]

It took around eight years for the movement to regain confidence following the 1979 defeats but only about eight months following the 1992 defeats. The single event which confirmed that home rule had not been removed from the agenda was a unique public demonstration. The 'Democracy Demonstration' was held in Edinburgh in December 1992 during a summit meeting attended by the heads of government of the European Community. The party political infighting which followed the demonstration induced pessimism amongst many supporters of self-government but a steadier, more sober assessment of prospects for change seems to have set in. The SNP victory in the Perth and Kinross by-election in May 1995 was not followed by predictions that Scotland would soon be free. Progress was maintained without the excesses, and the wild fluctuations between extremes of pessimism and optimism seem to be giving way to a more balanced outlook. But if the history of the movement teaches anything, it is that lurches of extreme optimism or pessimism are easily provoked.

Changing Contexts

British nationalism is now less potent than at any stage this century. The Perth and Kinross by-election demonstrated this forcefully. The Conservative candidate attempted to wrap himself in the Union Flag and the Conservative campaign was timed to take advantage of the 50th anniversary of the end of the second world war. Typical of this campaign was a leaflet issued on Victory in Europe Day:

> Monday is VE Day. Britain will commemorate the victory over nationalism and remember those who laid down their lives to save Europe from tyranny. The Second World War brought out all that is best in Britain. A community spirit. A determination to overcome adversity. And, above all, a recognition of the need for everyone to work together.
>
> Scots fought together with servicemen and women from England, Wales and Northern Ireland. The war was won because Britain was a United Kingdom.
>
> 50 years on we should take this opportunity to reflect on the fact that Scotland achieves far more working in partnership with the rest of the United Kingdom. There is far more that unites us than divides us.

The British nationalism expressed in Perthshire in early 1995 was backward-looking and bombastic. In addition, the Conservative candidate's support for increasing taxes on fuel, opposition to a minimum wage, and enthusiasm for the free market allied British nationalism with a social and economic programme that was unpalatable to most Scots. British nationalism was also weakened by the confusion over the state's international role. A major pillar of Britain's appeal this century has been its role as a world leader, or at least a perception that it performed such a role. Debates on Britain's relations with Europe in the context of the Treaty on European Union (Maaastricht) showed up deep divisions amongst British nationalists on British's future role. Protection of 'sovereignty' has been a concern of British rather than Scottish nationalists in recent years.

Even such a mainstay of Britishness as the monarchy looks tattered today. Again, the Perth and Kinross by-election suggested that all is not well. Roseanna Cunningham, the SNP candidate, was candid in her republicanism. Her victory probably signalled indifference towards the monarchy rather than support for republicanism or independence, but an opinion poll suggested that only 36% of voters in the constituency wanted to retain the monarchy as it was.[5] Far more important than the status of the monarchy was the voter's opposition to the Conservatives.

In chapter three it was argued that Britain was traditionally viewed as a union rather than a unitary state by its most ardent admirers. It was maintained that there had always been an attempt to take account of the Scottish dimension and that the Conservatives more than Labour had been the party of the union state. That situation has changed. The union state is necessarily a dynamic state which must respond to changed circumstances. The case for a Scottish Parliament is based on an appreciation that the modern democratic age requires a democratic component to be added to the national distinctiveness which has been the hallmark of British pluralism. Labour has inherited the Conservative view of the constitution. The Labour candidate in Perth and Kinross did well because he embodied the attitudes and outlook of Scottish Conservatives of the recent past. Strong support for the Union tempered by measures aimed at accommodating Scottish demands combined with social and fiscal conservatism to make 'New Labour' look and sound like old Conservatism. Labour's alternative of home rule within the Union remains a viable option for most Scots. Its proposals amount to a recasting of the constitution and redefinition of the relationship between Scotland and the rest of Britain. It remains untested and difficult to assess given the scant detail Labour is willing to provide.

The challenge for Labour is not only to devise a new constitutional structure but to give Scots a reason to support a reformed Union. The debate has not yet become polarised between the status quo and independence but few serious commentators would now insist that if this happened the Union would win. Labour's problem probably lies not just in the constitutional structure it has to offer but in its ability to deliver on other fronts as well. What is new Labour's vision of Britain's international role? Is the Trident nuclear weapon system more important than the restoration of benefits to 16 and 17 year olds? Can Labour reinvent Britain in a way that will make Scots feel proud and convince them that it can provide the opportunities it once did? Labour's alternative is too vague and uncertain. What remains clear is that any future Labour Government will face a challenge unknown to any of its predecessors. It is not just the future of the party which may be in doubt if it fails but the future of the state itself.

Another change which is potentially significant concerns the constitutional future of Northern Ireland. For much of the twentieth century, Scottish home rulers pointed to Northern Ireland as an example of home rule in action. The Government of Ireland Act, 1920 established an Assembly at Stormont. It developed out of the convoluted attempts to find a solution to the 'Irish problem' which a succession of British Governments confronted. As the Royal Commission on the Constitution, headed by Lord Kilbrandon, stated:

> Northern Ireland, by one of history's choicest ironies, is the one place where Liberal home rule ideas were ever put into practice – and by a solidly Unionist government. It can truly be said to have been given a constitution that it did not want and that was designed for another place.[6]

Its demise owed more to the inbuilt Unionist majority and the policies they pursued than to its institutional arrangements. But so long as Stormont and, indeed, Northern Ireland, was associated with sectarianism, Scottish home rulers were reluctant to draw parallels. The peace process has changed this. John Major's Government proposed to establish an elected Assembly in Northern Ireland. The Prime Minister who has argued against devolution to Scotland was proposing just this for Northern Ireland. He justified the inconsistency by stressing that Northern Ireland was exceptional. In doing so, he assumed a degree of homogeneity in the rest of the UK and implicitly accepted that Britain was a unitary rather than a union state, although Northern Ireland's relationship with Britain is on the basis of a union state.

The Demise of the Constitutional Convention

The Constitutional Convention was unprepared for the most likely outcome of the 1992 general election. There had been a suggestion that resistance would have to be organised. Two months before the general election, the convener of the Campaign for a Scottish Assembly said that the Convention would have to coordinate a form of resistance.[7] But nothing happened. The supremacy of Parliament remained sacrosanct for many who had earlier espoused Scottish popular sovereignty. Kenyon Wright continued to maintain that the Convention was the 'only way to get what Scots want – genuine constitutional change', and probably even believed it.[8]

Prime Minister John Major had pledged that the Conservatives would 'take stock' following the election, and embarked on a superficial review and consultation. This was mirrored in the Convention's reaction to the election. Kenyon Wright also said that the Convention would have to 'take stock', and it floundered around looking for a role for itself. The limitations and inflated claims of the Convention were fully exposed. It had never been a popular body which could call on public support. It had failed to devise a strategy to deal with the return of a Conservative Government, and it had made only limited progress in devising a scheme of home rule. This last role should have been its primary if not sole function.

Wright proposed a six-point plan which included establishing a shadow Scottish parliament to meet quarterly with all MPs, MEPs and perhaps elected regional and island councillors; a civic forum consisting of community representatives; an annual state-of-the-nation day when the shadow Parliament and civic forum would report to the Scottish people; an appeal to Europe and the international community on Scotland's case for constitutional change; cooperation with any genuine Government initiatives; and an effective campaign identifying the role each group could play in a common strategy.[9] His list read like a trawl of the history of the movement. All of it was intended to regain the initiative lost to the more radical groups which were emerging and none of it was concerned with the issues which the Convention should have addressed before the election.

A month later, the Convention agreed to draw up plans for a canvass of opinion in a 'representative part of Scotland' but, as Wright conceded, this was unlikely to worry the Government. The idea was simply a reaction to those bodies which called for a multi-opinion referendum and the need for a less elitist approach. Falkirk was chosen as a part of Scotland which was as representative as anywhere else. The ballot was held in December 1993, and voters were asked two questions:

> Are you in favour of the establishment of an elected Scottish parliament? If so, would you wish to be: a) within the UK; or b) independent of the UK?

28,000 ballot papers were distributed but under 8,000 were returned. With under 30 volunteers involved in collecting the papers during the winter weather, even the organisers admitted that it could have been better organised. Of those who responded, 88% voted in favour of a Scottish parliament with 54% in favour of a parliament within the UK and 46% in favour of independence.[10] The Conservative's Scottish chairman described it as a 'stunning belly-flop'. Local plebiscites had been held in the past and had succeeded in difficult times in engendering interest in the issue, but it was an inappropriate strategy in the post-1992 period. Just when more direct action was required the Convention proved itself to be incapable even of organising a ballot competently.

Problems within the Convention became difficult to hide soon after the election. Norman Hogg, Labour MP, suggested that it should be wound up and the leader of the Scottish Liberal Democrats argued that the Convention in its existing form had reached the end, and called for it to be widened into a mass movement.[11] The Liberal Democrats began to adopt a more independent line, largely due to a belief that the party's close association with Labour in the Constitutional Convention had done it electoral damage at the general election. Even Shadow Scottish Secretary Tom Clarke was critical of the Convention for having been 'largely detached from popular politics.'[12] But the Convention still had its uses for Labour in its battles with the SNP. Labour continued to accuse the SNP of being uncooperative for failing to join the Convention, while simultaneously claiming that the Convention lacked popular support and had run its course.

The one function which could be performed was eventually acknowledged when a 'Constitutional Commission' was set up to consider some of the outstanding issues which remained unresolved.[13] The Commission was chaired by the journalist Joyce McMillan. It reported in October 1994 making recommendations on the electoral system including the issue of gender balance and the constitutional implications of a Scottish Parliament for the rest of the UK and local government. In their submission, the Liberal Democrats argued for the abolition of the post of Scottish Secretary and a reduction in the number of Scottish MPs at Westminster to 60. They proposed a Scottish parliament of 140 members elected by single transferable vote with about 40 constituencies. They also took issue with proposals emanating from the Labour Party that there should be a statutory obligation for gender equality.

The Commission advanced the debate but reached few substantive conclusions. It recommended the Additional Member System with the first-past-the-post voting system using the existing Westminster constituencies to provide the base of representation. Additional members would be elected using the eight Scottish Euro-constituencies, each of which would return five Members of the Scottish Parliament (MSPs). It was felt that this would ensure a degree of proportionality and provide a total of 112 MSPs. There was no agreement, however, on whether the allocation of additional members would in itself be proportional or whether it should be used as a corrective to the disproportionality of the first-past-the-post section. The failure to reach agreement meant that the extent of proportionality was not tackled, and it might therefore still be possible for a party with under 40% of the vote to win an overall majority of seats – the very outcome which the Commission had intended should not occur. Much else in this section of the report consisted of laudable intentions rather than concrete proposals.

The section dealing with the constitutional implications of a

Scottish Parliament was equally vague. The issue of Scottish representation at Westminster was evaded with a recommendation against
an immediate reduction, but propounding a 'general debate on
patterns of Westminster representation during a period of decentralisation, which might lead to agreed legislation on the issue at a later
date'. It supported retaining the Secretaryship of State for Scotland
during the transition but was uncertain of the long-term future of the
post. It argued that the Convention should 'seek maximum moral
and political entrenchment of the existence and powers of a Scottish
Parliament and Executive' but, once more, was vague on how this
would be achieved. In line with the tone of the document, the
section discussing how best to protect local government amounted to
supporting declarations of intent rather than substantive proposals.

The Convention made little progress beyond that achieved before
the general election. Few members attended Convention meetings
and there was little media coverage. It still had an important function
but it was able to perform it only to a very limited degree. Key issues
remain to be tackled: relations with Westminster and Whitehall, the
financing of the Scottish Parliament, and the electoral system. By
failing to reach a decision, the Convention contradicted the Claim
of Right which had been adopted at its inaugural meeting in March
1989. It would not be the Scottish people, not even representatives of
the Scottish people, who would 'determine the form of Government
best suited to their needs'. Civil servants in London would play a far
greater role in making the decisions that would determine the future
constitutional arrangements for the government of Scotland than
had initially been intended, and then only if voters outside Scotland
decided not to vote Conservative.

SNP: The Return of Pragmatism

In the immediate aftermath of the election, the SNP exhibited those
characteristics common to parties which have just suffered a setback.
High hopes had once more been betrayed but the party had more
reason to be optimistic than had been the case after 1979. Divisions
were shallower and more transitory. The party had believed its own
hype. Nonetheless, the SNP was the only party in Britain to lose no
deposits; it had increased its share of the vote by 7.4% to 21.5% but

it managed to hold only the three seats won in 1987, with Jim Sillars defeated in Govan.

The reason the increased SNP vote failed to translate into seats was the party's inability to concentrate its support. Indeed, the SNP's support was even more evenly spread in 1992 than it had been at the previous election. The nature of the SNP campaign was partly to blame. It had campaigned as if it had a chance of winning throughout Scotland in line with 'Scotland Free by '93' slogan. Instead of targeting constituencies where it had its best prospects the SNP spread its resources too thinly. In seats where it was best placed to win, including the Scottish Secretary's seat of Galloway and Upper Nithsdale, its share of the vote rose less than in seats in which it had little hope.

The party's long-term objective had been to replace Labour and in this it made some progress, but the goal still looked distant. Its greatest advances were in Labour-held seats, but in no seat was the SNP less than 10% behind a sitting Labour MP after the election. The SNP appealed to sections of Scottish society which traditionally gave strong backing to Labour. The profile of SNP support now resembles Labour's to a greater extent than after any previous election, suggesting that it is making progress towards its long-term goal. The Catholic community had in the past been hostile to the SNP. By 1992 much of that suspicion had been dispelled and one of the most notable changes was the increased support for the SNP amongst Scottish Catholics, although the Catholic community remained overwhelmingly Labour supporting.[14] A different approach was adopted by the SNP when it came to the European elections in 1994; it targeted North-East Scotland and succeeded in taking it from Labour. The party not only had a new Euro-MP but won its highest share of the vote in any national election, higher even than its October 1974 level of support. This should be the way forward at the next election. While the long-term goal of the SNP was to replace Labour its most likely gains were from the Conservatives. Such gains would diminish the Conservatives' prospects of winning an overall majority and might place the SNP in the enviable position of being able to influence a minority Labour Government.

Withdrawal from or refusal to participate in cross-party campaigns on steel, poll tax and the Constitutional Convention prior to the 1992 election were understandable but gave the SNP an image of being uncooperative. Relations with other parties and organisations had always been a central issue in the SNP and continued to be so. The post-election chorus, as Jim Sillars noted, was for 'unity, unity', but the defeated MP argued that it would be far better if it became 'honesty, honesty', which had been lacking in 'those who have marched along the Con-Convention road, brains clogged with rhetorical trash about "claims of right"'.[15] Sillars had a point but his opponents both inside and outside the SNP dismissed his arguments as the exaggerated reaction of a defeated candidate. Though expressed in language unlikely to convert, his central conclusion was not without foundation. Unity built on empty rhetoric had all too often been a hallmark of the self-government movement. Less convincing was the view expressed by associates of Sillars such as Iain Lawson who told the SNP conference that autumn that Scotland was the 'numpty nation of the world', provoking Winnie Ewing in her presidential address to warn against blaming the electorate. Nonetheless, there was strong support for continuation of the more combative approach supported by Sillars from Gordon Wilson and Margaret Ewing MP.

Support for a multi-option referendum and Scotland United became the issue around which the fundamentalist-pragmatist division was fought. At SNP national council two months after the election, the party overwhelmingly endorsed Salmond's support for a referendum. Lawson's view that the following four years would result in either Labour destroying the SNP or the SNP destroying Labour lacked any credibility. The victory of the pragmatic view understated the extent of genuine distrust of a more cooperative approach and was partly due to Salmond's enhanced standing following his impressive performance during the election and partly to the fundamentalist tendency to alienate potential support. Nonetheless, support for a more pragmatic approach was gaining ground.

In early 1995, Salmond was helped in pursuing a more pragmatic line when *Scotland on Sunday* headlined an interview with him suggesting that the party had softened its position on devolution.[16] The story was inaccurate and mischievous, but the predictable reaction from fundamentalists within the party found less support than might have been expected. The headline was based on Salmond's view that devolution would be his second preference. In the event it proved advantageous when in a major debate between Salmond and George Robertson, Labour's Shadow Scottish Secretary, the latter was unable to answer when asked what his second choice would be.

A series of other events made the SNP appear more cooperative and Labour look sectarian. Shortly after the election, an invitation to Salmond to address the Scottish Trades Union Congress was withdrawn, allegedly at the insistence of the Labour Party's Scottish leadership. The civic dignity which Norman Irons brought to the office as Edinburgh's first SNP Lord Provost following the local elections in 1992 showed that the SNP in local government could be an asset to the party. Local election results in 1994 suggested that progress was being made in areas that the party most needed to do well in order to win parliamentary seats. Its best results came in Tayside Region where the party doubled its number of councillors and took control from Labour. At the elections for the new unitary local authorities in April 1995, the SNP won 26% and 181 seats compared with Labour's 44% and 613 seats, the Tories' 12% and 82 seats and the Liberal Democrats' 10% and 123 seats. The nationalists also found themselves in control of two councils – Perthshire and Kinross, and Angus – but still failed to make the necessary breakthrough in Labour dominated central Scotland. Electoral politics proved as frustrating as ever for the SNP at the close of the century. Polling well but with an even spread of support, the party awaited the breakthrough that never seemed to come. It seemed that Scottish voters were still willing to give Labour a chance, hoping the party would win at Westminster. So long as the Tories won there, the SNP breakthrough seemed a distant prospect. The Nationalists' best hope would come only after Labour had been returned to power.

Policies continued to be developed and once more the party debated the need for some coherent ideological expression of its views. The debate was less rancorous and more short-lived than previous ones. A proposal to endorse social democracy was supported by Salmond at the 1992 conference. Its main advocate was Andrew Doig who, like Salmond, had been a member of the '79 Group. Doig was critical of the style rather than the substance of SNP policies, arguing that he had no objection to existing policies, merely their presentation. He argued that the SNP should embrace the language and style of contemporary social democracy.[17] Conference voted to remit Doig's motion, effectively shelving it indefinitely. The party was seeking a language and style which it could use throughout Scotland as well as for crystalising its views. Its left-wing was reluctant to adopt social democracy as they preferred to call themselves socialists; fundamentalists felt that being a nationalist was sufficient.

The Perth and Kinross by-election generated a new variant which seemed acceptable to all. Roseanna Cunningham placed the SNP in 'mainstream Scotland', and her articulation of detailed policies cohered around a theme of seeking to create a 'decent Scotland'. Hers was an unmistakably left-of-centre message expressed in language which was acceptable throughout Scotland. For the first time, the SNP could chide Labour for presenting a right-wing message in rural Scotland which was very different from that offered by Labour in urban areas. Cunningham not only talked about class but described the monarchy as the 'pinnacle of the class system', while the Labour candidate refused to acknowledge the existence of class.

However, the SNP's progress was not steady. An event which emphasised the tensions within the party and its difficult relations with other organisations came during the debate on the Maastricht Treaty on European Union. Margaret Ewing, as SNP Parliamentary group leader, negotiated a deal with Scottish Secretary Ian Lang which would ensure that Scotland would get between six and eight members on the Committee of Regions, a new institution to be set up under the conditions of the Treaty. The SNP MPs voted with the Government on this matter, provoking attacks from Labour. There was an element of nonsense to the whole business but it opened up divisions within the SNP and allowed its Labour opponents to accuse it of siding with the Tories. Though the deal had been done by Ewing, Salmond was the target of opposition and internal attacks.

Labour used it as an excuse for withdrawing from cross-party talks and its Scottish party conference which came shortly after the vote was dominated by the issue. It seemed for a moment that Labour had found a way of reviving the memory of the SNP that brought down the Labour Government in 1979. For months afterwards, SNP acivists were confronted by Labour opponents with the accusation that they could not be trusted. But 1993 was not 1979. The Maastricht vote was on a minor matter and Labour's record of supporting the Tories was far more extensive than the SNP's. Additionally, the

SNP was by then unambiguously acknowledged to be a left-wing party. Salmond's greatest difficulties at this time came from within the party. Three members of his shadow cabinet resigned, and Sillars launched one of his blistering attacks. He had a point, but he was suspected of gloating. The party's national executive endorsed the leadership's motion welcoming the concession 'wrung out of Westminster' by only 13 votes to 11.

The episode was significant but not for the reasons paraded in the press. It demonstrated the dangers of portraying the Conservatives as political pariahs. While the SNP abandoned any notion of being equidistant between Labour and the Tories after 1979, it had found itself in an awkward position. This would become even more difficult in the event of the return of a Labour Government. If the SNP is to avoid going through the same lobbies as the Tories, this would amount to taking the Labour whip and the party's *raison d'être* would disappear. The Maastricht vote demonstrated that the SNP after 60 years still had not fully come to terms with itself as an independent party. Plaid Cymru also wrung out a similar concession from the Conservatives but the reaction in Wales was very different. Plaid was praised for its actions. In part this demonstrates one of the key differences between the two nationalist parties. Plaid is more comfortably independent and willing to do deals. This makes it both an independent political party and also a pressure group. Robert McIntyre's insistence in the late 1940s that the SNP had to become more self-confident and independent if Scotland was to do the same is an appropriate lesson from the Maastricht episode.

Unity and 'People Power'

A radical response seemed likely after the election.[18] As the results were coming in on election night, Charles Gray, leader of Strathclyde Regional Council, announced on television that he could envisage civil disobedience in the event of a fourth Conservative election victory. His views were immediately and brusquely repudiated by the party's Scottish leadership.[19] In Parliament, John McAllion disrupted proceedings in May during Scottish Question Time. In February 1994, Alex Salmond disrupted the proceedings at the committee stage of the bill designed to reorganise Scottish local government. His protest highlighted the existence on the committee of English Conservative Members with no constituency interest taking decisions on a purely Scottish matter. While Labour parliamentarians protested about Salmond's behaviour, the head of local government for Unison, the trade union whose members would be most affected by the legislation, was also complaining about the presence of English MPs on the committee.[20] But in time the prospect of parliamentary disruption diminished and talk of civil disobedience grew fainter.

New groups sprang up following the 1992 election. These were not dominated by the political elites. The most significant was Scotland United. Pop stars Ricky Ross and Pat Kane were instrumental in its establishment along with some nationalist-inclined Labour Party members. John McAllion, Labour MP, was a founding member and announced that 'no party on its own could deliver to the Scottish people. I will not wait for another five years.'[21] Rallies were held in Glasgow's George Square reminiscent of those in the 1920s. The message from these rallies was simple: the need for unity and the call to give the Scottish public a voice in the debate. A referendum became the rallying call for all the new groups which emerged.

The idea of a multi-option referendum had been germinating for some time before the election. Some SNP members had seen it as a way of uniting the opposition while allowing each party to maintain its distinct position. Alex Salmond had succeeded in gaining the support of the SNP national executive for a referendum after he became leader but by that time it was too late and a polarisation had occurred amongst supporters of constitutional change. Neither the SNP nor the Constitutional Convention was keen on the idea, preferring instead to push their own schemes. It emerged after the election only because there appeared to be no alternative, and it had the merit of allowing for the maximum degree of agreement.

Scottish Labour MPs voted in support of a government-sponsored multi-option referendum immediately after the election. Predictably, this was rejected by Scottish Secretary Ian Lang. The only option was to run an unofficial referendum which there was no prospect of Labour's Scottish or British leadership accepting. The acceptance of an official referendum had been easy. A referendum sponsored by Scottish local authorities was proposed. Scotland United supported such a course of action. In November, a report was issued by

Scotland United which estimated the cost of running a referendum at £2.6m, or £1.6m if a postal ballot was held, and included a series of proposals to raise funds.[22] It was an ambitious effort to address the issue which was dismissed by its opponents. Labour MPs who were involved came under pressure from the party's leadership to tone down their involvement. Scotland United embarrassed Labour by highlighting its inactivity and lack of ideas. In time, it faded away having failed to raise anything like the funds necessary, and having run up against the opposition of Scotland's Labour establishment.

Another group set up in the aftermath of the election was Common Cause. It too demanded a referendum although it never placed this at the forefront of its activity. Its preference was to hold 'civic forums' in various parts of Scotland to build on existing support for constitutional change. It was a less radical body than Scotland United and therefore less likely to attract the opposition of Labour's leadership. Another group which was set up was Democracy for Scotland (DfS), which established a vigil outside the Royal High School Building in Edinburgh, the site of the proposed Scottish Parliament. Democracy for Scotland committed itself to maintaining the vigil until such time as a Scottish Parliament is established.

The plethora of groups caused some concern. The danger of the energies of the movement being dissipated led to the establishment of the Campaign for Scottish Democracy, an umbrella body led by the trade unions. It was the Campaign which organised the Democracy Demonstration in Edinburgh in December 1992 during the summit meeting attended by the EC heads of government. This demonstration was attended by between 25,000 and 40,000 people, depending on whose estimates are believed. Either way, it was impressive. A number of speakers addressed the rally, including an anonymous woman who read out a 'Democracy Declaration' which concluded:

> When the eyes of the world are on our capital, Edinburgh, we are confident that the peoples and governments of Europe will recognise the appeal of its host nation. We therefore raise our demand without fear or favour – Scotland demands democracy.[23]

It was similar to the call by supporters of Scottish home rule in 1919, made to the world's political leaders deciding on Europe's future at

Versailles. This time the call had an undeniable democratic basis and Europe's leaders were meeting less than a mile away. In addition, the declaration demanded the recall of the Scots Parliament. The writer William McIlvanney addressed the meeting, saying that if the 61 opposition MPs were to walk out of Westminster something might happen. Alex Salmond was rapturously welcomed by the crowd when he demanded that Scotland should be set free.

The aftermath of the rally saw Labour backtracking on the demand for the recall of the Scots Parliament, which the SNP exploited to the full. McIlvanney and George Robertson, Labour MP, who was later to become Shadow Scottish Secretary, confronted each other in the press over the interpretation of the rally. Robertson's was the typical response of the metropolitan politician. He suggested that it was important not to get 'carried away' by the numbers who attended the rally. McIlvanney, formerly a staunch Labour supporter, accused Robertson of deliberately distorting its importance and believing that 'any form of political life outside London is a joke'. Labour would be reluctant to support a major rally of this type again.

The Meaning of Self-Government

One of the most significant developments since the 1992 election has been the manner in which the strategies employed by the self-government movement incorporated its objectives. They became more democratic, less elitist. The popular nature of the movement became more evident. The danger that a Scottish Parliament might replicate the Westminster model and simply exchange a British elite for a Scottish elite has always existed. If this happened it might improve the governance of Scotland but it would not amount to self-government. A more radical interpretation of self-government demands that any constitutional structure should allow for the totality of Scottish society and should ensure that power and the resources required to exercise power are evenly distributed.

In 1994, the Campaign for Scottish Democracy proposed the establishment of a Scottish Civic Forum, a name chosen in preference to Senate, bringing together representatives from all walks of life to debate issues of importance to Scotland. A consultative conference was held in June in the Royal High School. Alan Miller of the Scottish

Council for Civil Liberties and author of the Democracy Declaration explained that it was intended to hold regular meetings which would challenge the more conservative notions of democracy:

> We are repeatedly told that we live in a democracy because there is a plurality of political parties and universal suffrage. But I think all of us would agree that there are other forms which would be appropriate and would involve many of those who find themselves excluded from the present process.[24]

A speaker representing old age pensioners remarked that this was the first time they had been involved in debating Scotland's constitutional status. It was not the usual 'representative forum' which collected together Scotland's elected representatives but a more genuine example of grass-roots democracy. In March 1995, the Forum met again to discuss unemployment. The movement was linking issues affecting Scots in their everyday lives to the question of the nation's constitutional status.

The civic nationalism which has emerged as the dominant ideology of the movement combines the two elements of popular sovereignty – democracy and nationalism. There remain challenges to it from within and without the movement. A chauvinistic Scottish nationalism exists. Since 1992, two organisations – Settler Watch and Scottish Watch – have tarnished the movement with their anti-English statements and posters, and they have been condemned by the mainstream of the movement. In Perth and Kinross, the SNP took the unusual step of taking legal action to prevent such organisations from publicly endorsing the party. But however insignificant the support for these bodies, they are a reminder of the ugly face which nationalism can take when it fails to associate with its democratic twin.

Conclusion

A number of general conclusions can be drawn from this study. The context in which the national movement has found itself has been pre-eminent in determining its opportunities and influencing strategy. The precise definition of the goal or goals of the movement has changed and the ideological context has been important. In turn, this has influenced strategy. The definition of democracy has undergone dramatic changes this century and the opening up of its meaning has given strength to the self-government movement. There have been rapid changes in strategy and the relationship between the various approaches has been complex. As one approach has failed, it has given way to another. There had been almost a circular process of different strategies coming to the fore in succession. Each of the organisations in the movement has been better at criticising other sister organisations than they have been at understanding the nature of Britain or the British parties. It is striking how rarely the movement has taken account of its own history. Equally striking have been the high expectation and subsequent disillusionment. In part the disillusionment has been due to a limited appreciation of the weakness of each strategy, the history of the movement, and the strength of its opponents.

The study also demonstrates much about the nature of contemporary Britain, especially if viewed as a union rather than a unitary state. As a union state, Britain has always accepted the need to take account of Scottish distinctiveness but has failed to incorporate democratic accountability into that. The challenge for supporters of self-government who believe in the union state is to come up with a workable scheme and put it into effect. For supporters of self-government who believe in a Scottish state, the challenge is still to win majority support for their case. For both, the imperative is to find a *modus vivendi* which will allow them to articulate their views and compete without doing more damage to each other than their common enemy.

The main conclusion of this book, although others who may read it may draw a different conclusion, is that the movement has rarely been willing to acknowledge the difficulties it faces. Strategically, each of the approaches has had some validity, but at different stages its energies have been dissipated through intra-movement disputes, by following naive strategies, or as a consequence of failing to understand what can best be achieved by any given strategy. A pluralistic approach will always be necessary with different organisations respecting each other. The SNP is central to this if only because support for it alone carries with it a sanction and because the measurement of its success is generally seen as the measurement of the strength of the whole movement. But the SNP must always be aware that it is only a part, if the most important part, of the self-government movement.

The final word should be in keeping with one of the themes of the book. If self-government has any meaning it involves allowing those without a voice to be heard. The new groups that emerged spontaneously after the 1992 election were established by ordinary Scots beyond the control of political parties and existing groups. Democracy for Scotland (DfS) was established following a demonstration on the Kessock Bridge the day after the election, which in turn led to the vigil outside the old Royal High School in Edinburgh. Marking 1,000 days of the vigil, a previously unknown member of DfS explained its objectives in words which are a fitting conclusion to this book. These words not only embody the ideals of the movement but also the principles on which any successful strategy must be based. They have been ignored all too often this century:

> Representatives in the Scottish parliament should be representative of Scottish society as a whole and not dominated by lawyers, accountants and business men as Westminster is. The ultimate democratic goal should be people having the opportunity to take part in all levels of decision making. A cross periodically on a ballot paper is not the same as genuine democracy. Power should be devolved from the parliament and local authorities. More decisions should be taken by people locally.
>
> ... A Scottish parliament, if it is to be worth having, must have the political will and sufficient power to redress the impoverishment – economic, industrial, social and cultural – that has been caused by successive Westminster governments of whatever party to the people of Scotland. Let's make Scotland different. The Scottish parliament should generate an atmosphere which is different from the present Westminster system – one which is welcoming to all Scottish people, men and women alike. For the parliament to be a success, the Scottish people must take the initiative. You will need to show your support and become involved.[25]

1. Leszek Kolakolwski, 'Hope and hopelessness', *Survey*, Summer 1971, vol. 16, pp. 37–52.

2. *Herald*, April 24, 1992.
3. Muriel Gray, 'Judas Tory voters sell out for a tenner', *Scotland on Sunday* April 12, 1992.
4. Joyce McMillan, 'Remedy for a manic-depressive nation' *Scotland on Sunday* April, 1992.
5. *Scotsman*, ICM Poll, May 25, 1995. 15% of voters in Perth and Kinross supported the abolition of the monarchy and 44% wanted it further slimmed down.
6. The report of the Royal Commission on the Constitution (Kilbrandon), vol. 1, London, HMSO, Cmnd. 5460, p. 376, para. 1249.
7. *Scotsman*, February 14, 1992.
8. *Herald*, February 10, 1992.
9. *Ibid.*, April 19, 1992.
10. *Scotsman/Herald* December 14, 1993. The precise figures were 27,828 forms distributed with only 7,788 returned. 6,878 voters said they were in favour of a parliament and 910 were against.
11. *Herald*, August 6, 1992; *Scotsman*, September 15, 1992.
12. *Tribune*, October 1, 1992.
13. *Scotsman*, September 14, 1993.
14. For a detailed account of the nature of SNP support see Jack Brand, James Mitchell, Paula Surridge, 'Social Constituency and Ideological Profile: Scottish Nationalism in the 1990s', *Political Studies*, vol. 42, 1994, pp. 616–29.
15. Jim Sillars, 'Time for honest truths', *Scotsman*, April 25, 1992.
16. *Scotland on Sunday*, January 29, 1995.
17. Andrew Doig, 'Building on solid principles', *Scotsman*, August 24, 1992.
18. *Scotsman*, April 13, 1992.
19. *Herald*, April 11, 1992.
20. *Scotsman/Herald*, February 2, 1994.
21. *Scotland on Sunday*, April 12, 1992.
22. *What price democracy?*, Scotland United, 1992. Also press reports November 28, 1992.
23. *Scotsman*, December 10, 1992.
24. *Ibid.*, June 20, 1994.
25. Helen Allan, 'Keeping a watchful eye on the political will for change', *Scotsman*, December 27, 1994.

Chronology of
Scottish Self-Government, 1885–1995

14 August 1885
Royal assent given to the Secretary for Scotland Act establishing the Scottish Office.

May 1886
Establishment of the Scottish Home Rule Association (SHRA).

3–5 February 1887
Editorials in the *Scotsman* supporting Scottish home rule.

27 April 1888
Keir Hardie stands as the first independent Labour candidate in the Mid-Lanark by-election and includes support for Scottish home rule as part of his platform.

9 April 1889
Scottish home rule motion defeated in Commons by 200 votes to 79. Scottish MPs voted 17 to 22 against.

6 March 1891
Federal home rule motion in Commons moved but talked out.

29 April 1892
Federal home rule motion defeated by 74 votes to 54 in Commons. Scottish MPs vote 14 to 10 in favour.

23 June 1893
Scottish home rule motion defeated by 168 votes to 150 in Commons. Scottish MPs vote 37 to 22 in favour.

3 April 1894
Scottish home rule motion carried in Commons by 180 votes to 170. Scottish MPs vote 35 to 21 in favour.

29 March 1895
Federal home rule motion passed in Commons by 128 votes to 102. Scottish MPs vote 29 to 15 in favour.

25–27 March 1897
Founding annual conference of the Scottish Trades Union Congress (STUC).

7 January 1907
Formation of association to achieve devolution of Scottish affairs.

26 May 1908
Scottish home rule bill passes second reading in Commons by 257 votes to 102. Scottish MPs vote 44 to 9 in favour.

1 June 1908
Glasgow Herald describes Scottish home rule demands as a 'by-product of Irish agitation'.

27 April 1910
Some Scottish Liberal MPs form a 'Scottish Nationalist' group in Parliament.

29 June 1910
Scottish Liberal conference passes main resolution setting up the Scottish National Committee, with object of Scottish home rule.

23 October 1910
Scottish Liberal conference passes measure in favour of Scottish home rule.

6 July 1911
Young Scots Society issues manifesto in which devolution is seen as the most urgent reform after abolition of the Lords.

16 August 1911
Scottish home rule bill gets second reading by 172 votes to 73. Scottish MPs vote 31 to 4 in favour.

1 November 1911
Proposals for a National Convention on home rule issued by Scottish National Committee.

1912

Agriculture added to the responsibilities of the Scottish Office.

28 February 1912

Scottish home rule motion carried by 226 votes to 128 in Commons. Scottish MPs vote 43 to 6 in favour.

3 July 1912

Federal home rule bill gets second reading in Commons by 264 votes to 212. Scottish MPs vote 43 to 7 in favour.

27 April 1913

T. McKinnon Wood MP, Secretary for Scotland, guest at Young Scots Society annual dinner, states that they had to persuade their 'brethren south of the Tweed that it [Scottish home rule] was a question of practical politics, that what they were aiming at was for the advantage not only of Scotland but of the Imperial Parliament'.

30 May 1913

Scottish home rule bill gets second reading in Commons by 204 votes to 159. Scottish MPs vote 45 to 8 in favour.

15 June 1913

International Scots Home Rule League set up as the only organisation which people can join irrespective of party.

25 January 1914

First annual meeting of Scottish Home Rule Council agrees to include women in any scheme of representation to a Scottish Parliament.

25 January 1914

Annual meeting of International Scots Home Rule League reports that branches have been formed in America.

5 February 1914

Annual Committee of Convention of Royal Burghs remitted back report on Scottish self-government.

12 March 1914

Annual committee of Convention of Royal Burghs discusses second draft of sub-committee on self-government and votes to remove 'including women' as voters from report.

15 May 1914

Scottish home rule bill debated in Commons but sitting adjourned without a vote.

23 October 1917
Prime Minister Lloyd George meets parliamentary Committee of Trades Union Congress and indicates his support for Scottish home rule.

8 December 1918
Draft constitution approved for reconstituted SHRA.

1919/1920
Foundation of Scottish National League (SNL).

1919
Health (including housing) added to the responsibilities of the Scottish Office.

16 May 1919
Scottish home rule bill debated in Commons but talked out.

3–4 June 1919
Devolution motion carried by 187 votes to 34 in Commons. Scottish MPs vote 35 to 1 in favour.

16 April 1920
Scottish home rule bill introduced in Commons. Closure carried by 65 votes to 52. Scottish MPs vote 38 to 9 in favour.

3 April 1921
Annual meeting of SHRA agrees to form branches in Scotland and seek representation for Scottish Parliament in League of Nations.

28 April 1921
Relief of Parliament Bill, providing for the establishment of 'subordinate Parliaments in England, Scotland and Wales', introduced into Commons.

13 January 1922
SHRA congratulates Government on settling the Irish Question and notes the need for 'comprehensive scheme of self-government for the several nations of Great Britain'.

8 May 1922
Government of Scotland and Wales Bill presented in Commons but does not proceed.

26 May 1922
Government of Scotland Bill presented in Commons but talked out.

1 November 1923

SHRA sends letters to delegates to imperial conference in London pointing out that Tories have only 15 Scots MPs while Opposition has 59 but there are 347 UK Tories to 268 Opposition and asks, 'Is it because Scotland has been too constitutional in its methods of pressing for self-government that its demand has been ignored?'

9 May 1924

Government of Scotland Bill gets second reading but it is talked out after Labour Government refuses second day's debate.

15 June 1924

Resolution at SHRA meeting urges Parliamentary obstruction.

15 November 1924

First meeting of the Scottish National Convention (SNC) to draw up a scheme of devolution.

1926

Upgrading of Scottish Office to a Secretaryship of State.

22 February 1926

Scottish National Movement (SNM) set up following split in SNL.

13 May 1927

Government of Scotland Bill, based on SNC's proposals, is talked out at second reading.

14 May 1928

Foundation of National Party of Scotland (NPS) following conversations between SNL, SNM, SHRA and Glasgow University Scottish Nationalist Association.

23 June 1928

Inauguration of NPS in King's Park, Stirling.

29 January 1929

Midlothian and Peeblesshire, Northern. National Party of Scotland (NPS) contests its first by-election. Lewis Spence wins 4.5% of the vote.

30 May 1929

General Election. NPS contests 2 seats and wins 0.1% of Scottish vote.

7 May 1930

Convention of Royal Burghs sets up Scottish National Development Council to advise on economic affairs.

27 October 1931

General Election. NPS contests 5 seats and wins 1.0% of the vote.

June 1932

Foundation of Scottish (Self-Government) Party.

14 July 1932

Lord Beaverbrook publishes a letter on front page of *Daily Express* declaring his support for Scottish nationalism.

2 Feb. 1933

East Fife by-election. Novelist Eric Linklater wins 3.6% for the SNP and later parodies effort in novel *Magnus Merriman*.

2 November 1933

Kilmarnock by-election. Scottish Party contests the only by-election in its short history before merger with NPS, and wins 16.8% of the vote.

7 April 1934

First annual conference of the SNP

14 November 1935

General Election SNP contests 8 seats and wins 1.3% of the vote.

15 February 1936

Edinburgh office of the Secretary of State for Scotland opened in Edinburgh.

22 April 1936

Saltire Society founded.

October 1937

Publication of the report of the Gilmour Committee on Scottish Central Administration (Cmd. 5563).

25 May 1939

Royal assent given to legislation reorganising Scottish Office which was followed by opening of St. Andrew's House, Edinburgh.

10 April 1940

Argyll by-election. SNP wins 37% of vote.

11 September 1941

Secretary of State for Scotland Tom Johnston sets up Council of State consisting of all living former Scottish Secretaries 'for the purpose of surveying problems of post-war reconstruction in Scotland' and allows for meetings of the Scottish Grand Committee to take place in Scotland.

30 May 1942
Major split at SNP annual conference after Douglas Young is elected chairman. John MacCormick leaves to found Scottish Convention.

4 October 1942
First general meeting of Scottish Convention.

17 February 1944
Kirkcaldy by-election. SNP wins 41%.

3 May 1944
'Declaration on Scottish Affairs' (Leonard Declaration) signed by prominent Scots in favour of Scottish home rule.

12 April 1945
Dr Robert McIntyre wins Motherwell by-election for the SNP.

17 April 1945
Robert McIntyre holds up Parliamentary business when he refuses to be sponsored and provokes Commons debate.

24 June 1945
Scottish Convention asks candidates their views on home rule. 84 out of 168 reply; 57 favourable, only 3 against.

5 July 1945
General Election. SNP contests 8 seats and wins 1.2% of vote, loses Motherwell. Attlee's Labour Government elected. Scottish Council of Labour Party manifesto lists a 'Scottish Parliament for Scottish Affairs' as second preference. 23 of the 37 Scottish Labour MPs declare their support for home rule.

20 January 1946
Scottish Council (Development and Industry) formed.

28 November 1946
Scottish Tourist Board established.

22 March 1947
First Scottish National Assembly organised by Scottish Convention attended by a broad range of representatives from Scottish society.

2 July 1947
Scottish Daily Express opinion poll published showing 76% approve of the

establishment of a Scottish Parliament dealing with Scottish affairs while 13% disapprove and 11% don't know.

15 August 1947

Proclamation of Indian Independence and establishment of Pakistan following partition.

29 January 1948

Government issues a white paper on Scottish Affairs (Cmd. 7308) proposing changes in Parliamentary procedures and an enquiry into Anglo-Scottish financial relations.

18 February 1948

Paisley by-election. John MacCormick stands as a 'National' candidate with Liberal and Conservative support but Labour holds seat.

21 March 1948

Scottish National Assembly meeting.

23 May 1948

Church of Scotland report favours home rule.

5 July 1948

Inauguration of National Health Service.

7 July 1948

Stirling and Falkirk by-election. SNP wins 8.2% of the vote.

February 1949

Kirriemuir local plebiscite.

29 October 1949

Launch of Scottish Covenant.

. 3 November 1949

Scottish Unionists issue 'Scottish Control of Scottish Affairs', a manifesto advocating increased administrative devolution.

23 February 1950

General Election. SNP contests 3 seats and wins 0.4% of the vote. During the election, Winston Churchill as leader of the Conservatives plays the 'Scottish card' arguing that Scotland should never 'be forced into the serfdom of socialism as a result of a vote in the House of Commons'.

27 July 1950

Hector McNeill, Secretary of State for Scotland, rejects a plebiscite on home rule preferring the 'normal process of our parliamentary democracy'.

22 October 1950
Glasgow University students elect John MacCormick as rector.

26 October 1950
Scotstoun local plebiscite.

25 December 1950
Removal of Stone of Destiny from Westminster Abbey.

April 1951
Festival of Britain opens.

13 April 1951
The Stone of Destiny is returned to Westminster Abbey.

18 April 1951
Treaty of Paris signed establishing the European Coal and Steel Community.

25 October 1951
General Election. SNP contests 2 seats and wins 0.3% of vote. Conservatives under Churchill form a Government.

28 October 1951
Inaugural meeting of Scottish Covenant Committee.

17 February 1952
Royal Titles case begins.

14 March 1952
First BBC television broadcast in Scotland.

23 July 1952
Publication of Catto Report on economic links between Scotland and England suggests that Scotland receives 12% of UK expenditure and pays 10% of costs.

2 June 1953
Coronation of Queen Elizabeth broadcast on television and seen to symbolise national unity.

24 July 1954
Publication of report of the Royal Commission on Scottish Affairs (chaired by Lord Balfour) recommending transfer of electricity, food, animal health, roads and bridges to Scottish Office (Cmd. 9212).

26 May 1955
General Election. SNP contests 2 seats and wins 0.5% of vote. Conservatives win again.

30 May 1955
Announcement that Scottish Television Ltd., chaired by Roy Thomson, had been given contract to become Scotland's first commercial station.

28 October 1955
Nationalist Party of Scotland (NPS) formed, headed by Major Glendinning and Douglas Henderson.

1956
Start of Radio Free Scotland.

25 March 1956
Scottish Office takes over responsibility for roads.

26 July 1956
Nasser nationalises the Suez canal.

3 December 1956
Britain and France withdraw troops from Suez canal.

19 January 1957
Scottish Council of the Labour Party (SCLP) Executive comes out against home rule on 'compelling economic grounds'.

25 March 1957
Treaty of Rome signed by France, West Germany, Italy, Belgium, Luxembourg, and the Netherlands, establishing the European Economic Community from 1 Jan. 1958. Britain refuses to join.

17 February 1958
The Campaign for Nuclear Disarmament (CND) formed.

13 June 1958
Scottish Council of the Labour Party (SCLP) rejects support for a Scottish Parliament.

13 September 1958
SCLP conference rejects home rule. 'Scotland's problems can best be solved by socialist planning on a UK scale.'

12 May 1959
Scottish unemployment doubles due to end of national service and deflationary policies.

June 1959
Peebles local plebiscite.

8 October 1959
General Election. SNP contests 5 seats and wins 0.8% of vote. Conservatives returned again.

4 January 1960
Stockholm Convention establishing the European Free Trade Association is signed on the initiative of the UK.

4 February 1960
MacMillan makes his 'winds of change' speech in Cape Town.

20 February 1960
Scottish unemployment over 100,000.

1 November 1960
Prime Minister Harold MacMillan announces that a Polaris missile base will be set up in the Holy Loch, Scotland.

10 August 1961
Britain formally applies to join the EEC.

September 1961
Grampian Television, covering North-East and Highlands and Islands starts broadcasting.

16 November 1961
Glasgow Bridgeton by-election. SNP wins 18.7% of vote.

21 November 1961
Publication of Toothill Report on the Scottish economy.

1 December 1961
Launch of Scottish Plebiscite Appeal Fund.

11 April 1962
Establishment of the Scottish Development Department within the Scottish Office.

14 June 1962
West Lothian by-election. Billy Wolfe wins 23.3% for the SNP. Conservatives lose their deposit for the first time in 42 years.

February 1963
Jedburgh local plebiscite.

7 November 1963

Kinross and West Perthshire by-election. Home is elected Conservative MP to take up seat in Commons as Prime Minister. SNP wins 7.3%.

12 December 1963

Kenya becomes an independent republic within the Commonwealth.

1964

Regional Development Division set up in Scottish Development Department in Scottish Office. Scottish Transport Group set up.

15 October 1964

General Election. SNP contests 15 seats and wins 2.4% of vote. Labour elected to Government.

1 December 1964

Labour Prime Minister Harold Wilson announces that Polaris missile base Holy Loch is to be retained.

1965

Highlands and Islands Development Board (HIDB) established.

29 September 1965

First SNP party political broadcast.

9 December 1965

'National Plan' for Scotland witnesses Scotland treated as one unit.

31 March 1966

General Election. SNP contests 23 seats and wins 5.0 of vote. Labour re-elected to Government.

14 July 1966

Carmarthen by-election. Gwynfor Evans wins the seat for Plaid Cymru with 39% of vote.

19 October 1966

Russell Johnston, Liberal MP, introduces Scottish Self-Government Bill.

9 March 1967

Glasgow Pollok by-election. SNP wins 28.2% and allows the Conservatives to win the seat.

2 May 1967

Local elections. SNP do well winning 60,000 votes in Glasgow but no seats on the council.

2 November 1967

Hamilton by-election. Winnie Ewing wins seat for SNP from Labour with 41.6% of vote.

24 November 1967

Launch of 'Thistle Group' inside the Conservative Party arguing for home rule.

1967–68

Both BBC Scotland and STV start transmitting political programmes.

9 May 1968

SNP wins 30% of vote and 108 seats in local government elections. 37.2% of vote in Glasgow. Dr Robert McIntyre becomes Provost of Stirling.

18 May 1968

Ted Heath makes his 'Declaration of Perth' at Scottish Conservative Party conference and announces the establishment of committee under Sir Alec Douglas-Home.

18–21 September 1968

Liberal Party Assembly opposes a call for Scottish independence in favour of a federal scheme.

1968

Passenger road transport and sea transport transferred to Scottish Office Establishment of the Scottish Transport Group.

15 April 1969

Harold Wilson appoints a Royal Commission under Lord Crowther to consider the Constitution.

30 October 1969

Glasgow Gorbals by-election. SNP wins 25% but this is interpreted as a setback for the party.

6 May 1969

Local elections. SNP makes only modest gains which are interpreted as a setback.

19 March 1970

South Ayrshire by-election. Jim Sillars holds the seat comfortably for Labour and SNP win 20.4% of vote.

20 March 1970

Douglas-Home Committee, established by Ted Heath, reports recommending an elected 'Scottish Convention'.

18 June 1970

General Election. SNP contests 65 seats and wins 11.4% of vote.

Hamilton is lost but Western Isles is gained from Labour. Conservatives returned to power.

16 September 1971
Stirling and Falkirk by-election. SNP wins 34.6% of vote.

7–13 December 1971
Wendy Wood on hunger strike in protest at Conservative Government's refusal to establish a Scottish legislature as promised at the election.

22 January 1972
Prime Minister Edward Heath signs the Treaty of Accession to the EEC.

24 March 1972
Heath announces that Stormont Parliament is to be suspended and that direct rule is to be imposed on Northern Ireland.

1973
Scottish Economic Planning Department set up in Scottish Office.

1 January 1973
United Kingdom joins the European Community.

1 March 1973
Dundee East by-election. Gordon Wilson for the SNP wins 30.2% of vote and comes a close second to Labour.

March 1973
Launch of SNP's 'It's Scotland's Oil' campaign.

31 October 1973
Publication of Royal Commission on the Constitution (chaired by Lord Kilbrandon, following the death of Crowther) with Memorandum of Dissent from Crowther-Hunt and Peacock (Cmnd. 5460).

8 November 1973
Glasgow Govan by-election. Margo MacDonald wins seat for SNP with 41.9% of vote. But in Edinburgh North, Billy Wolfe, party leader, wins only 18.9%.

13 November 1973
State of Emergency is declared by Heath Government in reaction to economic and industrial relations crises. Imposition of three-day week. Minimum Lending Rate is increased to an unprecedented 13%.

28 February 1974
General Election. SNP contests 70 out of 71 constituencies and

wins 21.9% of vote. It loses Govan, holds the Western Isles and gains Argyll, Banff, Aberdeenshire East, Moray and Nairn from the Conservatives and Dundee East, Clackmannan and East Stirling from Labour.

12 March 1974

Queen's Speech includes a commitment that the Labour Government 'will initiate discussions on the Constitution and will bring forward proposals for consideration'.

13 March 1974

Lord Crowther-Hunt appointed Minister of State at the Privy Council with responsibility for devolution.

17 April 1974

STUC gives strong backing to devolution.

7 May 1974

First elections to Scottish regions. SNP wins 12.6% of the vote but contests no seats in Tayside.

3 June 1974

Publication of 'Devolution within the United Kingdom: some alternatives for discussion' white paper. Seven options put forward.

22 June 1974

Scottish Executive of the Labour party rejects devolution proposals.

17 August 1974

Special Labour Party in Scotland conference in Glasgow overturns Scottish Executive decision on devolution.

7 September 1974

Devolution white paper published.

10 October 1974

General Election. SNP wins 30.4% of vote holding seven seats won in February and gaining Angus South, Galloway, Perth and East Perthshire from the Conservatives and Dunbartonshire East from Labour.

1975

Industry powers transferred to Scottish Office.

21 February 1975

Margaret Thatcher's first visit to Scotland as Conservative leader. She asserts her support for a Scottish Assembly.

21 March 1975

Labour's Scottish conference defeats a resolution calling for wide-ranging powers for a Scottish Assembly and instead seeks an Executive with powers similar to Secretary of State for Scotland.

28 March 1975

Launch of Scottish Daily News newspaper cooperative.

5 June 1975

Referendum on European Community membership. SNP campaigns for a 'No' vote. Scotland votes with the rest of UK to stay in the Community. Only Shetland and the Western Isles vote against.

8 July 1975

Launch of Scottish Development Agency.

8 November 1975

Scottish Daily News ceases operation.

22 November 1975

Publication of 'Our Changing Democracy' white paper (Cmnd. 6348) advocating a 142-member legislative assembly with considerable powers retained by Secretary of State for Scotland.

18 January 1976

Launch of Scottish Labour Party led by Jim Sillars.

9 May 1976

'Keep Britain United' launched with mainly Conservative backing.

1 August 1976

Publication of 'Devolution to Scotland and Wales: Supplementary Statement' (Cmnd. 6585). Recommends at least two Assembly seats for all constituencies; that the Assembly alone should nominate the chief executive; the UK Government to be able to object to Assembly Bills only if causing 'unacceptable repercussions' on non-devolved matters, and unable to take back powers; judicial review of Assembly legislation to be allowed; Assembly power to surcharge rates dropped; SDA operations, administration of the courts, private law, regulation of teaching and legal profession to be devolved.

26 October 1976

ORC poll in the *Scotsman* showed 65% intending to vote 'Yes' in a referendum on the Government's plans for a Scottish Assembly with 16% intending to vote 'No' and 19% don't knows.

23 November 1976
Establishment of 'Scotland is British' by industrialists.

28 November 1976
Scotland and Wales Bill published.

1 December 1976
Conservative Shadow Cabinet decide to oppose Devolution Bill leading Alick Buchanan-Smith to resign as Shadow Scottish Secretary and Malcolm Rifkind as junior Scottish spokesman

8 December 1976
Government publish 'Devolution – the English dimension'.

16 December 1976
Scotland and Wales Bill given second reading by 292 votes to 247 after Government concedes referendums once the Bill is enacted.

7 January 1977
Conference in Newcastle organised by Tyne and Wear County Council under title 'Devolution – the Case Against'.

9 February 1977
ORC poll in Scotsman. 66% support Government's devolution proposals and 21% oppose with 13% undecided or unwilling to vote.

13 January *15 February 1977*
Committee stage of Scotland and Wales Bill on the floor of the House of Commons. Only amendment agreed is that Orkney and Shetland should each have one Assembly member.

19 February 1977
Motion on guillotine to ensure passage of devolution legislation is defeated by 312 votes to 283; 22 Labour MPs vote against and 15 abstain, effectively killing the Scotland and Wales Bill.

11 March 1977
Labour Party in Scotland call for an immediate referendum on devolution.

23 March 1977
Labour Government survives a no-confidence vote in the Commons after the Lib-Lab Pact is agreed.

28 March 1977

ORC poll in *Scotsman*. Britain-wide poll asked whether Government should go ahead with plans to give Scotland some form of self-government. 41% said Government should go ahead; 42% said it should not go ahead and 17% did not know but 70% agreed that Scotland should have a greater say in running its own affairs while 22% said it should not. Asked how many MPs Scotland should have at Westminster after devolution, 37% said same number as now; 14% said more than now; 22% said less; 11% said none at all; and 16% did not know. 47% of people in Britain disagreed with the proposition that Scotland is a 'nation in its own right' while 46% agreed that it is. 58% felt devolution would almost certainly lead to the break-up of the UK; 33% disagreed and 9% did not know.

15 April 1977

Ted Heath calls for Scottish Assembly with revenue-raising powers.

4 May 1977

SNP makes substantial gains in local government elections and Labour loses ground.

21 May 1977

Scottish Conservatives reverse their policy and oppose a directly elected Scottish Assembly.

26 July 1977

Lord President's statement in the Commons: separate Bills for Scotland and Wales in next session; Assembly with no revenue-raising powers; limited industrial powers; head of Executive retitled 'First Secretary'; premature dissolution of Assembly to be possible on vote of two-thirds of members; block grant to be fixed for 'a number of years' by percentage formula; 'independent advisory board' on devolution financing; 'Joint Council' between Government and Executive proposed.

4 November 1977

Scotland Bill given first reading in House of Commons.

14 November 1977

Scotland Bill given second reading by 307 votes to 263. Wales Bill passes its second reading by 295 votes to 264.

16 November 1977

Guillotine motion on devolution legislation is carried by 313 votes to 287.

22 November *1 February 1977*

Committee Stage of Scotland Bill. Clause 1 (declaring the unity of the UK) is removed by 199 votes to 184 on first day.

1978

Forestry Commission headquarters moved to Edinburgh.

25 January 1978

'Cunningham amendment' successfully moved by 168 votes to 142 in Commons stating that 'if it appears to the Secretary of State that less than 40% of the persons entitled to vote in the referendum have voted "Yes" . . . he shall lay before Parliament the draft of an Order in Council for the repeal of this Act'. Grimond amendment that if Orkney or Shetland vote "No" in referendum 'the Secretary of State shall lay before Parliament the draft of an Order in Council providing that . . . the Act shall not apply to them, and providing also for the establishment of a commission to recommend such changes in the government of that area or those as may be desirable' carried by 204 votes to 118.

26 January 1978

Launch of 'Yes for Scotland' campaign chaired by Lord Kilbrandon.

27 January 1978

Helen Liddell, Labour's Scottish general secretary issues circular to the party explaining decision not to participate in cross-party referendum campaigning.

14–15 February 1978

Report Stage of Scotland Bill in Commons. Tam Dalyell's amendment stipulating that if Parliament is dissolved before the referendum is held, it must be deferred until three months after polling day, approved by 242 votes to 223. Canavan amendment to remove 40% rule defeated by 298 votes to 248.

22 February 1978

Scotland Bill given third reading by 297 voted to 257.

23 February 1978

Scotland Bill given first reading in House of Lords.

14–15 March 1978

Scotland Bill given unopposed second reading in House of Lords.

4 April–17 May 1978

Committee Stage of Scotland Bill in House of Lords. Lords vote for an amendment proposing additional member voting system by 155 to 64.

Lords vote to withdraw from Assembly responsibility for abortion, aero-
dromes, forestry and afforestation, inland waterways and road passenger
service licensing.

13 April 1978
   Glasgow Garscadden by-election. SNP wins 32.9% but fails to take seat
from Labour.

26 April 1978
   Regional Council Elections. SNP win 20.9% of vote, Labour win 40%.

16 May 1978
   Lords vote by 102 to 93 for a Speaker's conference to consider the
number of MPs at Westminster after devolution.

31 May 1978
   Hamilton by-election. Margo MacDonald wins 33.4% for SNP but
Labour holds seat.

7 June 1978
   Report Stage in Lords begins.

20 June 1978
   Report Stage in Lords ends. Assembly committees required to reflect
party balance; purchase grants for libraries, museums and art galleries re-
served; requirement for 14 days' interval followed by second vote if Bill not
affecting Scotland carried by Commons only because of votes of Scottish
MPs; new Government clause on Orkney and Shetland to replace 'Grimond
amendment'.

29 June 1978
   Scotland Bill given unopposed third reading in Lords.

4 July 1978
   Commons timetable motion for consideration of Lords' amendments.

6–26 July 1978
   Consideration of Lords' amendments begins. Alternative voting system
defeated by 363 to 155 votes. Other amendments removing powers accepted by Commons. Government defeated on committee balance, second
vote in Commons and reservation of forestry.

27 July 1978
   Lords accepts Commons amendments.

30 July 1978
John Mackintosh, ardent supporter of Scottish self-government and Labour MP, dies.

31 July 1978
Royal Assent given to Scotland Bill.

26 October 1978
Berwick and E. Lothian by-election caused by death of John Mackintosh. SNP wins 8.8% and loses deposit. Isobel Lindsay is candidate. Labour hold seat.

1 November 1978
Callaghan announces 1 March 1979 as date for devolution referendums in Scotland and Wales.

12 February 1979
System Three poll for *Glasgow Herald*. 45% of Scots intending to vote 'Yes'; 35% 'No' with 20% undecided. Marks a major swing against devolution.

13 February 1979
Lord Home argues for a 'No' vote on the grounds that the Conservatives would produce a more powerful Assembly.

16 February 1979
ORC poll for the *Scotsman*. 49% of Scots agree that Scotland Act, 1978 should be put into effect; 33% said 'No'; 13% undecided and 4% would not vote.

23 February 1979
NOP poll for *Daily Record*. 44% intend to vote 'Yes' in referendum; 30% 'No'; 20% undecided and 6% will not vote.

1 March 1979
Referendum held. 51.6% voted 'Yes' and 48.4% voted 'No'. Of the total electorate, 32.9% voted 'Yes', 30.8% voted 'No' and 36.3% did not vote. Wales votes heavily against devolution proposals by 79.7% to 20.3%.

22 March 1979
Commons statement by Prime Minister James Callaghan declining to set a date for vote on order to repeal Scotland Act and calling for all-party consultations. Motion of no-confidence put down by the SNP Parliamentary group.

28 March 1979
Government defeated on Conservative motion of no-confidence by one vote. SNP MPs vote against Government.

3 May 1979

General Election. SNP lose nine seats, leaving them with only 2 with 17.2% of the vote. Conservatives under Margaret Thatcher win election.

7 June 1979

First directly elected European Community elections. SNP wins 19.4%. Winnie Ewing wins Highlands and Islands for SNP.

20 June 1979

Commons passes repeal order on Scotland Act by 301 votes to 206. Of the Scottish MPs, 43 vote against repeal, 19 in favour with 9 absent. George Younger, Secretary of State for Scotland, offers all-party talks to consider 'the scope for improving the handling of Scottish business in Parliament'.

26 June 1979

Wales Act is repealed.

18 August 1979

Inaugural conference of SNP '79 Group agrees the group's principles to be 'independence, socialism and a Scottish republic'.

1 March 1980

Campaign for a Scottish Assembly launched.

3 May 1980

Jim Sillars joins SNP.

28 May 1981

SNP annual conference votes in favour of civil disobedience.

16 October 1981

Jim Sillars, SNP vice-chairman, leads group of SNP activists who break into the Royal High School in protest against unemployment and constitutional question.

15 February 1982

Scottish Grand Committee meets in Royal High School, Edinburgh as part of Conservatives' alternative to devolution.

23 March 1982

Glasgow Hillhead by-election. Roy Jenkins takes the seat for Social Democratic Party. SNP wins 11.3%

2 April 1982

Argentina seizes the Falkland Islands claiming them as Argentine territory.

25 April 1982

British forces recapture part of Falklands Islands. Mrs Thatcher tells Britain to 'Rejoice. Rejoice'.

3–5 June 1982

SNP annual conference. Campaign for Nationalism set up in reaction to '79 Group. Gordon Wilson successfully moves to proscribe all groups within the party.

26 August 1982

SNP national council votes on expulsions of '79 Group members.

14 June 1982

End of South Atlantic Conflict when British forces capture Port Stanley, Falklands Islands.

16 September 1982

Margo MacDonald resigns from SNP.

1 March 1983

John Home Robertson, Labour MP, threatens Parliamentary disruption to press the case for Scottish Assembly.

9 June 1983

General Election. SNP wins 11.8% and hold their two seats, losing 53 out of 72 deposits.

14 June 1984

Euro-elections. SNP hold Highlands and Islands and win 17.8% of the vote.

13 September 1984

SNP annual conference votes for a directly elected constitutional convention by 264 votes to 28.

17 February 1986

Single European Act is signed by European Community member states moving Europe towards 'ever closer union'.

11 June 1987

General Election. SNP wins 14% of the vote, loses both the Western Isles and Dundee East to Labour but wins Moray, Banff and Buchan, and Angus South from Tories.

1 July 1987

Single European Act comes into force.

13 September 1987
Festival for Scottish Democracy organised by Labour Party and trade unions.

23 November 1987
Nigel Lawson, Chancellor of the Exchequer, attacks Scottish 'dependency culture' in a speech in Glasgow.

February 1988
Foundation of Scottish Labour Action, nationalist fringe group within the Labour Party.

11 March 1988
Scotsman poll shows 42% support non-payment of poll tax and 44% oppose non-payment.

15 March 1988
Alex Salmond, SNP MP, interrupts budget speech in House of Commons.

1 April 1988
Introduction of poll tax in Scotland.

13 July 1988
Launch of 'Claim of Right for Scotland' by group established by Campaign for a Scottish Assembly proposing a Constitutional Convention.

15 September 1988
SNP annual conference adopts a policy of poll tax non-payment and explicit support for independence in Europe.

21 October 1988
Donald Dewar, Shadow Scottish Secretary, agrees that Labour will participate in a Constitutional Convention.

10 November 1988
Glasgow Govan by-election. Jim Sillars wins the seat for the SNP with 48.8% of the vote.

14 March 1989
Jim Sillars attempts to disrupt budget speech in House of Commons but is prevented from doing so by Labour leader Neil Kinnock.

30 March 1989
First meeting of the Constitutional Convention.

15 June 1989

Glasgow Central by-election. SNP fail to take seat from Labour but wins 30.2% of the vote. European-Elections. SNP wins 26.9% of the vote and holds Highlands and Islands.

9 November 1989

Berlin Wall comes down.

10 March 1990

Scottish Council of the Labour Party votes to support an alternative to first-past-the-post voting system in elections to the Scottish Parliament.

16 April 1990

Dick Douglas, MP for Dunfermline West expelled from Labour Party after 42 years as a member after deciding to stand as an Independent Labour candidate in local elections in opposition to poll tax.

22 September 1990

Alex Salmond elected national convener of the SNP.

4 October 1990

Dick Douglas MP joins the SNP.

29 November 1990

Paisley North and South by-elections. SNP wins 29.4% in Paisley North and 27.5% in Paisley South but Labour holds the seats.

30 November 1990

Constitutional Convention publishes 'Towards Scotland's Parliament: a report to the Scottish people by the Scottish Constitutional Convention'.

23 March 1991

SNP ends its poll tax non-payment campaign following Government decision to end the tax.

7 November 1991

Kincardine and Deeside by-election. Conservatives lose seat to Liberal Democrats. SNP win 11.1% of the vote.

8 January 1992

Announcement of closure of Ravenscraig steel mill.

23 January 1992

Sun backs independence with front page headline, 'Rise now and be a nation again'.

29 January 1992
Scotsman/ITN poll showing 50% support for Scottish independence.

7 February 1992
The Treaty on European Union signed in Maastricht.

10/11 April 1992
Launch of Scotland United. Start of vigil outside Royal High School organised by Democracy for Scotland.

13 April 1992
Ian Lang rejects call for a multi-option referendum.

14 April 1992
Launch of Common Cause.

15 April 1992
Lord Fraser appointed as Scottish Office Minister responsible for constitutional affairs.

7 May 1992
District Council Elections. Conservatives marginally increase their vote to 23% SNP win 24%, hold onto Angus district. In Edinburgh, Labour loses overall control and relies on SNP support at price of appointment of the first SNP Lord Provost of Scotland's capital.

16 September 1992
'Black Wednesday', Britain leaves the European Exchange Rate Mechanism.

27 November 1992
Publication of Scotland United document 'What price democracy?' advocating a multi-option referendum.

12 December 1992
Democracy Demonstration in Edinburgh coinciding with European Union Summit.

8 March 1993
SNP vote with Government in Commons on Maastricht Bill.

9 March 1993
Government publish 'Scotland in the Union: a partnership for good' (Cm. 2225) advocating cosmetic changes in response to Government's exercise in 'taking stock' of Scotland's status as part of the UK.

1 November 1993
Maastricht Treaty comes into force.

December 1993
Falkirk local plebiscite.

15 December 1993
Downing Street Declaration between Irish and UK Governments is published.

6 April 1994
Archbishop of Canterbury causes controversy by saying that Britain is 'an ordinary little nation'.

5 May 1994
Last regional elections before abolition of regional authorities. SNP wins 26.8%.

9 June 1994
Euro-Elections. SNP wins 32.6% of the vote; holds Highlands and Islands and gains North-East Scotland from Labour.

18 June 1994
Civic Forum held in Royal High School to discuss creating a Scottish Senate/Civic Forum.

30 June 1994
Monklands East by-election caused by the death of John Smith, Leader of the Opposition. Labour holds seat. SNP wins 44.9% of the vote.

12 February 1995
'Great Debate' organised between Alex Salmond, SNP leader and George Robertson, Labour's Shadow Scottish Secretary. Salmond emerges as clear winner.

3 April 1995
Court of Session in Edinburgh bans 'Panorama' interview with Prime Minister as it could prejudice the local elections to be held in Scotland.

6 April 1995
Elections to new unitary local authorities. SNP wins 26.3% of the vote and outright control of three of the 29 new authorities: Moray, Angus and Perth and Kinross.

25 May 1995
Perth and Kinross by-election. Roseanna Cunningham elected SNP MP with 40.4% of the vote.

Bibliography

A range of sources were used in writing this book. Papers held in the Scottish Records Office, Charlotte Square, Edinburgh, and the Public Records Office, Kew, London were consulted. In addition private papers in Churchill College, Cambridge and in the National Library of Scotland (NLS) Edinburgh were used. The papers of the Scots Secretariat held in the NLS were an invaluable source. The *Glasgow Herald* was the main newspaper source though the *Scotsman* was important in covering the last thirty years. In addition the following papers were consulted:

Airdrie and Coatbridge Advertiser
Courier and Advertiser
Daily Express
Daily Record
Daily Record and Mail
Dumfries and Galloway Standard
Dumfries Standard
Dundee Advertiser
Economist
Forward
Glasgow Evening Citizen
Glasgow Evening Times
Guardian
Observer
Picture Post
The People

Press and Journal
Radical Scotland
Scotland on Sunday
Scots Independent
Scottish Daily Mail
Spectator
The Sun
Times
Tribune

Official publications

Balfour (Chairman) (1954), *Report of the Royal Commission on Scottish Affairs* Cmnd. 9212 (London, HMSO).

Census Scotland 1951, Vol. II, Population of Towns and Larger Villages and of Urban and Rural Scotland

Kilbrandon (Chairman) (1973), *Report of the Royal Commission on the Constitution* (Cmnd. 5460 (London,MSO).

Scottish Home Department (1948), 'Scottish Affairs' Cmd. 7308 (Edinburgh, HMSO)

Scottish Office (1993), 'Scotland in the Union: a partnership for good' Cm. 2225 (Edinburgh, HMSO).

Books and articles

Alexander, K. J. W. (1970), 'The Economic Case against Independence', in Neil MacCormick (ed), *The Scottish Debate*, (London, Oxford University Press).

Alford, B. W. E. (1975), *Depression and Recovery? British Economic Growth, 1918–39*, (London, Macmillan).

Almond G. and Verba, S. (1965), *The Civic Culture*, (Boston, Little Brown).

Anon. (1996), 'Home Rule for Scotland', *Scottish Review*, July.

Arblaster, Anthony (1987), *Democracy*, (Milton Keynes, Open University Press).

Ascherson, Neal (1977), 'The Strange Death of Devolution', *Scotsman* March 4.

Bachrach, Peter and Baratz, Morton (1962), 'The Two Faces of Power', *American Political Science Review*, vol. 56.

Barber, Benjamin (1984), *Strong Democracy: Participatory Politics for a New Age*, (Berkeley, University of California Press).

Barker, Peter (1992), 'Legitimacy in the United Kingdom: Scotland and the Poll Tax', *British Journal of Political Science*, vol. 22.

Barry, Brian (1983), 'Self Government Revisited', in David Miller and Larry Siedentop (eds.), *The Nature of Political Theory*, (Oxford, Oxford University Press).

Barry, Brian (1989), *Democracy, Power and Justice: essays in political theory*, (Oxford, Clarendon Press).

Beitz, Charles (1979), *Political Equality: an essay in democratic theory*, (Princeton, Princeton University Press).

Beller, Dennis and Belloni, Frank (1978), 'The Study of Factions', in Frank Belloni and Dennis Beller (eds.), *Faction Politics: Political Parties and Factionalism in Comparative Perspective*, (Oxford, ABC-CLIO).

Benn, Tony (1989), *Against The Tide: Diaries 1973–76*, (London, Arrow Books).

Berelson, Bernard et. al. (1954), *Voting*, (Chicago, University of Chicago Press).

Beveridge, Craig and Turnbull, Ronald (1989), *The Eclipse of Scottish Culture*, (Edinburgh, Polygon).

Birch, Anthony H. (1989) *Nationalism and National Integration* (London, Unwin Hyman).

Bochel, J. Denver, D. and Macartney, A. (eds.) (1981), *The Referendum Experience: Scotland 1979*), (Aberdeen, Aberdeen University Press).

Bogdanor, Vernon (1979), *Devolution*, (Oxford, Oxford University Press.

Bogdanor, Vernon (1980), 'The 40 Per Cent Rule', *Parliamentary Affairs*, vol. 33.

Bogdanor, Vernon (1981), *The People and the Party System: the referendum and electoral reform in British politics*, (Cambridge, Cambridge University Press).

Bogdanor, Vernon (1983), *Multi-party politics and the Constitution*, (Cambridge, Cambridge University Press).

Bold, Alan (1990), *MacDiarmid*, (London, Grafton).

Brand, Jack (1981), 'A National Assembly' *Crann Tara*, No. 13, Spring.

Brand, J. Mitchell, J. and Surridge, P. (1994), 'Social Constituency and Ideological Profile: Scotish Nationalism in the 1990s', *Political Studies* (vol. 42).

Brass, Paul (1976), 'Ethnicity and Nationality Formation', *Ethnicity*, vol. 3, no. 3.

Bruce, George (1986), *'To Foster and enrich'; the first fifty years of the Saltire Society*, (Edinburgh, Saltire Society).

Bryce, James (1888), *The American Commonwealth*, vol. 3 (London, Macmillan).

Bryson, Bill (1994), *Made in America*, (London, Secker and Warburg).

Bute, Marquess of (1889), 'Parliament in Scotland', *Scottish Review*, October.

Butler, David (1983), *Governing Without a Majority*, (London, Collins).

Butler, David and Kitzinger, Uwe (1976), *The 1975 Referendum* (London, Macmillan).

Cairncross, Alec (1992), *The British Economy since 1945*, (Oxford, Blackwell).

Callaghan, James (1988), *Time and Chance*, (London, Fontana).

Camilleri, Joseph and Falk, Jim (1992), *The End of Sovereignty?*, (Aldershot, Edward Elgar).

Cobban, Alfred (1969), *The National State and National Self-Determination*, (London, Collins).

Cohen, Joshua and Rogers, Joel (1983), *On Democracy: Towards a Transformation of American Society*, (Harmondsworth, Penguin).

Cohen, Robin (1994), *Frontiers of Identity: The British and the Others*, (London, Longman).

Coleman, William (1984), *The independence movement in Quebec, 1945–80*, (Toronto, University of Toronto Press).

Colley, Linda (1992), *Britons: Forging the Nation 1707–1837*, (London, Yale University Press).

Connor, Walker (1973), 'The Politics of Ethnonationalism', *Journal of International Affairs*, vol. 27, No. 1.

Conroy, Harry (1992), 'Constitutional Convention's Campaign', *The Scottish Government Yearbook, 1992*.

Conservative Central Office (1981), *The First 10 Years*, (London, Conservative Party).

Coupland, Sir Reginald (1954), *Welsh and Scottish Nationalism*, (London, Collins).

Crossman, Richard (1977), *Diaries* vol. 2, (London, Hamish Hamilton).

Cunningham, Frank (1987), *Democratic Theory and Socialism*, (Cambridge, Cambridge University Press).

Cunningham, George (1989), 'Burns Night Massacre', *The Spectator*, 28 January.

Dahl, Robert (1956), *A Preface to Democratic Theory*, (Chicago, University of Chicago Press).

Dalton, Russell J. and Kuechler, Manfred (eds.) (1990), *Challenging the Political Order*, (Cambridge, Polity Press).

Dayell, Tam (1977), *Devolution: the End of Britain?*, (London, Jonathan Cape).

Deacon, David and Goulding, Peter (1991), 'When Ideology Fails: The Flagship of Thatcherism and the British National and Local Media', *European Journal of Communication*, vol. 6.

Dicey, A. V. (1886, 1973), *England's Case Against Home Rule*, (Richmond, Richmond Publishing).

Dicey, A. V. (1890), 'Ought the referendum to be introduced into England?', *Contemporary Review*, April.

Dodd, Walter F. (1962), 'Constitutional Conventions' in Edwin R. A. Silgman (ed.), *Encyclopaedia of the Social Sciences*, (vol. 3 (New York, Macmillan).

Drucker, Henry (nd.), *Breakaway: the Scottish Labour Party*, (Edinburgh, EUSPB).

Eisinger, Peter (1973), 'The Conditions of Protest Behavior in American Cities', *American Political Science Review*, vol. 67.

Esman, Milton (1977), 'Perspectives on Ethnic Conflict in Industrialized Societies', in Esman (ed.), *Ethnic Conflict in the Western World*, (London, Cornell University Press).

Farley, Lawrence (1986), *Plebiscites and Sovereignty*, (London, Mansell Publishing Ltd).

Ferguson, William (1990), *Scotland: 1689 to the Present*, (Edinburgh, Mercat Press).

Finlay, Richard (1992), '"For or against?": Scottish Nationalists and the British Empire, 1919–39', *The Scottish Historical Review*, vol. 61.

Finlay, Richard (1994), *Independent and Free, Scottish Politics and the Origins of the Scottish National Party, 1918–1945* (Edinburgh, John Donald).

Fleisher, Martin (ed.) (1973), *Machiavelli and the nature of political thought* (London, Croom Helm).

Foulkes, G. Maxton, J. Canavan, D. Robertson, J. H. and Marshall, D. (nd.), *Defending Scotland Against Thatcher: An action plan for the Labour Movement*, (authors).

Franklin, V. P. (1992), *Black Self-Determination: A Cultural History of African-American Resistance*, (New York, Lawrence Hill).

Fraser of Allander Institute (1989), *Scotland and Independence: an economic perspective*, Glasgow, Fraser of Allander Institute.

Fraser, Graham (1984), *René Lévesque and the Parti Québécois in Power*, (Toronto, Macmillan).

French, Stanley and Gutman Andres (1974), 'The Principle of National Self-Determination', in Virginia Held, Sidney Morgenbesser and Thomas Nagel (eds.), *Philosophy, Morality and International Affairs*, (Oxford, Oxford University Press).

Gamble, Andrew (1994), *Britain in Decline*, Fourth edition (Houndmills,

Macmillan).

Gamson, William (1975), *The Strategy of Social Protest*, (Homewood, Il., Dorsey).

George, Stephen (1990), *An Awkward Partner: Britain in the European Community*, (Oxford, Oxford University Press).

Grant, Wyn (1989), *Pressure Groups, Politics and Democracy in Britain*, (Hemel Hempstead, Philip Allan).

Gray, Alasdair (1992), *Why Scots should rule Scotland*, (Edinburgh, Canongate Press).

Green, Philip (1985), *Retrieving Democracy* (London, Methuen).

Grieve, C. M. (1922), 'Scottish literature and Home Rule', *Scottish Home Rule: monthly organ of the SHRA*, vol. 3, no. 5.

Griffiths, N. (1989), 'Retrospect and Prospect' in Owen Dudley Edwards (ed.), *A Claim of Right for Scotland*, (Edinburgh, Polygon).

Hadfield, Brigid (1989), *The Constitution of Northern Ireland*, (Belfast, SLS Legal Publications).

Hamilton, Ian (1990), *A Touch of Treason*, (Moffat, Lochar Publishing Ltd).

Hamilton, Ian (1991), *The Taking of the Stone of Destiny*, (Moffat, Lochar Publishing).

Hanham, H. J. (1969), *Scottish Nationalism*, (London, Faber).

Harvie, Christopher (1977, 1994), *Scotland and Nationalism*, (London, Routledge).

Harvie, Christopher (1981, 1993), *No Gods and Precious Few Heroes*, (London, Edward Arnold).

Haworth, J. 1968), *The National Party of Scotland and the Scottish Self-Government Movement: 1928–1939*. (Syracuse D.SS., United States of America).

Heberle, Rudolf (1951), *Social Movements*, (New York, Appleton-Century-Croft).

Held, David and Pollitt, Christopher (1986), *New Forms of Democracy*, (London, Sage).

Hogan, Michael J. (1987), *The Marshall Plan: America, Britain, and the reconstruction of Western Europe, 1947–1952*, (Cambridge, Cambridge University Press).

Hogwood, Brian (1977), 'Models of Industrial Policy: The Implications for Devolution', *Studies in Public Policy*, Strathclyde University Centre for the Study of Public Policy, no. 5.

Hogwood, Brian (1986), 'If consultation is everything then maybe it's nothing . . . , *Strathclyde Papers on Politics and Government*, no. 44.

Holland, Robert (1991), *The Pursuit of Greatness: Britain and the World Role, 1900–1970*, (London, Fontana).

Janda, K. (1980), *Political Parties, a cross national survey*, (New York, Free Press).

Jenkins, J. Craig (1983), 'Resource Mobilization Theory and the Study of Social Movements', *Annual Revue of Sociology*, vol. 9.

Jenkins, Peter (1988), *Mrs Thatcher's Revolution*, (London, Pan Books).

Jordan, A. G. and Richardson, J. J. (1987), *Government and Pressure Groups in Britain*, (Oxford, Clarendon Press).

Keating, Michael and Bleiman, David (1979), *Labour and Scottish Nationalism*, (London, Macmillan).

Kee, Robert (1972), *The Green Flag: a history of Irish Nationalism*, (London, Weidenfeld and Nicolson).

Kellas, James G. (1971), 'Scottish Nationalism' in David Butler and Michael Pinto-Duschinsky, *The British General Election of 1970*, (London, Macmillan).

Kellas, James G. (1989), *The Scottish Political System*, Fourth edition, (Cambridge, Cambridge University Press).

Kellas, James G. (1991), *The Politics of Nationalism and Ethnicity*, (Basingstoke, Macmillan).

Kemp, Arnold (1993), *The Hollow Drum*, (Edinburgh, Mainstream).

Kennedy, Ludovic (1967), 'Yours for Scotland' *Spectator*, November 10.

Kennedy, Ludovic (1989), *On my way to the club*, (London, Collins).

Klandermans, Bert (1986), 'New Social Movements and Resource Mobilization: The European and the American Approach', *International Journal of Mass Emergencies and Disasters*, vol. 4.

Klandermans, Bert and Tarrow, Sidney (1988), 'Mobilization into Social Movements: synthesizing European and American Approaches', *International Social Movement Research*, vol. 1.

Kolakolwski, Leszek (1971), 'Hope and Hopelessness', *Survey*, vol. 17, Summer.

Kornhauser, William (1959), *The Politics of Mass Society*, (New York, Free Press).

Krouse, Richard (1982), 'Two Concepts of Democratic Representation: James and John Stuart Mill', *The Journal of Politics*, vol. 44.

Leckie, Ross (1988), 'Implications for Industry', in Michael Fry (ed), *Unlocking the Future*, (Edinburgh, Conservative Constitutional Reform Forum).

Lijphart, Arend (1977), *Democracy in Plural Societies* (New Haven, Yale University Press).

Linklater, Andro (1992), *Compton Mackenzie*, (London, Hogarth Press).

Linklater, Magnus and Denniston, Robin (eds.) (1992), *Anatomy of Scotland*, (Edinburgh, Chambers).

Lippman, Walter (1925), *The phantom public*, (New York, Harcourt Brace Jovanovich).

Lipset, S. M. and Rokkan, S. E (1967), 'Cleavage structures, party systems and voter alignments', in S. M. Lipset and S. E. Rokkan (eds.), *Party Systems and Voter Alignments*, (New York, Free Press).

Lukes, Steven (1974), *Power: a radical view*, (London, Macmillan).

McAdam, D. McCarthy, J. D. and Zald, M. N (1988), 'Social Movements' in Neil Smelser (ed.), *Handbook of Sociology*, (London, Sage).

MacCormick, John (1955), *Flag in the Wind*, (London, Victor Gollancz).

MacCormick, Neil (ed.) (1970), *The Scottish Debate*, (London, Oxford University Press).

MacCormick, Neil (1981), *Legal Right and Social Democracy*, (Oxford, Oxford University Press).

MacCormick, Neil (1991), 'Is Nationalism Philosophically Credible?' in W. Twining (ed.), *Issues of Self-Determination*, (Aberdeen, Aberdeen University Press).

McCrone, David (1992), *Understanding Scotland: the sociology of a stateless nation*, (London, Routledge).

McCrone, Gavin (1969), *Scotland's Future: the economics of nationalism*, (Oxford, Basil Blackwell).

McEwen, Sir Alexander (1938), *Towards Freedom*, (London, William Hodge & Co. Ltd),

McKay, Donald (ed.) (1977), *Scotland 1980: the economics of self-government*, (Edinburgh Q Press).

Mackintosh, John P. (1968), *The Devolution of Power*, (London, Penguin).

Mackintosh, John P. (1974), 'The New Appeal of Nationalism', *New Statesman*, 27 September.

Mackintosh, John P. (1982), 'The trouble with Stephen Maxwell', *Question*, 15 April 1977 reprinted in Henry Drucker (ed.), *John P. Mackintosh on Scotland*, (London, Longman).

MacPherson, C. B. (1984), *Democratic Theory: Essays in Retrieval*, (Oxford, Clarendon Press).

Macwhirter, Iain (1990), 'After Doomsday . . . The Convention And Scotland's Constitutional Crisis', *Scottish Government Yearbook 1990*.

Margolis, Michael (1979), *Viable Democracy*, (Harmondsworth, Penguin).

Margolis, Michael (1983), 'Democracy: American style', in G. Duncan (ed.), *Democratic theory and practice*, (Cambridge, Cambridge University Press).

Marshall, T. H. and Bottomore, Tom (1992), *Citizenship and Social Class*,

(London, Pluto Press).

Mayo, Henry B. (1960), *An Introduction to Democratic Theory*, (Oxford, Oxford University Press).

Meehan, Elizabeth (1993), *Citizenship and the European Community*, (London, Sage).

Melucci, Alberto (1985), 'The Symbolic Challenge of Contemporary Movements', *Social Research*, vol. 52.

Mény, Yves (1991), *Government and Politics in Western Europe*, (Oxford, Oxford University Press).

Mény, Yves and Wright, Vincent (eds.) (1985), *Centre-Periphery Relations in Western Europe*, (London, Allen & Unwin).

Michie, Alistair and Hoggart, Simon (1978), *The Pact: the inside story of the Lib-Lab government, 1977–78*, (London, Quarter).

Middleton, K. W. B. (1954), 'New Thoughts on the Union Between England and Scotland', *Juridical Review*, vol. 61.

Milbrath, Lester (1965), *Political Participation*, (Chicago, Rand McNally).

Miller, David (1988), 'The Ethical Significance of Nationality' *Ethics*, vol. 98.

Miller, W. Brand, J. and Jordan, M. (1980), *Oil and the Scottish voter, 1974–79*, (London, Social Science Research Council).

Milward, Alan (1992), *The European Rescue of the Nation-State*, (London, Routledge).

Mitchell, James (1990), *Conservatives and the Union*, (Edinburgh, Edinburgh University Press).

Mitchell, James (1991), 'Constitutional Conventions and the Scottish National Movement: Origins, Agendas and Outcomes', *Strathclyde Papers on Government and Politics*, No. 78.

Mitchell, William (1892), *Home Rule for Scotland and Imperial Federation*, (Edinburgh, Scottish Home Rule Association).

Mitchell, William (1892), *Is Scotland to be sold again? Home Rule for Scotland* (Edinburgh, Scottish Home Rule Association).

Mitchell, William (1893), *Home Rule All All Round: or Federal Union. Letter to Right Hon. H. H. Asquith*, (Edinburgh, Scottish Home Rule Association).

Mitchison, Naomi (1986), *Among You Taking Notes . . . The Wartime Diary of Naomi Mitchison, 1939–1945*, (Oxford, Oxford University Press).

Morgan, Kenneth (1981), *Rebirth of a Nation, Wales 1880–1980*, (Oxford, Oxford University Press).

Morgan, Kenneth (1985), *Labour in Power, 1945–51*, (Oxford, Oxford University Press).

Morgan, Kenneth (1992), *The People's Peace: British History, 1945–1990*, (Oxford, Oxford University Press).

Morris, Aldon D. and Mueller, Carol McClurg (eds.) (1992), *Frontiers in Social Movement Theory*, (London, Yale University Press).

Murray, Véra (1976), *Le Parti Québécois: de la fondation à la prise du pouvoir*, (Montreal, Hurtubise).

Nairn, Tom (1988), *The Enchanted Glass: Britain and its Monarchy*, (London, Radius).

Nodia, Ghia (1994), 'Nationalism and democracy', in Larry Diamond and Marc F. Plattner (eds.), *Nationalism, Ethnic Conflict, and Democracy* (Baltimore, John Hopkins University Press).

Panebianco, Angelo (1988), *Political Parties: Organization and Power*, (Cambridge, Cambridge University Press).

Parsons, Wayne (1988), *The Political Economy of British Regional Policy*, (London, Routledge).

Pennock, J. Roland (1979), *Democratic Political Theory*, (Princeton, Princeton University Press).

Peters, B. G. (1977), 'Insiders and outsiders: the politics of pressure groups influence on bureaucracy', *Administration and Society*, vol. 9, no. 2.

'Petition Nationale de l'Ecosse', (1919) In *Scottish Review*, vol. 42, Spring.

Philip, Alan Butt (1975), *The Welsh Question: Nationalism in Welsh Politics, 1945–1970*, (Cardiff, University of Wales Press).

Phillips, Anne (1991), *Engendering Democracy*, (Cambridge, Polity Press).

Popper, Karl (1960), *The Open Society and Its Enemies*, (London, Routledge and Kegan Paul).

Potter, A. (1961), *Organised Groups in British National Politics*, (London, Faber).

Price, Vincent (1992), *Public Opinion*, (London, Sage).

Pryde, George (1960), *Central and Local Government in Scotland Since 1707*, (London, Historical Association).

Robbins, Keith (1988), *Nineteenth Century Britain: integration and diversity*, (Oxford, Clarendon Press).

Rokkan, Stein and Urwin, Derek (eds.) (1982), *The Politics of Territorial Identity: Studies in European Regionalism* (London, Sage).

Rokkan, Stein and Urwin, Derek (1983), *Economy, Territory and Identity*, (London, Sage).

Rose, Richard (1982), *Understanding the United Kingdom*, (London, Longman).

Rudolph, Joseph and Thompson, Robert (1985), 'Ethnoterritorial Movements and the policy process: accommodating nationalist demands in the developed world', *Comparative Politics*, vol. 17, no. 3.

Ryan, Alan (1973), 'Two concepts of Politics and Democracy: James and

John Stuart Mill', In Martin Fleisher (ed.), *Machiavelli and the nature of political thought*, (London, Croom Helm).

Schumpeter, Joseph (1987 edition), *Capitalism, Socialism and Democracy*, (London, Counterpoint).

Scott, Andrew Murray and Macleay, Iain (1990), *Britain's Secret War: Tartan Terrorism and the Anglo-American State*, (Edinburgh, Mainstream).

Scott, Paul (ed.) (1993), *Scotland: a concise cultural history*, (Edinburgh, Mainstream).

Scottish Council Research Institute (1974), *Economic Development and Devolution*, Edinburgh, SCRI.

Shattschneider, E. E. (1975, 1960), *The semi-sovereign people*, (Hinsdale, Illinois, The Dryden Press).

Sillars, Jim (1986), *Scotland: the Case for Optimism*, (Edinburgh, Polygon).

Sillars, Jim (1989), *Independence in Europe*, (Edinburgh, SNP publication).

Simpson, David (1970), 'Independence: the Economic Issues', in Neil MacCormick (ed.), *The Scottish Debate*, (London, Oxford University Press).

Smith, Anthony (1991), *National Identity*, (London, Penguin).

Speck, W. A. (1993), *A Concise History of Britain, 1707–1975*, (Cambridge, Cambridge University Press).

Tamir, Yael (1993), *Liberal Nationalism*, (Princeton, New Jersey, Princeton University Press).

Tarrow, Sidney (1994), *Power in Movement*, (Cambridge, Cambridge University Press).

Teghtsoonian, Katherine Anne (1987), *Institutional structure and government policy: responding to regional nationalism in Quebec, Scotland and Wales*, (Stanford, Stanford University Ph.D., USA).

Tilly, Charles (1985), 'Models and realities of popular collective action', *Social Research*, vol. 52.

Waddie, Charles (1892), *An Inquiry Into the Principles of National and Local Self Government*, (Edinburgh, Scottish Home Rule Association).

Wambaugh, Sarah (1920), *A Monograph on Plebiscites*, (London, Oxford University Press).

Wambaugh, Sarah (1993), *Plebiscites since the world war*, vols. I & II, (Washington, Carnegie Endowment for International Peace).

Wambaugh, Sarah (1943), 'Plebiscite' *Encyclopedia of the Social Sciences* (New York, Macmillan).

Weiner, Martin (1971), *Between Two Worlds: the political thought of Graham*

Wallas, (Oxford, Oxford University Press).

Weir, Stuart and Hall, Wendy (eds.) (1994), *Ego trip: extra-governmental organisations in the United Kingdom and their accountability*, (London, The Democratic Audit of the United Kingdom).

Whiteley, P. and Winyard, S (1983), 'Influencing Social Policy: the effectiveness of the poverty lobby in Britain', *Journal of Social Policy*, vol. 12.

Williams, Francis (nd.), *Fifty Years' March*, (London, Odhams Press Ltd).

Wolfe, Billy (1973), *Scotland Lives*, (Edinburgh, Reprographia).

Wood, Wendy (1970), *Yours sincerely for Scotland*, (London, Arthur Barker).

Wright, L. C. (1969), 'Some Fiscal Problems of Devolution in Scotland', in Wolfe, J. N. (ed.), *Government and Nationalism in Scotland*, (Edinburgh, Edinburgh University Press).

Wolfe, J. N. (ed.), *Government and Nationalism in Scotland*, (Edinburgh, Edinburgh University Press).

Index